FILM IN THE MIDDLE EAST AND NORTH AFRICA

Film in the Middle East and North Africa

—— CREATIVE DISSIDENCE ——

EDITED BY JOSEF GUGLER

UNIVERSITY OF TEXAS PRESS ❧ AUSTIN

Copyright © 2011 by the University of Texas Press
All rights reserved

First edition, 2011

Requests for permission to reproduce material
from this work should be sent to:
Permissions
University of Texas Press
P.O. Box 7819
Austin, TX 78713-7819
www.utexas.edu/utpress/about/bpermission.html

The paper used in this book meets the minimum requirements
of ANSI/NISO Z39.48-1992 (R1997) (Permanence of Paper).

Transliterations of film titles are those commonly
used in Anglophone resources.

Library of Congress Cataloging-in-Publication Data

Film in the Middle East and North Africa : creative dissidence /
edited by Josef Gugler. — 1st ed.
p. cm.
Includes bibliographical references and indexes.
ISBN 978-0-292-72327-6 (cloth : alk. paper)
1. Motion pictures—Political aspects—Middle East. 2. Motion pictures—
Political aspects—Africa, North. 3. Motion pictures—Social aspects—Middle East.
4. Motion pictures—Social aspects—Africa, North. 5. Middle East—In motion
pictures. 6. Africa, North—In motion pictures. I. Gugler, Josef.
PN1993.5.M53F55 2010
302.24'430956—dc22

2010035087

TO DIRECTORS WHO, AGAINST ALL ODDS,
TAKE UP JUST CAUSES.

As for recognition of my life's work, I have to say that none of the 33 films I have directed to date has been easy to do. At first I had a hard time winning recognition and acceptance, and I owe a lot to foreign critics like Jean-Louis Bory, who organized screenings of my films at UNESCO Headquarters in Paris. It was a way of paying tribute to the work being done in a country like Egypt, whose cinema was usually regarded with condescension rather than admiration. Many people in Europe thought that all we could do was make light comedies—with belly dancing scenes, obviously—though some of us were working hard and making more worthwhile films, often on shoestring budgets. That is why I feel I am sharing my prize with all the film-makers from poor countries who are still having great difficulty in making films in their own countries.

YOUSSEF CHAHINE
commenting on receiving the Lifetime Achievement Award at the Fiftieth Cannes Film Festival in 1997, *UNESCO Courier,* September 1997

CONTENTS

PREFACE XI

Creative Responses to Conflict
JOSEF GUGLER
1

PART 1
Regime Critics Confront Censorship in Iranian Cinema
ERIC EGAN
37

The Hidden Half (Tahmineh Milani):
Love, Idealism, and Politics
FAKHREDDIN AZIMI
63

Marriage of the Blessed (Mohsen Makhmalbaf):
The Wounds of War and the Betrayal of the Revolution
ERIC EGAN
75

Under the Skin of the City (Rakhshan Bani-Etemad):
Under the Surface Contrasts
RINI COBBEY
85

Stray Dogs (Marziyeh Meshkini):
Cruelty and Humanity amid Hardship in Afghanistan
ERIC EGAN
95

PART 2
Tolerated Parodies of Politics in Syrian Cinema
LISA WEDEEN
104

The Dupes (Tawfik Saleh):
Three Generations Uprooted from Palestine and Betrayed
NADIA YAQUB
113

The Extras (Nabil Maleh):
Lovers Suffer the Twin Repressions of Patriarchal
Culture and a Police State
JOSEF GUGLER
125

PART 3
Lebanese Cinema and the Representation of War
LINA KHATIB
134

In the Shadows of the City (Jean Khalil Chamoun):
Reconciling the Diverse Legacies of a Collective Memory
EDWARD GIBEAU
147

PART 4
Israeli Cinema Engaging the Conflict
NURITH GERTZ AND YAEL MUNK
154

Kedma (Amos Gitai):
The Birth of Two Nations at War
NURITH GERTZ, GAL HERMONI, AND YAEL MUNK
167

Avanti Popolo (Rafi Bukaee):
Battle Cry of the Fallen
JUDD NE'EMAN AND YAEL MUNK
177

PART 5
A Chronicle of Palestinian Cinema
NURITH GERTZ AND GEORGE KHLEIFI
187

Waiting (Rashid Masharawi):
A Scattered People Waiting for a Shared Future
NADIA YAQUB
199

Tale of the Three Jewels (Michel Khleifi):
Children Living and Dreaming amid Violence in Gaza
NURITH GERTZ AND GEORGE KHLEIFI
209

Paradise Now (Hany Abu-Assad):
Narrating a Failed Politics
NADIA YAQUB
219

PART 6
Political Film in Egypt
WALTER ARMBRUST
228

Destiny (Youssef Chahine):
Liberal and Fundamentalist Islam Clash amid the Splendor
of Twelfth-Century Andalusia
JOSEF GUGLER
253

Closed Doors (Atef Hetata):
The Attractions of Fundamentalism
JOSEF GUGLER AND KIM JENSEN
261

PART 7
Cinema and State in Tunisia
FLORENCE MARTIN
271

Bedwin Hacker (Nadia El Fani):
A Hacker Challenges Western Domination of the Global Media
JOSEF GUGLER
285

PART 8
From State Production to *Cinéma d'Auteur* in Algeria
ROY ARMES
294

Days of Glory (Rachid Bouchareb):
Another Vision of French History
OLIVIER BARLET
307

Hamlet of Women (Mohamed Chouikh):
Village Chronicles from a Time of Terrorism
DENISE BRAHIMI
315

PART 9
Morocco:
A National Cinema with Large Ambitions
KEVIN DWYER
325

Ali Zaoua, Prince of the Streets (Nabil Ayouch):
The Harsh Life of Street Children and the Poetics of Childhood
JOSEF GUGLER
339

CONTRIBUTORS 349
FILM INDEX 353
NAME INDEX 361

PREFACE

This book would not have been possible but for the creativity of film directors from across the Middle East and the Maghreb. Persevering against all odds, they have established a rich heritage of extraordinary films. Time and again they have offered fresh perspectives on crucial issues confronting the region by giving image and voice to dissident views. We dedicate the book to them.

I thank the eighteen contributors from three continents who agreed to join our venture, endured my unending demands, responded to my critical comments, and taught me a great deal. I am grateful to the directors and producers who provided me with films, illustrations, and information.

This collection grew out of a course I developed at the University of Connecticut in response to the aftermath of 9/11, the invasions of Afghanistan and Iraq, and the ongoing debate over the Israel/Palestine conflict. I am greatly indebted to Lynne Goodstein, who encouraged me to teach this course in the Honors Program, to a large number of colleagues who readily agreed to participate when the course morphed into a film and lecture series, and to my students whose comments and questions wonderfully concentrated my mind.

Many people helped along the way. Jim Burr at University of Texas Press has been most supportive from the time when we first discussed this project. But for the wizardry of Alex Bothell, many illustrations would be in worse shape; others would have been abandoned altogether as unsuitable for printing. My special thanks to Livia Alexander, Salma Abu Ayyash, Talat Azimi, Lana Babij, Stephen Bustamente, Daniel Buttrey, Maha Darawsha, Mohamed Faizal, Niloo Fotouhi, Nadia Hlibka, Janet Jordan, Géraldine Le Chêne, Gérard Le Chêne, Joseph Natale, Dominique Olier, Rasha Salti, Lynn Sweet, and Alex Williams, who assisted me in various ways.

I cherish the support my wife and our daughters gave me in spite of my sins of absence and distraction as I allowed myself to be absorbed by this endeavor.

Children are prominently featured in many films from the region; for them all royalties will be donated to UNICEF.

JOSEF GUGLER

We strove for consistency in transliterations, except that we have adhered to the transliteration of the names of characters used in the English subtitles of films and the transliteration of the names of directors and actors used in the anglophone world by distribution companies. Arabic transliterations follow American University in Cairo Press guidelines; thanks to the American University in Cairo Press for taking on this task.

FILM IN THE MIDDLE EAST AND NORTH AFRICA

Creative Responses to Conflict

JOSEF GUGLER

> After the revolution I concluded that it's not enough to go from one totalitarian regime to another... I realized that what was needed for us to achieve social justice and freedom is cultural change—to change people's perceptions of one another, and their perception of power.
> MOHSEN MAKHMALBAF (1997, IN BÉAR 2008, 124)

Images and voices from the Middle East and the Maghreb are little seen and heard abroad. As far as films are concerned, some are feted at film festivals, but only a few are shown in art houses and on select television channels, and home video distribution remains extremely limited.[1] Western productions dominate the screens of the world, and the political consequences are serious—most especially for a region as deeply embroiled in conflict with Western interests as the Middle East.[2] The lack of public interest parallels a dearth of scholarly attention, with the notable exceptions of Iran and Israel. Not a single scholarly article has been devoted to many of the films featured in this volume.[3]

Films from the Middle East offer representations at variance with those that predominate in much of the Western media. Locally produced stories and images call into question common assumptions about the region's history, cultures, and people. Such films demonstrate commonalities and differences across a region that is all too often subject to unwarranted generalizations. Analysis of the economic, political, and cultural contexts in which directors produce them reveals the complexity of societies that tend to be characterized rather superficially from afar.

Nine essays present the region's major national cinemas.⁴ They devote special attention to the work of directors who have given image and voice to dissent from the discourses of authoritarian regimes, of patriarchy, of fundamentalist movements, and of the West. They explore the interactions of the aspirations of directors, the pressures exerted by producers and sponsors, and the restrictions imposed by governments, religious authorities, and custom. The country essays are complemented by in-depth discussions of eighteen films that have been selected for both their excellence and their critical engagement with pressing current issues.

Fiction films are the focus of this volume.⁵ Fiction films are unrivaled in their impact on viewers. They provide an immediacy of experience rarely found in documentaries and that the written word cannot match. They bring foreign settings alive in images, sound, characters, and story. Their dramatic stories elicit emotional responses, and their characters engage empathy.⁶ The empathy elicited becomes particularly important when they reach audiences who start out with negative views of other societies and cultures. Such is the case for many outside observers of the Middle East.

The long history of Iranian cinema, its international renown, and the remarkable films of directors confronting the state earned it a special place in this volume. Three of the featured Iranian films focus on successive phases in the history of the clerical regime and demonstrate the complexity of Iranian politics; the fourth offers penetrating commentary on contemporary Afghanistan. The other major emphasis is on the Israel/Palestine conflict, the overarching political issue in the Middle East. Generations old, the conflict continues to shape the present. Palestinian directors, Israelis, and an Egyptian working in Syria present their perspectives on successive stages in the conflict from 1948 to the present in six featured films.

Nineteen scholars rallied to the project.⁷ About half the contributors are film scholars, while others range across literary studies and the social sciences to two film directors and a novelist. Beyond differences in disciplinary orientation, there is considerable variation among contributors in the perspectives that inform their writing. They offer an illuminating range of approaches to the cinemas of the region.

Egypt, Iran, and Israel boast established commercial cinemas. Elsewhere in the Middle East and the Maghreb, most film directors find themselves in extremely difficult circumstances. Commonly they develop their own scripts; they embark on what are usually protracted searches for funding; they proceed on minuscule budgets; they try to avoid censorship, and when that fails, they engage in difficult negotiations with censors; they take on multiple production roles, recruiting actors, sometimes training amateur actors, assembling crews; and they struggle to get their films distributed. They are truly filmmakers. If they face multiple constraints, they exert much more control over their productions than directors of high-budget films. Theirs is a *cinéma d'auteur*, and it comes at a price—few manage to produce more than one film a decade. But extraordinary directors have left their mark, pursuing their visions despite the severe constraints. Iranian cinema has secured worldwide attention, but there are treasures to be discovered elsewhere in the Middle East and the Maghreb.

The *auteur* directors, more often than not, dissent from political regimes, patriarchal customs, religious movements, and Western interference in the region. They may be characterized as intellectuals *cum* artists critically engaged in politics. Iranian director Rakhshan Bani-Etemad puts it thus in Nader Takmil Homayoun's documentary *Iran: A Cinematographic Revolution* (*Iran: Une révolution cinématographique*, 2006): "The responsibility on my shoulders is totally different to that of a Western filmmaker. Whether I like it or not, it's a responsibility I must take."

These directors have managed time and again to overcome daunting obstacles to give image and voice to dissent in powerful films, even if some had to remain less than explicit. Where they pioneered, commercial cinema has sometimes followed. Their films offer perspectives on issues central to the Middle East and the Maghreb today that reflect the political orientation of much of the intellectual class. We explore their perspectives alongside the political, cultural, and commercial constraints within which they create their films.

The region spanning the Middle East and the Maghreb may invite generalizations, but when it comes to cinema, the contrasts are striking. The circumstances of film production vary widely across the region. At the same time, assumptions about the relationship of economic resources and film production are readily confounded. And so are assumptions about the relationship between political regimes and censorship. The contributions to this volume reflect the diversity of the region's cinemas. Here I will sketch differences and recurrent patterns while touching on some important films produced in Afghanistan, Iraq, Libya, and Turkey.

The Economics

Local markets for films are extremely limited in most countries. Only Egypt and Iran have populations that exceed forty million, and incomes are low in all the principal film-producing countries except Israel (see the accompanying table). At the same time, film production is confronted with formidable foreign

Population, Income, and Film Production

Country	Population (millions) 2008	GNI at PPP per head[1] 2008	Production of feature-length fiction films								
			1920s	1930s	1940s	1950s	1960s	1970s	1980s	1990s	2000–2008	Total
Algeria	34	$7,940[2]					9	40	38	54	47	188
Egypt	82	$5,460	14	94	326	530	449	460	573	393	294	3,133
Iran	72	$10,840[3]		9	3	138	437	559	389	546	554	2,635
Israel	7	$27,450							169[4]	107[4]	107[4]	...
Lebanon	4	$10,880		1	3	12	71	40	51	23	36	237
Morocco	31	$4,330					3	16	38	43	96	196
Palestine	4	...						3	5	10	18	36
Syria	21	$4,350	1	2	1	1	18	84	25	27	13	172
Tunisia	10	$7,070					4	19	19	28	37	107

[1] Purchasing power parity (PPP) converts currencies to U.S. dollars according to their purchasing power, i.e., one dollar has the same purchasing power over domestic Gross National Income (GNI) as the U.S. dollar has over U.S. GNI. For comparison, the U.S. Gross National Income per capita was $46,970 in 2008.
[2] Estimate
[3] For a period other than 2008
[4] Israeli films shown in Israeli theaters; the few coproductions are not shown.
... Missing data

SOURCES

Demographic and economic data from World Bank (2009). Film production for Syria compiled from Qasim (2009, 1160–1161); for all other Arab countries compiled from Armes (2008, 2010b, 2010c; films categorized as documentaries by Armes have been omitted); for Iran provided by Egan (2010); for Israel provided by Central Bureau of Statistics (2010).

competition. Powerful producers in the West, Japan, Hong Kong, and India are firmly established in the region, even if a number of countries put restrictions on them.[8] The Arab-language film market in turn is dominated by the Egyptian film industry. Films from the Maghreb are further hampered by the language barrier that their Arabic vernacular presents for viewers elsewhere in the Arab world. They do, however, enjoy a measure of support from the Maghrebi diaspora in France.

Most directors depend heavily on subsidies throughout the Middle East and the Maghreb. Governments have played an important part in funding national cinemas and encouraging the production of quality films. The fortunes of national cinemas have waxed and waned with such support. Foreign government agencies, television networks, and foundations also have provided major support for film production in many countries.

Egypt has established one of the world's principal film industries in spite of its poverty. Hollywood on the Nile has produced more than three thousand feature films since 1924. Private investment created a commercial and export-oriented genre based on a star system. It developed a strong local flavor, even if Hollywood was a source of open or hidden inspiration. Egyptian films dominate national screens, assisted by government measures that restrict imports—from India and Hong Kong in particular. Producers in the 1940s and 1950s accommodated their Arab export markets with Levantine rhythms, characters, and locations; since the 1980s they have bowed to the moral conservatism of the Gulf region (Shafik forthcoming).

The Egyptian film industry was nationalized in 1960. However, private productions continued to predominate. The overall level of production decreased as Syrian, Lebanese, and Jordanian producers and distributors withdrew from Egypt and invested in Lebanon instead. Most of the significant films of the 1960s were public-sector productions, as Armbrust notes in this volume, but the General Film Organization, plagued by corruption and nepotism, accumulated huge debts and did not manage to produce more than thirteen films a year. Politically committed leading directors left in frustration. Among them were Youssef Chahine, who went to Lebanon, and Tawfik Saleh, who moved to Syria. Public feature-film production was terminated in 1971 (Shafik forthcoming).

The exodus of foreign producers and distributors from Egypt in the early 1960s gave a boost to Lebanese production, which in turn made extensive use of Egyptian stars and technical talent (ibid.). But the boost was limited and short-lived. The small country never established a commercial cinema.

In Syria, soon after Hafez Assad came to power in 1970, the National Film Organization brought together directors from across the Arab world who set out to establish the "Alternative Cinema" in opposition to commercial Arab, and notably Egyptian, cinema (Shafik 2007, 154). Funded by the National Film Organization, they produced several films that earned international recognition. Film production took off in the early 1970s but dropped back after a few years, perhaps because of the conflicted relationship between directors and the regime that controlled all film production until recently.

Iran, with a large population that is not as poor as most in the region, has a long-established commercial cinema. But it was public funding by the clerical regime that allowed a flourishing of quality productions that have established Iranian cinema as the one cinema in the region to gain worldwide recognition. The poetics that characterize many Iranian films have charmed foreign viewers, while directors who offered critical perspectives on political developments in Iran found a ready response overseas. A large, well-educated exile community constitutes a major part of the international market for Iranian films.

In Iraq, novice Mohamed Al Daradji's *Ahlaam* (2005) marks a promising new beginning after the fall of the regime of Saddam Hussein. Al Daradji wrote, co-produced, directed, and shot the film on a shoestring budget of $300,000.

Affluent Israel has established a cinema that joins private and public finance, and quite a few Israeli films have received international recognition. Amos Gitai, however, established himself as the Israeli director best known on the international scene with European financing secured after he exiled himself in France in 1983 to return to Israel only ten years later.

Libya usually is not perceived as a film-producing country, but Muammar al-Gaddafi provided crucial funding for the region's two most important epics. *The Message* (*Mohammed, Messenger of God/al-Risala*, 1976) and *Lion of the Desert* (1981) address themes central to the Middle East and the Maghreb: the birth of Islam and the resistance to colonialism. They are probably the biggest productions anywhere in the region, except perhaps for some of Chahine's, featuring famous actors, using elaborate sets, staging large battle scenes, and employing dramatic scores by Maurice Jarre. *The Message* appears to be the only film in the region to have been shot in two languages, an Arab version and an English version, with different actors using the same sets. The director of these two remarkable films defies ready categorization. Born in Syria, Moustapha Akkad started out with these two films, then went on to produce a series of horror movies in Hollywood.

Film production in the Maghreb has not been commercially viable except for some comedies.[9] Public funding has flowed and ebbed in a somewhat chronological sequence across the three countries, and this is reflected in production figures (see table). Virtually all Algerian features were produced by government agencies until 1984, and for a while they outnumbered the combined production of Algeria's neighbors. They included notable films, prominent among them *Chronicle of the Years of Embers* (*Waqa'i sanawat al-djamr* / *Chronique des années de braise*, 1975). Mohamed Lakhdar-Hamina's œuvre won the Palme d'Or at the Cannes Film Festival and to this day remains the only film from Africa or the Arab world to be so honored. Some films were co-produced with foreign directors, among them Youssef Chahine, who directed three in the 1970s, all set in Egypt. In Morocco, production increased substantially once nearly all features received government funding from 1980 onward. Production has been further boosted with an increased level of funding since the 1990s. Similar funding was initiated in Tunisia in 1981, but its impact was not apparent until state support became more generous in 2001.

European support—from government agencies, television networks, and foundations—has provided the other main source of funding in the region, often in conjunction with government support (Armes forthcoming). France is preeminent among foreign supporters as it pursues its twin goals of promoting the use of the French language, *la francophonie*, around the world and of enlisting broad support for its defense of the "cultural exception" to free-trade agreements, that is, that cultural products should receive special encouragement and protection so as to promote diversity on the global level. The prime beneficiaries of French support have been films from the Maghreb, which commonly use the language of the former colonial power. It probably helps that many directors reside in France and others have good connections there.

Descendants of Maghrebi immigrants in France have established, along with first-generation immigrants, a flourishing cinema that partakes of the government's support for the French film industry. These directors tend to focus on the situation of the immigrant community. Some of their films follow immigrants back home. Others are set entirely in the Maghreb. The *cinéma beur* found its apotheosis in Rachid Bouchareb's *Days of Glory* (*Indigènes*, 2006). The film was a box-office success, earned its leading actors jointly the Best Actor award at Cannes, and was nominated for an Oscar.[10]

Technological changes in distribution have profoundly affected film consumption throughout the region. First television, then video cassettes, and most recently DVDs have become strong competitors of film theaters. If local television channels offered limited fare, satellite transmissions greatly expanded television programming, and piracy of transmissions made them available to much of the population. Piracy similarly expanded access to home video.

Box-office receipts plummeted; many film theaters closed, and others let their technical equipment and facilities deteriorate, further discouraging potential viewers. These developments dealt a serious blow to film production, but they also offered some benefits. With local television production came technical facilities, opportunities for training, and jobs. Television companies purchased and/or co-produced films; some governments mandated such support for locally produced films. Cinema audiences have expanded afresh in recent years with the establishment of movie complexes in many countries. It remains to be seen whether efforts to combat DVD piracy will be effective and enable producers to benefit from this potentially major source of revenue.

Technological change is coming to film production in the form of digitalization. Compared to production on 35 mm film, digital production assures substantial savings: cameras and film stock are cheaper, smaller crews are required, and laboratories are eliminated altogether; also, digital video allows immediate review, reducing shooting time and hence the cost of actors, crew, and facilities. However, until cinema theaters make the expensive transition to digital projection, much of the savings in production is lost in transferring digital film to 35 mm film. For the most part, directors have been reluctant to forgo the quality of 35 mm film. While a few established directors have made the occasional digital film, they tend to be minor works. It was left to newcomer Nadia El Fani to venture forth with an impressive digital production, *Bedwin Hacker*, in 2002.

The Politics

The political significance of film has been recognized at least since *The Birth of a Nation* hit the screens in 1915. And political authorities have sought to take advantage of the medium's political potential since the Soviet Revolution, if not before. Censorship is ubiquitous in the Middle East and the Maghreb. At its most comprehensive, film production is suppressed altogether. The Arab Gulf countries have ample resources to finance film production, and they present a promising market: for decades they were the principal foreign market for the Egyptian film industry. But only recently have some Gulf countries produced a few films.

Producers and sponsors choose which directors to support and what scripts to consider, and producers can use their power to shape the final product. Directors are induced to propose scripts that are likely to get funding. The extent to which producers and sponsors exert their power varies greatly. But that power is there, whoever funds cinema. The heated debate about the distorting effect of foreign funding is ongoing; meanwhile, there can be no doubt that film production in the Middle East and the Maghreb would be much diminished without such funding. And while repressive regimes and government bureaucrats might be expected to be the most obvious enemies of cinema that challenges the status quo, such assumptions are not always borne out.

In Syria, the National Film Organization commissioned, approved, and funded all film production from 1969 until recently. Yet Syrian cinema is renowned for the critical stance its directors have taken time and again vis-à-vis the regime. Usually the attacks on the regime are coded, and many allusions remain opaque to foreign viewers, but they are readily apparent to the Syrian public. However, *Sacrifices* (*Sunduq al-dunya*, 2002) by Oussama Mohammad, famous for the scathing critique of the Syrian regime in his earlier *Stars in Broad Daylight* (*Nujum al-nahar*, 1988),[11] is said to remain hermetic even for Syrian intellectuals (Wright 2006). Unusually explicit is Nabil Maleh's *The Extras* (*al-Kompars*, 1993), a breathtaking denunciation of the repressive regime. The film tells of illicit love in a patriarchal culture and of illicit discourse under a tyranny. In an interplay of reality and fantasies, daydreams, and hallucinations, *The Extras* effectively conveys the fears that haunt those who break cultural taboos and just about anybody living in a police state.

Commentators have tended to dismiss the political significance of such criticism, suggesting that it is tolerated and even encouraged by the regime simply as a way of letting off steam. For example, miriam cooke has cast this interpretation in terms of "commissioned criticism" and has written of films that "run the risk of enabling the injustice to persist" (2007, 72–77, 120). Wedeen rejects such "safety valve" interpretations as functionalist, proposing a conflict analysis instead. She gives intellectuals opposing the regime a measure of agency: "Artistic transgressions are the site of *politics*, of the dynamic interplay between the regime's exercise of power and people's experiences of and reactions to it" (Weeden 1999, 89).

Government funding obviates the need to pander to popular tastes. At the Syrian film festival in New York, Oussama Mohammad commented that he preferred the yoke of the National Film Organization to the tyranny of commercial cinema (Mohammad 2006). And scripts benefit from rewrites while directors wait for years until they finally get the opportunity to shoot the films. The few films produced in Syria thus gain international recognition time and again. It took fourteen years for Mohammad's second film to be released, but *Sacrifices* won wide acclaim, including the Special Prize of the Jury at the Paris Biennale of Arab Cinema. Such successes bring credit to a regime that can present itself as the sponsor of quality cinema. Still, the government has sharply curtailed film production. Since the golden age of Syrian cinema in the 1970s, production has dropped to a trickle of two or three films a year, suggesting a stand-off between the regime and strong-willed directors. Recently the government allowed independent productions outside the National Film Organization. One of the first such films, Hatem Ali's *The Long Night* (2009), is extraordinarily explicit, featuring, in their prison setting, four men who have been jailed for decades for acts of conscience.

In Iran, as in Syria, government funding allowed directors to escape the dictates of commercial production. Unlike Syria, such funding consistently supported a large output of films. Quite a number of directors produced works that gained international recognition for Iranian cinema such as no other of the region's cinemas enjoys. At the same time, Iranian cinema also is constrained by censorship. Government regulations impose strict cultural norms. Women have to appear veiled even in domestic settings; men and women cannot touch, not even husband and wife. More constricting is political censorship. Nevertheless, Iranian directors have taken critical aim at the clerical regime time and again. That took courage, manipulation, and compromise.

Mohsen Makhmalbaf's *Marriage of the Blessed* (*Arusi-ye khouban*, 1989) presents a reckoning with the revolution ten years after its victory. Set at the end of the devastating Iran-Iraq War, the film contrasts the suffering of war veterans and the destitute with the wealth of profiteers. The religious leaders' egalitarian slogans on city walls are contradicted by graffiti such as "Volunteer combatant, a lion in battlefields, a victim in town." The protagonist, a shell-shocked photojournalist, wants to "work for Islam," but his photographs of urban poverty are censored by his newspaper. Eventually, at the lavish wedding his rich father-in-law has put on, he screams: "Robbed food tastes delicious." In Takmil Homayoun's documentary *Iran: A Cinematographic Revolution*, Makhmalbaf tells of getting permission to make the film by submitting to the censors a screenplay filled with revolutionary slogans but shooting a different script and of getting the film released by showing the censors a longer version of the film in which he had replaced all the "disturbing scenes" with revolutionary statements. Only much later, when the film ran in cinemas with the "real scenes" put back in, did the authorities catch on.

Tahmineh Milani, in an interview with NBC's Ann Curry, tells of being threatened by the country's top censor when she challenged him early in her career. The stress took its toll, and she gave birth to twins prematurely; one of them died after a couple of days.[12] Milani nevertheless confronted the clerical regime with *The Hidden Half* (*Nimeh-ye penhan*) in 2001. The film has been promoted and tends to be interpreted as a critique of the position of women, the half of the Iranian population that clerical dictate seeks to hide literally as well as figuratively. But there is also the hidden half of the love story, the man's side of the story we are never told. Most prominent is the film's historical dimension, its focus on the secular half of the anti-Shah movement that was suppressed by the Islamic Revolution and remains hidden in the clerical regime's version of Iranian history. *The Hidden Half* was the first Iranian film to speak of those events, and Milani did have to curtail scenes. Thus she could not convey that the clerical regime had many students killed (Auer 2006).[13] Still, she was arrested in August 2001 to face trial and possible execution on several charges, including "sympathizing with counter-revolutionary grouplets" in her film; intervention by then President Mohammad Khatami got her released. If directors managed to produce critical films during the Khatami era, their room for maneuver became much more restricted when Mahmoud Ahmadinejad acceded to the presidency in 2005, as Egan spells out in this volume.

Directors manage to produce critical films in Iran and Syria, then face further struggles getting them released. Both regimes are usually prepared to have these films shown at international festivals but often restrict their domestic distribution. Some of the very films that won awards abroad could not be shown in Iran. In Syria, a common pattern is for critical films to appear only at the Damascus International Film Festival. Still, in both countries, films do circulate all year round—underground.

In Israel, a number of directors, among them several Israeli Arabs, regularly produce films that critically address Jewish-Arab conflicts within Israel as well as the Israel/Palestine conflict.[14] They usually draw on government support, like other Israeli productions, and several have been submitted for Academy Awards. Still, such critical films have faced obstacles, as Shohat spells out for the 1980s (2010, 241–242). Some foreground Palestinians as well as Israelis. Much of Amos Gitai's vast *œuvre*, fiction as well as documentary, has been devoted to the conflict. His *Kedma* (2002) is set in Palestine as the State of Israel is about to be established in 1948. Gitai gives voice to survivors of the Holocaust who have come to the Promised Land to find themselves in the middle of war and to Arabs who have to flee their ancestral homes. Rafi Bukaee's *Avanti Popolo* (1986) ranks with the classics of antiwar cinema. Set at the end of the Six Day War in 1967, it has Israeli and Egyptian soldiers recognize their common humanity. Inasmuch as the Egyptian soldiers are played by Arabs living in Israel and are identified as such by local viewers because of their accent, they can readily be seen to represent a suffering minority—like Jews have been for centuries. Ari Folman's *Waltz with Bashir* (*Vals im Bashir*, 2008) shares the antiwar message and goes on to denounce the complicity of the Israeli army in the massacre of Palestinian refugees at Sabra and Shatila in 1982.

In Egypt, explicitly political films have become quite common since the early 1990s even in commercial cinema. Three issues dominate: fundamentalism, denunciations of Israel and/or the United States, and critiques of Egyptian politics that are remarkably explicit. Films about fundamentalism are constrained by strict censorship. As Walter Armbrust spells out in his essay in this volume, no endorsement of Islam as a political alternative is allowed in cinema. Films can criticize Islamic fundamentalism as a political movement, but even then they are subject to restrictions. Various signifiers of Islamic identity have become a common sight in public places but are suppressed in nearly all Egyptian films. An acknowledgment of these new realities would entail a more differentiated depiction of Islam than has prevailed in Egyptian cinema so far.

Films about Israel and/or the United States are subject to few restrictions; they can even implicate the regime's policy of normalization with Israel. Armbrust argues that these films have to be understood in the context of regional conflicts. He further suggests that these films be thought of as a "politicsploitation" genre. Anti-Israeli and anti-American films, like the "blaxploitation" cinema, employ crude stereotypes—national stereotypes in this case. They are predicated on making audiences feel good about themselves by reversing the stereotypes propagated by the more powerful. American affirmation of moral commitments becomes American hypocrisy in Egyptian politicsploitation cinema.

More or less veiled regime critiques could be found in Egyptian cinema for a long time, while the country was ruled by a monarchy subject to British interference, during the regime of Gamal Abdel Nasser, and in the post-Nasser era. In recent years the critiques have become quite explicit as films denounce political corruption and police brutality. The depiction of torture in films such as *The Yacoubian Building* ('*Imarat Ya'qubyan*, Marwan Hamid), the highest-grossing film in Egypt in 2006, and *Chaos* (*Heya fawda*, 2007), Youssef Chahine's last film, directed jointly with Khaled Youssef, is particularly striking.[15] One might consider the political import of these films to be undercut by implausible developments and caricatured portrayals that put them at a remove from reality and give salience to their fictional character. But the crowds they draw raise the question of how such fantasy shapes the popular imagination. When viewers applaud as *Chaos* concludes with an uprising against the corrupt police officer who has terrorized the neighborhood, a vision of Egypt's corrupt and oppressive regime being toppled cannot be far from their minds.

In Lebanon, numerous films have been produced in response to the trauma of the Civil War. Jean Khalil Chamoun's *In the Shadows of the City* (*Taif al-madina*, 2000) is perhaps the finest example. The poignant story of a twelve-year-old boy growing up a witness to fifteen years of war centers on early love and family, all the while effectively rendering the grim reality of those years. As the child becomes a man, the film bears witness to the deepening sectarian divisions along with the spreading physical destruction. He lives in what soon becomes a separate Muslim community, but the significant relationships he establishes beyond the sectarian divide give a human face to The Other. Chamoun, like many of his fellow Lebanese filmmakers, wanted to break the amnesia about the Civil War that had engulfed Lebanon and to assuage the continuing social tensions. Recent developments in Lebanon have confirmed the importance of the task they assigned themselves.

In Tunisia, the autocratic regime of Ben Ali that has perpetuated itself for more than two decades has stifled any critique. However, denunciation of his predecessor Habib Bourguiba does pass. Thus Nouri Bouzid, in his autobiographic *The Golden Horseshoes* (*Safa'ih min dahab/Les sabots en or*, 1989), has flashbacks of the torture he suffered in prison. Tunisian cinema is perhaps the most restricted of any in the region with regard to current national politics, but it enjoys a degree of freedom in the cultural realm that sets it apart from other Arab cinemas. Directors have been able to address sexuality and display a modicum of nudity. In 1986 Nouri Bouzid, in *Man of Ashes* (*Rih essed/L'homme de cendres*), told of two young men coping with the experience of having been abused by their master. In 2002 Nadia El Fani introduced bisexual women protagonists in *Bedwin Hacker* and overcame censors' objections to a brief display of a semi-nude woman.

The Algerian government controlled the production and distribution of films outright from independence until 1984. Initially most films were devoted to the War of Liberation; then the agricultural revolution was brought to the screen. A few films did set out to demystify the regime's ideology of the past and the present, employing a rich dose of humor. Merzak Allouache pioneered this alternative view with *Omar Gatlato* (*Umar Qatlatu al-Rudjla*, 1977), which dwells on the disenchantment of the post-revolutionary generation growing up in Algiers. Then in the early 1980s, just as the government was about to give up its control over film production, it released two similarly critical films. Mahmoud Zemmouri's *The Crazy Years of the Twist* (*Sanawat al-twist al-majnuna/*

Les folles années du twist, 1983) tells the story of people caught between the conflicting demands of the liberation movement and the French army, making short shrift of the unending tales of heroism and selfless commitment during the struggle for independence. And Ahmed Rachedi satirized the bureaucracy in *Monsieur Fabre's Mill* (*Tahunat al-sayyid Fabre*/*Le moulin de M. Fabre*, 1984).

The events of October 1988, when the authoritarian regime violently repressed young demonstrators who had taken to the streets, prompted vigorous responses from filmmakers. Mohamed Chouikh highlights the betrayal of the liberation struggle in *Youssef: The Legend of the Seventh Sleeper* (*Youcef kesat dekra sabera*/*Youcef, la légende du septième dormant*, 1993). When his protagonist, an amnesiac veteran living in the colonial past, sets out to find the families of his fallen comrades, he refuses to accept that the corrupt party leaders, the bosses who mistreat their workers, and the fundamentalists who oppress the very women who participated in the struggle represent a post-colonial present. Malik Lakhdar-Hamina's *Autumn—October in Algiers* (*Uktubur fi-l-Jaza'ir*/*Automne—Octobre à Alger*, 1993) features an artist censored by the repressive regime and his brother who has turned fundamentalist and seeks to impose the strictures of his beliefs on his family; they both get caught up in the bloody events of October 1988.

Morocco has seen dramatic change in recent years. In 2000, *Ali Zaoua, Prince of the Streets* (*Ali Zawa*/*Ali Zaoua, prince de la rue*) brought the misery of street children to public attention, but Nabil Ayouch refrained from social, let alone political, critique. A few years later, with King Mohammed VI opening up for inquiry and public discussion the repression that characterized the regime of his father, Hassan II, a series of films was released about what have become known as *les années de plomb*, the Years of Lead, and their aftermath.[16]

The *cinéma beur* of first- and second-generation Maghrebi immigrants in France has been little inhibited in protesting discrimination against immigrants. Rachid Bouchareb's *Days of Glory* is one of the rare films whose political impact was immediate and patently obvious in various ways.

The Directors

Most filmmakers in the Middle East and the Maghreb have devoted some of their films to criticize the discourses and actions of political regimes, of patriarchal authorities, of religious movements, of the West. Oftentimes, however, they have been compelled to retreat from outspoken critiques to fare less objectionable to the powers that be.

Mohsen Makhmalbaf's political biography paradigmatically represents the history of the Iranian Revolution. In 1972 the fifteen-year-old established an underground group that distributed anti-Shah leaflets. Two years later Makhmalbaf attacked a police officer.[17] Makhmalbaf was injured in the attack, arrested, and jailed until he was freed with the advent of the revolution in 1978. The first films made by the autodidact in the early 1980s reflect his religious morality; they were even screened in mosques.[18] Shortly, however, Makhmalbaf became critical of the religious regime that had entrenched itself in power, and he produced a series of films denouncing social injustice under the new dispensation, *Marriage of the Blessed* foremost among them. Shortly after, Makhmalbaf began filming outside Iran. *Time of Love* (*Nobat-e asheghi*, 1990) was shot in Turkey and *The Silence* (*Sokut*, 1998) in Tajikistan; since 2002 all his films have been shot abroad, as have those of his wife and his daughters. When protests erupted in Iran in 2009 in response to the regime's handling of the presidential election and demonstrations were violently repressed, Makhmalbaf took on the role of spokesperson for the opposition. *Inter alia* he addressed the European Assembly in Strasbourg.

Refused permission to establish a film school, Makhmalbaf had trained his family and a few friends in his Makhmalbaf Film School.[19] His wife Marziyeh Meshkini and his daughters, Samira and Hana, continued his critical thrust. Among them the three women have directed seven fiction films, the four most recent ones devoted to Afghanistan. Meshkini's *Stray Dogs* (*Sag-haye velgard*, 2003) powerfully conveys the state of a country devastated by three decades of war. When the film invokes the neorealist tradition with a reference to Vittorio De Sica's *Bicyle Thieves* (*Ladri di biciclette*, 1948), it calls attention not just to stylistic parallels but to similarities in context. If neorealism had thematic roots in a critical examination of Italian society after World War II and if it was grounded in the material constraints of production companies struggling to survive, Afghan society is in utter disarray and the circumstances of filming in Afghanistan are extreme. Samira Makhmalbaf's *Two-Legged Horse* (*Asbe du-pa*, 2008) apparently incurred the wrath of fundamentalists: its filming was interrupted by a bombing.

The emergence of women directors in Iran under the clerical regime has been spectacular. The prominent role they have taken in film production may be seen as a response to the assault by the clerical regime on the position of women. Rakhshan Bani-Etemad and Tahmineh Milani are among the most prominent Iranian filmmakers, and they have produced pointed critiques of the regime.

The situation of Syrian directors is extraordinary. Most trained in "socialist" Eastern Europe. On their return they became civil servants at the National

Film Organization—and proceeded to critique Syria's "socialist" regime more or less openly in their films. Oussama Mohammad, for one, has commented that among the many influences during his tenure at Moscow's VGIK in the 1970s was that of Soviet filmmakers who produced films that voiced critiques of authority, the regime, and the official discourse (Salti 2006, 44).

Nabil Maleh studied in Czechoslovakia and returned to Syria in 1964. Unlike most of his Syrian peers, he did not become a civil servant at the newly established National Film Organization. He was among the few Syrians involved in the establishment of the pan-Arab Alternative Cinema, and his *The Leopard* (*al-Fahd*, 1972) was one of the two first full-length fiction films produced by the group, to international acclaim. His productive career was interrupted when he left Syria in 1981 to return only in 1992 to shoot *The Extras*, an exceptionally explicit critique of the authoritarian regime. At the turn of the millennium, Maleh was closely involved in the movement of prominent Syrians that sought to bring liberalization to Syria.

Jean Khalil Chamoun found his calling when the Civil War broke out in Lebanon. As established filmmakers fled the fighting, the recently returned novice director stayed on to become, in joint productions with Mai Masri, the foremost chronicler of the protracted tragedy in a series of documentaries. Eventually Chamoun proceeded to produce *In the Shadows of the City*.

Amos Gitai started out with documentaries critically examining the legacy of the Israel/Palestine conflict. Hostile reactions prompted Gitai to leave for France, where he remained for ten years. With European financing he moved on to a series of fiction films that established him as an international celebrity. *Kedma* won the Palme d'Or at Cannes. The film distinguishes itself for giving voice to both Jews and Arabs in the crucial confrontation of 1948.

Rafi Bukaee developed *Avanti Popolo* from his graduation project. The film earned the Golden Leopard's Eye at Locarno and, against strong political opposition, became the Israeli submission to the Academy Awards. Bukaee went on to produce films and directed only one more before his untimely death in 2003.

Palestinian directors have devoted themselves to influencing international opinion in support of the struggle of the Palestinian people. Many exiled themselves to Europe, where they have found most of the funding for their films. A considerable part of their efforts has gone into documentary films, but they also have produced notable fiction films. Michel Khleifi was the first to bring international recognition to Palestinian cinema. Born and raised in Nazareth, he studied theater and television in Belgium. His first film, *Fertile Memory* (*al-*

Dhakira al-khasba, 1980), financed by German and Dutch television networks, was considered innovative not just in the context of Palestinian filmmaking, but in comparison to Arab documentary films in general. Khleifi's *Wedding in Galilee* (*Urs al-Jalil*, 1987), a Belgian-French-German co-production, brought international acclaim, winning the Critics' Prize at Cannes, the Tanit d'Or at Carthage, and the Golden Seashell at San Sebastián. It was the BBC's turn to provide most of the funding for *Tale of the Three Jewels* (*Hikayat al-jawahir thalath*, 1994). The film was shot in Gaza still under Israeli occupation, and the Israeli army stipulated that no scenes showing weapons or demonstrations could be filmed. One day after Khleifi started filming, the Hebron massacre occurred; the country was in uproar; there were curfews, demonstrations, and violent deaths. The shooting schedule was canceled, and the entire project was in doubt. When the filming finally resumed, the crew members were considered mad; they became known by the locals as "The Fools" (Gertz and Khleifi, in this volume).

Unlike most established Palestinian directors, Rashid Masharawi was born in the Occupied Territories and raised there, in the Shati refugee camp in Gaza. When he was twelve, he moved to Tel Aviv and lived there illegally to help support his parents and his seven siblings after his father developed diabetes. He worked as a construction worker, as a waiter, as a dishwasher. At the age of nineteen Masharawi completed his first short. Over the next decade he directed a half-dozen more shorts while making a living building film sets (Gertz and Khleifi 2008, 43–45, 214). His first feature, *Curfew* (*Hatta ish'ar akhar*, 1994), was informed by his experience of life under Israeli occupation. The film was screened at the Critics' Week at Cannes and brought Masharawi international recognition. In 1996 Masharawi established the Cinematic Production and Distribution Center in Ramallah. Its Mobile Cinema brought films to children in refugee camps (Cinema Production Center, n.d.). The experience is reflected in *Ticket to Jerusalem* (2002), co-produced by the center, the story of a man who persists against all odds in his mission to screen films for Palestinian children. The oppression of the occupation is all-pervading, the dread that disaster might suddenly strike constant. *Waiting* (*Intizar/Attente*, 2005) in turn reflects Masharawi's experience of waiting to return to the ancestral home in Jaffa that his parents fled in 1948. *Laila's Birthday* (*'Eid milad Laila*, 2008) lightens the mood by bringing humor to a story of the frustrations of everyday life in Ramallah.

Hany Abu-Assad did not formally study cinema, either. He started out as an airplane engineer in the Netherlands and proceeded to produce films for cinema and television. His first feature film was an inconsequential comedy set in a Dutch middle-class milieu. *Rana's Wedding* (*al-Quds fi yawm akhar*, 2002), produced by the Palestinian Ministry of Culture with the help of funds secured from the Gulf states, brought him international recognition. Abu-Assad and Bero Beyer wrote *Paradise Now* (*al-Janna al-an*, 2005) in 1999, but it took them five years to get to shoot after they had secured funding from Dutch, Israeli, German, and French producers. Filming in Nablus, the crew was caught between the Israeli army and various Palestinian factions. Six European crew members departed after an Israeli missile hit a nearby car, the local location manager was kidnapped, and gunmen ordered the crew to leave. Filming resumed after three weeks, but five days later a landmine exploded three hundred meters from the set, and Abu-Assad moved the set to Nazareth, his birthplace in Israel (Abu-Assad 2005).

Beyond Egypt's popular cinema, several directors articulated social concerns and political critique in films that found international recognition. Tawfik Saleh, Youssef Chahine, and Salah Abu Seif became the principal directors of "Egyptian Realism."[20] Saleh was the only one to focus on political issues and adhere to a realist approach throughout his life's work, a total of seven feature films. Saleh ran into problems with censorship and bureaucracy in Egypt and eventually moved to Syria. There he joined directors from several other Arab countries to establish the "Alternative Cinema." Saleh's *The Dupes* (*al-Makhduʿun*, 1972) and Maleh's *The Leopard* were the group's first full-length fiction films. *The Dupes* won the Tanit d'Or at Carthage and was screened as a Critics' Selection at Cannes. From Syria, Saleh moved on to Iraq, where he produced his last film, *Long Days* (*al-Ayyam al-tawila*, 1980), on the life of Saddam Hussein—at a time when the dictator was still widely respected as a progressive leader.

Egypt's colonial experience brought education imported from Britain, but many intellectuals turned to the United States, which was seen as an anti-colonial power. Youssef Chahine is one of those educated at a prestigious British-style school who later trained in the United States. The internationally acclaimed director has sought to critically engage the West, notably in his autobiographic *Alexandria . . . New York* (*Iskanderija . . . New York*, 2004). And while his *Destiny* (*al-Masir*, 1997) is a denunciation of Islamic fundamentalism, it starts out with a man burned at the stake by the Inquisition. In his contribution to *September 11* (*11'09"01—September 11*, 2002), a compilation of shorts by eleven directors from around the world, Chahine engages in a dialogue with an American Marine killed in Beirut in 1982 that addresses the question of Westerners who ask, either from profound ignorance or in cynical hypocrisy, "Why do they hate us?"

Chahine was prompted to produce *Destiny* by his clash with Egyptian fundamentalists who had attacked him over his preceding film, *The Emigrant* (*al-Mohager*, 1994). Already he had been distressed to see young actors he had nurtured renounce acting as incompatible with their newfound fundamentalist beliefs. The example of one such actor informs a central story line in *Destiny*. Another major story line recalls the persecution and stabbing of Egyptian Nobel laureate Naguib Mahfouz.

Atef Hetata also has experienced the threats of fundamentalists from close by. Both his parents, Nawal el-Saadawi and Sherif Hetata, have been placed on death lists by fundamentalists. Hetata's first feature film, *Closed Doors* (*al-Abwab al-moghlaka*, 1999), gives voice to the secular, progressive, feminist viewpoints that his parents had championed for decades.

Maghrebi directors have moved back and forth between the two shores of the Mediterranean. Such is the case of Nabil Ayouch, who was born in Paris, the child of a French mother and a Moroccan father. For many years he spent half his time in Morocco, and in later years he moved there (Barlet 2003). *Ali Zaoua* (2000) focuses on an aspect of Moroccan society not readily acknowledged: its story of street children was a new departure for Moroccan film and indeed Arab film. The film earned the Stallion of Yennenga, the top prize at FESPACO, the Pan-African Film and Television Festival of Ouagadougou, and numerous other awards. Ayouch has come to prominence as a producer in Morocco. His production company, Ali n' Productions, joined with the National Radio and Television Company to form The Film Industry—Made in Morocco, which announced in 2007 that it planned to produce thirty feature films over a two-year period.

Nadia El Fani has moved between Tunis and Paris, where she was born to a French mother and a Tunisian father. She was not able to attend film school and learned her craft as an assistant to a string of directors for close to ten years. Eventually she produced her first short and established her own production company, Z'Yeux Noirs. *Bedwin Hacker*, her first feature, broke new ground in more ways than one. The film shatters stereotypes about Islamic societies by projecting an Arab world that not only contrasts with Western depictions but also is quite different from the world commonly presented in Arab films. In particular El Fani subverted stereotypes about Arab women by moving beyond the denunciation of gender inequality to show women who are very much in control in the world at large. She brings to the fore a key issue in globalization: Western domination of global media. And she pioneers a high-tech theme in Arab film and keeps her viewers in suspense with complex spy action. El Fani had to struggle with more or less explicit censorship all along: the difficulties of securing funding for the prize-winning script, the cuts demanded by the Tunisian Ministry of Culture, and the four-year delay until the film was released in Tunisia.

Nearly all Algerian directors, like their fellow intellectuals, sought refuge in France from fundamentalist threats in the 1990s.[21] Mohamed Chouikh and his wife, Yamina Bachir-Chouikh, were notable exceptions. They stayed in Algeria during *les années de violence*, the Years of Violence, even after her brother was killed. Chouikh added to his *œuvre* with films that established him as perhaps the finest Algerian director. Bachir-Chouikh, who had edited his films, and Chouikh responded to their experiences in quite different ways in her *Rachida* (2002) and his *Hamlet of Women* (*Douar nssa/Douar de femmes*, 2005).

Large numbers of Algerians, Moroccans, and Tunisians have settled in France. Among the many directors of their *cinéma beur*, Paris-born Rachid Bouchareb stands out. The director of a half-dozen feature films, he also has become an important producer of independent films. Some of his films range far beyond the confines of France and the Maghreb, and several have earned prestigious awards. His *Days of Glory* addresses the Maghreb, honoring the generation of his grandfather, who fought for the liberation of France in 1944–1945, and challenges the French to rewrite their history. In the sequel, *Outside the Law* (*Hors-la-loi*, 2010), he seeks to have French colonial history rewritten from the Sétif massacre in 1945 to the struggle of Algerian nationalists in France and the Paris massacre of peaceful demonstrators in 1961.

Themes of Dissent

Most of the directors who produce outside commercial cinema give voice and image to dissent in some if not all of their films, and so do some directors of commercial films. If certain themes stand out, their salience varies across borders, inviting an examination of their specific political and cultural contexts. We have seen already that films critical of political regimes can be found in every country and that their critiques have been remarkably forceful even where they faced repression. Some of these critiques have been quite explicit; others have had to remain rather subtle. Films problematizing gender relations have been produced in most countries for a long time. Some entail regime critique as they decry legislation and policies discriminating against women. Most critique patriarchal traditions that are upheld, or indeed resuscitated, by narrow interpretations of fundamentalist teachings. Denunciation of such patriarchal traditions is a major element in some of the films attacking Islamic fundamentalism that have appeared in recent years, usually in countries where the movement turned violent. Apart from such anti-fundamentalist films, directors have largely avoided portraying religion in their works, but then censorship commonly prohibits any material that might be deemed disrespectful of Islam.

Colonialism has been the focus of major films in Algeria and Libya, countries marked by protracted armed struggles against the European colonizers. Surprisingly few films from the region have addressed Western imperialism since the days when nationalist films denouncing British interference were common in formally independent countries such as Egypt and Iraq. Palestine is the pan-Arab theme *par excellence*. A substantial number of films have been devoted to the Palestinian cause throughout the Arab world and beyond. Kurds, not unlike Palestinians, are in search of their country. Their plight and their aspirations have inspired films by several directors, most of them of Kurdish descent.

GENDER

Gender issues recur in the cinemas of the Middle East and the Maghreb; they are conspicuous in the cinemas of Iran and Tunisia. The films denouncing the subordinate position of women in Iran may be seen as a reaction to the sustained effort of the clerical regime to roll back gains women had made. Among those responding to this attack have been prominent male directors like Dariush Mehrjui and Jafar Panahi, but two women directors stand out. Much of the large *œuvre* of Tahmineh Milani is devoted to gender issues, and Rakhshan Bani-Etemad has produced several films with the same focus. Most of the gender-oriented films are set among the middle class, but Bani-Etemad's *Under the Skin of the City* (*Zir-e pust-e shahr*, 2001) takes viewers into a working-class milieu where political discontent is rife and youth are alienated. A working mother holds her family together against the odds. She is involved in an unending struggle to support her family and protect her children as they reach adulthood in a patriarchal world where corruption, crime, and political repression are rampant.

A half-century after Tunisia promulgated legislation that profoundly reshaped women's rights, the position of Tunisian women within the family, their educational opportunities, and their professional achievements continue to be well ahead of those of women elsewhere in the Arab world. As in Iran, women are relatively well represented among filmmakers; and strong women feature in many Tunisian films, whether produced by women or men. Such strong female characters remain, however, usually largely confined within the family context as the clichéd powerful matron. Nadia El Fani's *Bedwin Hacker*, in contrast, no longer defines the protagonist in terms of her position within the family but as an independent woman. A technology wizard, she challenges Western domination of global media, interfering with satellite transmissions in cyberspace. With a French secret-service agent in hot pursuit of her, *Bedwin Hacker* has the qualities of a thriller at times, all the while subverting stereotypes about Islamic societies, most especially as concerns gender relations.

RELIGION

The Middle East is the heartland of Islam, but only in a few instances do films exalt religion. Overtly religious films are produced in Iran. Mohsen Makhmalbaf, for one, started out directing such films. In Egypt, Muslim religious films were produced in the 1960s and 1970s.[22]

Moustapha Akkad's *The Message* tells the story of The Prophet. Production in Morocco came to a halt when the producers withdrew their support, but Libyan leader Muammar al-Gaddafi stepped into the breach, and the film was completed in Libya. *The Message* offers a faithful reenactment of the events surrounding the life of The Prophet. For Muslim viewers the film illustrates the foundation story of their faith. Distribution was, however, restricted in some Arab countries because of protests by Muslim groups, even though the film had passed muster with religious authorities in Cairo and Beirut. In Morocco, on the other hand, the film was even dubbed in the Berber language. Muslims take for granted that representations of The Prophet, and for that matter his closest family, cannot be shown or heard. For others the absence of the principal protagonist lessens the dramatic impact of the story, and it becomes a somewhat dry history lesson.

Elsewhere filmmakers have denounced Islamic fundamentalists, most notably in Afghanistan, Algeria, and Egypt, countries where conflict with the authorities led to violence.[23] Most of their films forcefully condemn fundamentalists. Leaders are depicted as power-hungry and/or corrupt and their followers as blind adherents at best. Fundamentalists are shown to impose abhorrent rules, on women in particular, and to be responsible for deplorable violence. If such films challenge the tenets of some Muslims, they make it all too easy for Westerners simply to be outraged and to applaud the directors. And indeed, many of these films have been readily distributed in the West, quite unlike most of the films originating in the Middle East and the Maghreb.

Osama (2003) by Siddiq Barmak, Afghanistan's best-known director, was released to wide acclaim. The film is a searing indictment of the Taliban, denouncing their ideology and exposing brutality and corruption under their regime. *Osama* won the Golden Globe Foreign Film award and numerous others. And it is one of the rare films to draw comment from Western politicians; it was endorsed by George W. Bush as well as Hillary Clinton. But the subjugation of women continues to be part of post-Taliban Afghanistan, as *Stray Dogs* dramatically conveys.

Algerian directors have produced notable films in response to the rise of fundamentalism. Already in the 1990s *Youssef: The Legend of the Seventh Sleeper* and *Autumn—October in Algiers*, while condemning the regime, criticized fundamentalists who seek to impose their beliefs on others. In *Bab el-Oued City* (*Bab al-wad al-humah*, 1994), Merzak Allouache denounced the fundamentalists as they turned violent yet acknowledged their grievances, in particular the bloody repression of the 1988 demonstrations. These directors produced their films under precarious circumstances as violence spread in the early 1990s.

Only when the violence subsided could filmmakers address the civil war that pitted Islamists against the military regime that had denied them electoral victory in 1991. Allouache returned from self-imposed exile to shoot *The Other World* (*L'autre monde*, 2001), in which he effectively conveys the horrors of war-torn Algeria through the reactions of victims and witnesses rather than gruesome pictures. Yamina Bachir-Chouikh in turn produced *Rachida*, a dramatic condemnation of the atrocities committed by fundamentalists in which women appear as resilient victims. Mohamed Chouikh undertook to revisit the civil war at a time when many fundamentalists had laid down their arms in response to a government amnesty. Unlike most films addressing fundamentalism, Mohamed Chouikh's *Hamlet of Women* is conciliatory, offering a nuanced treatment. His villagers fight off the insurgents—and they fear government. He gives voice to the grievances that made a man join the insurgents. The story involves a reversal of gender roles that problematizes gender stereotypes while at the same time providing a source of humor that lightens this return to a painful past. *Hamlet of Women* won the top prize at Vues d'Afrique, the Montreal African film festival.

In Egypt the rise of Islamic fundamentalism as both a political ideology and a social practice has been a significant theme in commercial cinema since the early 1990s, as Armbrust sets out in his essay in the present volume. Armbrust focuses on two films of particular interest. *The Yacoubian Building* denounces fundamentalism as well as political corruption and repression, and it links them: favoritism embitters the protagonist of one of the several stories told in the film. He ends up being recruited by the fundamentalists, and his arrest and torture lead him to join the armed wing of the fundamentalist organization. Ahmad al-Badri's *I Am not with Them* (*Ana mish ma'ahum*, 2007), a romantic love story, acknowledges that the place of religion in society is widely debated in Egypt, as it is elsewhere in the Muslim world. These are commercial productions aimed primarily at the Arab market. Youssef Chahine in *Destiny* (1997) and Atef Hetata in *Closed Doors* (1999) sought to reach beyond local audiences, and both relied on foreign funding.

Destiny is arguably the finest film by Egypt's most distinguished director, who won a Lifetime Achievement Award at Cannes when the film was shown there in competition in 1997. The epic is set in the late twelfth century in the splendors of Córdoba, Andalusia's foremost city, bringing to life the flourishing Muslim civilization. Chahine offers a twofold critique of fundamentalist ideology. The film revolves around the life and teachings of the renowned Muslim philosopher Averroës, also known as Ibn Rushd. *Destiny* shows a humanist Averroës confronting the fundamentalists of the day with the affirmation "No one can claim to know the whole truth." Chahine complements the philosopher's teachings with his own philosophy of life, that life is to be lived—and enjoyed—to the fullest. Song and dance sequences, seamlessly integrated into the action, express Chahine's response to fundamentalism. *Destiny* is a thoroughly entertaining film of a sage and lovers of life confronting life-denying fundamentalists hungry for power.

In his debut feature, Atef Hetata attacks fundamentalism as did Chahine, but *Closed Doors* does what *Destiny* failed to do: the film effectively conveys the attractions of the fundamentalist creed and the community established around it. Set in Cairo during the 1991 Gulf War, the complex story of the coming of age of a boy raised by his divorced mother moves beyond the personal to detail the social, economic, and political ills of Egyptian society that make fundamentalism an appealing creed. Still, Hetata, like Chahine, chooses to present an undifferentiated picture of fundamentalist leaders. The clerics appear manipulative and their motives suspect. Neither director seems prepared to consider the fundamentalist faith at face value.

COLONIALISM AND IMPERIALISM

Colonialism has been the focus of major films where there was a protracted armed struggle. Moustapha Akkad created what is perhaps the foremost Middle Eastern film on the anti-colonial struggle in the Arab world. *Lion of the Desert* (1981) tells of the long resistance to the Italian conquest of Libya. The $35 million budget, rivaling those of its most expensive Hollywood contemporaries, was largely bankrolled by Muammar al-Gaddafi. The film was banned in Italy on the grounds that it was "damaging to the Italian army" (Popham 2007); only in 2009 did Italian television screen it during a state visit of Muammar al-Gaddafi. The film features dramatic battle scenes but may appear drawn-out to Western viewers. Gaddafi is preparing another epic on the Libyan resistance to Italian imperialism, *Years of Torment*. The film, budgeted at more than $40 million, is to be based on his own writing and directed by another Syrian, Najdat Anzour (ibid.).

During the Algerian War of Liberation, Chahine devoted a film to the cause. *Jamila, the Algerian* (*Jamila*, 1958) is based on the story of a heroine of the struggle, Djamilah Bouhired, one of the three women bombers depicted in *The Battle of Algiers*.[24] When the government of newly independent Algeria began producing films in the 1960s, most of them told of the war. The most famous film of the nascent Algerian cinema, though, the epic *Chronicle of the Years of Embers*, is set in the two decades leading up to the beginning of the war in 1954. Even the finest Algerian productions on the War of Liberation were overshadowed by *The Battle of Algiers* (*La Battaglia di Algeri*, Gillo Pontecorvo, 1966). Although directed by an Italian, *The Battle of Algiers* may be considered an Algerian film inasmuch as Saadi Yacef, the leader of the insurgency, was involved with the script, co-produced the film, and played himself in a key role. Gillo Pontecorvo's masterwork stands out among accounts of the anti-colonial struggle in the region; it is a classic among depictions of anti-colonial struggles anywhere in the world. *The Battle of Algiers* is as relevant to asymmetrical warfare today as it was a half-century ago. As the captured Front de Libération Nationale (FLN) leader Larbi Ben M'Hidi puts it in the film, in response to a journalist questioning the insurgents' bomb attacks on civilians:

> Isn't it even more cowardly to attack defenseless villages with napalm bombs that kill many thousands of times more? Obviously, planes would make things easier for us. Give us your bombers, sir, and you can have our baskets [in which the bombs were hidden].

Pontecorvo persuasively presents the rationale for "terrorism" in response to overwhelming military might and dramatically demonstrates the effectiveness of torture in extracting secrets from its victims, while suggesting the loss of legitimacy entailed in both strategies.

Pontecorvo's object lesson of how the French won the battle and lost the war gained fresh relevance when the United States invaded Afghanistan and Iraq, faced guerrilla warfare, and resorted to torture. The Pentagon's Office of Special Operations and Low-Intensity Conflict, for one, thought so, screening the film in August 2003, three months after the commander in chief had declared "Mission Accomplished."

In response to the U.S. invasion of Iraq, documentary filmmakers have produced an impressive array of films. Hollywood was slower to respond, and its films focus, as usual, on Americans. In distinct contrast, Al Daradji's *Ahlaam* is the story of two patients and a doctor at a psychiatric hospital in Baghdad where Al Daradji worked as a volunteer in 2003. Part of the gripping film is set in 1998, telling of repression under Saddam Hussein and bombing by the United States and Britain. Then the story resumes in 2003 with the fall of Baghdad. The horrors of the mayhem unleashed by the U.S. invasion become palpable as the three protagonists struggle to reach their very different goals. Al Daradji dramatically conveys the experiences of Iraqi civilians as bombs rained on Baghdad, Baathist snipers killed civilians in the streets, looters took advantage of the lawlessness, and American soldiers were unable to communicate with the population.[25]

PALESTINE

The establishment of Israel and the exodus of Arabs in 1948 was experienced by Arabs as a profound tragedy, the *Nakba*. The ensuing conflict has rent the Middle East for more than six decades. A substantial body of film has been devoted to the Palestinian cause across the Arab world as well as in Iran and Israel.[26] Egyptian director Yousry Nasrallah tells of the *Nakba* in "The Departure," the first half of his epic *The Gate of Sun* (*Bab el shams*, 2004). Based on the eponymous novel by the distinguished Lebanese author Elias Khouri, it was shot in Syria and Lebanon with actors and crew from around the Arab world.[27]

With *Kedma*, acclaimed Israeli director Amos Gitai gave voice to the two sides opposing each other in 1948. An Arab refugee confronts Israeli soldiers and prophesies strife without end, while a recently arrived Holocaust survivor, walking among the dead and wounded after a battle, protests that he does not want to be part of the history being written.

The Dupes stands out among the films devoted to the Palestinian cause across the Arab world. Featured in this volume with Syrian cinema, it is very much a pan-Arab production. Egyptian director Tawfik Saleh drew on the most important novella by Ghassan Kanafani, the distinguished Palestinian writer; the film was produced under the auspices of Syria's National Film Organization, and it was shot in Syria and Iraq. *The Dupes* follows three Palestinians who are propelled by economic or political reasons to migrate to Kuwait in search of work. A fellow Palestinian in Baghdad offers to take them across the border to Kuwait. These men represent three generations of Palestinian refugees, and their stories tell of their losses in 1948 and their precarious positions ten years later. The film denounces the hypocrisy and weakness of Arab regimes that proclaim their solidarity with the Palestinian people but have abandoned them.

Palestinian directors have sought to sensitize the outside world to the oppression suffered by Palestinians and to make foreigners understand that Israeli military might narrowly circumscribes the avenues Palestinian resistance can take. Rashid Masharawi's *Waiting* takes viewers to Palestinians living in Jordan, Syria, and Lebanon who continue to wait for the return to their homeland. A visit to the memorial site for the victims of the Sabra and Shatila massacre in Beirut brings home the precarious position of Palestinian refugees in their "host countries": Palestinian women and children were slaughtered by Lebanese militia, and more than twenty years later only a simple plaque commemorates them.

In 1967 the combined armies of Egypt, Jordan, and Syria suffered a dramatic defeat in the Six Day War. It was all the more traumatic for taking the Arab world by surprise, and it tarnished the stature of Gamal Abdel Nasser as the foremost nationalist leader of the Arab world. A number of Arab films reacted to that shock, prominent among them Chahine's *The Choice* (*al-Ikhtiyar*, 1970), *The Sparrow* (*al-'Usfur*, 1973), and *Return of the Prodigal Son* (*Awdat al-ibn al-dal*, 1976).[28] A few years later, novice Israeli director Bukaee addressed the war with *Avanti Popolo*. He features a desperate Egyptian soldier, an actor in civilian life, who recites Shylock's monologue in *The Merchant of Venice* as he pleads with Israeli soldiers to recognize their common humanity. Eventually the former enemies proceed together chanting "Avanti Popolo," the classic song of communist and socialist parties. *Avanti Popolo* reflects the reversal of roles: after their victory in 1967, Jews, once victims, become occupiers; Palestinians experience oppression in their own land, as if a minority.

Tale of the Three Jewels by Palestinian Michel Khleifi tells of life in Gaza under Israeli occupation in the early 1990s, lightening the mood by focusing on children, introducing the dreams of one of them, and offering an ambiguous ending. With *Paradise Now* Hany Abu-Assad presents Western audiences with a Palestinian perspective on what is commonly put beyond the bounds of argument by being branded "terrorism" while humanizing those who make the ultimate sacrifice by giving their lives for the cause. Where *The Battle of Algiers* articulates the strategic rationale for attacks on civilians in a struggle against overwhelming military might, *Paradise Now* conveys the rationale of suicide bombers living under oppression. The film's very title focuses attention on individual motivation. Its reference to rewards in the afterlife, however, plays to Western preconceptions. It obscures the political context foregrounded in the film, and it is misleading inasmuch as some suicide bombers are secular, as is one of the film's protagonists. *Paradise Now* won the Golden Globe Best Foreign Film award and numerous others, and it was nominated for an Oscar.

Just about all Palestinian directors adopt a mode that is by and large realist, quite close to the documentary, but Elia Suleiman takes an altogether different approach. His *Chronicle of a Disappearance* (*Sijill ikhtifa'*, 1996) and *Divine Intervention: A Chronicle of Love and Pain* (*Yad ilahiya*, 2002) stand apart by two distinctive features: minute portrayals of what passes for a normal life and flights of escapist fantasy. The "normal" life Suleiman affectionately portrays is the daily life of his parents in their Nazareth home in *Chronicle of a Disappearance* and that of his widowed father in a neighborhood rent by petty conflicts in *Divine Intervention*. The films then turn to the political context of Palestinians' daily life in altogether different ways. *Chronicle of a Disappearance* employs humor, ridiculing Israeli police who are manipulated by Suleiman's lover at will. *Divine Intervention* speaks of struggle, and the flight into fantasy becomes even more explicit. E.S.—Elia Suleiman played by himself—throws an apricot pit out of the car window at a tank, and the tank explodes; his lover strides through a roadblock, the Israeli soldiers are paralyzed as they watch her, and the watchtower collapses in an explosion. In the film's magnificent climactic scene, the lover becomes a ninja freedom fighter, spiraling into the air, warding off gunfire from her Israeli enemies, eliminating them all, and downing a helicopter.

These films respond to the frustrations of Palestinians living as second-class citizens in Israel and under Israeli occupation elsewhere. Suleiman has told of the euphoria of a Ramallah audience upon seeing the watchtower collapse (Wood 2006, 220). His films also can be seen as an expression of despair—the despair that normal life is an illusion for Palestinians and that there is no prospect of overcoming Israeli military might.

Suleiman went on to tell of his own life and that of his family since 1948 in *The Time that Remains* (2009). Drawing on the recollections of his father and his mother's letters, he presents a series of vignettes of the Suleimans and with it a history of Nazareth. Restrained acting, bordering on caricature, illustrates that history rather than bringing it alive. Suleiman again offers his viewers ironic gags, but he provides only faint echoes of the flights of fantasy that took viewers beyond the tableaux of his parents' life in his two preceding films, and the sense of laconic despair has become all-pervading—from Suleiman's grandfather, the mayor of Nazareth, who signed the surrender to the Israeli army; to Suleiman's father who was savagely beaten by Israeli soldiers and left for dead; to Suleiman himself who, as in his previous films, remains a silent witness.[29]

In the summer of 2006, Israel launched a devastating assault on Lebanon. Philippe Aractingi started shooting *Under the Bombs* (*Taht al-qasf/Sous les bombs*, 2007) even as Israeli planes were wreaking havoc. Much of the film has a documentary character, most strikingly the powerful opening sequence of a bombing. *Under the Bombs* poignantly conveys the disaster that befell the Lebanese, showing fear and panic, the despair of the bereaved, and the physical destruction wrought, rather than gruesome pictures.

KURDISTAN

Kurds, like Palestinians, are in search of their country. Their plight and their aspirations have inspired a number of films. Path-breaking was the powerful *Yol* (1981), which shared the Golden Palm at Cannes, where it also won the Critics' Prize. Kurdish-Turkish director Yilmaz Güney wrote the script while imprisoned, then entrusted the direction to his friend Şerif Gören. After Güney escaped from prison, he processed the film in France. The story follows five prisoners on furlough; one of them returns to "Kurdistan," as an intertitle puts it. The fields are blooming, but shots are ringing out from his village, where military police have cornered two guerrillas. The nights are filled with the sound of gunfire. When the army brings the dead for identification during the day, the villagers dare not recognize them for fear of retribution. Several more films focusing on the Kurdish conflict were produced in Turkey after its return to civilian rule. Prominent among them is Yeşim Ustaoğlu's *Journey to the Sun* (*Güneşe yolculuk*, 1999), which takes viewers from the discrimination Kurds experience in Istanbul to the devastation of the Kurdish countryside. Ustaoğlu had to find funding for the film in the Netherlands and Germany, but she was allowed to shoot it in Turkey. She and her film were showered with prizes at the two principal Turkish film festivals. However, distribution in Turkey proved difficult.[30]

Iranian productions devoted to Kurds commonly condemn the regime of Saddam Hussein, yet they remain silent on the position of Kurds in Iran. Samira Makhmalbaf's *Blackboards* (*Takhte siah*, 2000) drew worldwide attention to the plight of Iraqi Kurds when it garnered the Jury Prize at Cannes. Bahman Ghobadi established himself as a major director with four films in the span of just seven years. They were produced and largely funded in Iran. Ghobadi's films bring the Kurds into the cultural discourse both as subjects of his films and himself as a Kurdish filmmaker who has gained international recognition. *A Time for Drunken Horses* (*Zamani bara-ye masti-ye asbha*, 2000), set on the Iran-Iraq border, is shaped by a stark contrast between caring child workers and the men who exploit them—Ghobadi is anything but romanticizing his compatriots. *Marooned in Iraq* (*Songs of My Motherland/Avaz-hayé sarzamin-e madariyam*, 2002), shot in Iran, speaks of the suffering of the Kurdish people at the hands of Saddam Hussein. *Turtles Can Fly* (*Lakposht-ha ham parvaz mikonand*, 2004) shows refugee children in Iraq in desperate poverty; the child protagonist is a rape victim who raises her little brother but succumbs to utter distress. *Half Moon* (*Niwemang*, 2006) celebrates Kurdish music while denouncing the severe restrictions on women singing in public in Iran.

Hiner Saleem enjoyed funding by the Regional Government of Iraqi Kurdistan for *Kilometre Zero* (*Kilomètre zéro*, 2005). The film is set in Iraq at the time of the U.S. invasion. It has returning Kurdish exiles commenting that they know the United States is an imperialist power and they would have preferred the Swiss or the Swedish, but nobody else came. If Kurds appear as victims in most films devoted to them, that is not the case in Saleem's *Dol* (2007). This film stakes out the claim to a state bringing the Kurdish people together by having viewers partake of the life of Kurds in three countries: life under military boots in Turkey, exhilaration at liberation and grief over the suffering of the past in Iraq, and armed resistance in Iran.[31]

Creative Dissidence against the Odds

To sum up, apart from the established film industry of Egypt, film production in the Middle East and the Maghreb depends heavily on subsidies. Even in Iran, with its large market, and in Israel, with its relatively affluent population, government funding plays a significant role. Elsewhere the fortunes of film production have waxed and waned as government policies have changed over time. Foreign funding has enabled the work of Palestinian directors and much of the recent work of directors such as Youssef Chahine, Amos Gitai, and the Makhmalbafs. It likewise has aided filmmaking throughout the Maghreb.

Outside the commercial cinemas of Egypt, Iran, and Israel, most film directors have to surmount formidable obstacles to secure funding, to produce their films, and to get them distributed. Against all odds, they have produced outstanding works. Many of their films have successfully competed in international film festivals. However, very few have enjoyed general release overseas, even while distribution for home viewing and institutional use has improved.

Most of these *auteurs* give voice to dissent, as do some of those working in commercial cinema. These intellectuals *cum* artists have managed to produce trenchant critiques, some more explicit than others, a testimony to their engagement and their courage. They offer fresh perspectives on crucial issues confronting the region today, perspectives that are shared by much of the intellectual class.

NOTES

I wish to thank, without implicating, Roy Armes, Kevin Dwyer, Eric Egan, Lisa Wedeen, and the anonymous reviewers for helpful comments on earlier versions.

1. Very few of the films featured here have enjoyed general release in the anglophone world; most have had only limited exposure at film festivals and art houses. Some are available in the United States on home video; others are distributed for institutional use. However, as of this writing, *Avanti Popolo* is available only in Hebrew, *Hamlet of Women* is not in distribution, and *Waiting* is only in theatrical distribution.
2. The sketches of and comments on Hollywood productions in Shaheen's encyclopedic *Reel Bad Arabs: How Hollywood Vilifies a People* (2009) constitute a devastating indictment of the role played by the world's predominant media industry in projecting negative images of the Arab world. An eponymous documentary based on his study (Sut Jhally, 2006) offers the most extraordinary examples of the rampant vilification of Arabs. Shaheen's subsequent study *Guilty: Hollywood's Verdict on Arabs after 9/11* (2008) demonstrates how this industry continues to project images that further poison international relations at a time of crisis. Khatib (2006) compares the politics of Hollywood and Arab films. Particularly striking are her observations on the contrasting use of space: while Hollywood films convey mastery of space by the Western protagonists, Egyptian and Palestinian films present an insider view.

3. Armes (2008, 2010b) and Qasim (2009) list most Arab films. Armes gives information on the directors; Qasim provides information on the production team and a short summary of the story of each film.
4. Turkish cinema is not included in this collection, and in this introduction I just touch briefly on a couple of Turkish films focusing on the Kurdish issue. Turkish cinema is one of the major cinemas of the region, with both a large body of work and a number of directors who have gained international recognition. The omission is a matter for regret, even if it may be justified on several grounds. One argument turns on the question of the extent to which Turkey, while geographically largely within Asia, is culturally part of Europe. Kemal Atatürk sought to transform the country into a European nation three generations ago, and conflicts over his reforms fuel current debates over Turkey's application to join the European Union. Another consideration is that Turkey has remained marginal to the conflicts that ravage the Middle East. This may change if the simmering conflict between Turkey and the increasingly autonomous Kurdish region of Iraq comes to a head. In the end, there were practical matters of keeping this volume manageable in terms of the efforts required and the publisher's concern over the length of the book. On Turkish cinema see Dönmez-Colin 2008 and Suner 2010.
5. Full-length fiction films used to be called feature films, but feature-length documentaries have become quite common. At the same time, the boundaries between the two genres have become blurred. Major directors like Jean Khalil Chamoun and Amos Gitai work in both genres. If Western fiction is quite distinct from local productions, such is not the case for Western documentaries: they often draw on public and/or private funding that frees them from commercial considerations, and many directors share local perspectives and have come to give image and voice to them.
6. Rosenstone has argued (1995), with reference to historical film, that film is not only different from written discourse, and necessarily so, but that this very difference constitutes an important contribution; he posits historical film as a History *sui generis*. The argument can be extended to films complementing conventional analysis of foreign societies and cultures.
7. Two film scholars working under a repressive regime may have been compelled by their precarious position to withdraw after initial indications that they would be happy to collaborate.
8. Dwyer (2007) sets out the formidable challenge globally operating media corporations present to countries that are small and poor, with Morocco as his example.
9. On the box-office success of comedies in the Maghreb see Armes 2010a, 7, 18, 22. In spite of such successes, comedies are rarely produced outside the commercial cinemas of Egypt, Iran, and Israel. Their scarcity probably reflects the priorities of both directors and the national and foreign public agencies that provide financial support.

10. *Beur* is French slang for a descendant of immigrants from the Maghreb. On the *cinéma beur* see Tarr 2005 and Armes forthcoming.
11. On *Stars in Broad Daylight* see Wedeen in this volume.
12. NBC. 2009. *Inside Iran*, June 7
13. Exiles can speak whereof those who stay have to remain silent. In *For a Moment, Freedom (Ein Augenblick, Freiheit*, 2008), Arash Riahi interweaves three stories of people who emigrate to escape persecution in Iran. Their diverse experiences convey the dangers they face not only crossing the border illegally but also from Iranian secret-service agents in Ankara, their efforts to convince U.N. officials to grant them refugee status and to get foreign countries to allow them to immigrate, their struggles to survive in the meantime, and the disaster that awaits those who are forced to return to Iran. All the while the drama is leavened with a good dose of humor.
14. In the 1989 edition of *Israeli Cinema: East/West and the Politics of Representation*, Shohat provided a rich account of the beginnings of the "Palestinian wave" in Israeli cinema that was rather critical; in her 2010 revision she presented a comprehensive overview of a more recent documentary cinema that has actively intervened in the revisionist debate over the representation of Israeli history.
15. Khaled Youssef tells of negotiating with the censors and cutting ten seconds. They were replaced by a black screen, signaling to viewers what had to be omitted (Barlet 2008).
16. For a brief discussion of five Moroccan films that evoke the trauma of the Years of Lead see Bakrim 2005. Only one of them, Faouzi's Bensaidi's *A Thousand Months (Alf shahr/Mille mois*, 2003), is in distribution.
17. Makhmalbaf revisited that episode in a fictionalized account, *A Moment of Innocence (Nun va goldoon*, 1996), recruiting the police officer he had stabbed to coach the police officer in the film. With the film Makhmalbaf disowned his revolutionary past, depicting himself and a woman accomplice as idealistic dreamers living in a world of fantasy.
18. Makhmalbaf's mother, Esmat Jam-pour, acted in three of his early, "Islamic" films.
19. Among the distinguished graduates of the Makhmalbaf Film School are Ebrahim Ghafouri, who shot most of the films of the Makhmalbaf family from 1995 to 2005; Makhmalbaf's brother-in-law Akbar Meshkini, who designed the sets of most of the family's films since 1998; and his son Maysam Makhmalbaf, who has produced most of the family's films since 2000.
20. On Egyptian Realism see Shafik 2007, 128–143.
21. Salim Aggar devoted a documentary, *Ça tourne à Alger* ["Filming in Algiers"] (2007), to the very few directors who continued filming in Algeria. Among others, Malik Lakhdar-Hamina tells of the hazards of filming *Autumn—October in Algiers* (1993), and Belkacem Hadjadj (*Once upon a Time/Il était une fois/Machaho*, 1995) reconstitutes an encounter with insurgents at a roadblock in the middle of the night when he, his crew, and actors feared for their lives.

22. Coptic films have appeared in Egypt in recent years, their distribution restricted by law to churches (Shafik forthcoming).
23. A number of Israeli films likewise have critically portrayed Orthodox Judaism.
24. On *Jamila, the Algerian* see Fawal 2001, 80–88.
25. Mohamed Al Daradji's documentary *War, Love, God & Madness* (2008) tells the story of filming *Ahlaam* in Baghdad in 2004. Actors and crew were shot at in the streets. Insurgents kidnapped and tortured Al Daradji and three crew members, shot one of them, and eventually lined them up for execution, to be saved only by the siren of a passing police car. Militia kidnapped and tortured them in turn. Finally handed over to U.S. troops, they were subjected to violence and abuse until the Dutch embassy intervened due to Al Daradji having Dutch as well as Iraqi citizenship.
26. Hafez (2006), Massad (2006), and Sadr (2006, 215) touch on numerous Arab and Iranian films that focus on Palestine.
27. On *The Gate of Sun* see Elbendary and El-Assyouti 2005.
28. On *The Choice, The Sparrow*, and *Return of the Prodigal Son* see Fawal 2001, 88–116.
29. On Suleiman see Abu-Remaileh 2008, Dabashi 2006, and Gertz and Khleifi 2008, 171–189. On *Chronicle of a Disappearance* in particular see Bresheeth 2007.
30. Comments on Handan İpekçi's *Hejar* (*Big Man, Small Love/Büyük Adam, küçük aşk*, 2001) and the prizes the film garnered are promising, but at this time *Hejar* is only available in the Turkish original or with Japanese and Chinese subtitles. For a detailed, critical discussion of the portrayal of Kurds in Turkish cinema see Dönmez-Colin 2008, 91–109.
31. For brief accounts of films devoted to Kurds, including films not mentioned here, see Bozarslan 2006; Shafik 2007, 43, 238–240; and Suner 2010.

REFERENCES

Abu-Assad, Hany. 2005. "Q&A with director Hany Abu-Assad." The interview is no longer posted at http://wip.warnerbros.com. A somewhat different version is available in the French press book, *Paradise Now*. Haut et Court.

Abu-Remaileh, Refqa. 2008. "Palestinian Anti-Narratives in the Films of Elia Suleiman." *Arab Media and Society*, May. http://www.arabmediasociety.com/?article=670.

Armes, Roy. 2008. *Dictionary of African Filmmakers*, Bloomington: Indiana University Press.

———. 2010a. "Cinema of the Maghreb." *Black Camera* 1 (1): 5–29.

———. 2010b.: *Arab Filmmakers of the Middle East: A Dictionary*. Bloomington: Indiana University Press.

———. 2010c. Personal communication to the author, January 11.

———. Forthcoming. "The Filmmaker and the State in the Maghreb." In *African Cinemas: A Continental Approach*, ed. Josef Gugler.

Auer, Claudia. 2006. "Interview with Tahmineh Milani: Between Censorship and a Smash Hit." http://qantara.de/webcom/show_article.php/_c-544/_nr-14/i.html.
Bakrim, Mohammed. 2005. "Le cinéma marocain à la recherche du temps perdu." http://africine.org/?menu=art&no=5992&rech=1.
Barlet, Olivier. 2003. "A propos de *Ali Zaoua*: entretien avec Nabil Ayouch." http://www.africultures.com/php/index.php?nav=article&no=2897.
———. 2008. "*Le Chaos* face à la censure: Entretien d'Olivier Barlet avec Khaled Youssef." http://www.africultures.com/index.asp?menu=affiche_article&no=7212&rech=1.
Béar, Liza. 2008. *The Making of Alternative Cinema*. Vol. 2, *Beyond the Frame: Dialogues with World Filmmakers*. Westport, CT: Praeger.
Bozarslan, Hamit. 2006. "La représentation des kurdes dans le cinéma." In *Créations artistiques contemporains en pays d'Islam: Des arts en tensions*, ed. Jocelyne Dakhlia, 201–207. Paris: Edition Kimé.
Bresheeth, Haim. 2007. "Segell Ikhtifa/Chronicle of a Disappearance." In *The Cinema of North Africa and the Middle East*, ed. Gönül Dönmez-Colin, 168–178. London: Wallflower Press.
Central Bureau of Statistics (Israel). 2010. Personal communication to the author.
Cinema Production Center. n.d. "Rashid Masharawi." http://www.cineprod-center.com/home.htm.
cooke, miriam. 2007. *Dissident Syria: Making Oppositional Arts Official*. Durham, NC: Duke University Press.
Dabashi, Hamid. 2006. "In Praise of Frivolity." In *Dreams of a Nation*, ed. Hamid Dabashi, 131–160. London: Verso.
Dönmez-Colin, Gönül. 2008. *Turkish Cinema: Identity, Distance, and Belonging*. London: Reaktion Books.
Dwyer, Kevin. 2007. "Moroccan Cinema and the Promotion of Culture." *Journal of North African Studies* 12 (3): 277–286.
Egan, Eric. 2010. Personal communication to the author, January 5.
Elbendary, Amina, and Mohamed El-Assyouti. 2005. "To Begin at the Beginning." *Al-Ahram Weekly*, January 13–19. http://weekly.ahram.org.eg/2005/725/cu4.htm.
Fawal, Ibrahim. 2001. *Youssef Chahine*. World Directors. London: British Film Institute.
Gertz, Nurith, and George Khleifi. 2008. *Palestinian Cinema: Landscape, Trauma, and, Memory*. Edinburgh: Edinburgh University Press; Bloomington: Indiana University Press.
Hafez, Sabry. 2006. "The Quest for/Obsession with the National in Arabic Cinema." In *Theorising National Cinema*, ed. Valentina Vitali and Paul Willemen, 226–253. London: British Film Institute.
Khatib, Lina. 2006. *Filming the Modern Middle East: Politics in the Cinemas of Hollywood and the Arab World*. London: I. B. Tauris.
Khoury, Elias. 2005. *Gate of the Sun*. Translated by Humphrey Davies. Brooklyn, NY: Archipelago Books.

Massad, Joseph. 2006. "The Weapon of Culture: Cinema in the Palestinian Liberation Struggle." In *Dreams of a Nation*, ed. Hamid Dabashi, 30–42. London: Verso.

Mohammad, Oussama. 2006. Public discussion at ArteEast Syrian film festival, notes taken by Josef Gugler, New York, May.

Popham, Peter. 2007. "Gaddafi Turns Screenwriter for $40m Epic about Italian Invasion." *The Independent*, November 3.

Qasim, Mahmud. 2009. *Mawsuʿat al-aflam al-ʿarabiya, Arabic Films Encyclopedia, 1927–2009*. Published at the author's expense.

Rosenstone, Robert A. 1995. *Visions of the Past: The Challenge of Film to Our Idea of History*. Cambridge: Harvard University Press.

Sadr, Hamid Reza. 2006. *Iranian Cinema: A Political History*. London: I. B. Tauris.

Salti, Rasha. 2006. "Critical Nationals: The Paradoxes of Syrian Cinema." In *Insights into Syrian Cinema: Essays and Conversations with Contemporary Filmmakers*, ed. Rasha Salti, 21–44. New York: ArteEast and Rattapallax Press.

Shafik, Viola. 2007. *Arab Cinema: History and Cultural Identity*. Revised edition. Cairo: American University in Cairo Press.

———. Forthcoming. "Popular Egyptian Cinema: Industry and Society," in *African Cinemas: A Continental Approach*, ed. Josef Gugler.

Shaheen, Jack G. 2008. *Guilty: Hollywood's Verdict on Arabs after 9/11*. Northampton, MA: Olive Branch Press.

———. 2009. *Reel Bad Arabs: How Hollywood Vilifies a People*. Revised edition. Northampton, MA: Olive Branch Press.

Shohat, Ella. 2010. *Israeli Cinema: East/West and the Politics of Representation*. Revised edition. London: I. B. Tauris.

Suner, Asuman. 2010. *New Turkish Cinema: Belonging, Identity, and Memory*. Tauris Third World Cinema. London: I. B. Tauris.

Tarr, Carrie. 2005. *Reframing Difference*: Beur *and* Banlieue *Filmmaking in France*. Manchester: Manchester University Press.

Weeden, Lisa. 1999. *Ambiguities of Domination: Politics, Rhetoric, and Symbols in Contemporary Syria*. Chicago: University of Chicago Press.

Wood, Jason. 2006. *Talking Movies: Contemporary World Filmmakers in Interview*. London: Wallflower Press.

World Bank. 2009. *World Development Report 2010*. http://econ.worldbank.org/WBSITE/EXTERNAL/EXTDEC/EXTRESEARCH/EXTWDRS/EXTWDR2010/0,,contentMDK:21969137~menuPK:5287748~pagePK:64167689~piPK:64167673~theSitePK:5287741,00.html.

Wright, Lawrence. 2006. "Disillusioned." In *Insights into Syrian Cinema: Essays and Conversations with Contemporary Filmmakers*, ed. Rasha Salti, 45–65. New York: ArteEast and Rattapallax Press.

1

Regime Critics Confront Censorship in Iranian Cinema

ERIC EGAN

> [A] film's life is longer than a government's life ... I have gone from politics to cinema to tell people many things.
> MOHSEN MAKHMALBAF (2008, 226–227)

> I think that the history of Iranian cinema is very much linked with that of Iranian intellectualism, which in turn, is a movement linked with the history of modern Iran.
> BAHRAM BEYZAI (2006, 27)

> My films are never shown so I do not know what the [Iranian] public thinks.
> ABOLFAZL JALILI (2006, 44)

> What the artist wants is different from what the politicians want. Artists search a way to converge diverse elements. Our job is to find a meeting point. On the other hand, politicians look for diversities.
> ABBAS KIAROSTAMI (2006, 54)

> Now we have had a revolution and nothing has changed.
> DARIUSH MEHRJUI (2006, 74)

As these comments from leading filmmakers illustrate, to approach an understanding and critical engagement with the cinematic medium in Iran requires an examination of the complex social, political, and historical conditions that have informed Iranian culture in general and cinema in particular. Iranian cinema operated for the first seventy-nine years of its life under a system of monarchical rule before being forced to adapt to the changed ideological strictures of the new Islamic regime in the wake of the 1979 Revolution.

Iranian cinema has functioned as an integral part of the complex and tortuous narrative of twentieth-century Iranian history. In this respect it has shown itself responsive to social and political change, with filmmakers attempting to articulate a moral and political vision through an intimacy and familiarity with indigenous cultural forms to be engaged as sites of struggle and contested meanings. As a result, Iranian cinema has, since its inception, operated within a complex conflux of Persian, Western, and Islamic influences. Whether a monarchical dictatorship or Islamic theocracy, culture, art, and communication have, in the absence of autonomous democratic political activity, been used by those in power to propagate their visions of Iranian society, enforce nationalist or religious sentiments, and legitimate the right to rule. At the same time, this position is critiqued and problematized by artists using various media as a means of challenging notions of cultural absolutism.

The Early Years

The history and development of cinema in Iran prior to the Iranian Revolution in 1979 provides the first step in setting the terms of debate and constructing a template explicating recurrent issues that have informed the cinematic landscape and its development as an art form. The key issues that were to become constant and defining features of the development of the medium—censorship, religious disapproval, and centralized government control—became quickly established in the early days of its introduction into the country. Brought to Iran in 1900 by the fifth shah of the Qajar Dynasty, Mozaffar al-Din Shah, cinema, unlike its development in the West, began life as a plaything for the royal court and elites of Iranian society. These early films were primarily short newsreels documenting the activities of the shah and the royal family and may be counted as the first examples of state-sponsored film. This set something of a precedent, which in a sense was to be expected given the highly centralized and autocratic structure of government in Iran; film was commissioned, controlled, and seen to be in the service of the state. It was not until cinema moved from the court into the public arena as a form of mass entertainment that this relationship became problematic and began to provoke reactions from other elements within a deeply traditional society.

The first public cinema in Iran was established by Mirza Ebrahim Khan Sahafbashi in 1903 and immediately provoked a storm of protest. The clergy issued a *fatwa* against the new medium, deeming it a threat to Iranian values. These protests forced the government to bow to religious pressure, resulting in the eventual closure of Sahafbashi's enterprise. Throughout this period the cinema was caught between those wishing to promote and expand the medium as a means of mass entertainment and the more conservative religious elements in society who wished to limit its spread. Lacking a coherent policy, a weak government saw itself merely reacting to events as expediency demanded. This was reflected throughout the country as a whole, which by the end of World War I was in political, social, and economic crisis. In the midst of this chaos a young army officer, Reza Khan, staged a *coup d'état* and installed himself as shah in 1925, establishing the Pahlavi Dynasty that was to rule the country until it was overthrown by the Revolution of 1979. He set out to create a strong, centralized government that would put the country on a path of secularizing and modernizing reforms, challenge the authority of the clergy, and bring Iran into the modern world. The cinema would form a vital element of this modernization drive.

Shortly after the inauguration of the new regime, the government decreed that one of the functions of the cinema would be to promote the latest European methods of agriculture (Sadr 2006, 13). This highlighted the government's awareness of the power of the new medium and the view that film should serve in promoting the activities and ideology of the state. Such a policy required strict control of the medium. The government introduced a censorship program that began with the banning of *Grass* (1924), a documentary on Iranian nomadic tribes made by American filmmakers Merian C. Cooper and Ernest B. Schoedsack. The reason given was that the film offered a picture of a traditional way of life at odds with the modern and progressive outlook of the new regime. Censorship became a codified part of state policy with the introduction of a bill in 1930 requiring all cinema managers to acquire an exhibition permit in order to screen films.

The same year Avanes Ohanian established the country's first cinema school and succeeded in making the first Iranian feature film, a comedy titled *Abi and Rabi* (*Abi va Rabi*, 1930). Two years later he made *Haji Agha, Cinema Actor* (*Haji Agha actor-e cinema*, 1932), the story of a religious man initially antagonistic and suspicious of cinema who becomes won over by the new medium. The film was a reflection of wider debates in society and established a thematic preoccupation that was to become a constant in Iranian cinema: the clash between the traditional and the modern. This theme was reiterated the following year when the first Iranian talkie, *The Lor Girl* (*Dokhtar-e Lor*, Abdolhossein Sepanta, 1933), was released. Shot and produced in India, this film has the distinction of establishing the form, particularly in terms of the stock characters and social types portrayed, of much of the commercial cinema that came to dominate Iranian screens after World War II and up to the 1979 Revolution.

The Lor Girl tells the story of a government official sent to quell rebellious tribes in the Lorestan region of the country. While there he meets and falls in love with the independent and strong-willed Golnar, whom he rescues from tribal captivity and brings to the city. The film modeled elements that would pervade much of Iranian commercial cinema: the chivalrous hero, guided by a social conscience and strong moral codes of friendship and community, and the independent heroine, whose honor must be protected from the advances of villains, framed within a love story that contrasts modern values with traditional values and the rural with the urban. Indeed, *The Lor Girl* illustrates the connectedness of cinema with currents in society and in a sense reflected official ideology in its drive to modernize the country and suppress rebellious tribes. This was a point not lost on the government officials who were impressed by the film and through the Ministry of Culture approached its producer to make a film on the famous Iranian poet Ferdowsi.

Such government intervention and undertakings should be seen as attempts to use the cinema as a means of promoting a progressive image of the country and to effect a cultural change. Known as Pahlavism, this was an effort by the shah to legitimize his rule ideologically and culturally by laying claim to the glories of the ancient kings of the Persian Empire and turning the emotive force of secular Iranian nationalism into a cult of monarchy. This was done to counteract the influence of the clergy, promote the idea of continuous kingship, and legitimate the new Pahlavi Dynasty by using culture as a tool of the political system.

A series of further censorship laws was passed in 1934 and 1935 that placed cinema under the direct control of the Department of Police and gave it the power to alter any film deemed politically or ethically inappropriate. In 1938 the first cinema bill was passed; it required production permits and forbade any subject matter censors considered contrary to the security, respect, and dignity of the nation. These developments established the official attitude toward cinema and the arts in general: the state sought to control cultural activities through direct intervention and a more subtle form of ideologically conditioned censorship. However, the lack of an economic and technical infrastructure hampered the development of an indigenous industry. As a result, only nine indigenous films were made in the 1930s. The majority of Iranian screens showed foreign films. Moreover, even these films operated under and were subject to strict censorship. Under such conditions and given the economic, social, and cultural consequences of World War II, the industry, such as it was, entered a period of stagnation.

PART 1: IRANIAN CINEMA

The Postwar Years, 1945–1963

The war and postwar years were a time of tumultuous change in Iran. British and Soviet forces occupied the country for the duration of the war, forcing Reza Shah to abdicate in 1941. Iran entered a brief period of democracy when his son Mohammad Reza Shah assumed the throne. This era of relative freedom was brought to an abrupt end with the oil nationalization crisis of 1951–1953 and toppling of nationalist leader Mohammad Mosaddeq and his elected government in a CIA-sponsored coup in August 1953. These tumultuous events resulted in the shah consolidating his position and strengthening his control on power and was, over the next two and a half decades, to see Iran move into the orbit of American political and cultural influence. This period was marked by the rise of the indigenous commercial film industry and increased foreign cultural influence in the import and production of films, as well as continued government interference.

The incipient format of the indigenous commercial cinema can be seen in Esmail Kushan's production *The Tempest of Life* (*Tufan-e zendegi*, 1948), directed by Ali Daryabegi. It tells the story of Nahid and Farhad. Nahid's father refuses to allow the pair to be together and forces her to marry a wealthy merchant of dubious character. Farhad, heartbroken, dedicates himself to his work and soon becomes successful and rich. After a series of incidents the young lovers are reunited before eventually marrying and living happily ever after. The melodramatic love story, simplistically located in traditional cultural mores, formed the template of what came to be known as Film Farsi.

Most Iranian commercial films were Film Farsi. These films were heavily influenced by Egyptian and Indian song and dance films and melodramatic American B movies. Through Kushan's Pars Film Studio output, which in turn encouraged a proliferation of local studios, the indigenous industry began to find its feet and entered a period of rapid development. A country that had produced only 11 feature films up until 1948 produced some 336 films from seventy-three local studios by the end of 1965 (Issari 1989, 197). Most of these films were low-quality melodramas and comedies made purely for commercial gain. Despite the often poorly executed treatments and formulaic and simplistic storylines, however, Film Farsi must be seen as an important and integral part of Iranian cinematic history.

Film Farsi productions were conceived and made purely for consumption by local audiences, who generally showed themselves enthusiastically receptive to the stock elements of comedy, action, and Persian singing and dancing. These films reflected, however simplistically, elements of wider social, historical, and political changes occurring in the country at the time. The large number of productions with themes such as the simplicity of rural life and the promotion of traditional values, in contrast to the perceived sinister complexity of large cities, can be seen as an attempt to articulate anxieties about the pace of change.

In a period of rapid modernization exemplified by the 1963 Revolution of the Shah and the People, or the White Revolution,[1] many Iranians felt dislocated and unable to keep up in a society that, buoyed by the rise in oil prices and the resulting influx of petro dollars into the economy, was hurtling into the sphere of international capitalism and Western influence. This inevitably resulted in a restructuring of traditional social bonds. Amid the fistfights and posturing that structured Film Farsi, in its own way the genre represented an attempt to express the local and knowable concerns and desires of its audience. Indeed, the central character of the *luti* (lumpen rogue) became an exaggerated representation of Iranian masculinity with a strict code of honor and morality, an antihero with an anarchic sense of justice who rejected all forms of Westernization and stood as a standard-bearer of what mainstream audiences saw as traditional Iranian values.

By this time cinema had become the main form of cultural entertainment for the majority of the population. The rapid development of the medium and the increasingly autocratic nature of the state meant that it was never far from controversy or government interference. What began to emerge from officialdom was a dual policy of regressive and enlightened steps as the government sought to control the medium but also contribute to its development as a serious art form. The former was most clearly evidenced in 1950 with the establishment of a Screen Commission consisting of representatives from the Ministries of the Interior and Education and the Departments of Publications and Propaganda and of Police. The commission set out a rigid code of conduct for all aspects of film production, distribution, and exhibition. Among the articles and guidelines were some that outlawed anything that the authorities considered offensive to Islam or the monarchy, incited political turmoil, or corrupted public morals.

The application of these laws was often haphazard, with less attention paid to works that potentially would corrupt public morals than to those seen as insulting the monarchy. Indeed, it is hard to imagine the survival of the commercial sector, with its high quotient of risqué content and violence, if films had been subjected to the letter of the law. These codes and restrictions were augmented in 1965, then reinforced in 1968 when the Ministry of Arts and Culture took direct control of the Screen Commission. Among the new categories subject to censorship were films that insulted the military, incited riots and rebellion, or damaged the prestige of the country by denigrating its culture and portraying it as backward. These new restrictions reflect the official policy and ideology of a government that by this time had developed a large and sophisticated military and intelligence machine and had quelled all forms of dissent.

Despite the restrictive measures, certain developments contributed to the emergence of a politically, socially, and artistically engaged cinematic movement. The first steps lay in the efforts and visual arts projects undertaken by some foreign embassies to establish a newsreel and documentary program to expand their nations' information services and promote their cultural and infrastructural activities. One of the lasting legacies of this foreign influence came with the documentary and newsreel productions of the U.S. Information Services (USIS) and Syracuse University in the 1950s that marked a turning point both technically and aesthetically for future indigenous film production. This undertaking produced a large number of educational documentaries as well as a weekly newsreel that was shown in local cinemas; the films addressed such topics as the activities of the shah, development programs, and improved health and agricultural methods.

In one respect these films were designed to produce a Western consumerist cultural view that reflected Pahlavi designs for the country (Naficy 2002, 257). Yet they also must be seen as a continuation of the state's view of cinema from its inception as a form of private sponsorship for and by the ruling elite and as a means to promote state ideology. These newsreels were to have a telling influence on the local film industry. By the time the Syracuse team left in 1959, Iran had the most up-to-date audio-visual center in the Middle East, with well-trained and technically proficient filmmakers about to emerge. In addition, these cinematic undertakings enhanced the notion of the filming of and engagement with reality, elements that were to become hallmarks of the unprecedented artistic flourishing of Iranian cinematic talent in the 1960s and 1970s.

The New Wave: From White Revolution to Islamic Revolution

The emergence of a socially and politically engaged cinematic movement by filmmakers eager to explore and expand the medium's possibilities must be viewed within the context of the tumultuous changes taking place in the country. This was a period of unprecedented cultural development in the arts as a whole and the desire among a new generation of filmmakers to break with the repetitious and simplistic formula of Film Farsi. While Film Farsi acted as a catalyst to develop a new form of artistic cinema, attention also must be given to the influence of the contemporary political and cultural developments, both official and unofficial, in Iran. Part of the shah's modernization program, with its drive to achieve unprecedented levels of economic and industrial growth, was a desire to foster a form of "high culture" ideologically in tune with the advent of a "new civilization." It would serve the dual purpose of promoting the appearance of a liberal and vibrant cultural environment to the outside world through investment in "serious" art while at the same time restricting access through censorship and state controls.

The regime established an infrastructure to foster, promote, and control works of "high" artistic quality. The National Film Board, under the direction of the Ministry of Culture and Arts, was to be responsible for administering the film production activities of the entire country. The ministry also controlled the newly established National Iranian Radio and Television, which in addition to promoting the country's visual media culture provided regular employment and training in television for those working in the cinema industry. The commitment to establish a sustainable infrastructure capable of high-quality cinematic output was served by the creation in 1963—likewise through the Ministry of Culture and Arts—of the College of Dramatic Arts (Mehrabi 1984, 388). Similarly, the Iranian Young Cinema Society, established in 1974, was intended to familiarize amateur students of cinema with professional techniques.[2]

Other state-sponsored institutions like the Institute for the Intellectual Development of Children and Young Adults and its cinema department, Telfilm,[3] and the Film Industry Development Company financed the majority of New Wave films and nurtured the talent of directors including Abbas Kiarostami, Amir Naderi, Bahram Beyzai, Parviz Kimiavi, and Bahman Farmanara. A fund was established to begin a massive building and development program for movie studios and theaters. Through its control of the cinematic medium, the regime selectively promoted films of a critical nature, screening them to select audiences at prestige events such as the Tehran International Film Festival or in film festivals abroad while banning them from wider exhibition on domestic screens.[4]

Given the lack of a genuine form of political opposition capable of expressing grievances or articulating the changed social conditions, it was perhaps inevitable that artists would come to occupy a socially active role, attempting to fill the political vacuum. Forugh Farrokhzad in poetry and Sadeq Chubak, Housang Golshiri, and Gholam Hossein Saedi in literature and theater set about experimenting with form and content to examine the changed circumstances of the social environment. Many of these artists collaborated with the new voices emerging in the cinema. This collaborative adaptation is one of the distinct attributes of the New Wave cinema as artists together explored the psychology of complex characters, the cinematic medium itself, and the Iranian cultural past and present.

Groundbreaking films like *Siyavosh at Persepolis* (*Siyavosh dar Takht-e Jamshid*, Fereydoun Rahnema, 1964) employed theatrical stylistic forms and a complex series of cultural and filmic codes that presented an entirely fresh approach to filmmaking in which time and place are irrelevant phenomena. *Siyavosh at Persepolis* centers on Crown Prince Siyavosh, who after a falling-out with his father leaves Iran and settles in Turan, or modern-day Turkey. There he marries the daughter of King Afrasyab and is killed in a plot by the king's scheming and jealous son. The film combines this ancient story with documentary-style scenes of foreign tourists visiting the ruins of Persepolis in the present, creating a work in which past, present, future, legend, theater, and a myriad of filmic forms are combined in a dense intertextuality that was new to Iranian cinema. Such self-reflexivity and mixing of historical and cultural forms was evident in other films as well, such as *The Mongols* (*Mogholha*, Parviz Kimiavi, 1973) and *Prince Ehtejab* (*Shahzadeh Ehtejab*, Bahman Farmanara, 1974).

The Mongols takes a highly stylized Godardian approach in comparing the coming of television in Iran to the destructive Mongol invasion of the thirteenth century, making oblique reference to the Western cultural invasion that was seen as a result of the shah's modernization program. This question of the influx of Western values and the feeling of cultural dislocation they induced was reflected in other intellectual currents, such as Jalal Al-e Ahmad's highly influential book *Gharbzadegi* (*Westoxification*, 1962), and became a thematic preoccupation of many New Wave films.[5] Searing social commentary was also evident in *Prince Ehtejab*. Based on Houshang Golshiri's acclaimed novel, the film focuses on a dying prince recalling the extravagances, cruelty, and ruthlessness of his and his ancestors' rule. A harsh indictment on the abuse of power, it drew heavy parallels to the shah's regime.

Sohrab Shahid Saless, in his hugely influential landmark films *A Simple Event* (*Yek ettefaq-e sadeh*, 1973) and *Still Life* (*Tabiat-e bijan*, 1974), developed a poetic realism with a sparse, slow, and naturalistic style to depict real locations, local people, their culture, social conditions, and daily struggles and to capture the routine and rhythm of their lives. Nasser Taghavi's *Tranquility in the Presence of Others* (*Aramesh dar huzur-e digaran*, 1973) presents a picture of

Iranian society as one plagued by decadence, corruption, and rootlessness to which despair and self-destruction are the only answers. The film follows a retired army colonel who comes to Tehran to visit his daughters. Seeing that they are living decadent lives and feeling unable to adapt to the new environment, he blames himself for what he perceives as their immorality and corruption. He falls into despair and dies in deep depression in a mental hospital. Such films articulate a form of social commitment based on self-realization and a belief that the creative process can open up a space where more ideal social relations can be discussed and allowed to flourish. The cinematic language that articulates these social concerns originated in a more personal politics embedded in local contexts and cultural forms. The central and most famous film in this regard is Dariush Mehrjui's *The Cow* (*Gav* 1969).

Based on a short story by Gholam Hossein Saedi taken from his collection *Azabadaran-e Bayal* (The Mourners of Bayal), *The Cow* looks into the relationship between a farmer and his cow. Following the cow's death, the distraught farmer begins to take on the cow's characteristics before eventually succumbing to madness and death. The film was initially banned for what was seen as its unflattering depiction of rural poverty. After it won accolades at the 1970 Venice Film Festival, it was allowed onto Iranian screens on the condition that it attach a disclaimer stating that the events portrayed took place prior to the modernization undertakings of the Pahlavi regime. As an important and highly influential film that is credited with bringing Iranian cinema to world attention, much has been written about *The Cow*, from its groundbreaking realist aesthetic (Issari 1989, 240) to its portrayal of a society of superstition, fear, distrust, and grinding poverty in the midst of what was supposed to be an era of modernization (Mirbakhtyar 2006, 52) to the analogies it draws with an economy overdependent on one saleable commodity (Sadr 2006, 133). While all these elements are evident, the far-reaching influence of the film lies in its success in creating a uniquely Iranian form of realist cinema that strongly influenced many post-revolutionary films.

Deeply embedded in the diverse cultural strands of Iranian culture, *The Cow* combined the ritualistic, the epic, and the metaphorical. Structured like a mourning ritual, the film portrays a realism that contains elements of expressionism and surrealism, exhibiting an air of foreboding and apprehension. The combination leads to a heightening of the "senses so that even the slightest tremble is registered as a jarring change" (Dabashi 2007, 114), which in turn draws attention to the unstable and fabricated nature of reality. This is a reality based on indigenous cultural ritual forms with allusions to pre-Islamic and

Islamic elements,[6] yet these are counterbalanced by the performed nature of rituals that have become routinized and devoid of meaning. It is the intertwining of cultural elements and their interaction with a refracted vision of a fluid and volatile reality that was to have a huge influence on post-revolutionary cinema.

In a different vein but equally influential in the development of a more highbrow but commercially accessible cinema was Massoud Kimiai's *Qaisar* (1969). This story of an individual who sets out to avenge the rape of his sister and death of his brother combines and transforms many elements of Film Farsi to present a bleak and noirish vision of a cynical society beset by crime and disaffection; yet it also portrays the oppressiveness of honor and traditional beliefs and the impotence of rebellion. These were elements that Kimiai was to continue to explore under changed ideological conditions after the revolution in films such as *Protest* (*Eteraz*, 2000), which deals with the disillusionment, hopelessness, and clash of differing generational belief systems during the Khatami era.

This type of cinema, more narrative, genre-driven, and readily accessible to a large domestic audience, can be seen to have influenced the socially critical work of Mohsen Makhmalbaf and Jafar Panahi as well as the genre-oriented *engagé* films of the late 1990s. The legacy of the New Wave lies perhaps in this commitment to issues of social and political concern. Through a focus on the flexible structures of representation that originate in and recognize the complexity and diversity of national and indigenous cultural experiences, these films gave voice and expression to oppositional discourses in questioning absolutist ideologies and beliefs.

By the mid-1970s the Iranian film industry was in crisis. The regime had become aware of the growing discontent in society at large and was increasingly sensitive to criticism in cinema. Official institutions like the Ministry of Culture and Art withdrew financial support. Increasingly harsh and arbitrarily applied censorship led to many films being drastically cut or shelved indefinitely. Production dropped from ninety-one films in 1971 to just eighteen in 1978. At the same time, rising costs of production and promotion, high taxation, and runaway inflation created a situation in which many producers moved from production to the lower-cost, less risky enterprise of importing cheap foreign films for distribution.

The voices of discontent and protest that had been growing against the shah's rule and culminated in his overthrow and exile in 1979 dealt the final blow to the industry. Associated with the ills of the Pahlavi regime and seen as a symbol of Western infiltration and corruption, cinema became a target of attack for zealous revolutionaries. Some 180 theaters were destroyed in Iran. In Tehran only 7 out of a total of 118 theaters remained intact by 1978 (Akrami 1987, 138). With the triumph of the revolution and the return from exile of its charismatic leader, Ayatollah Khomeini, cinema and the country as a whole entered a new and uncertain future.

Cinema in the Era of War and Revolution, 1979–1988

The first decade of the Islamic Revolution, from the toppling of the shah in 1979 to the death of Ayatollah Khomeini in 1989, could be considered one of the most turbulent periods in Iran's long history. During this time Iran experienced the catastrophic problems of war, economic crises, and social and cultural upheaval. Having assumed absolute power, the clerics set about the task of implementing Khomeini's revolutionary ideology whereby the tenets of the faith constituted the rules of government and members of the *ulama* (the clergy) exercised authority as the political elite. The media were to help create a new Islamic society, as expressed in Ayatollah Khomeini's declaration that cinema, radio, and television should be used as instruments of education for the advancement of society rather than misused as a "vice," as happened under the previous regime and kept "our young people in a state of backwardness" (Khomeini 1981, 258).

The institutionalization and control of culture and the means of its dissemination were codified and laid out in Article 175 of the new constitution of the Islamic Republic. It decreed that the media would disseminate and observe Islamic norms and promote the interests of the country. The revolution resulted in the total collapse of the Iranian film industry. Many leading producers, actors, and directors went into exile, and those who remained were beset by uncertainty as to what would be permissible under the new ideological system. This caution was reflected in the paltry number of films made in the early years following the revolution. Most of these stuck to a propagandist formula of castigating the former regime and lauding the achievements of the revolution.[7] The new regime took its first steps to revive and bring the medium under centralized control in 1980 with the introduction of a points system, from 1 to 4, that allowed Iranian producers to import an equivalent number of foreign films to the grading their films received. A producer who earned four points would be allowed to import four films; a two-star rating would give a producer the right to import two films, and so on. The measure was introduced to prevent Iranian producer-distributors from harming the industry by cashing in on the comparative cheapness of foreign-made films—an average of $50,000 against $150,000 for a film made in Iran at the time. The hope was that this would encourage producers to make more quality films of their own. The points system was soon followed by the all-too-familiar imposition of state control over content, in this case under the 1981 Censorship Act.

Henceforth physical contact or romantic relationships between the sexes were forbidden, all female characters were required to adhere to Islamic dress codes, and all material deemed insulting to Islam or the Islamic Republic was prohibited. Strict enforcement of these codes is evident: in the first three years following the revolution, 513 foreign films of a total 898 reviewed were banned (Naficy 2000, 106). The situation was little better for domestic productions: of a total of 40 films made in the first four years after the revolution, 23 were banned by the authorities (Motavalli 1983, 56). Indeed, these measures and others reflect larger currents in society; some 175 newspapers were shut down in 1981, and universities were closed in order to "Islamicize" the education system. Official control further tightened in 1982 when the Iranian parliament devised "Guidelines to Govern the Policies of the Iranian National Radio and Television." These stated that the goal of all media should be to adhere to and promote the principles of independence, freedom, and the Islamic Republic. While these principles and declarations established the framework within which the media were to operate, it was not until the following year that the government took the first constructive steps toward rebuilding a shattered industry.

The Farabi Cinema Foundation (FCF) was established in 1983 under the auspices of the Ministry of Culture and Islamic Guidance. It was charged with the enforcement and regulation of government cinematic policy, the centralization of state control, and the promotion of a new form of cinema. The FCF set out the parameters of what was acceptable in all areas of cinematic activity by putting in place a series of regulations to control film production, distribution, and exhibition. In the area of production, the FCF was responsible for the import and export of films, the leasing of filmmaking equipment, and the provision of financial credit. In 1986 it introduced a system of classification and censorial regulations for all films. This system required each production to gain screenplay approval before being granted a production permit. On completion the finished film is sent to the Council of Film Reviewing, which issues it an exhibition permit, bans it outright, or subjects it to modifications. An exhibition permit is granted according to a four-point grading system. The grade a film receives determines the exposure it will have, the type of theaters where it will be shown—in conjunction with an equivalent grading system for cinema theaters introduced in 1987—and its access to promotional and advertising resources.

The foundation set out to promote and support a form of cinema that would project Islamic values and revolutionary ideals. Other institutions including the Foundation of the Oppressed and the Art Institute of the Islamic Propaganda Organization established film units to provide training and finance for young revolutionaries in the visual arts.[8] Through these efforts the regime conveyed, albeit as a vaguely defined notion, its general desire to establish an Islamic cinema "that would play its role in propagating Islam, just like the mosque" (Al-lamehzadeh 1997, 130). For the most part these early efforts resulted in poorly made films that dealt with jurisprudential issues, revolutionary political sloganeering, and themes like the righteous man, his path to God, and Quranic religious or philosophical debates on sin and repentance, destiny and fate, good and evil. Simplistic and didactic in tone, these films embodied the first stage in producing official art as part of the regime's larger Islamicization project of society at large, from the institutional level to that of individual psychology. The aim of this sociocultural undertaking was to create an ideal revolutionary citizen dedicated to the state and its Islamic ideology. This vision was perhaps best realized in the cinema by the appearance of the war genre, which did not exist in Iranian cinema before the revolution.[9]

The Cinema of the Sacred Defense arose during the eight-year war with Iraq that began in 1980. In that period cinema became a tool of government propaganda in preserving revolutionary morale, castigating the enemy, and keeping the country fighting.[10] War began to dominate Iranian cinema screens, with many of the films merely serving as a means of transmitting unsubtle official sloganeering in support of Islam and the Islamic Republic. Within the context of the regime's socialization policy, these films provided the perfect format for the portrayal of the Islamic man as the stoic defender of the faith while at the same time reproducing (officially sanctioned) Shia cultural forms such as martyrdom and sacrifice. The importance of the war film as a conveyor of state ideology can be clearly seen in the government's establishment, five years after the war ended, of the Association for the Sacred Defense to continue supporting filmmakers who produced works on the Holy Defense. The end of the war in 1988 and the death a year later of the revolution's spiritual leader, Ayatollah Khomeini, marked a turning point for the Islamic regime. The ruling elite recognized that change would have to occur if the Islamic system was to be maintained and a shattered country with massive economic and social problems was to be rebuilt.

Cinema in the Era of Reconstruction, 1989–1997

A new administration led by Ali Akbar Hashemi Rafsanjani began to focus on economic and infrastructural reconstruction and a less confrontational approach to Iran's foreign relations. The lessening intensity of the revolutionary fervor resulted in some easing of restrictions in the sociocultural sphere. This led to the growth of the theater, the revival of traditional Iranian classical music, and an increase in the number of journals and newspapers from 102 in 1988–1989 to 369 in 1992–1993 (Schirazi 1998, 137). For the cinema this new era brought the abolition in 1988 of the need to gain screenplay approval before beginning a project. However, this seemingly progressive step merely placed censorship responsibility into the hands of producers, making them ever more cautious in the projects they chose. These steps must also be seen within the context of the tightening of restrictions by the High Council of Culture. Reiterating the terms of the 1985 law governing media, it decreed that any material that officials determined to be socially and politically divisive to the unity of the nation, advocate Western values, or promote morally corrupting behavior would be banned. However, the efforts of the FCF over the previous decade had begun to bear fruit.

What had been a moribund industry was now producing between forty and fifty films a year. Many of those who had received training were now emerging as artists experimenting with the language of form and content, and the reappearance of certain pre-revolutionary filmmakers added new currents and quality to the industry. The latter included Dariush Mehrjui, whose commercially oriented comedy *The Tenants* (*Ejarehneshin-ha*, 1987) became the highest-grossing Iranian film of all time at the domestic box office; Nasser Taghavi's *Captain Khorshid* (*Nakhoda Khorshid*, 1987), a loose adaptation of Ernest Hemingway's *To Have and Have Not*; the experimental poeticism of Amir Naderi's *Water, Wind, Earth* (*Ab, bad, khak*, 1989); and the compassionate, humanistic, and poetic realism of Bahram Beyzai's *Bashu, the Little Stranger* (*Bashu, gharibeh kuchak*, 1986). Directors including Ebrahim Hatamikia and Mohsen Makhmalbaf began to look critically at the decade of war and revolution. Using the war genre as a means of focusing on the problems of veterans, Makhmalbaf's *Marriage of the Blessed* (*Arusi-ye khuban*, 1989) examined the social and political problems besetting the country and asked difficult questions concerning the sacrifices that were made and the direction of the revolution.[11]

Perhaps of greatest significance was the active role taken by the FCF in aggressively promoting "superior Iranian films" on the world stage. This undertaking arose from the desire to present a more liberal and moderate face to the outside world and resulted in the number of screenings of Iranian films at international festivals rising from 88 in 1989 to 415 in 1993 (Duagoo 1993, 64–67). Iranian films became staples of the international festival circuit and were soon seen to have certain clearly identifiable traits. These included a slow, meditative, realism-inflected aesthetic countered by a self-reflexive consideration of the nature of the image and its construction, the collapse of the division between fiction and reality, an emphasis on children as the main characters, a depiction of real events, and a location within a rural milieu. For many this type of filmmaking soon became repetitious and formulaic, a form of Orientalist curiosity composed of beautiful landscapes and esoteric silences.[12] The point that such criticism misses is the diversity of approach in the application of many of these elements.

The focus on children, for example, ranges from the constructed realism in combination with spiritual and symbolic elements in Abbas Kiarostami's *Where Is the Friend's House?* (*Khaneh-ye dust kojast?*, 1987) to the poetic and abstract desire and longing in Abolfazl Jalili's *Dance of Dust* (*Raqs-e khak*, 1992) to his harsh documentary-inspired indictment of a cruel and dehumanizing society in *Don* (1999) to the simplistic and moral life lessons of Mohammad-Ali Talebi's *Tick Tack* (1994) to the plight of immigrants and the economic hardship of children on the margins of society in films such as *Djomeh* (Hasan Yektapanah, 2000) and *Baran* (Majid Majidi, 2001). These films, while radically different in style and tone, present the picture of a world that is extremely aggressive and even hostile to children. Moving beyond the simple pillorying of ideological or political positions, such films portray the strength of social and human experience that offers a new testimony about humankind.

The censorship restrictions that followed the revolution made the focus on adult relationships difficult and may have encouraged a move to the less contentious—at least in the mind of the censor—world of children. Here Iranian filmmakers have attempted to explore the conflict between human innocence and the cumulative pressures of social experience. They have transcended the political particularities of the moment to express deeper layers of a unique Iranian cultural and historical experience and such dimensions of human existence as the tragic, death, love, conscience, and social responsibility.

This cinema is attuned to the dangers of didacticism and seeks to set forth a myriad of voices in counteracting and challenging the worst excesses of a repressive society. It draws on morality, ethics, and stoicism rooted in deep-seated cultural contours. While the desire of the regime may have been to change foreign viewers' image of Iran and make them question their attitudes toward the country (Tahami 1993, 4), the attitude of the regime to these films was once again one of repressive tolerance. Many of the films lauded on foreign screens were banned in Iran.[13] This contradictory cultural policy in relation to domestic and international audiences has its precedent in policies of the Pahlavi regime.

New technologies like satellite television and the Internet changed the cultural arena. A generation that had grown up under the Islamic regime rejected the Islamic socialization project, and a burgeoning movement of intellectuals called for reform of the system and the introduction of some form of democracy and civil society. These voices and the articulation of such concerns were to become more pronounced as the Rafsanjani administration came to an end. Initial reforms in the cultural sphere had been rolled back as conservative elements reasserted control in a bid to offset the perceived onslaught of Western cultural decadence. They imposed stricter rules, implemented increased bureaucratic and supervisory controls on production, and threatened to ban any film seen as portraying an unfavorable image of the country.

These restrictions formed part of a larger crackdown in which by the mid-1990s most reformist newspapers were banned or closed down, hundreds of intellectuals and supposed dissidents were imprisoned or executed, and tens of thousands were arrested for what the authorities called "social corruption." These measures highlighted the dissent being voiced in society at large: it was more persistent and articulate than before and came from diffuse sources. It questioned authoritarian rule through a language that called for the recognition of individual rights, the establishment of a civil society, and the need for a separation of religion and politics.

Cinema in the Era of Reform, 1997–2005

The currents of dissent culminated in the landslide election of the former reformist Minister of Culture Mohammad Khatami as president in 1997. He conducted his election campaign on a policy platform with a priority of implementing the rule of law and developing a civil society (Ansari 2000, 96). In 1997 the cinema of reconstruction reached its pinnacle with Abbas Kiarostami's *The Taste of Cherry* (*Tam-e gilas*, 1997) winning the Golden Palm at the Cannes Film Festival (Elena 2005, 123). From this point on, the focus, form, and thematic preoccupations in Iranian cinema began to change. Previously emphasis was placed on the technical and ideological aspects of film production and the promotion of a "quality cinema" primarily for export.

By contrast, the Khatami era saw a cinema emerge that was more openly concerned with critical subject matter and social and political problems such as poverty, corruption, and the abuse of power. The focus on children and rural settings was altered to a concentration on more adult themes such as divorce, extramarital affairs, alienation, drug addiction, teenage pregnancy, and their playing out in an often hostile urban environment. With the easing of censorship restrictions and a desire to express complex problems and openly address social issues, many filmmakers put aside the symbolic and esoteric in favor of more straightforward, commercially oriented narratives. The cinema of this era had greater appeal to commercial domestic audiences and was defined by genre conventions, particularly comedy, melodramas, and family films; it was primarily concerned with the notion of youthful rebellion and the status and problems of women in society.

The most startling of the new voices to emerge were those of women filmmakers who came to the fore during this period. Their emergence was all the more dramatic given that prior to the revolution the only films directed by women were *Marjan* (1956) by Shahla Riyahi, the short documentary *The House Is Black* (*Khaneh siah ast*, 1962) by the poet Forugh Farrokhzad, and *The Sealed Soil* (*Khak-e sar beh mohr*, 1977) by Marva Nabili (Dabashi 2007, 382–386). Now a new generation of female artists and filmmakers articulated the problems, concerns, and difficulties of life in a religiously and culturally codified and hierarchically structured society. They sought to examine the complexity of subjects defined as objects in a society that is constructed to deny and erase, or make difficult, their identities as individuals. This undertaking necessitated the realistic depiction and representation of women who previously occupied roles of simplistic dualism or archetypes of "chaste or unchaste dolls" (Lahiji 2002, 215–226). Filmmakers like Rakhshan Bani-Etemad, Tahmineh Milani, Samira Makhmalbaf, and Marziyeh Meshkini sought to give voice to this silence.

In films like *Nargess* (1992), about a complex love triangle, or *The May Lady* (*Banoo-ye ordibehesht*, 1998), which highlights the desires of a middle-aged divorced woman and questions the officially constructed notion of the ideal woman, Bani-Etemad examines the plight of women in society. Combining a documentary-infused aesthetic with complex psychological investigations, she uses her characters to reflect and examine pressing social concerns. Her films present not just a more realistic portrayal of women as individuals but of a society, as shown in *Under the Skin of the City* (*Zir-e pust-e shahr*, 1999), in which families are betrayed, mothers are abandoned, and promises, both personal and political, are meaningless.[14] The more commercially oriented Milani has used genre and a more straightforward narrative style in tackling socially contentious issues. Her work has ranged from comedy to family drama and social critique. Some have generated much comment and debate, among them *Two Women* (*Do zan*, 1999) and *The Fifth Reaction* (*Vakonesh-e panjom*, 2003), which portray women trapped and powerless under an unyielding patriarchal system, and *The Hidden Half* (*Nimeh-ye penhan*, 2001), which questions political and personal beliefs.[15]

The overall government strategy with regard to cinema was to promote and bolster the domestic market and place greater emphasis on the private sector. These commitments were delineated in the Third Development Plan, which outlined means to improve productivity, establish an organization to promote a national cinema, develop a visual media system throughout the country, and establish a research and training program for all aspects of the cinema industry (Mohammadi 2002, 6). The FCF began to provide producers in the private sector with access to more facilities and help in promoting and distributing their films abroad. The government introduced further reforms by removing the barrier of film ranking, giving more power to producers and cinema owners that resulted in films' greater exposure to market forces and increasing reliance on the box office (Mahmoudi 2006, 24).

Perhaps the most striking undertaking was the relaxation of the censorship codes, a move that allowed filmmakers to tackle more risqué and taboo subjects. Banned films like Ali Hatami's *Haji Washington* (1982), Dariush Mehrjui's *The Lady* (*Banoo*, 1992), and Mohsen Makhmalbaf's *A Moment of Innocence* (*Noon va goldun*, 1996) finally received screening permits. The government announced its intention to redress the country's shortage of cinema screens by beginning a comprehensive theater construction program.[16] These efforts were enhanced by the decision to leave cinema policies unchanged for five years, thus replacing the ministry's fifteen-year-old policy of annual declarations, to create an atmosphere of stability that freed filmmakers from the uncertainty and capriciousness of official whims. *Hemlock* (*Shokaran*, Behrooz Afkhami, 2001), *Maxx* (Saman Moqaddam, 2005), *The Lizard* (*Marmulak*, Kamal Tabrizi, 2004), *The Girl in the Sneakers* (*Dokhtari ba kafsh-haye katani*, Rasoul Sadr Ameli, 1999), and *I'm Taraneh, 15* (*Man Taraneh, panzdah sal daram*, Rasoul Sadr Ameli 2002) were box-office hits that provoked controversy and protest, highlighted changing forms and subject matters, and illustrated the fine line between the permissible, the critical, and the officially acceptable.

The Lizard is an instructive example of the complex battle between official narratives and counternarratives. Taking a comedic and satirical swipe at the hypocrisy of the clergy and the blind belief of their followers, the film tells the story of an escaped convict who inadvertently becomes a respected religious figure through his simplistic, down-to-earth, common-sense preaching. The film became the biggest box-office success in the twenty-five years of the Islamic Republic as well as creating a wave of protest and official condemnation that resulted in its being withdrawn from exhibition after only three weeks. The articulation of its message operates on the border of socially engaged criticism and an endorsement of official values. On the one hand it suggests that the individual is eventually transformed by his encounter with the spiritual and that if the clergy are to survive they must accept criticism and become more attuned to the people's needs. On the other it posits that the Quran is open to all who seek it and that individuals can find their own paths to God.

These questions centering on the clash between an officially sanctioned versus a more individualistic approach to religion were very much in tune with the intellectual debates occurring throughout the Khatami era of issues such as individual freedom and the separation of religion and politics. However, the idea of the individual finding a path to the divine can be construed, in the context of a system that posits the learned jurists (*mujtaheds*) as the source of all power, both spiritual and political, as an attack on the absolute power structure of the Islamic Republic.

Similarly, *I'm Taraneh, 15* tackles contentious social issues within the context of a critical and constructive engagement with traditional and officially endorsed values (Dönmez-Colin 2004, 173). The story follows a teenage girl from a broken home who becomes pregnant after a temporary marriage (*sigheh*) and who, despite social pressures, decides to keep the child and raise it as a single mother; the film is calling on the rights of the individual to be respected and for freedom of expression in contradistinction to traditional values. It also can be seen to echo official attitudes in its highlighting of a moral choice that endorses spiritual growth and motherhood. In this respect it could be said to bear a certain resemblance to the Islamicized cinema that emerged in the years immediately after the revolution with its emphasis on self-sacrifice and decency standing against selfish and immoral behavior.

Indeed, the notion of an "Islamic cinema" acting as a vehicle for the promotion of official ideology and propaganda has been transformed in the minds of the authorities. They began to champion a form of cinema that would eschew dogmatism in favor of examining the spiritual relationship between individuals and God and the promotion of Islamic moral values. Toward this end the FCF established a Department of Spiritual Cinema in 2003 to promote a form of cinema that explores the essence of being and the enigmatic, mystical, and supernatural world of divine origin (Danesh 2007, 73). With its emphasis on dreams, miracles, the supernatural, and religious symbolism, it bears a marked resemblance to the type of filmmaking promoted during the early years of the revolution. Its relevance lies in chiming with the emergence of the socially engaged cinema and in operating within the margins of criticism and moral values. The social cinema of the Khatami era embodies an amalgamation of elements from Film Farsi in its commercial orientation, from Islamic cinema in its belief in the supremacy of moral good and self-sacrifice, and from New Wave films in their examination of pressing social issues.

At the same time, some members of the older, pre-revolutionary generation of filmmakers returned to filmmaking after years of silence and produced works on the fate of the artist and on censorship, offering an often searing indictment of an immoral society in freefall. Such was the case of Bahman Farmanara in *Smell of Camphor, Fragrance of Jasmine* (*Bu-ye kafur, atr-e yas*, 2000) and *A House Built on Water* (*Khaneh-e ru-ye ab*, 2002) and Parviz Kimiavi in *Iran Is My Land* (*Iran sara-ye man ast*, 1999). The emergence of new filmmakers added to a vibrant and increasingly diverse industry.[17] Bahman Ghobadi set out to chronicle the experience of Kurds in *A Time for Drunken Horses* (*Zamani bara-ye masti-ye asbha*, 2000), *Marooned in Iraq* (*Avaz-haye sarzamin-e madariyam*, 2002), and *Turtles Can Fly* (*Lakposht-ha ham parvaz mikonand*, 2004). Marziyeh Meshkini in *Stray Dogs* (*Sag-haye velgrad*, 2004) and Hassan Yektapanah in *Djomeh* (2000) depicted the suffering of Afghans.[18]

The increasingly outspoken views of the press and the perceived liberalization of the cultural sphere caused alarm in the conservative ruling faction, resulting in the closure of many newspapers and tighter controls on the media in general. As part of this clamp-down, a new cinema law was drafted in 2000 to remove the permit requirement for screening a film and place the responsibility for the production and screening of their films onto the producers and directors. Those within the industry voiced concern that this proposal rendered them defenseless against the judiciary and in fact increased the arbitrary power of the latter to intervene directly in screening decisions. These fears were well founded: for the first time ever the Iranian judiciary intervened to ban Saman Moghaddam's film *Party* (2001) deeming it insulting to those martyred during the war. These measures were bolstered by a stricter application of the censorship laws. Under such conditions filmmakers including Mohsen Makhmalbaf moved abroad, while others including Jafar Panahi and Abolfazl Jalili experienced the familiar pattern of having their works win awards abroad yet be banned in Iran. This reflected the situation in a society at large pervaded by a sense of frustration and despair as the high expectations for reforms under the Khatami administration ended in widespread disillusionment.

The election in 2005 brought the hard-line conservative Mahmoud Ahmadinejad to office and with him his promise to restore Islamic government. While the new minister for cultural affairs stated the need for a liberal attitude in filmmaking and to accommodate different viewpoints (Omid 2006, 176), the traditional problems of government control of the medium, censorship, and adverse economic conditions have continued to beset the industry. Perhaps a good indication of the changing of official attitudes toward the medium was the publication in 2007 of a two-year study by the cultural commission of the Majles (Iranian parliament) on the state of the Iranian film industry. It was extremely critical of the reforms introduced under the Khatami administration as promoting Westernization and desecrating Islamic values. The report criticized the content of many films made during this period for their concentration on what were deemed to be negative social issues such as divorce, drug addiction, and suicide. This view in essence has formed the template of the Ahmadinejad administration's approach to cinema.

The conservative ideological orientation has resulted in an increase in religious and revolutionary themes in films, a reduction in the activities of independent filmmakers, the almost total elimination of Iran's presence in international festivals,[19] and production of films with mass appeal and a strong ideological flavor. Such attitudes are familiar to an Iranian cinema that traditionally has functioned in an often hostile environment and yet has produced new generations of artists and cinematic movements that have continued to subvert, undermine, and question notions of censorship; they examine the responsibility of the artist to his or her art and society at large and the uneasy relationship with the state. Historically the absence of a civil society in Iran and the implementation of repressive official policies have stifled the terms of public debate to such an extent that it has fallen to the artist to act as the critical conscience and give voice to those unable to speak. This has been and continues to be the driving force of the best of Iranian cinema where the medium is used as an engaged mode of expression and an instrument of social change.

PART 1: IRANIAN CINEMA

NOTES

1. This was the cornerstone of the shah's modernization program. Its main points centered around land reform, workers' rights, and women's suffrage. Many of the reforms were never implemented or poorly executed.
2. This institution was closed following the revolution and reopened in 1985. Since then it has established fifty-nine offices across the country. Some 40,000 students have graduated from the institution in a variety of cinematic fields, and many of their works have been aired on Iranian television.
3. Set up in 1969 under the auspices of the Ministry of Culture and Arts, the institute allowed Iranian youth the opportunity to experiment with the medium. It produced some one hundred films, including works from Abbas Kiarostami, Dariush Mehrjui, and Bahram Beyzai, until 1979.
4. The film festival was established by the Ministry of Culture and Arts in 1972 as a gala event to promote Iranian cinema and the regime itself by showcasing the best films on an international stage in front of some of the world's leading cinema personalities.
5. Al-e Ahmad's work attacked the rapid Westernization that he perceived Mohammad Reza Shah to be inflicting on the country. However, its main theme was the sense of Iranians' own deep alienation and the fear that they were in danger of losing their unique cultural identity. As a counterweight to this rootless Westernization, he called for a reaffirmation of Iranian identity grounded in the Persian language and Shia Islam.
6. In Zoroastrianism, the pre-Islamic religion of Iran, the cow is the symbol of a good world composed of truth, piety, and just rule, a connection between divine conception and human action. In the Quran, Surah II, known as "The Cow," declares that righteous conduct and surrender to the will and purpose of God are the manifestations of true religion.
7. For a full list of the films of this period see Maghsoudlou 1987.
8. This was a religious foundation Khomeini established to promote economic justice and look after the needs of the poor. Its responsibilities extended to cinema production and exhibition, and up until the 1990s it was the largest owner of film theaters in the country.
9. In the 1950s a few films were produced with the support of the military; they were propagandistic in nature and intended to inculcate nationalistic feelings and support for the army and the monarchy (Mirbakhtyar 2006, 25–26).
10. A large number of government institutions produced films about the war; these included the Art Institute of the Islamic Propaganda Organization, the War Department of Channel 1, the television group of the Islamic Revolutionary Guard Corps, the Cinematic Institute of the Mostazafan Foundation, the film section of the Ideological and Political Department of the Army, the Shahid Television Group, and the Revayat-e Fath documentary group.

11. On *Marriage of the Blessed* see the essay devoted to the film in this volume.
12. The filmmaker Bahram Beyzai referred to this type of filmmaking as "fake folklore that make[s] it look as if Iran were a quiet country where everything is good, people are innocent, we have God" (Dupont 2001, 17).
13. This position is reflected in a statement by Ayatollah Khamenei, Khomeini's successor as the country's spiritual leader: "It does not impress me if we win foreign awards because these films often have dubious agendas" (in *Ettelaat*, January 4, 1995).
14. On *Under the Skin of the City* see the essay devoted to the film in this volume.
15. On *The Hidden Half* see the essay devoted to the film in this volume.
16. In 2004 the Ministry of Culture and Islamic Guidance made approximately 30 billion tomans ($3.4 million) available for this purpose. Despite the opening of ten new theaters in the first six months of the year, the availability of exhibition space remains dismally inadequate throughout the country.
17. The year 2000 marked a record, with twenty directors realizing their first features.
18. On *Stray Dogs* see the essay devoted to the film in this volume.
19. In Ahmadinejad's first four years in power, only two Iranian films, Saman Salur's *Lonely Tune of Tehran* (*Taraneh tanhai-ye Tehran*, 2008) and *Nobody Knows about Persian Cats* (*Kasi az gorbe-haye irani khabar nadareh*, 2009) by Bahman Ghodadi, were screened at the Cannes Film Festival. Both were denied production permits, shot illegally, and privately submitted to the festival. The screening of the latter film drew strong protest from the Ministry of Culture and Islamic Guidance.

REFERENCES

Akrami, Jamsheed. 1987. "The Blighted Spirit: Iranian Political Cinema in the 1970s." In *Film and Politics in the Third World*, ed. John D. H. Downing, 131–145. New York: Praeger.

Al-e Ahmad, Jalal. 1982 (1961–1962). *Plagued by the West* (*Gharbzadegi*). Translated from Persian by Paul Sprachman. Delmor, NY: Center for Iranian Studies, Columbia University.

Allamehzadeh, Reza. 1997. "Iran: Islamic Visions and Grand Illusions." In *Film and Censorship: The Index Reader*, ed. Ruth Petrie, 129–132. London: Continuum International.

Ansari, Ali. 2000. *Iran, Islam, and Democracy: The Politics of Managing Change*. London: Royal Institute of International Affairs.

Beyzai, Bahram. 2006. "The Other Side of the Story." In *Cinemas of the Other: A Personal Journey with Film-Makers from the Middle East and Central Asia*, ed. Gönül Dönmez-Colin, 27–40. Bristol: Intellect Books.

Constitution of the Islamic Republic of Iran. 1997. Tehran: Department of Translation and Publication, Islamic Culture and Relations Organization.

Dabashi, Hamid. 2007. *Masters and Masterpieces of Iranian Cinema.* Washington, DC: Mage.

Danesh, Mehrzad. 2007. "Religious Cinema in Iran: The Green Path." *Film International* 13 (1–2): 68–74.

Dönmez-Colin, Gönül. 2004. *Women, Islam, and Cinema.* London: Reaktion Books.

Duagoo, Mohammad-Mehdi. 1993. "Government Policies." *Cinemaya: The Asian Film Quarterly* 22 (Winter): 64–67.

Dupont, John. 2001. "Film Takes Iranians Back to a Dark Time." *International Herald Tribune*, February 16.

Egan, Eric. 2005. *The Films of Makhmalbaf: Cinema, Politics, and Culture in Iran.* Washington, DC: Mage.

Elena, Alberto. 2005. *The Cinema of Abbas Kiarostami.* London: Saqi.

Issari, Mohammad Ali. 1989. *Cinema in Iran 1900–1979.* Metuchen, NJ: Scarecrow Press.

Jalili, Abolfazl. 2006. "Treading the Thin Line: Fiction as Documentary." In *Cinemas of the Other: A Personal Journey with Film-Makers from the Middle East and Central Asia,* ed. Gönül Dönmez-Colin, 40–46. Bristol: Intellect Books.

Kiarostami, Abbas. 2006. "Life and Nothing but . . . Reality without Interruption." In *Cinemas of the Other: A Personal Journey with Film-Makers from the Middle East and Central Asia,* ed. Gönül Dönmez-Colin, 50–58. Bristol: Intellect Books.

Khomeini, Ruhollah. 1981. *Islam and Revolution: Writings and Declarations of Imam Khomeini (1941–1980).* Translated from Persian by Hamid Algar. New Jersey: Mizan Press.

Lahiji, Shahla. 2002. "Chaste Dolls and Unchaste Dolls: Women in Iranian Cinema since 1979." In *The New Iranian Cinema: Politics, Representation, and Identity,* ed. Richard Tapper, London: I. B. Tauris.

Maghsoudlou, Bahman. 1987. *Iranian Cinema.* New York: New York University Press.

Mahmoudi, Alireza. 2006. "Iran's Popular Cinema under a Reformist Government Responding to Perpetual Needs." *Film International* 12 (4): 20–28.

Makhmalbaf, Mohsen. 2008. "Filmmaking in Iran Today." In *Mohsen Makhmalbaf: From Discourse to Dialogue,* ed. Fernando González García, 223–229. Madrid: Junta de Andalucía, Consejería de Cultura.

Mehrabi, Massoud. 1984. *Tarikh-e sinema-ye Iran.* Tehran: Mahnameh Film Press.

Mehrjui, Dariush. 2006. "Dariush Mehrjui: From Social Realism to Dramas of the Interior." In *Cinemas of the Other: A Personal Journey with Film-Makers from the Middle East and Central Asia,* ed. Gönül Dönmez-Colin, 75–83. Bristol: Intellect Books.

Mirbakhtyar, Shahla. 2006. *Iranian Cinema and the Islamic Revolution.* Jefferson, NC: McFarland.

Mohammadi, Ali. 2002. "The Impact of Globalization on Iranian Cinema." *Asian Cinema* 13 (1): 3–17

Motavalli, John. 1983. "Exiles." *Film Comment* 19 (4): 56–59.

Naficy, Hamid. 2000. "Iran." In *The International Movie Industry*, ed. Gorham Kindem, 98–117. Carbondale: Southern Illinois University Press.

———. 2002. "Cinematic Exchange Relations: Iran and the West." In *Iran and the Surrounding World: Interactions in Culture and Cultural Politics*, ed. Nikki R. Keddie and Rudi Mathee, 254–281. Seattle: University of Washington Press.

Omid, Jamal. 2006. "Iran." In *The International Film Guide 2006*, ed. David Rosenthal, 176–180. London: Guardian Books.

Sadr, Hamid Reza. 2006. *Iranian Cinema: A Political History*. London: I. B. Tauris.

Schirazi, Asghar. 1998. *The Constitution of Iran: Politics and State in the Islamic Republic*. Translated from Persian by John O'Kane. London: I. B. Tauris.

Tahimi, Massoud. 1993. "Making Ends Meet." *Film International* 1 (2): 4–7.

The Hidden Half*
Love, Idealism, and Politics

FAKHREDDIN AZIMI

The Hidden Half, Tahmineh Milani's sixth and most successful film, attracted international attention following her unexpected arrest and brief detention a day after giving an interview to a pro-reform newspaper in late August 2001.[1] In the interview she spoke, among other things, about the necessity of dialogue in Iranian politics and society; the need to listen; and the communication divide between individuals, especially along gender lines, and within the larger society between people and government, between victors and vanquished—alluding to one of the main themes of *The Hidden Half*. She spoke of the need for Iranians to address the bitter legacy of the traumatic revolutionary years, especially the repressive and poisonous political climate and conflicts of the years of cultural revolution, and the silencing of opposition voices, still largely taboo subjects in the Islamic Republic.[2]

Milani's brush with the judicial authorities was part of the ongoing friction between forces identified as "conservatives" and "reformers" in Iranian politics, an attempt by the former to strike a blow against President Mohammad Khatami and his reformist agenda, as well as a warning to other filmmakers not to transgress political and social limits in their work. Milani was the first filmmaker arrested in years. Four charges, all potentially carrying the death penalty, were brought against her, including the charge of "sympathizing with counter-revolutionary grouplets" in her film. Following intervention by the president's office, she was released after two weeks on $250,000 bail.[3] The controversy surrounding Milani and *The Hidden Half* perhaps afforded the film more attention

---

* *The Hidden Half/Nimeh-ye penhan*. 2001. Film written and directed by Tahmineh Milani. Based on Farideh Golbu-Kardavani's novel *Bad az eshq* ("After Passion"). Produced by Arta Film (Iran) and Iranian Film Society (Iran). Distributed in the United States by Facets. 108 minutes.

Design by Metronome Studios

Tahmineh Milani, after her release from prison, with Mohammad Nikbin, male lead, producer, architect partner, and husband. Courtesy Mohammad Nikbin

than it might otherwise have received. However, Milani is one of a handful of women filmmakers whose work—both art-house and popular—is often regarded among noteworthy examples of modern Iranian filmmaking.

Basing her screenplay loosely on Golbu-Kardavani's novel *Bad az eshq* (*After Passion*), Milani took a story set in the 1960s and deftly transferred it to Iran in the early 1980s. *Bad az eshq* is a coming-of-age love story written in the form of an expiatory memoir of a woman who, having reached a moment of emotional crisis in her life, decides to tell her husband of an ardent, platonic, and ill-fated love affair she had as a university student. The melodramatic story is innocuous, apolitical, and conventional—a sentimental requiem for the endurance of passionate youth.

Combining love story and melodrama with the political and the social, in *The Hidden Half* Milani skillfully uses the novel's basic framework—the story of a young girl's journey of emotional maturation—and the device of the memoir to recount a textured, complex, politicized narrative not merely of the resilience of love but also of idealism, fortitude, and solidarity against the sociopolitical backdrop of the momentous and transformative events that followed the collapse of the Pahlavi monarchy. Onto the pale canvas of the novel Milani has woven a compelling narrative with a distinct political edge and social depth, exploring themes of conjugal relations and keeping and revealing secrets within marriage.

The chief protagonists of the film are Fereshteh (played by Niki Karimi), a university student of poor, provincial origins, and the urbane journal editor and intellectual Roozbeh Javid (played by Milani's husband, Mohammad Nikbin). Fereshteh is unsettled in the impersonal, chaotic, metropolitan Tehran of the immediate post-revolutionary years. She is bright and idealistic, wanting to change the world but also keen to understand it; she is inquisitive but also restrained; driven but also held back by inexperience, by personal, social, and moral impulses, and by affiliation with a radical leftist revolutionary organization. She steadily comes to realize how the issues of gender and class crisscross in the context of the struggles to resist the distinctly paternalistic clerical exclusionism unfolding in post-revolutionary Iran.

Roozbeh Javid is a man with a certain mystique. He possesses a seemingly stoic serenity, a self-confidence born of wealth and status, an impeccable if affected elegance, a conspicuously cosmopolitan deportment. A gentle, discreetly reassuring voice gives him a particularly appealing presence, a certain gravitas. He appears to share the inflated self-image typical of Iranian intellectuals in the 1970s and the aversion of the more high-minded among them to calculated conformism and sycophancy. There is an implicit assumption that his wisdom transcends the dark cloud of mundane zealotry descending on revolutionary Iran. He and his circle, especially the writers who frequent his office, such as the former political prisoner Ms. Pahlavan, represent an older generation of middle-class intellectuals who lived through the post-1953 consolidation of Pahlavi authoritarianism, a generation of intellectual-activists who came to believe in the distinct specificities of Iranian history and culture as opposed to the sweeping generalities informing their successor generation's ideologically driven view of sociopolitical change.

1953

The personal odysseys of the man and the girl share one crucial dimension: their lives have been punctuated by tragedy and adversity. The man "lost" his sweetheart, Mahmonir, who like himself was a member of the pro-Soviet Tudeh Party's youth organization. She is presumed to have died in the clashes of August 19, 1953, a day of infamy in the collective memory of Iranians that ended in the Anglo-American-engineered overthrow of the democratically elected government of Dr. Mohammad Mosaddeq. A veteran parliamentarian, Mosaddeq was widely viewed by Iranians as a steadfastly democratic opponent of royal autocracy and a champion of constitutionalism, Iranian nationalism, and sovereign rights vis-à-vis British imperialism. Having nationalized the British-controlled oil industry and reined in the shah, Mosaddeq's government was toppled by crowds hired, instigated, and mobilized by thugs in the pay of local agents of the American and British intelligence services.[4]

The coup had a lasting impact on Iranian politics and society, as it widened the rift between the people and the ruling class. The post-1953 authoritarian state made approaches to its opponents, seeking to co-opt and neutralize them while otherwise suppressing them. Wishing to avoid the loss of credibility that their complicity in the erosion of constitutional rule would entail, the intellectuals generally shunned open cooperation with the regime, as did many university students. Their scope for civic engagement, however, became increasingly restricted. Still, any attempt by the state to depoliticize them only increased their politicization.

Throughout the 1960s and 1970s, the chronic disempowerment of the public by a myopically authoritarian regime supported by the West deepened public resentment. Whenever secular constitutionalist groups attempted to represent and address the growing undercurrent of public resentment and to persuade the regime to change course, they were relentlessly suppressed. The state's marginalization and emasculation of secular reformists benefited Islamist groups whose existing organizational networks of mosques and other religious venues gave them an unsurpassed opportunity to mobilize. They looked to the leadership of Ayatollah Ruhollah Khomeini, an atypical activist Shiite divine who in the 1960s combined oppositional constitutionalist, nationalist, and Islamist discourses to emerge as an implacable and fearless opponent of the Pahlavi regime.

Eventually, public resentment and revulsion overwhelmed the royalist regime in the late 1970s when as a result of clumsily managed attempts at political reform it began to lose its sense of direction and its assumed invincibility. Following an interlude of uneasy and untenable moderation immediately after the revolution, the growing political radicalization that earlier had led the secular leftists and Islamists to forge a tactical coalescence against the shah resulted in confrontation. The leadership of Khomeini and the fragmentation of the secular forces facilitated the defeat of the latter in the post-revolutionary period when the winners—the radical Islamists—claimed all the material and symbolic spoils, and their vanquished opponents were systematically incapacitated, marginalized, and demonized. This is the backdrop against which the central drama of this film unfolds.

1979

Having acquiesced to a marriage of convenience following the disappearance of his beloved Mahmonir, Roozbeh Javid meets, a quarter of a century later, Fereshteh, the student-activist, who bears an uncanny resemblance to his lost love. Like many members of her generation animated by liberationist-egalitarian ideas, Fereshteh is attracted by a leftist ideology and movement. Her organizational affiliation gives her a sense of purpose, but it also demands unquestioning compliance. She only receives clichéd answers from a disciplinarian apparatchik, Nasrin, who links the small cell of which Fereshteh is a member with the upper echelons of the organization; Nasrin seeks to assert her authority but is privately rarely taken seriously by the free-spirited members of the cell. They are young girls animated by a passionate interest in political change and liberation as well as by more intimate and powerful human emotions and concerns.

The benign mischief and irrepressible *joie de vivre* natural to youth discreetly defies ideological straightjackets; it resists the demands of ideology as spontaneously as it does the edicts of theology. At one meeting of the cell, Fereshteh wonders if all revolutionaries look the same and are so obviously recognizable. She asks if they are also required to read the histories of other societies and revolutions, as her cell members are encouraged to do. She wistfully muses that she would like to wear makeup sometimes and escape from the rigidity of the political organization. Meanwhile her friend Zohreh—a fine-arts student from a comfortable background—when questioned about the appropriateness of having a picture of Gary Cooper on her wall next to those of Mosaddeq, Che Guevara, and Ho Chi Minh, replies in her carefree manner that she loves them all, "and fortunately there is enough room for all of them." Clearly, youthful passions and ideological zealotry share an apparent intensity but little else.

In the context of growing social restlessness and political radicalization, an exclusionist culture of confrontation began to emerge in 1979 that sharply constricted the sphere of tolerant politics. The politically repressive monarchy was replaced, following a chaotic interlude, by a new authoritarian regime that revealed itself to be intolerant of opponents. It abhorred secular values, denigrated women's rights, and displayed little hesitation in excluding, even eliminating, any group that might have claimed a role in the widespread popular movement to bring down the shah or a share of the revolutionary spoils. Ill-equipped and fragmented, the secular revolutionaries sought to confront their Islamist counterparts but ended up paying a high price. Unable to adapt themselves to the new realities, secular leftist activists strove to resist clerical exclusionism and consequently suffered unflinching suppression or elimination by the very forces they had helped to empower. An entire generation bore the brunt of the repression in lost or shattered lives, extensive incarceration and ill treatment, forced deracination and flight from the country, desolation, resignation, or conformism in the face of the emerging clerical state apparatus with its pervasive security forces and punishing penal system.

During the anti-Shah protests of the late 1970s, many women, including female affiliates of certain secular political groups, had donned the *chador* as a symbol of resistance and defiance against what they saw as the shallow Westernization and modernity of the monarchist regime. What they had voluntarily chosen as a revolutionary or oppositional symbol would later become an obligatory uniform, coercively enforced by the new rulers. Narrowly interpreted strictures of Islamic law and norms of chastity as defined by the clerical regime reduced women to a state of dependency on their male guardians. The loss of autonomy had far-reaching sociolegal and moral implications.

Fereshteh's life is rapidly overwhelmed by the cataclysmic events. Her educational, intellectual, and emotional development is ruptured. Her world is populated by figures like Rastegar, the nefarious, ever-present security agent who plagues her at the university; by watchful revolutionary guards; by female vigilantes; and by thugs loyal to the Islamist regime who harass and attack her

Fereshteh the student confronted by a female vigilante in 1979

and her comrades. Milani manages to capture the tense atmosphere of political struggle that prevailed on campuses, where secular student activists were constantly under attack and in perpetual fear of arrest or expulsion from the university. They fiercely opposed the closure of the universities that the regime pursued as a key component of a ruinous cultural revolution.

The universities were eventually reopened following large-scale purges of students and faculty a few years after war broke out with Iraq in 1980. Many who, like Fereshteh, were activists in a previous period were denied reentry and the chance to complete their education. Milani's protagonist is also thwarted in her initial attempt to reapply to enter the university by the malevolent Rastegar, but she eventually succeeds in finishing her degree due to the intervention of her future husband.

Amid political struggle, falling in love may prove therapeutic but is rarely unproblematic, especially in a tense sociopolitical context. Fereshteh's story is at a certain level a narrative of conflict between ideological loyalty on the one hand and emotional longing on the other. On a deeper level, she and Roozbeh are both affected by the constraints of politics and of culture and convention, pride and principle. But while Roozbeh and those around him appear to have greater room for maneuver, Fereshteh finds her voice and asserts her agency when she is out of their orbit and propelled onto her own trajectory. In the face of daunting personal and political predicaments and pressures, she emerges sobered and confident, not cowed. In her memoir she tells her husband: "My difficulties made me what I am."

The infatuation of younger women with older men—particularly intellectual types with their tantalizing perceived learning and culture—has been a common feature of the interrelations between the sexes among the more educated in modern Iran. Fereshteh is attracted to Roozbeh for his intellect, experience, assumed refinement, and cultivation. She is irresistibly drawn to the man by his apparent wisdom and sophistication, by the sense of calm composure he exudes, and by his seemingly unthreatening, unobtrusive desire to protect her as the political situation becomes increasingly dangerous and opposition to the revolutionary government more costly. In his judgment, her political activities—amounting to little more than distributing anti-government pamphlets—are too dangerous; they are ultimately an inconsequential gesture in the face of a self-righteously merciless regime. He wants to help her by arranging for her departure to England, thereby saving her from the very real danger facing political activists. She hesitantly agrees until she discovers that he is married. This brings the painful realization that, as with her political adventures, she has become embroiled in a relationship more convoluted and with wider repercussions than she could have imagined.

2000

Roozbeh's scheming wife has little difficulty in emotionally blackmailing Fereshteh and persuading her that she should shun a married man. Fereshteh believes the wife's story of her loveless marriage to Roozbeh, and it is only years later at a chance meeting with Roozbeh, when he reminds her that she did not hear his side of the story, that she realizes that she might not have heard the whole truth, that she might have acted hastily and impulsively—and judged harshly. Roozbeh's side of the story, never revealed to Fereshteh or the viewer, may be seen as another hidden "half," underlining Milani's core contention about the need for attentiveness to the narratives of others. This dimension of the film transcends a facile feminist reading of it reinforced by the manner in which it is represented in posters and publicity, particularly in the West.[5]

Twenty years have elapsed. Fereshteh is now a mature married woman, the wife of a well-placed, decent, if unexciting, government official. The flame of Fereshteh's past love may not have been completely extinguished but has been well concealed over the years. Her husband has been assigned by the Office of the President to investigate the case of a female prisoner now facing execution. The woman has appealed to the president, asking for her case to be reviewed— her "last chance to remain alive," as she puts it. Fereshteh's long-submerged activist solidarity is unexpectedly rekindled when she accidentally comes upon the woman's dossier.

Already at an emotionally delicate moment in her life, having just met Roozbeh once more, Fereshteh is moved to commit her own life story to paper; she writes her memoir to reveal to her unsuspecting husband the carefully subsumed secrets of her earlier life. The act of revisiting and revealing the tormenting, unforgettable emotional-political entanglements of her past is not merely intended for personal expiation—an act of self-revelation, a moment of catharsis, a form of healing confession. Fereshteh seeks to distance herself from the past altogether and to persuade her husband to try to understand why she and those like her acted as they did in their youth. Her immediate hope is to help a woman in peril whose fate could be drastically affected by the decision of her husband. She shows solidarity with a woman whom she assumes to have been judged harshly—just as she, Fereshteh, had once harshly judged another person.

For both Fereshteh and Roozbeh, their love had seemed deep and mutual, yet they abandoned one another or rather resigned themselves to forced separation. The man, although in a position to know, imagine, or find out why she shunned him, simply succumbed to resignation and seemed to accept another defeat in the face of fate. He made little apparent effort to contact her, search her out, and explain his side of the story; there was no pestering or pursuit. Was he simply accustomed to being pursued? Did he expect not to be so easily abandoned? Was he too self-centered or given to that gentlemanly composure and self-control expected from a man of his standing? It could be conjectured that he wished to avoid imposing himself on her; he was not overly averse to risk but wanted to avoid any lapses that could prove socially costly. Did he ultimately and simply act as a man who knew that the forces of circumstance were stronger than his will?

As for the young Fereshteh, settling into a routine marriage and the ravages of time were unlikely to have fully extinguished her passion for a man she so deeply admired. But she had concluded that her love for him was a chronicle of failure foretold, a hopelessly lost cause. Rekindling her submerged political commitment through her attempted intervention on behalf of the woman prisoner may make the past—the struggles, loves, passions, risks—worthwhile if it could save a life in danger of being wasted by the moralistic but ethically indifferent quasilegal and bureaucratic banalities that had destroyed or maimed so many lives in the past.

NOTES

I would like to thank Josef Gugler for inviting me to contribute this essay and for his helpful and perceptive comments on an earlier draft.

1. Born in Tabriz in 1960, Tahmineh Milani is an architect by training and with her husband and fellow architect, Mohammad Nikbin, designed part of the Tehran metro system. Nikbin took the role of the male lead in *The Hidden Half*, which they co-produced. Nikbin went on to produce Milani's three subsequent films.
2. Although Milani's arrest did not receive extensive coverage in the Iranian press, news of it provoked an immediate uproar among women's activists in Iran and led to international petitions on her behalf. The episode is well documented in both English and Persian sources such as Scott 2001. Until *The Hidden Half*, Milani was considered a nonpolitical filmmaker, and commentators have noted that since her experience with this film, she has moved away from political themes to concentrate

on the condition of Iranian women. An outspoken public figure, she has strongly criticized the circumstances and arrangements in Iranian society that allow or tolerate injustice, discrimination, and abuses against women and children. For background and discussion of Milani's filmmaking see Mazra'eh 2001.

3. Milani's arrest came as a shock, with much speculation as to the motives behind it. Made in accordance with the officially stipulated and enforced rules, the film completed a scheduled four-week screening in Tehran without interference from the courts and did not attract more than the usual attention in the Iranian media. It was boycotted, however, by some judges when screened at the Fajr Film Festival, Iran's premier showcase for new films, in February 2001.

4. For an analysis of the coup of 1953 see Azimi 2004; for the broader historical context of major political developments in modern Iran see Azimi 2008.

5. Editor's note: The sleeve of the DVD issued in the United States, reproduced here, is based on the image of the Iranian poster but obscures part of it behind a gauze curtain. Focusing attention on half of Fereshteh's face, it suggests a feminist critique of the condition of women who remain half-hidden. A close look behind the curtain reveals an oblique view of Fereshteh in the trench coat of her militant student days; in that context the frontal half of her face appears as the young woman in love.

REFERENCES

Azimi, Fakhreddin. 2004. "Unseating Mosaddeq: The Configuration and Role of Domestic Forces." In *Mosaddeq and the Coup of August 1953*, ed. Mark J. Gasiorowski and Malcolm Byrne, 27–101 Syracuse, NY: Syracuse University Press.

———. 2008. *The Quest for Democracy in Iran: One Hundred Years of Struggle against Authoritarian Rule*. Cambridge, MA: Harvard University Press.

Golbu-Kardavani. Farideh. 1998. *Bad az eshq*. Tehran: Ketabsara.

Mazra'eh, Hamid. 2001. *Fereshteh-haye Sukhteh: Naqd va barressi-ye film-haye Tahmineh Milani*. Tehran: Varjavand.

Scott, Stephanie. 2001. "Tahmineh Milani Talks Back: A Feminist Filmmaker Forges Ahead and Fights for Freedom in Iran," *NewEnglandFilm.com*, December 1. http://www.newenglandfilm.com/news/archives/01december/milani.htm.

Courtesy Makhmalbaf Film House

*Marriage of the Blessed**
The Wounds of War and the Betrayal of the Revolution

ERIC EGAN

Mohsen Makhmlabaf stands as one of the most contentious, controversial, and eclectic artists to emerge in Iran since the revolution. His films are a reflection of the complex political, social, and cultural upheavals that have taken place within the country since 1979. He has constantly sought to stretch himself as an artist and explore difficult and often incendiary themes and issues, from the propagandist and dogmatic religious stance of his early work, the searing social commentary of works such as *The Peddler* (*Dastforush*, 1987) and *The Cyclist* (*Bicycleran*, 1989), the reflective examination of self and cinema in films including *Once upon a Time Cinema* (*Nasseredin Shah actor-e cinema*, 1992) and *A Moment of Innocence* (*Noon va goldun*, 1996), the poetic lyricism of *Gabbeh* (1996) and *The Silence* (*Sokut*, 1998), to the philosophical musings in his current cycle of exile films, *Sex and Philosophy* (2005) and *Scream of the Ants* (2006). *Marriage of the Blessed* (*Arusi-ye khuban*, 1989), along with *The Peddler* and *The Cyclist*, marked the end of a cycle of films that I refer to as the *mostazefin* trilogy. Having as their focus the plight of the dispossessed and oppressed masses (*mostazefin*) that formed the vanguard of the revolution (Egan 2005, 100), these films stand as documents on the state of the nation during a decade of war and revolution. They succeed in chronicling the soul of a people abandoned, hopes betrayed, and promises broken, through an examination of the conditions of the poor and dispossessed to whom the revolution had promised the inheritance of the world.

In *Marriage of the Blessed*, Makhmalbaf uses and reconfigures the war genre as a means of critically engaging with a whole host of social problems besetting

---

* *Marriage of the Blessed/Arusi-ye khuban*. 1989. Film written and directed by Mohsen Makhmalbaf. Produced by Open City Entertainment (Iran). Distributed in the United States by Facets. 70 minutes.

the country. In essence he sets out to question the failed promises of the revolution, challenge regime rhetoric, and reevaluate deeply held notions of martyrdom and the "Islamic man." Makhmalbaf posits a picture of a dislocated society caught between idealism and realism, spiritualism and materialism. At the same time, the film is an examination of cinematic form in which the employment of a panoply of techniques visually represents a fractured and distorted society. In it Makhmalbaf also questions the image and its ability to truthfully represent reality and dramatize the psychological and spiritual dilemmas that the country faced in the aftermath of militarism. *Marriage of the Blessed* depicts the incomprehension and loss of faith, the distortion of ideological grand narratives, and the failure of the Islamicization process in its design for a new society of justice and equality built on the tenets of faith. In this respect it is symptomatic of the best of Iranian cinema in its use of national trauma and local cultural forms "to make a global spectacle beyond its immediate borders" (Dabashi 2007, 180).

For Makhmalbaf the film represents the culmination of a move away from the arid religious dogmatism of his early works to a more balanced search for social justice. The dedicated advocate of the regime, attempting to articulate this support through an "Islamic cinema," had become an outspoken critic, accusing it of betraying the revolution by abandoning those who had sacrificed themselves for its ideals (Devictor 2008, 273–277).

The trusted insider now began shedding and questioning the blind adherence to staunchly held absolutist beliefs. This inevitably led to conflict, censorship, and controversy with those in power for whom an unswerving, unquestioning faith meant a worldview that was either for or against the revolution. Makhmalbaf is aware of the nuance and subtlety needed by the artist in navigating his way through such a system. His films of this period operate within ideological currents that centered on questions regarding the future direction of the revolutionary state, the broken promises of the revolution, and the corruption of revolutionary ideals.

Such a stance positions the film within the debates occurring between various factions of the ruling elite at the time and shows the fine line between "official criticism" and something that could be deemed "anti-regime." While Makhmalbaf does criticize the situation in the country, he is careful to do so within "acceptable" guidelines and not directly attack the system itself. This is achieved by focusing on the experiences of its central character as "someone who believes in justice and the revolution that he took part in" (in Goudet 1996, 25). Makhmalbaf is examining the betrayal of the revolutionary ideals and a call for the existing system to make good on its promises—reform of the system, not its overthrow.

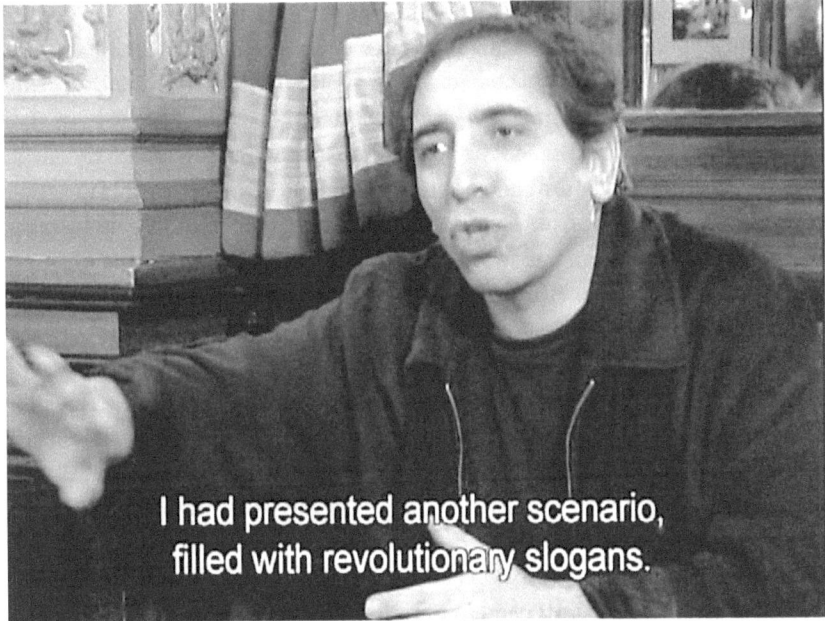

Mohsen Makhmalbaf explains how he misled the censors. Frame from Nader Takmil Homayoun's 2006 documentary *Iran: A Cinematographic Revolution*

Marriage of the Blessed tells the story of Haji, a returned war photographer suffering from shell shock who is unable to assimilate back into society. Scarred both physically and psychologically by his experiences at the front, he cannot come to terms with a society he sees as beset by materialism and exploitation. This leads him to question the sacrifices made during the war, the perceived betrayal of the promises of the revolution, and the hollowness of official rhetoric. This point is clearly illustrated in the opening of the film when we see a line of graffiti, "Volunteer combatant a lion in battlefields a victim in towns," scrawled across a wall. Haji is the embodiment of this rhetoric, an internal exile suffering paralysis, erasure, and fracturing of the self. Makhmalbaf has taken the notion of the "Islamic man" as the stoic defender of the faith, defined by official ideological notions of martyrdom and sacrifice, and transformed him into a traumatized individual in the face of the reality of experienced life.

The heroics of the battlefield are replaced by the somnambulism of the returnee haunting the margins of a new society that is the antithesis of the ideals for which he fought. It was the war, and in particular the notion of the martyr (*shahid*), that defined the image of the Islamic Republic and its desire to conflate the individual, citizen, and nation into one. Within this context the returning veteran is the physical embodiment of this notion of sacrifice, the fictive representation of death. Haji dwells in a complex combination of absence and presence, a living ghost trapped within a series of distorted and distorting images searching for meaning and context. Makhmalbaf uses the story of Haji to make sense of a world caught between idealism and realism and to reconcile these conflicting poles through an interrogation of the image with Haji acting as direct witness (at the front) and mediated witness (the photographs he takes with his camera). He is a transcendental subject using the camera and image as a spiritual guide to reconstitute the self in a journey toward truth.

The feeling of self-loss and the identity of the individual trapped between opposing ideological poles is illustrated when Haji is in the hospital undergoing an MRI scan. In the waiting room his fiancée, Mehri, accidentally spills some liquid on a photograph of him. In her attempts to wipe it up, the image of the picture begins to fade. The film itself then switches from color to black and white, reflecting the Manichean dualism of the world in which Haji finds himself trapped. From then on we follow him on a journey to find meaning in society and reconstitute the image of the self. This search for meaning is encapsulated when Haji takes his camera onto the streets of a Tehran depicted as a nightmarish urban void in the throes of death and decay.

Descending into the drug-infested and crime-ridden slums of the city, Haji imagines that he sees crowds of angry demonstrators. In one scene they are carrying placards of Ayatollah Motahhari, and in another they are carrying images of Ali Shariati. Both men greatly influenced the language of revolution and the hopes for a new society. The former proposed an inclusive vision of Islam based on the psychological transformation of all pious believers on the path to righteousness and oneness with God (Rahnema and Nomani 1990, 42). The latter espoused the creation of an Islamic utopia through social revolution that would lead to a classless society of Muslims ruled by enlightened intellectual thinkers (Rahnema 1998, 292–294).

These are the ideological foundations of the belief system that Haji is trying to capture in a bid to reconstitute the self and give meaning to his sacrifices. He raises his camera, the shutter clicks, and the imagined images of the placard-carrying demonstrators disappear. In this instant the idealism and ideological foundations of the revolution are supplanted by an empty frame. This is a complex image that functions as both a question—What becomes of a society without ideals?—and suggestive answers: their replacement by a nothingness or the emptiness of materialism. Training his camera on the problems afflicting society, he attempts instead to document the betrayal of these ideals and their substitution by self-annihilation, loss, and dislocation.

Haji's journey through the streets of Tehran also allows for the reconfiguration of the notion of the martyr. In contrast to its official association and promotion by the regime as self-sacrifice, the term in its literal sense means witness, the one who struggles against all forms of oppression and injustice. With his sorrowful heart and "anxious eye," Haji documents the crime, poverty, and drug addiction of the failed utopia. His camera bears witness to the reality behind revolutionary rhetoric. However, when he attempts to have his photographs published, he experiences frustration and censorship; the newspaper editor tells Haji that he cannot hope to solve social problems with a few photographs.

The film presents the picture of a society whose ideals have been replaced by the exploitive materialism of a new class of "entrepreneurs." In the marriage registry office, secret land deals are proposed by speculators and black marketeers; in the bazaar Haji's father-in-law complains about the price and quality of watermelons, an ironic echo of Ayatollah Khomeini's assertion that "we did not make this revolution for cheaper melons." Indeed, Haji comes to the conclusion that it is people like his father-in-law who will destroy the revolution from the inside. The return of the petit bourgeoisie is shown not only as the betrayal of the supposed revolutionary ideals of sacrifice, equality, and justice but as symptomatic of a society in conflict and at the edge of psychic crisis and collapse. The martyr stands, as a witness and a reminder of these symptoms, on the margins of that society, whose institutional powers and orthodox truths are found to be insecure. This critical position and the instability of meaning suggest an alternative possibility beyond the empty prescriptions and dictates that govern everyday reality.

Makhmalbaf has used the notion of the dislocated war returnee as a catalyst, inducing instability in the structures of personality, family, and society to reconfigure accepted and orthodox rationales. This commitment extends to the level of form, where he employs myriad techniques such as distorted framing devices, wide-angle lenses, claustrophobic close-ups, iris shots, and a restlessly moving camera in presenting the individual trapped in a fragmented world not of his own making. In its depiction of the extremes of human behavior, the staccato and jagged rhythms of its editing, and the undermining of a stable visual world, *Marriage of the Blessed* posits a worldview in which the discovery of the self is a journey that must be taken alone and a life without devotion to an ideal is one that leads to selfishness and vanity.

Makhmalbaf's cinema is tortured, informed by an unfolding social process that acts as a means of discovery and movement away from abstract ideological absolutes that consume the individual to an assertion that meaning in life is something that each individual has the ability to attain only through suffering. The design of his cinema, with its passionate response to problems of social and cultural identity, is dynamic and in constant flux, marked by tensions, setbacks, and contradictions rather than a static and consistent development of a single theme. His films are for the most part shaped by a central organizing problematic. The driving force in examining this problematic is the value afforded the autonomous individual struggling against and trapped by ideological dogma, be it political, patriarchal, or religious. This in turn opens up the possibility for a series of inquiries into the notion of the self in contradistinction to social relations that stress group ties and obligations or autonomy that is constantly challenged by the need for conformity.

The reconfigured society and the place of the individual within it are clearly shown in the marriage ceremony scene. Here the new materialists and war veterans come side by side to form a microcosm of Iranian society and illustrate the debates taking place within the ruling elite concerning the future direction of the revolution. The clerics still relied on this support and loyalty coming from the *mostazefin*, but even here a split was discernible. A dual system began to operate whereby the leadership employed an increasingly hollow-sounding rhetoric as an assurance of their devotion and commitment to the cause of the *mostazefin*. In reality, an ideological shift had taken place as the government aligned itself more and more with the middle classes in a bid to establish the mosque and the bazaar as the twin pillars of the state in order to emphasize the economic sphere and the need to rebuild the country in the aftermath of war. The term *mostazefin* now ceased to be a divisive economic category depicting the deprived masses; instead it became an inclusive political term to describe all supporters of the regime and all those fighting oppression, regardless of class (Abrahamian 1993, 52).

In his speech at the wedding Haji refers to the dualism in society by welcoming guests with mismatched cars, socks, and wives. Then he proceeds to an anti-materialist outburst, inviting the guests to eat the food robbed from the poor. This induces a fit, highlighting his inability to adapt to new circumstances and his confinement within memory, and results in his being hospitalized. More importantly, it marks his transformation from an active observer of society in a search for meaning to one who has now become a passive object of observation. This change occurs when he escapes from the hospital and starts to live on the streets and the margins of society, becoming the subject of another photojournalist's report.

Haji as creator of the image has now become the subject of the image. This marks the final stage in his feeling of powerlessness and disenfranchisement,

Haji addresses the wedding guests.

as he has lost the ability to control the image and, by extension, thought, belief, and ideology. The attempt to uncover a changed "reality," the search for an understanding of the self, and the questioning of the truth and worth of held beliefs have resulted in a voyage of self-discovery that for Haji has led to frustration, alienation, and self-annihilation. This point is suggested in the film's contemplative final image, a high-angled, long-held freeze frame showing the sprawling cityscape of Tehran over which we hear the sound of gunfire. This final image stands as a distillation of the issues raised in the narrative while at the same time offering an unresolved ending that allows the narrative to live on in the viewer's mind.

The freeze frame acts as a final melancholic photographic image embroiled with notions of presence, absence, and death. It is the aura of the static image that throws the passing of time and existence into relief. Haji is constructed by and attempting to define himself by a memory that privileges the fleeting motionless image over direct visual representation of duration. In other words, he attempts to capture, preserve, and suspend reality by recourse to the contemplative, frozen image of the still photograph. Throughout the film, narrative flow and movement are constantly disrupted by disorientating and disconnected images of frozen life that highlight the instability of both spatial and temporal relations. This has the effect of dislodging the cause-effect progression of the narrative as the basis from which situations disclose actions and moving the film into the realm of thoughts, dreams, and memories.[1]

The hallucinatory images and dreamlike atmosphere of *Marriage of the Blessed* reflect the desire to engage in a debate about ideals through a character who operates on the level of the spiritual. The spatial indeterminacy of Haji's quests through the labyrinthine streets of the city ends with the film's final image, which places the viewer back into the realm of idealism and deeply held beliefs. The sound track would suggest that Haji has decided to go back to the front, the world of the spiritual and ideals, in a form of self-annihilation and a rejection of the new society. This notion of self-annihilation is reflective of Ali Shariati's idea of a return to self in which the individual would gain self-knowledge, particularly in terms of national identity, before embarking on the path to self-annihilation or martyrdom. Haji has returned and sought to make sense of himself and his position in society and found himself dislocated. Having rejected the new society, he is left with only his ideals and self-annihilation, either on the battlefield or in the slums. The discovery of the empty rhetoric of the new society shows the hollowness of the officially constructed notion of the martyr, who is now both a victim on the battlefield and a victim in the city.

NOTES

1. The Iranian poster reproduced here conveys the hallucinatory atmosphere of the film while highlighting its salient themes through the interaction of Iranian and Islamic symbols. The battlefield at the bottom of the poster, set in a (yellow) desert landscape, has at its center a *mihrab*, signifying the sacred character of this place of suffering. It thus represents the belief system embodied in the figure of Haji. The battlefield is dominated by a floating, angel-like wedding dress that promises a release for Haji from the realms of ideals into a more prosaic existence in the "real" world. The bowl and the pomegranate seeds spilling from it recall the scene in the film when Haji's betrothed, startled by a dove released into her path by her disabled brother, tosses a bowl of pomegranate seeds into the air. The dove and the seeds also signify hope and promise. In Iranian culture the pomegranate stands as a symbol of abundance and strength as well as a symbol of a joyous future. It is placed on a ceremonial cloth during wedding celebrations. The Quran mentions pomegranates as growing in the gardens of paradise and as an example of the good things that God creates. The symbolic significance of the dove also has its roots in both Islamic and pre-Islamic Persian culture. In Islam the dove and the pigeon clan

are respected because they are believed to have assisted the Prophet Muhammed in distracting his enemies outside the cave of Thawr at the beginning of the great *hijra*. In Zoroastrian religion the dove is a portent of good omens—it is the companion on the flight of creation of the earth angel Spenta Armaiti, who brings the gifts of harmony and peace to the world. In the film, however, these meanings are negated as the seeds are spilt, and the promise of a joyous married future for Haji is not fulfilled—quite like the promises of the revolution that were broken.

REFERENCES

Abrahamian, Ervan. 1993. *Khomeinism: Essays on the Islamic Republic*. Berkeley: University of California Press.

Dabashi, Hamid. 2007. *Iran: A People Interrupted*. New York: New Press.

Devictor, Agnès. 2008. "*Marriage of the Blessed*: An Overload of Meaning and Images in Crisis." In *Mohsen Makhmalbaf: From Discourse to Dialogue*, ed. Fernando González García, 273–284. Madrid: Junta de Andalucía, Consejería de Cultura.

Egan, Eric. 2005. *The Films of Makhmalbaf: Cinema, Politics, and Culture in Iran*. Washington, DC: Mage.

Goudet, Stephanie. 1996. "Entretien avec Mohsen Makhmalbaf," *Positif* 422 (April): 21–26.

Rahnema, Ali. 1998. *An Islamic Utopian: A Political Biography of Ali Shariati*. London: I. B. Tauris.

Rahnema, Ali, and Farhad Nomani. 1990. *The Secular Miracle: Religion, Politics, and Economic Policy in the Islamic Republic of Iran*. London: Zed Books.

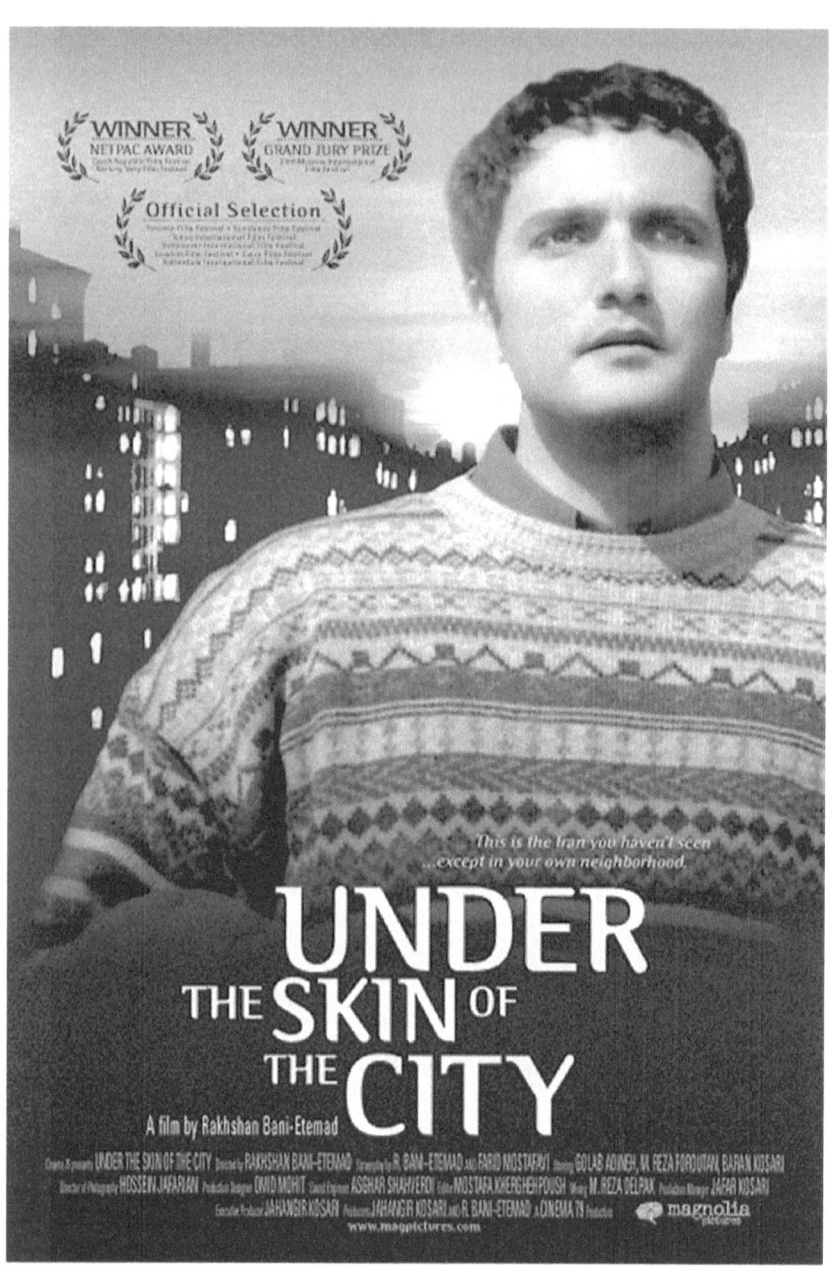

Courtesy Magnolia Pictures

*Under the Skin of the City**
Under the Surface Contrasts

RINI COBBEY

> ... the internal tug-of-war between rebellion and
> resignation, progressivism and conservatism...
> HAMID NAFICY (2001, 574)

The "First Lady of Iranian Cinema" is a popular and fitting title for director Rakhshan Bani-Etemad.[1] Besides the obvious reference to her prominence as a filmmaker, the term can connote a social role that balances between politics and family. Bani-Etemad's work as a whole reflects this tension, and she addresses it directly in *Under the Skin of the City*. The film frames the story of one Tehran family's everyday existence, bracketed by opening and ending scenes that show interviews being recorded for a political documentary. Bani-Etemad foregrounds the relationships between individual and shared (even mass) experiences and between what one sees on the surface and what is going on behind the scenes, "under the skin."

The central narrative of the film follows a short time in the life of Tuba's family. A factory worker by day, Tuba is mother to four young adult children and wife to an invalid husband. In the introductory scenes Bani-Etemad shows the life of the not especially oppressed. This family has access to employment, education, political expression, a home, and—importantly—each other. The first time the family members appear together they are going out for pizza when Tuba just as well could have cooked at home. They are not destitute, but the

---

* *Under the Skin of the City/Zir-e pust-e shahr*. 2001. Directed by Rakhshan Bani-Etemad and written by Bani-Etemad and Farid Mostafavi. Produced by Cinema 79 (Iran). Distributed in the United States by Wellspring. 93 minutes.

film makes clear that they live within sight of the edge. Tuba finds the pizzeria too fancy; her elder son, Abbas, finds their home nearly a shack. Any financial emergency that comes up is barely manageable. Tuba works to maintain the stability they have; Abbas works to gain more.[2]

Abbas's work is running errands for a garment manufacturer. His younger brother, Ali, cuts school to distribute political protest literature on the street. Their sister Mahboubeh attends high school with her best friend from next door, listening to popular music and whispering about boys. An older sister, Hamideh, pregnant with a second child, lives with her husband, Rahmat, their young daughter, Tala, and Rahmat's mother. Tuba's husband, Mahmoud, spends his days at home, debilitated by a leg injury and his own disillusioned spirit.

Members of the family get along well, and this is manifested in their everyday endearing exchanges and their aggressive support for each other in the face of outside challenges. When Abbas and Ali are introduced, the older brother is called upon to bail out the younger one, who has been arrested for fighting in the street with political opponents. As the family members return home one afternoon, each reacts protectively to the presence of Tala and Hamideh, who has been beaten by Rahmat. Another evening, Abbas returns to his parents' home with presents to share, and they laugh and play together.

Even fractious Ali, most vocal in his dissatisfaction with present-day life, is a committed member of the close-knit family: he tutors his mother, who is trying to learn to read, helps his sister search for a missing friend, and follows his brother in the climactic scene of the film out of a desire to protect him. Ali is motivated by the dual drives of family and broader social allegiance, regularly articulating the underlying injustices that cause the individual pains his loved ones suffer.

An overarching tension builds throughout the film between maintenance of the status quo to survive and the search for a better way of life against powerful obstacles. Each time a character makes a well-intentioned decision to significantly change the way things are, a dramatic loss ensues. The film is rather ambivalent about the tactic of taking more moderate steps by working within established systems for whatever change is accessible.

In contrast to Tuba, who takes a conservative approach to everyday life, Abbas is a dynamic, optimistic character in an active quest to move up in the world. He has a stable job with some handy benefits, but he really wants something with a much bigger and faster payoff. With greater returns comes greater risk, and Abbas believes it is worth the gamble to sacrifice what his family currently has—a home they own, reliable employment, relative freedom and safety—for a major improvement. Motivated by his commitment to the family and a future with the office worker he seeks to court, Abbas pursues a promising opportunity. He will obtain a passport and visa to go work in Japan and make enough money to return home to buy a bigger and better home for his family and live comfortably ever after. All he needs is a little up-front money to get the visa. This he can get by selling the family home to an interested developer. The family may need to find a place to rent in the meantime, but the proceeds hold the key to breaking free from the status quo.

Tuba adamantly opposes this plan. When she cannot persuade either her husband or her son that owning their home is not worth risking for the possibility of owning more, she hides the deed to the house. When Tuba chooses to conserve the home, Abbas seeks aggressively to improve, and his father goes along with the son, things fall apart one by one, and the family's relatively stable life is seriously jeopardized.

While this plot unfolds, two subplots involving Tuba's daughters develop. Each manifests the same tension between conserving an imperfect but arguably manageable status quo and dramatically altering everyday reality for a desired improvement. Both subplots feature physical violence in a family context.

Hamideh's bruised face and presence in her parents' home rile her supportive siblings, who shout that she should leave her husband and that they would confront him themselves. Tuba's response is to work within established social structures to find a compromise. Instead of either welcoming her daughter long-term into the safety of her home or sending her straight back to her violent husband, Tuba takes her daughter and granddaughter to their home, where she confronts not Hamideh's husband, but her mother-in-law. Hanging laundry side by side, the two older mothers talk about reasons for and resistance to Rahmat's violence. Tuba encourages her son-in-law's mother to hold him accountable for his actions and to look out for Hamideh and her daughter, just as she instructs Hamideh to be more careful. Rahmat's mother is more frightened of the threat of homelessness—as they exist on the economic edge—than of her son's anger. Tuba reassures her that she will find a place for them in her own home if it comes to that. A distasteful solution, this submission nevertheless illustrates one avenue toward surviving under the weight of personal and cultural oppression—women looking out for women and helping each other when the actions of men are overpowering.

The other subplot involves Tuba's next-door neighbors, among them Masum, the best friend of Mahboubeh, Tuba's younger daughter. Masum's

Tuba interviewed on television

relationship with her older brother, Ahmad, is altogether different from the relationship Mahboubeh has with her brothers. Ahmad is suspicious, censorious, and abusive. He is also, Ali alleges, a hypocrite dealing in drugs while imposing stifling moral standards on his sister. When Masum is caught having attended a concert, Ahmad beats her. Masum runs away from home, disappearing into an underground culture of disaffected Tehran youth involved in illegal activities and leading physically and psychologically harsh lives in an attempt to survive apart from their established family structures. As in Hamideh's case, Tuba had counseled the girls to show restraint and not to do anything that would irritate the violent man. Mahboubeh takes a more aggressive approach. After witnessing the extreme circumstances in which Masum put herself to get away from Ahmad, Mahboubeh verbally confronts Ahmad, then slaps him.

Masum's dramatic attempt to find a better way by running away parallels Abbas's fall into illegal activity in his attempt to make a better life. The last we see of either character, each is running away from increasingly dangerous situations into the unpromising unknown.

Framing all this individual and family-level conflict is the larger social and political structure. The film opens with Tuba on screen twice: in the frame of Bani-Etemad's movie and on the monitor of a camera crew interviewing women factory workers about an upcoming national election. Tuba's story is set during the run-up to the parliamentary elections in 2000, a time of political promise following the election of reformist Mohammed Khatami as president in 1997.

When we last see Tuba, at the end of the film, she is again facing a film camera and confronting the (fictional) documentary filmmaker: "Who the hell do you show these films to, anyway?"

With these book-ending scenes of Tuba talking and the documentary filmmakers soliciting and capturing her perspective, we are shown once more that Tuba's situation is satisfactory and holds promise. She has access to representation, both political and more broadly through the media. However, the nature of Tuba's performance reveals shortcomings in both contexts. In the opening scene she talks to the camera about her hope for progress—better working and living conditions, for women in particular—but her delivery is stilted and awkward. The camera cuts and, against a black screen, the audience of *Under the Skin of the City* hears a cacophony of voices of women workers who comment on their reality much more freely and express their frustrations with working and living conditions. At the end of the film, Tuba painfully and freely gushes her anger and sadness; since the last time she was interviewed, she has encountered homelessness, violence, and the potential loss of both her sons. She demands that the filmmaker try to capture what is in her heart, not just the outer world of her status as a worker and of politics. The camera, however, once again fails to capture this honest expression.

This is the language and performance of melodrama, a cinematic form seemingly polar in opposition to documentary. Yet, in her career, which alternates between documentaries and narrative features, it is a distinction Bani-Etemad transgresses at times. To quote Hamid, *Under the Skin of the City* "animates an essential question of political filmmaking: how to balance fidelity to social reality with the often more compelling and convincing dictates of dramatic fiction" (2003, 50).

The documentary sequences in *Under the Skin of the City* recall similar scenes in Bani-Etemad's *The May Lady* (*Banoo-ye ordibehesht*, 1998). That film was released five years earlier, but *Under the Skin of the City* appears as a prequel. The "May Lady" is a documentary filmmaker and divorced woman struggling not, as is the case for nearly all of Bani-Etemad's central characters, with her economic status but rather with the intertwined conflicts between motherhood, romantic love, and professional success. In the course of searching for the "perfect woman" to feature in her next film, the May Lady meets some of the women she filmed for past documentaries, among them Tuba, who had been working at a factory. Tuba pleads for help from the May Lady, as she has ended up with one son in jail and one on the run. It is not clear how the filmmaker can help, but it is evident she feels a pull and a sense of conflict as she

Rakhshan Bani-Etemad on the set. Courtesy Rakhshan Bani-Etemad

looks back over older footage of Tuba and wonders what her role was and is in this woman's dramatic, hard life.

Underlying the more prominent themes of family relations, work conditions, and political opportunities is the self-reflective question of the power of personal stories told—to whom?—in the context of larger social systems in need of critique. This is one of the functions of the movie melodrama: to treat, often tragically, the personal story of an individual and her family as microcosms of larger social struggles. As Schatz puts it, melodrama is "at once celebrating and severely questioning the basic values and attitudes of the mass audience" (1981, 223). Hamid observes (2003) that the members of Tuba's family represent the spectrum of political positions in contemporary Iran, from the father, once a revolutionary and now disenchanted, to the disenfranchised daughters suffering severe abuse, from the economically and politically upwardly mobile sons to the ultimately disillusioned mother who holds little power. Neighbor Masum and the crowd she joins may be considered as occupying one more position on that spectrum, rebelling not so much against the political order as against cultural dictates. Bani-Etemad does not spell out these connections for her audience; rather, she develops an emotionally evocative narrative through plot, performance, sound, and images.

Bani-Etemad's films destabilize the possibility of any form of film simply "telling it like it is." Besides the inherent self-critique a film within a film offers, her aesthetic techniques reveal their own craftedness, even more so when viewed in a context of the majority of seemingly more "natural" filming techniques. In conjunction with the wide, gritty shots that straightforwardly present Tehran as a busy, dusty city overflowing with hard-working families, *Under the Skin of the City* includes a few carefully framed angles that provoke layers of interpretation. For example, a view through a chain-link fence suggests loss of freedom for the character; and camera positions push against censorship rules related to women's veiling and to touching between men and women. Similarly, the juxtaposition of a sound track almost entirely devoid of extranarrative music against three scenes featuring dramatic musical cues emphasizes not only the importance of these plot points but also the nondocumentary nature of the whole story.

At only three points in the film music from outside the scene's action accompanies the visuals, and each of these is the point at which a character is making the choice to take a drastic step to change a tragic situation. During two of these scenes, the presence of music is so subtle as to be mistakable for ambient sounds of a passing train or the rhythmic droning from a road and a truck engine. As low, nonmelodic, industrial-sounding tones, they underscore the scene's danger and the darkness of the choices portrayed. The first accompanies Masum's decision to run away as she meets Mahboubeh one more time over the wall separating their homes. The next accompanies Abbas's decision to take a drug-running offer. The third and most dramatic and obvious use of extranarrative music is a mix of tones with various instruments and ethereal harmonies when Abbas's efforts for improvement dramatically disintegrate.[3]

The end of the movie is ambiguous on a couple of levels. Abbas is getting away, and Tuba is picking up the pieces. She stands in front of the camera with her voting card in hand. An official system is in place—for representation, for survival. Yet the story, as emphasized in its melodramatic climaxes and viewed in light of *The May Lady*'s revelations, presents a picture of a society in which cultural restraints on women's lives coincide with a general malaise across the demographic strata. None of the promises, Tuba's final speech pronounces, from the revolution to the recent political reforms, has been fulfilled. In the first interview, the camera is meddling, getting in the way of true expression. In the second interview, the camera is inadequate, unable to capture reality or to effect any direct change.[4] Nonetheless, Tuba will vote and the filmmaker persists.

In this movie about the contrasting strategies of making the best of the status quo and taking risks in the search for improvement, Bani-Etemad highlights how individual people and families are embedded in the social and political system. The political limits the personal. But the power to survive is in the personal, which is why Bani-Etemad, even in her documentaries,[5] is drawn to stories of individuals and families, not to slogans or overly simplified, direct critiques.[6] *Under the Skin of the City* presents what is possible with film while discouraging overconfidence in the simple fact of dramatic representation.

NOTES

1. See for instance Thomas 2003.
2. Editor's note: The U.S. poster, reproduced here, promotes *Under the Skin of the City* by foregrounding Abbas, played by heartthrob star Mohamad Reza Forutan. The Iranian poster shows him towering over his family and his sisters. In distinct contrast, the cover of the English and Persian DVD issued in Europe has Tuba hovering over her children, conveying her role in holding the family together. The altogether different French poster evokes the city as an engulfing environment: in a somewhat abstract black and white composition, a man and two smaller women, all faceless, appear lost in a towering cityscape.
3. Ambient music accompanies some scenes, as when music is playing from a radio. One scene, showing Abbas dancing for and with his mother, begins with music seeming to match the live action but increasing in volume without narrative logic or a visual match. This music is upbeat and certainly cues and matches the emotions of the moment, whether we understand it as coming from within the story or without.
4. It is possible to read both documentary scenes as reflecting not the ineptness of the filmmakers and failing equipment but as their active attempts to craft and censor the "reality" they supposedly present. This ambiguity allows Bani-Etemad to layer her film with promises made and failed and with inherent confusion in the systems of representation.
5. Bani-Etemad's *Our Times* (*Ruzegar-e ma*, 2002) begins as a documentary about many—the joyful exuberance of young people voting and the inspiring story of scores of women running for president—but becomes the story of one woman's complex struggle for survival.
6. Thus Bani-Etemad's oft-quoted insistence that she is not making feminist films but films about women and humanity (Naficy 2001, Safaee and Parsa 2007).

REFERENCES

Hamid, Rahul. 2003. "Under the Skin of the City." *Cineaste* 28 (4): 50–51.

Naficy, Hamid. 2001. "Veiled Voice and Vision in Iranian Cinema: The Evolution of Rakhshan Banietemad's Films." In *Ladies and Gentlemen, Boys and Girls*, ed. Murray Promerance, 37–53. Albany: SUNY Press.

Safaee, Hamed, and Vahid F. Parsa. 2007. "Tehran, the City that Forgets." *TehranAvenue.com*, May. http://www.tehranavenue.com/article.php?id=693.

Schatz, Thomas. 1981. *Hollywood Genres*. McGraw Hill.

Thomas, Kevin. 2003. "Under the Skin of the City." *Los Angeles Times*, April 4. http://www.calendarlive.com/movies/reviews/cl-et-skin4apr04,0,7365335.story.

Design by Mehrdad Zonnour. Courtesy Makhmalbaf Film House

*Stray Dogs**
Cruelty and Humanity amid Hardship in Afghanistan

ERIC EGAN

Marziyeh Meshkini's second feature film, *Stray Dogs*, must be understood as part of a wider social project and cinematic narrative undertaken by the Makhmalbaf Film House (MFH). Set up in 1996 by her husband, Mohsen Makhmalbaf, the MFH has functioned as a film training school and production house. Based on a collaborative approach, it has succeeded in producing a number of remarkable and internationally renowned films by several members of the Makhmalbaf family. These works are socially committed and exhibit a myriad of moral, political, and narrative ambiguities derived from combining a realist and poetically symbolic aesthetic (Egan 2005, 189–190).

A central strand of the Makhmalbafs' endeavor has been an ardent commitment to the plight of Afghanistan and its people. This has inspired the production of four feature films—*Kandahar* (*Safar-e Qandehar*, Mohsen Makhmalbaf, 2001), *At Five in the Afternoon* (*Panj-e asr*, Samira Makhmalbaf, 2003),[1] *Stray Dogs*, and *Buddha Collapsed out of Shame* (*Buda az sharm foru rikht*, Hana Makhmalbaf, 2007)—as well as two documentaries, *Afghan Alphabet* (*Alefba-ye afghan*, Mohsen Makhmalbaf, 2002) and *Joy of Madness* (*Lezate divanegi*, Hana Makhmalbaf, 2003), that are part of a larger enterprise to use cinema as a means of education and regeneration and as "a mirror for society to look at its faults" (Mohsen Makhmalbaf in Calhoun 2004, 22).[2] The narrative trajectory of these feature films begins with *Kandahar* and continues with *Five in the Afternoon* in depicting a melancholic portrait of a society in freefall (McGill 2004, 33), but fragments of hope are found in individuals who actively struggle against repressive social and cultural strictures. *Kandahar* depicts an outsider

---

* *Stray Dogs/Sag-haye velgard*. 2003. Written and directed by Marziyeh Meshkini. Produced by Makhmalbaf Film House (Iran) and Wild Bunch (France). International distribution by Wild Bunch (France). 93 minutes.

trying to break into a closed society where nothing is as it seems, while *Five in the Afternoon* portrays the efforts of an insider to break out of oppressive patriarchal cultural forms.

Stray Dogs continues this investigation of Afghan society by adopting a harsh, stripped aesthetic that empties objects of meaning and depicts the heartbreaking impotence of struggle. It is a form of cinema that takes those who struggle as its theme, shows the process that generates the problems, and questions the means of representing and portraying these problems. Meshkini achieves this through a simple narrative of two siblings, Zahed and his sister, Gol Ghotai, and their daily battle to survive amid the harsh poverty of post-Taliban Afghanistan. Visiting their imprisoned mother, they are allowed to stay over as "night prisoners." When authorities stop this practice, the children decide to attempt a series of robberies with a view to being caught, arrested, and permanently imprisoned alongside their mother.

The opening scene of *Stray Dogs* depicts hoards of children scavenging in a garbage dump. Framed against a barren, desolate, post-apocalyptic landscape, the scene continues as a group of children with flaming torches chase a stray dog. The baying crowd forces the animal into an underground cave, where the children attempt to burn it alive. They accuse it of being simultaneously an English dog hunting Taliban, a Russian looking for nuclear bombs, and finally an American responsible for killing the father of one of their friends. The frightened animal trapped underground by flames and the children trapped above in a devastated, forsaken netherworld create the image of a hell that is all-pervasive. The scene serves as a summation of an ardent, complex, meta-cinematic film that operates within a series of external narrative forces and an internal dialogue. The film has a complex formal structure that serves to highlight and critically engage with the origins and influences of its own intertextual construction.

Meshkini's film exhibits a hybridity of form that is problematized and self-questioning. From this perspective the opening image of the garbage heap serves as the "overdetermined depot of social meanings where hybrid multi-chronotoic relations are reinscribed" (Stam 2003, 40). This image allows for a critical vantage point from which to define and illuminate a society and reflects the essence of Meshkini's filmic work. Such a portrayal shows the devastation wrought by external political interference as well as the destructive nature of internal cultural and religious mores. Feral children and a pock-marked landscape are the products of and testimonies to this history that Meshkini's camera probes by reducing objects to unstable entities in search of meanings that have become warped, suspect, indecipherable. She presents a work that

Children struggling to survive

is derived from and problematizes the notion of transnational aesthetics: the film questions the application, interpretation, and historiography of cinematic intertextuality.

In *Stray Dogs* Meshkini reflects and examines the multilayered nature of historical formations shaped by intricate linkages between local forces (patriarchy, religion) and international forces (invasion and war). The film suggests ways of understanding and inhabiting the cultural function of these forces. This necessitates a questioning of objects and their altered meanings within specific and changing contexts. The transformation of objects is achieved through reducing their cultural meanings to a utilitarian physicality in which the spiritual has through necessity become supplanted by the material in the struggle for survival.[3] As a result, books become fuel for a fire, prayer beads are merely decorative objects to be hung around the neck of a dog, marriage alleviates hunger, and cars become homes. The displacement of cultural significance from objects renders humankind to the level of mere existence in which the elements of civilization are remnants of the past transformed by the needs of the present into empty vessels of survival. The reduction and reappropriation of objects into new forms become a point of contrast with the suffering derived from tradition.

The children's mother is in prison because she remarried, thinking her first husband dead, for economic survival. Upon his return from fighting what he considered a holy war, she is imprisoned and condemned as an adulterer. The family's suffering increases when the children's father is seized as a suspected terrorist and removed to the U.S. prison at Guantanamo Bay. He refuses to pardon his wife despite the pleading of his children, and they are left alone and bereft. The contrast between ideals and reality, the material and the spiritual condemns all to suffering and hardship. Meshkini portrays the effects through a complex and questioning realist aesthetic of exploring, discovering, and confronting. She achieves such an aesthetic through a carefully constructed *mise en scène* with expressionless figures carefully placed in static frontal shots lacking depth. Movement is stilted, somnambulistic, and affected. Dialogue is emotionless, and the editing is often fractured, leaving empty frames of contemplation when the camera continues to record after people leave the frame.

Meshkini imbues the images with a self-consciousness and strangeness that give them something of a photographic aura that connotes both a presence and absence. The sequences in the bazaar when the children give wood to the kebab seller and when they buy prayer beads are filmed photographs, static and hallucinatory, detached images of contemplation. This fractured temporal and spatial realm imbues the images with a dreamlike quality and posits them as disconnected and open-ended episodic fragments of fleeting and at the same time frozen moments in time. The disconnectedness and instability of space—reflective of Afghanistan as a country—is highlighted by Meshkini's use of repetition: the numerous journeys to the prison gate, the toiling among trash heaps. Such recurrence and reiteration, while emphasizing the struggle, drudgery, and stoicism of the fight for survival, also serve as means to reevaluate the depiction of a given "reality." As a result, alternative realities are allowed to be presented and negotiated in subtly changing forms.

The scene in which the children attempt their first robbery is a prime example of Meshkini's approach. The children follow a *burka*-clad woman through labyrinthine alleyways to steal her basket. The scene begins with traditional narrative suspense-building techniques of accelerating shot-reverse-shots and point of view from Zahed to the basket. Zahed grabs the basket and is pursued by the woman before he is caught and beaten by her. Prior to this, however, strict adherence to classical narrative structures is broken by a decentered, objective, low-angled shot of two young girls peering from behind a barred window. At first the spatial relationship is unclear until the girls are shown watching from the alleyway where the robbery is taking place. The breaking of the tension and narrative drive of the scene undermines the application of traditional editing and framing techniques by introducing an element that appears external and superfluous. On closer examination, though, the shots of the girls serve as both a complication of formal application and a silent intertextual form of thematic comment.

Within the narrative of the film the shots of the girls enhance the notion of imprisonment. This is a place where mothers, fathers, children, and even television sets are physically and mentally locked behind bars. The silent and forlorn image of the girls also can be read as an allusion to the imprisoned girls in *The Apple* (*Sib*, Samira Makhmalbaf, 1997) and to emphasize the placement of *Stray Dogs* within the tradition of children in Iranian cinema. A key element in Iranian cinema has been a focus on children, their stoicism and perseverance in an often cruel and hostile world they do not understand but try to survive and at times make anew. Children's suffering calls into question the repressive and hierarchical structures of social relations and their functions within society. Films including *Djomeh* (Hassan Yektapanah, 2000), *Delbaran* (Abolfazl Jalili, 2001), and *Baran* (Majid Majidi, 2001) represent the plight of Afghans within Iranian society. They use the notion of the dispossessed individual to comment on the social formations and workings of Iranian society.

Meshkini has taken a recognizable filmic form and transformed it by reinscribing "national" as a term no longer confined to territorial boundaries. The notion of the dispossessed nation is distilled in one particular scene of heartbreaking beauty that encapsulates the traumatic and tortured history of Afghanistan. In the scene we see the preparation for the burial of an old woman who has died of hypothermia. Her corpse is framed against a blazing fire while a pickaxe hacks at the barren soil. Amid the tears and mourning of her family we hear the sound of a jet plane overhead, and the scene ends with a high-angled, contemplative shot over the city. The scene has a dreamlike quality and emotive power that resist sentimentality by showing the human suffering in a nation's tragic history. It is an attempt to imbue the abstract idea of Afghanistan, chessboard of the Great Game, terrorist enclave, with the reality that political actions do not happen in a vacuum and can have real and devastating consequences.

Taking the filmic text as a series of proliferating, overlapping, and contested narrative strategies, Meshkini has engaged in a dialogue with another culture by using an understanding of national and international cultural forms to reperceive and rethink her own cultural constellation. This is one of the main aims in the cinematic project of the entire Makhmalbaf family, whose sense of active social responsibility is coupled with a view of Afghanistan as a surrogate of the Islamic Republic (Dabashi 2008, 219). Indeed, Mohsen Makhmalbaf's essay "The Buddha Was Not Demolished in Afghanistan: He Collapsed out of Shame" stands as a manifesto, at times angry, at others despairing, of their cinematic projects in Afghanistan, a country inextricably linked to Iran, culturally and historically. Afghanistan stands as an image of the past, present, and future

Marziyeh Meshkini on the set of *The Day I Became a Woman* (2000).
Courtesy Makhmalbaf Film House

of Iran. At the center is the family as the cornerstone of the social order. For the maintenance and cohesion of this order, tradition requires the submission and unquestioning obedience of each member of the kinship group to an all-powerful leader.

The family, through the figure of the strong patriarch, creates the hierarchical structure of the ruler and subject. Throwing off the destruction of a communist invasion and the oppressive brutality of the Taliban regime has resulted in a situation in which the very foundations of society have been problematized. The question is now what comes in its place and how to refashion this structure from the rubble of its destruction. Thus a picture emerges of a society in which the family has been shattered and imprisoned and children take on the role of adults in trying to remake it, free from cultural, traditional, and patriarchal tyranny, based on the principles of tolerance and forgiveness. The cinematic form used to examine these issues is a type of "obsessive framing" (Chaudhuri and Finn 2006, 164): different views of the same object are achieved through a close juxtaposition of shots and the unresolved tension between different forms that creates ambiguity in the rendering of reality. The key to these points exists in the encounter with Italian neorealism, specifically in *Bicycle Thieves* (*Ladri di biciclette*, 1948).

After two failed robbery attempts, the children in *Stray Dogs* go to a local cinema that is showing Vittorio De Sica's searing allegory of the human condition and treatise of hope, loss, and redemption. The children watch the film to discover how to steal and get caught. Here once again is the realm of the utilitarian function of art and the effect context has on its reception and the transformation of meaning. The engagement with *Bicycle Thieves* questions the glib Eurocentric assertion of locating Iranian film within a neorealist aesthetic that makes it accessible and readable and easily co-optable in the international film-festival circuit (Bradshaw 2006, 6). Meshkini tackles this assertion head-on, inserting De Sica's film into the narrative as a site of reference in a transformative process that highlights similarities in the context of difference.

The emergence of Italian neorealism in the years following World War II arose from the need to break with the cultural heritage of fascism. While never a straightforward homogeneous or unitary phenomenon, it did in different ways, through its denouncement of war and focus on social problems, redefine the coordinates of national cultural identity through a commitment to the representation of human reality and a reformist impulse. This is very much the ideological landscape inhabited by *Stray Dogs*, and Meshkini herself has noted the similarities in context between postwar Italy and present-day Afghanistan (Meshkini 2004, 37). The inclusion of *Bicycle Thieves* functions therefore to highlight the intertextuality of film while problematizing its application in different contexts.

Meshkini has attempted to highlight the constructed nature of filmic reality by removing the dramatic arcs and aura of narrative inevitability that result in diffuse sentimentality and tear-jerking melodrama, which undermine attempts at penetrating social criticism (Meshkini 2004, 38).[4] She has, in showing, highlighting, and questioning the constructed nature of depictions of reality, conversely succeeded in its faithful observance by producing an estranging antirealist effect. Such an enterprise is clearly illustrated as the children are watching the film in the theater.

At the point when the bicycle is about to be stolen on the screen, there is a cut and flash forward to the children waiting on the street to seize the moment when they will put into practice what they have learned from the film. The music from the film plays over the shot before a cut back to the movie theater for the denouement. The shot of the children waiting in the street is then repeated, this time without the music. Emotional manipulation is jettisoned by drawing attention to the absence of the music, and the image, through repetition, is presented as estranged and revelatory. This sequence presents a *mise en scène* that functions to observe and describe its own constructed nature. In doing so it reverses the relationship between meaning and appearance in which the latter is being constantly presented as a strange discovery, a moment of revelation.

Meshkini's approach represents a cinematically underdeveloped country and discovers the language by which it can express itself. Thus, *Stray Dogs* shows that the new image of reality has to be and is constructed through a questioning of the given forms of Western cinema and the recognition of the need to define the filmmaker's relationship to these forms and their subject. *Bicycle Thieves* presents the image of an uncaring society in which the actions of the individual to reinstate dignity and escape poverty result in the loss of all dignity. *Stray Dogs* uses the robbery of the bicycle not as holding the deluded promise of a means of escape or the restoration of dignity but as a symbol of heartbreaking despair where the result or aspiration is the replacement of one prison (a hostile social environment) with another (actual incarceration behind bars).

The final images, of Zahed imprisoned for his crime, crying for his mother and stamping his feet in childish rage and impotence before descending to silence, and of his sister alone, a tiny figure framed outside the huge, looming prison gate trying once again to get inside, stand as the haunting and visceral condemnations of a fallen world in which all are implicated. This Meshkini has achieved through the recognition of her own multilayered cultural and historical formations and her capacity to explore and explode the linkages between the local and international to highlight and "alleviate the sufferings of human beings" (Meshkini 2004, 39).

NOTES

1. Samira Makhmalbaf's *Two-Legged Horse* (*Asbe du-pa*, 2008) was also filmed in Afghanistan. She states that she chose to make it there after being refused a shooting permit in Iran (Samira Makhmalbaf 2008). She has cited language similarities, cultural parallels, and the universal human story that could have taken place in many countries, of which Afghanistan is but one.
2. After shooting *Afghan Alphabet*, Mohsen Makhmalbaf established the Afghan Children Education Movement (ACEM), which has launched more than eighty projects in the country, including reconstructing an orphanage in Kabul, building three schools in Herat, and supporting medical and health initiatives as well as establishing the beginnings of an Afghan film industry. ACEM has funded twenty Afghan filmmakers to attend film courses and provided funding for Siddiq Barmak's award-winning film *Osama* (2002).

3. Meshkini's first film, *The Day I Became a Woman* (*Roozi keh zan shodam*, 2000), highlights this point. It takes the notion of the instability of meaning and the transformative nature of objects in what is at times a surreal examination of three stages in the lives of women. In the first sequence a head scarf becomes a sail, and a makeshift sundial becomes a marker denoting the end of childhood. The second episode takes the image of a bicycle as a confrontation with tradition, the possibility of freedom, and an impotent form of rebellion. The final section of the film shows a plethora of consumer goods unmoored from their appropriate settings that act as a substitute for a life unlived.

4. Editor's note: The Iranian advance poster reproduced here, holding out the promise of melodrama and tears, was rejected by the Ministry of Culture. The final poster showed just a grim face of Gol Ghotai, but the film was barely allowed to be screened in Iran (Maysam Makhmalbaf 2009). On the French poster Gol Ghotai determinedly walks with her boisterous mutt in the lead; the cover of the U.S. DVD uses the same image. The Italian poster is a variation of this image that has Gol Ghotai smiling and her similarly cheerful little brother sitting by her side.

REFERENCES

Bradshaw, Peter. 2006. "Stray Dogs." *The Guardian*, August 18.

Calhoun, David. 2004. "Afghan Aftermath." *Sight and Sound* 14 (2): 20–24.

Chaudhuri, Shohini, and Howard Finn. 2006. "The Open Image: Poetic Realism and the New Iranian Cinema." In *Screening World Cinema*, ed. Catherine Grant and Annette Kuhn, 163–182. London: Routledge.

Dabashi, Hamid. 2008. *Makhmalbaf at Large: The Making of a Rebel Filmmaker*. London: I. B. Tauris.

Egan, Eric. 2005. *The Films of Makhmalbaf: Cinema, Politics, and Culture in Iran*. Washington, DC: Mage.

McGill, Hannah. 2004. "Iranian House Style." *Sight and Sound* 14 (4): 32–36.

Meshkini, Marziyeh. 2004. "The Entire World Is My Home," *Film International* 10 (4): 36–40.

Makhmalbaf, Maysam. 2009. Personal communication with Josef Gugler, December 13.

Makhmalbaf, Mohsen. 2001. "The Buddha was not Demolished in Afghanistan: He Collapsed out of Shame." Makhmalbaf Film House. March. http://www.makhmalbaf.com/doc/060123175313English.doc.

Makhmalbaf, Samira. 2008. "Interview with Samira Makhmalbaf." Makhmalbaf Film House. http://www.makhmalbaf.com/articles.php?a=491.

Stam, Robert. 2003. "Beyond Third Cinema: The Aesthetics of Hybridity." In *Rethinking Third Cinema*, ed. Anthony R. Guneratne and Wimal Dissanayake, 31–49. London: Routledge.

2

Tolerated Parodies of Politics in Syrian Cinema

LISA WEDEEN

In Arabic, the word *tanfis* means "letting out air" and is used by many Syrians to describe the perception that politically critical television serials and films operate as "safety valves," allowing people to vent frustrations and displace or relieve tensions that otherwise might find expression in political action. This claim has been echoed by scholars asserting that tolerated or authorized critical practices function to preserve a repressive regime's dominance rather than undermining it. Others, by contrast, inspired by Mikhail Bakhtin's analysis of "carnival," celebrate the chaos-promoting effects and political potential of licensed rituals ...

Abstract juxtapositions of the "safety valve" formulation versus the idea of "resistance" obscure the ambiguity of these practices, which, however, are no less political for being ambiguous ... My observation of permitted comedies in Syria suggests, contrary to the dichotomous functionalist safety valve debate, that political parodies, feature films, and jokes are where Syrian political vitality resides and where critique and oppositional consciousness thrive. Artistic transgressions are the site of *politics*, of the dynamic interplay between the regime's exercise of power and people's experiences of and reactions to it ... [1]

Whereas cartoons and slapstick comedies enjoy a mass audience, Syrian films tend to appeal to the bohemian intellectual community; it may be that the limited audience for feature films is what permits them to be produced at all, despite the censorship. Many films critical of the regime have been produced by the National Film Organization, but not all have gained Syrian distribution rights. Censors approve production on the basis of a script that usually omits incendiary language or cinematic directions that might later be included in the actual film, but could be construed as blatantly critical. When a film is completed, the National Film Organization hosts an opening night to which dignitaries and some of the intellectual community are invited. Only after the premiere do government censors decide on the fate of its distribution. Some films emerge from the censors' offices to be shown to a general audience. Those that gain acceptance tend to be ones that have won recognition in Europe, are not particularly critical of the regime, or situate their criticisms in scenarios predating the Ba'thist era.

The National Film Organization was originally established in 1969 by the Ba'thist Regime of Salah Jadid to produce state propaganda films, but under Asad the Film Organization has not served that function.[2] Instead, artists have tended to struggle with the regime for control over cinematic signification, i.e., over representing the intersections between politics and everyday life. In 1974, four years after coming to power, Asad dismissed the Organization's director, Hamid Mar'i, and appointed a replacement who banned the production of documentary films. The regime, however, continued to permit critical films in fictional form, and has actually sponsored their production. As a result, the production and discussion of films have grown to become a center of intellectual life and discourse, especially when compared to other outposts of the intelligentsia such as the university. In the 1970s, film clubs (*nawadi al-sinama*), which exist in every Syrian city, became gathering places for Syria's intellectual elite and centers of secular oppositional activity.

The activities of the film clubs were sharply curtailed in the spring of 1980 as part of the regime's extensive efforts to eliminate opposition to its rule. Some of Syria's foremost film makers went into exile at this time. Yet despite increasing state intervention, a new group of internationally recognized, politically critical film makers emerged in the 1980s, under the auspices of the National Film Organization.[3] Some of the films they produced do not have an overtly political content. Others, although produced by the National Film Organization, have not been shown to general audiences because of their biting political commentary.

Nujum al-Nahar (*Stars of the Day*, 1988) is perhaps the most politically critical film ever to have been made in Syria. Usama Muhammad, the film's director, initially sent the film abroad, where it won first prize at the Festival of Valencia and the International Festival of Rabat. The film was well-received at Cannes and gained commercial distribution in France, Spain, Germany, and Switzerland. In May 1989, Muhammad screened the film in Damascus at a special preview for an audience that included government officials and military officers.

The censors decided neither to ban the film nor to approve it for distribution. Instead, the film remains in a curiously liminal position, neither available for general distribution, nor officially condemned.

Muhammad's film is an insightful and revelatory critique of the Syrian regime. Although taking the relatively safe form of a fictional narrative, the film's plot is a thinly disguised metaphor for political power and for Asad's cult. Muhammad, an ʿAlawi, depicts the moral crisis of a rural ʿAlawi family, some of whose members have moved to the city and have become involved in urban life and corrupt officialdom. As characters, they represent the regime's vulgarity and brutality. The main male protagonist, Khalil (played by real-life film director ʿAbd al-Latif ʿAbd al-Hamid), looks uncannily like Asad. Khalil is the controlling, manipulative, stingy brother and the *de facto* patriarch of the family. On his wall is a map of Lattakia, the region where most of Syria's ʿAlawi population originates. The dialect the family members speak is distinctively ʿAlawi and the language they invoke explicitly connects patriarchal family life to martial rule and political violence. A tire also hangs on the wall of Khalil's home, symbolizing *dulab*, a method of torture practiced in Syria. Khalil works as a telephone operator and listens in on people's calls. His sunglasses, and those of his brothers and male relatives, further signify their involvement in the security forces. Khalil's twin sons, dressed identically, repeat the same formulaic slogan in unison at key points in the movie:

> Papa bought me a rifle. Me and my brother are small children. We learned how to join the Army of Liberation. In the Army of Liberation we learned how to protect our homeland. Down, down with Israel. Long live the Arab nation.

In the context of the film, the slogan operates to parody the emptiness and tedium of official discourse, just as the character of Khalil, the brutal buffoon who looks like Asad, serves to mock the actual president and profane his cult. The attack on Asad's cult is made particularly explicit when Kasir, Khalil's deaf brother, arrives in Damascus. The capital city is papered with enormous pictures of a famous singer, who is also Kasir and Khalil's cousin. The style of the pictures and their strategic location on facades of public buildings make clear the reference to Asad's cult. Since Syrian directors film on location, the mechanics of taking down pictures of Asad and replacing them with images of, in this case, an actual Syrian singer, were exceptionally daring. Muhammad claims that he filmed those shots during a state holiday, and that members of his film crew charged with the task of taking down Asad's posters and replacing them with others knew the risk they were taking and were sympathetic to Muhammad's project.⁴ These same crew members worked for the secret police, according to Muhammad, but in his estimation, they had come to admire Muhammad's project and to respect his critical sensibilities.

The film's title is a pun that invokes both the Arabic expression "I'll have you seeing stars at noon"—a threat of violence similar to American cartoon depictions of characters "seeing stars" when they get knocked out—and also Syria's contemporary political celebrities, or "stars of the day." The film suggests that there is no place to stand in contemporary Syria. The countryside, although filmed to show off its breathtaking beauty, is boring and unlivable or overrun with petty familial disputes and with the attitudes that Muhammad characterizes as "backwardness." The capital city is corrupt and the site of regime domination. The Arab nation may have informed collective fantasies of political belonging in the past, but what remains are vapid slogans. A sense of displacement, of being trapped and deadened, is dramatized by Kasir's experiences upon his arrival in Damascus. He becomes immediately stuck in the middle of a terrible, cacophonous traffic jam. In search of his cousin, the famous singer whose image is everywhere but whose person he cannot locate, Kasir visits two symbolically freighted sites in the city: a store in which birds in cages are for sale, and a tombstone engraver's workshop.

The film also suggests that there is no one with whom to identify positively. The sympathetic characters in the film are helpless victims: Sana', Khalil's sister, successfully refuses to wed her cousin whom she does not know and to whom she is not attracted, but when she falls in love with a humble Arabic teacher, Khalil forces her to marry a regime-identified thug, a relative who rapes her when she tries to run away from him. The grandfather is kind and wise, but bedridden and ineffectual. Kasir, Khalil's most endearing brother, is deaf because he was beaten by his father as a boy. Although his deafness distances him from his violent brothers, he too internalizes the family's norms, and, in one effort to conform to the brutality of his male relatives, delivers a merciless beating to Sana's lover.

It is, in short, an extraordinary film that uses the symbols and language of the regime in order to subvert the regime's system of signification. It transgresses all of the boundaries of the acceptable, and unlike those cultural critics who indicate what they cannot represent, *Nujum al-Nahar* represents what it must not show. There is little distance between Asad and official corruption or arbitrary power in Muhammad's film: *Nujum al-Nahar* is an explicit attack on Asad's public glory.⁵ It is also a defense of art, of the possibility of a politically engaged, aesthetically sophisticated visual experience that self-consciously struggles against internalized censors only to confront actual external ones.[6]

The film, although never shown commercially in Syria, has had wide underground circulation among intellectuals and some general exposure at Syrian cultural festivals. Other films have been officially distributed, however, that are punctuated with moments of profound political criticism and can also be said to occupy, in less encompassing form, the border between the officially tolerated and the taboo.[7] I will elaborate on two.

Nabil Malih's *al-Kumbars* (*The Extras*, 1993) lacks the breathtaking aesthetics of some other Syrian films, but politically it is remarkably daring. That the film was distributed commercially, Malih claims, was a matter of luck. An official from the Cairo film festival asked a key Syrian official why the film was not being commercially shown, thereby embarrassing the regime into releasing it.[8] The film is certainly shockingly explicit in its condemnation of political life, and the six *al-Kindi* theaters in Syria (the government theaters where art films are shown) were packed with viewers during its four-month run. The film has also been shown at international film festivals and at human rights events . . .[9]

In *Waqa'i' al-'am al-muqbil* (*Chronicles of the Coming Year*, 1986), director and writer Samir Zikra visits some of the same themes we have already encountered in other critical depictions of Syrian political experience. Produced by Syria's National Film Organization, *Chronicles* was banned from distribution in 1986 but shown three years later in a public theater. Munir Wahba, the protagonist, has aspirations to form and conduct a national orchestra. The film documents the everyday frustrations of dealing with the bureaucracy's philistine, corrupt officials. Statements such as, "The director is here. Play now and tune up later," capture Zikra's representation of official vulgarity. The film also highlights the patently spurious quality of Syrian discourse. In one scene at the "Ninth World Conference for the Deaf held in Palestine," an official lauds the "outstanding support the deaf, dumb, and blind of Syria have enjoyed." He announces, "The World Organization for the Deaf honored his Excellency, President of the Organization of Association for the Support of the Deaf, Dumb, and Blind in Syria by bestowing the highest medal upon an Arab official in the field of deaf and dumb education and by awarding . . . a medal of honor." As the official continues his speech, one character informs another that a car has run over one of the deaf students. The spurious content of the speech is revealed not only by its juxtaposition to one deaf person's actual death, but also by the mention of Palestine, which signifies both the false promises of the regime and the lost hopes of many Syrians.[10]

Most important, the film offers a critique of political power that invokes the imagery of personal omnipotence familiar to the cult in order, once again, to subvert it. A scene depicting a dreadful dream of the protagonist, Munir, exemplifies the renegotiations of Syria's symbolic universe in ways designed to undermine rather than uphold official power.[11] Munir dreams:

> The Sultan and his associates are in a large, luxurious room, which is filled with the smoke of water pipes. They are laughing obscenely. In front of them a man who has been seated on a stump, his hands tied, kneels down. "Take him," orders one of the rulers. Two men take the captured man away. His groans of pain are audible, but his torture is not shown. Instead, we see the Sultan and his men laughing raucously. The camera approaches the laughter and zooms in on the laughing men. One man is eating a large hunk of meat with his fingers. Another's laugh exposes the absence of teeth at the side of his mouth.
>
> "Bring him," the Sultan orders. "Bring him," echo the others. The servants enter with the man. His body, naked from the waist up, is marked with deep lacerations. He is positioned on the stump, his back once again to the camera. The laughter continues unabated.
>
> "You were telling a joke about us. Tell us a joke," the Sultan orders, as he rips off a large drumstick from the carcass on a platter and tosses it to one of his friends. "Make us laugh even if it's about us." All are laughing. The Sultan tosses the drumstick to another who catches the leg and orders the tortured victim to speak. The beaten man raises his eyes and looks at the Sultan who returns the gaze and commands: "A joke."
>
> The tortured joker responds: "Listen to this. I just remembered it." The joker begins to tell his joke, but the sound is cut off and the audience is unable to hear. The Sultan and his men, however, do hear the joke, and they are outraged. As the joker finishes his joke, the sound returns. The rulers are silent, and it is the laughter of the joker which fills the room. The Sultan draws his sword, exclaiming: "You bastard. You are laughing at the Ottoman Sultan, Commander of Land and Sea, Sultan of all Times." He approaches the victim, who is still laughing. The sword cuts off the joker's head, which rolls onto the floor. But even decapitation fails to silence the laughter: it is the joker, smile intact, who enjoys the last laugh.

This scene uses so many conventional subterfuges that it draws attention to the very need to use them to disguise criticism: Zikra's critique of authoritarian, arbitrary power is bracketed in the context of a dream; the men are not contemporary leaders, but Ottoman pashas; and the dangerous joke remains unheard. The spectators' imaginations, not the film itself, construct the joke's subversive content. This scene represents censorship in ways that both protect the audience from being implicated (by not letting them hear the joke) and also paradoxically implicate the audience by inciting them to imagine its content. The scene thus evokes the imagined or real watchguard positioned next to each viewer, and also seduces viewers to draw on their own jokes and circumvent their internalized censors, without which the scene could hardly make sense.

The scene operates as a metaphor for Asad's cult. . . . Munir's thoughts are presented in the world of dreams, where he cannot control (and therefore cannot be held fully accountable for?) his subversive thoughts. And yet even in the most private, inaccessible part of himself, his unconscious, the content of the joke remains censored and unknown. What we do know is that the joke is dangerous and titillating because its subject matter is the sultan himself, whose self-proclaimed omnipotence has somehow been threatened by the joker. In fact, we do not need to know *the* joke; any of a number of jokes profaning Asad will serve for this struggle over symbolic meaning. The room is not big enough for both "heads," the head of state and the mind of a subversive joker, and as the latter head rolls, it is nevertheless the joker's laughter that resounds in the room. The sultan is capable of killing the joker, but not of stifling his laughter. People can never be fully silenced and controlled, the film suggests. And articulations that undermine the symbolic power of the leader also undermine his effectiveness. The joker has refused to operate within the politics of "as if." Even his death cannot alter the fact of his transgressive power.

NOTES

This essay is slightly abridged from Lisa Wedeen, *Ambiguities of Domination: Politics, Rhetoric, and Symbols in Contemporary Syria* (Chicago: University of Chicago Press, 1999), 88–89, 112–120. © The Regents of the University of Chicago. By permission of the University of Chicago Press. The title has been modified, and endnotes 1, 6, and 9 have been added by the editor. Textual omissions are indicated by ellipses.

On Syrian cinema under authoritarian rule see also Rasha Salti (ed.), *Insights into Syrian Cinema: Essays and Conversations with Contemporary Filmmakers* (New York: ArteEast and Rattapallax Press, 2006); Mayyar al-Roumi, "Le cinéma syrien: Du militantisme au mutisme," *EurOrient* 10 (2001): 1–25; and Meyar al-Roumi's documentary *Un cinema muet* ("A Silent Cinema", 2001).

PART 2: SYRIAN CINEMA

1. Editor's note: Wedeen, in *Ambiguities of Domination* (1999, 90–92), spells out how transgressive practices under authoritarian conditions such as those in Syria can be politically significant in several ways that transcend a simple "safety valve" interpretation.
2. Syrian film production dates back to the 1920s. In the late 1940s, encouraged by Lebanese financing and distribution, Syrian filmmakers began to produce several films a year, predominantly light comedies and musicals. A new Syrian army studio also produced some serious films, and during the union with Egypt from 1958 until 1961, the government set up a short-lived state film studio within the new Ministry of Culture.
3. Muhammad Malas won first prize at the festivals of Valencia and Carthage for his first feature film, *Ahlam al-Madina* (*Dreams of the City*, 1984). His second feature film, *al-Layl* (*The Night*, 1992), also won international recognition and appeared at the San Francisco Film Festival in 1994. Both of these films situate their narrative in the pre-Baʿthist era, but whereas *Ahlam al-Madina* managed to win the censor's approval in Syria, *al-Layl* was only shown to general Syrian audiences in 1996. Two other politically relevant films appeared in the late eighties: *Layali Ibn Awa* (*Nights of the Jackal*, 1989) by ʿAbd al-Latif ʿAbd al-Hamid, and *Nujum al-Nahar* (*Stars of the Day*) by Usama Muhammad, completed in 1988.
4. Interviews with Usama Muhammad, 1996.
5. For a discussion of Muhammad's views on the role of cinema, see Usama Muhammad, "al-Karasi kharij salat al-ʿard," in *al-Hayat*, March 21, 1995, page 18. In this article he likens cinema to a medical scope, penetrating the difficult and decisive areas of our lives. It is both the "stripping of the soul" and the "beauty and awfulness of this stripping."
6. Editor's note: On *Stars in Broad Daylight* see also Rasha Salti, "Stars in Broad Daylight," in *The Cinema of North Africa and the Middle East*, ed. Gönül Dönmez-Colin (London: Wallflower Press, 2007), 100–109.
7. Muhammad Malas's film *al-Layl*, for example, was recently shown in Syria, after years of postponement. For the most part *al-Layl* does not offend official historical understandings of the loss of Palestine and the creation of the state of Israel, but it does use the context of Syrian military coups in the 1940s to criticize the pomp and pretense of martial rule more generally. The film centers on a family in the Golan Heights town of Quneitra, and it weaves complex interrelationships among political events, neighborhood quarrels, and personal sensibilities to produce a textured, aesthetically appealing portrait of what Malas calls "the generation of the fathers," of pre- and post-independent Syria. Malas's film does take some political risks. Most notably, his depiction of sacrifice suggests explicitly that citizens' sacrifices will be appropriated by military men whose bogus ceremonies overwhelm people's actual political commitments. As the main protagonist says, "The fear is that we'll

sacrifice and die, and afterwards some bastards will come to negotiate over our corpses"—a line that has been cut from Syrian versions of the film. A shot of a military officer saluting while standing between two gigantic rams' horns, which opens and closes the film's narrative, reiterates this theme of appropriation and futility.

8. Author's interview, 1996.
9. Editor's note: For a discussion of *The Extras* see the essay on the film in this volume.
10. See Samir Zikra's *The Half Meter Incident* (1981) for a description of the ways in which Syrian media announcements deceived Syrians during the 1967 War.
11. The verbal description of this dream is my own.

*The Dupes**
Three Generations Uprooted from Palestine and Betrayed

NADIA YAQUB

It is difficult to place *The Dupes* within the national film industries of Arab cinema. The film is based on the novella *Men in the Sun* by Palestinian writer Ghassan Kanafani, directed by one of Egypt's preeminent directors, Tawfik Saleh,[1] funded by Syria's National Film Organization (NFO), and shot in Iraq as well as Syria (Saleh 2006b). It depicts events in pre-1948 Palestine and in 1958 Jordan, Iraq, and Kuwait. Indeed, the transnational and pan-Arab nature of the film's content and production are very relevant to its significance in Arab film history. Based on a highly acclaimed work of modern Arabic literature, *The Dupes* plays significant roles as a major work within Syrian and Arab cinematic history, a vehicle for the representation of Palestinians and their struggle, and an accomplished example of politically committed art. The film won the Tanit d'Or at the 1972 Carthage Film Festival and was nominated for the Golden Prize at the Moscow International Film Festival in 1973.

Men in the Sun is a story of three Palestinian men who attempt to cross the borders of Iraq and Kuwait to find work in oil-rich Kuwait.[2] The year is 1958, ten years after the 1948 Arab-Israeli war. Abou Kaiss, an older peasant, wants money to purchase a few olive trees and send his son to school. Assad is a political activist on the run from the Jordanian police. Marwan, a boy of fifteen, must leave school and provide for his mother and younger siblings after his father and older brother abandon their responsibilities toward the family. The three men meet in Basrah, where a fourth Palestinian, Aboul Kheizaran, offers to smuggle them into Kuwait inside a water tank. The men agree but perish in the heat of the tank when Kuwaiti border guards detain Aboul Kheizaran with

---

* *The Dupes/The Duped/ al-Makhduʿun*. 1972. Written and directed by Tawfik Saleh. Based on Ghassan Kanafani's novella *Men in the Sun*. Produced by the National Film Organization (Syria). Distributed in the United States by Arab Film Distribution. 107 minutes.

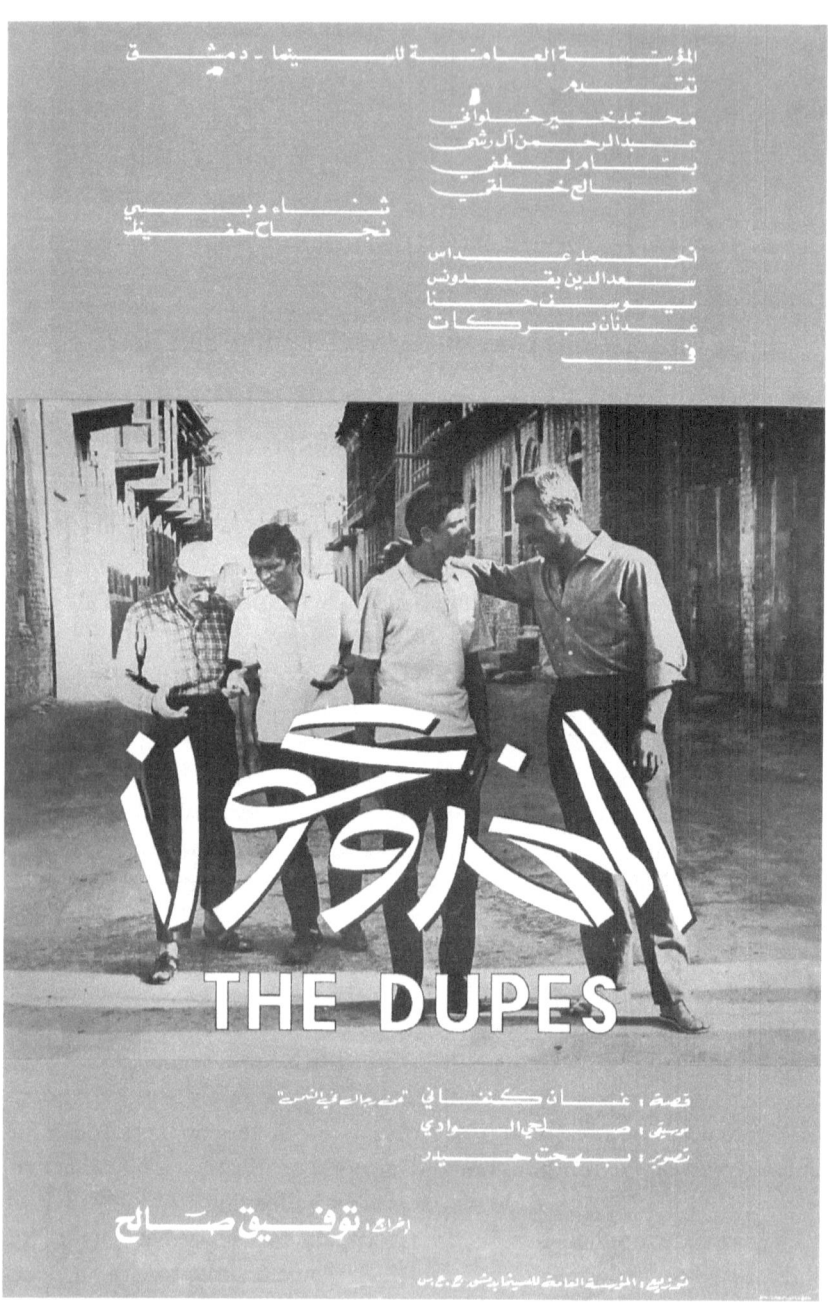

Design by M. Arnaout. Yale University Library

jokes about his reported sexual escapades in Basrah. The novella was inspired by a real incident in which forty immigrants suffocated in a tank while trying to cross the Kuwaiti border (Hennebelle and Khayati 1977, 135).[3]

The Dupes closely follows the plot of the novella and its structure, notable for its many flashbacks. The treatment of the narrative, however, differs in a number of ways. While Kanafani employs a spare prose style and eschews extensive description, Saleh uses the visual possibilities inherent in film to communicate a strong sense of place. At the same time he makes the message more salient by adding politically explicit dialogue and modifies it by changing the ending of the film to suit the political context of the early 1970s rather than the early 1960s, when the novella was written.

Published in 1963, Men in the Sun is a seminal work of Palestinian literature, the first significant work of fiction to follow the 1948 war. The book appeared shortly before the formation of the Palestine Liberation Organization (PLO) in 1964 and was a call to action on behalf of the Palestinian cause. Forced into exile ten years previously, by 1958 all the characters in the novel have abandoned the idea of return to Palestine and are seeking individual economic solutions to their problems. Their failure and deaths can be understood as the inevitable consequence of their tragic decision to literally turn their backs on the homeland—they head east toward Kuwait rather than west toward Palestine—and figuratively on the idea of Palestine and a sense of shared national identity.

When he wrote Men in the Sun, Kanafani was a member of the Arab National Movement, a pan-Arab socialist organization. In 1967 he became a spokesman for the Popular Front for the Liberation of Palestine, a Marxist-Leninist group that viewed the struggle for Palestine as part of a larger effort against Western imperialism in the Arab world. This larger political perspective is evident in the novella. Economics is foregrounded in details such as how much cash each man has, how much the smugglers at the Jordanian-Iraqi border charge, and Aboul Kheizaran's price. Agreements and decisions are calculated in economic terms without regard to personal ties. Marwan's father abandons his family for the financial security of a concrete house. Assad is cheated out of twenty dinars in Jordan by a man who fought alongside his father in 1948. Likewise, although Abou Kaiss and Aboul Kheizaran come from the same village and fought in the same battle in 1948, Aboul Kheizaran exploits the older man for personal gain. Financial transactions replace relationships based on familial structures and camaraderie, complementing the desert landscapes and atmosphere of political bankruptcy that permeate both the book and the movie; they are an integral part of the dystopic environment in which the characters move.

Looming over the economic landscape of the Arab world in the early 1960s was the development of the oil resources of the Arabian Peninsula, resources that were exploited in a systematic way through concessions to British and American oil companies only after World War II. As McLarney notes (2009), both the time of the novel's action, August 1958, and the time of its writing, January 1962, were highly charged politically. The former date coincided with the formation of the United Arab Republic (UAR), a first step in the realization of the Arab nationalist dream of a politically unified Arab world, as well as the Iraqi revolution that brought to power Abd al-Karim Qasim, a leader more interested in Iraqi nationalism than pan-Arabism. The latter date, on the other hand, followed the creation in 1960 of the Organization of Petroleum Exporting Countries (OPEC) a non-Arab transnational organization; the dissolution of the UAR in late 1961; and increasing tensions between Egyptian president and pan-Arabist Gamal Abdel Nasser and the leaders of oil-rich Arab states. The novella's irony arises in part from Kanafani's decision to set this story of economic exploitation and moral bankruptcy in 1958, when hopes for the emergence of an effective transnational Arab politics were at their peak.

None of these events are mentioned explicitly in either the novella or the film. Rather they are evoked through repeated references to time, 1958, and place, the Shatt al-Arab, the confluence of the Euphrates and Tigris Rivers and eastern border of the Arab world. The historic event that does arise repeatedly in the work is the 1948 war. For each of the Palestinian characters 1948 is an unaddressed trauma, the root cause of a personal predicament that is never confronted directly. Abou Kaiss has lost everything—home, livelihood, child—and he is too old to rebuild. Assad has lost his father. Marwan, though too young to remember pre-1948 life, bears the consequences of the communal breakdown that resulted from the war. Aboul Kheizaran has lost his manhood and, as a result, any sense of family or community. By creating characters whose predicaments are shaped by 1948 and situating them in a time and place that evoke the accomplishments and subsequent setbacks of the Arab national movement, Kanafani implicitly draws a connection between the two. Just as the Palestinian characters fail to confront the losses they incurred in 1948, Arab failure both in the 1948 war and on behalf of the Palestinian refugees afterward is the unaddressed wound at the heart of Arab nationalism.

Another historical moment never mentioned in the film but very much in the mind of the filmmaker is Black September 1970, the civil war between Palestinian guerillas and the Jordanian monarchy that led to the expulsion of the

PLO and its fighters from Jordan. "I wanted to show and say something about those Palestinians. The historical and political issues and the inhuman way they were and are treated by the whole world became the most important reason to make the film" (Saleh 2006b). This new political landscape led Saleh to alter the ending of Kanafani's novella. In the original, the men die in the tank silently. Aboul Kheizaran draws attention to that silence through his chastisement: "Why didn't you knock on the sides of the tank? Why didn't you say anything?" he asks (Kanafani 1999, 74). The criticism of the passivity of the Palestinian leadership implicit in the scene was highly controversial when the work first appeared. By 1971, when Saleh filmed *The Dupes*, however, Palestinian political groups had become key players in Arab leftist politics and were engaged militarily in demanding Palestinian rights. Kanafani's ending was no longer relevant to a time when Palestinians were vocal about their rights and aspirations but were either ignored or repressed by conservative Arab governments and the international community.

Saleh uses both cinematography and dialogue to allude to the political background that frames the writing of the novella and the events narrated within it. In an early scene Abou Kaiss lies on the ground near the Shatt recollecting a similar moment from pre-1948 Palestine when he imagines that he can hear the heartbeat of the earth. Kanafani describes the sand, the white-hot sky, and black birds circling overhead. Saleh adds a lush grove of palm trees, which is geographically accurate, as the Shatt is famous for its palm forests, and evocative of Iraq, as the palm tree is its national symbol. Images of the Shatt are interwoven with the story of Master Selim, the secular schoolteacher in Abou Kaiss's village who is an embodiment of the forward-thinking revolutionary. Saleh himself says of Master Selim that he is *la voie à suivre*, the path to follow (Cheriaa 1973, 15) that is otherwise missing from the world of the film. In *The Dupes* his modernity and education are signaled in his appearance—he sports glasses and Western clothes and haircut—and in his actions: he does not know how to pray, but he knows how to shoot a rifle and dies a hero's death in 1948. His revolutionary modernity is specifically coded in Arab nationalist terms in the lesson he teaches Abou Kaiss's son about the geography of the Shatt.

Ironically, the Shatt is not just a symbol of Arab nationalism in the film but also the locus for the individualist capitalism that Kanafani and Saleh criticize. In *The Dupes*, the three men negotiate with Aboul Kheizaran over his plan to smuggle them into Kuwait against a backdrop of the waterway and its maritime traffic, including oil tankers. At the film's end, Aboul Kheizaran removes the three corpses from the water tank and throws them onto a garbage heap in Kuwait in front of a backdrop of oil installations. The economics of inter-Arab relations is simultaneously raised and critiqued in these images.

Noteworthy, too, are images of both pre- and post-1948 Palestinian life. *The Dupes* is one of the first films to address the Palestinian question in a serious way. Until 1968, when the PLO founded its film unit, there were virtually no cinematic images from a Palestinian perspective; what footage did exist had been shot by the British, Zionists, Israelis, or the United Nations (Antonius 1978, 123). Abou Kaiss's memories of pre-1948 Palestine are depicted in idyllic rural scenes. Farmers tend to their olive trees in images evoking the association between Palestinian identity and an enduring physical relationship with the land that was a major theme in Palestinian art of the 1970s and 1980s (Boullata 2000, Shammut 1989). Abou Kaiss's home is marked with cultural artifacts—hand-woven carpets and cushions, an alcove stacked with mattresses—that suggest large families and the accommodation of guests, the baking of bread on a traditional oven, and cozy family meals around a communal tray. Abou Kaiss's recollection of home are intercut with his memories of ten years of humiliating exile in which institutions and charity, registration and soup lines replace family life and meaningful work.

As a Syrian rather than a Palestinian film, *The Dupes* was not only part of a new post-1967 Palestinian consciousness but a milestone in the development of a new Arab cinema and the byproduct of the complex relationship between Arab politics and the Palestine question. *The Dupes*, along with Shadi ʿAbd al-Salam's *The Mummy* (*The Night of Counting the Years/al-Mumiya*, 1969) and Youssef Chahine's *The Sparrow* (*al-ʿUsfur*, 1973), led to the development of a new realism in Arab cinema in the wake of the Arab defeat in 1967 (Bouzid 1995, 244–245). In the early 1970s Damascus became the center for this progressive pan-Arabist filmmaking. In fact, Tawfik Saleh moved there precisely because the politically explicit films he wanted to create were not possible in Egypt at that time. Palestine was at the heart of this movement; from 1969 to 1972 three of the five feature-length films produced by the NFO were about Palestine (Shafik 2007, 155). However, the connection between the production of films about Palestine and progressive Arab politics was not straightforward. Palestine was exploited by Arab governments as a means of distracting their populations from domestic problems. In fact, Saleh himself only came to direct *The Dupes* after his first screenplay was denied funding by the NFO (Saleh 2006a). After it was made, and despite its critical success, *The Dupes* was heavily censored; it was screened for two just weeks in Damascus and was not shown at all in Egypt or Iraq (Hennebelle and Khayati 1977, 138; Rosen 1989, 35).[4]

Preparing for the final border crossing

The politics addressed in *Men in the Sun* has significant generational and gendered dimensions that Saleh adeptly highlights. Among the four Palestinian characters are two victims, Abou Kaiss and Marwan, and two individualists, Assad and Aboul Kheizaran. Old, illiterate, and unprepared for the challenges of the modern world, Abou Kaiss is the victim of the failed politics of the past. His flashbacks suggest that the rural class he represents was losing its footing in the world even before 1948. His school-age son already knows more than Abou Kaiss does about the world outside the village and is not shy about demonstrating his superior knowledge. This fact is key, for it suggests that pre-1948 was not a utopian society to which Palestinians should aspire to return. Rather, it was already the site of social and economic upheaval about which there was debate and confusion. The scene suggests that even if Abou Kaiss had not lost everything in 1948, his later years in Palestine would have been marked by anxiety, for he is a victim not only of the Arab loss in 1948 but also of the failure of Palestinian and Arab leaders *before* 1948 to prepare their populace for the modern era. Marwan, in contrast, is the sacrificed future. He comes from the generation that should be educating itself to take on the social and political challenges to come. However, because of the failure of older men, boys like Marwan are forced to abandon their aspirations to meet the immediate economic needs of their loved ones.

Tawfik Saleh (left) and the Tunisian film critic Tahar Cheriaa at a demonstration in Frankfurt in 1973. From Khémaïs Khayati, *Cinémas arabes: Topographie d'une image éclatée* (Paris: L'Harmattan, 1996). Courtesy Khémaïs Khayati

Significantly, both Abou Kaiss and Marwan are motivated to travel to Kuwait because of the intensity of their commitment to their families. Their ability to look beyond their individual desires draws them to each other. During the tanker ride through the desert Marwan and Abou Kaiss are always together, either on top of the tank or in the cab. When the three men emerge from the tank after crossing the Iraqi border and before attempting the Kuwait crossing, Marwan instinctively crawls to where Abou Kaiss lies exhausted on the ground. Saleh's camera lingers over the physical connection between the two as Marwan rests his head on the older man's leg. Similarly, Marwan clings to Abou Kaiss's legs as the truck barrels through the desert and rests his head on the older man's shoulder when the two join Aboul Kheizaran in his cab.

Saleh draws the connection between these two men and their shared victimhood most strikingly through their clothing. Aboul Kheizaran suggests to the men that they remove their shirts before entering the water tank to make the heat more bearable. All three do so, although Assad does not remove his until he is in the tank, out of sight of Aboul Kheizaran. Eventually both Abou Kaiss and Marwan strip to their underpants, but Assad retains his trousers. When the men emerge from the tank, the visual contrast is striking. Assad looks like a laborer, but Marwan and Abou Kaiss, in briefs soiled by their sweat and the rust inside the tank and so loose around their hips and legs that they barely cover their private parts, have been utterly stripped of both their cultural identity and their masculinity.

This scene derives its power at least in part from the intricate ways in which Saleh has used clothing throughout the film to communicate cultural, class, and gender identity. Master Selim's secular, modern attire is notable because it contrasts with that of other men in the village. In one striking scene he sits in his suit, white shirt, and tie in the village guesthouse where men are talking and smoking. The guesthouse, with its mats and cushions, its brazier, coffee grinder, and water pipes, is the embodiment of an Arab male space. All the men save Master Selim wear long robes and elegantly arranged headdresses. The difference between Master Selim's dress and that of the other men mirrors and reinforces their differences in outlook and education—they speak of prayer, while he speaks of armed struggle and teaches his charges about their Arab heritage.

Headdresses in particular are emblematic of Arab male authority, particularly traditional authority, throughout the film. However, they only carry this significance when worn for style and character rather than utility. Like the other men in his village, Abou Kaiss wears a flowing *kufiya* and ʿ*iqal* (a ring of black rope that men wear on top of their headscarves) in the pre-1948 men's guesthouse, but in the post-1948 scenes he rarely has one, and when he does, he wears it wrapped tightly around his head like a bandage as protection from the heat of the desert. Assad's headscarf is highly symbolic, for it belongs to Abu Abed, the smuggler who had promised to take him from Amman to Baghdad. In a scene whose significance is cued by its repetition in the film, Abu Abed gives the scarf to Assad for protection during his desert walk. At the very moment when he abandons Assad, cheating his old companion's son, he symbolically relinquishes his claim to traditional Arab male honor. Tawfik Saleh has spoken of the desert in *The Dupes* as a symbol for the "desert" of time through which the Palestinians have passed since 1948 (Hennebelle and Khayati 1977, 137), and the way in which the men wear their headdresses reinforces this association. In the desert these markers of Arab masculinity are stripped of their cultural significance, while their inadequacy as protection from the sun is emphasized.

Like Abou Kaiss and Marwan, Assad and Aboul Kheizaran are also victims of 1948. However, they turn their backs on their social and familial responsibilities in favor of individual economic gain. Saleh emphasizes this point by adding two flashbacks to the novella's narrative in which Assad and Aboul Kheizaran each rejects the urgings of a friend who wants him to continue the political struggle rather than leave for Kuwait and its economic opportunities. Assad and Aboul Kheizaran are united by their sterility, as well—Aboul Kheizaran because of his war wound and Assad because of his refusal to marry. Just as Marwan and Abou Kaiss are paired in the film, a special bond links Assad and Aboul Kheizaran. They too spend much of the desert journey together, and their conversation reveals that they share an appreciation for the cynical and the mercenary. When Aboul Kheizaran opens the tank after the fateful crossing of the Kuwaiti border, it is Assad's name he calls out, not Abou Kaiss's, despite his prior acquaintance with the latter.

The sterility of Aboul Kheizaran and Assad points to a major theme of the narrative: the disruption contemporary politics has caused to Arab Palestinian masculinity. The opening scene of Kanafani's novella is quite sensual. Abou Kaiss lies on the ground at the edge of the Shatt, remembering his land in Palestine and its association with the smell of his wife's hair. In *The Dupes* this scene is contextualized within Abou Kaiss's trek through the desert. The film begins with him as a speck on the horizon walking toward the camera to fall exhausted under the palm trees of what is clearly not Palestinian soil. Abou Kaiss's almost erotic relationship with the land contrasts sharply with the final scene, in which Aboul Kheizaran pulls the men from the tank like a midwife at a still birth. In analyses of the novella much has been written about the significance of Aboul Kheizaran's emasculation, especially in light of the punning around the words *qa'id*, which means both "driver" and "leader," and *qawwad*, which means "pimp" (McLarney 2009, Zalman 2006). The double meaning encourages the reading of his character as a representation of emasculated Palestinian and/or Arab leadership.[5]

But Aboul Kheizaran's character does not have to be read allegorically to impart a meaningful commentary on gender and Palestinian politics. As Amy Zalman notes (2006, 48), national loss is coded in the novella as a particularly male trial and the task of compensating for that loss a male endeavor. Kanafani's story, and in particular Aboul Kheizaran's inability to counter the Kuwaiti border guard's sexual teasing, makes clear that the old way of being a Palestinian man is no longer viable but that Palestinians have not yet found a way, or have been prevented from finding a way, to be honorable men in the post-1948, oil-rich Arab world.

An important theme running through *Men in the Sun* and *The Dupes* relates to the passage of time. There are repeated references to the ten years since

1948, ten years of stagnation and humiliation. This long span contrasts with the urgency inherent in the minutes that pass while the men are in the tank. The message of the novella, written fourteen years after 1948, is clear: time is running out. Decisive action must be taken now. The urgency of this message is redoubled in Saleh's film, which came out ten years after Kanfani's novella and five years after the 1967 war. It is ironic that more than thirty years after Saleh completed *The Dupes*, a Palestinian director, Rashid Masharawi, should feel the need to address the same theme in his film *Waiting* (*Attente/Intizar*, 2006).[6]

NOTES

1. The director's first name is also transliterated as Taufik, Tawfiq, or Tewfik, his last as Salih.
2. An earlier Syrian production, *Men under the Sun* (*Rijal tahta as-shams*, 1970), directed by Mohammad Chahine, Marwan Mouazzen, and Nabil Maleh, is also about the Palestinian question, but it bears no relationship to Kanafani's novella.
3. Editor's note: The poster the National Film Organization issued for *The Dupes* used only black and blue, for economy's sake perhaps. The picture of Abou Kaiss, Assad, Marwan, and Aboul Kheizaran in Baghdad and the text remain rather indistinct. A dramatic contrast is created by the white Arabic and English titles on the poster reproduced here, the French title on another version. A French poster produced in France shows a sketch of the three would-be migrants sitting together exhausted after their first border crossing in the water tank.
4. Censorship of the film was not limited to the Arab world. It was screened at Cannes but did not open in Paris as planned (Hennebelle and Khayati 1977, 126).
5. Aboul Kheizaran's name also suggests emasculation. *Khayzuran* means reed and refers metaphorically to the slender waist of a beautiful woman in medieval Arabic poetry. The Kuwaiti guard emphasizes this point by calling him Aboul Kheizaranah, a feminized form of the word.
6. On *Waiting* see the essay devoted to the film in this volume.

REFERENCES

Antonius, Soraya. 1978. "The Palestinian Cause in the Cinema," review of *La Palestine et le cinéma* by Guy Hennebelle and Khemaïs Khayati. *Journal of Palestine Studies* 7 (2): 120–125.
Boullata, Kamal. 2000. *Istihdar al-makan: Dirasa fi al-fann al-tashkili al-filastini al-muasir*. Tunis: al-Munazama al-Arabiya li-al-Tarbiya wa-al-Thaqafa wa-al-Ulum.

Bouzid, Nouri. 1995. "New Realism in Arab Cinema: The Defeat-Conscious Cinema." *Alif: Journal of Comparative Poetics* 15: 242–250.
Cheriaa, Tahar. 1973. "Tewfik Saleh et 'Les Dupes.'" *Positif* 151 (June): 9–16.
Hennebelle, Guy, and Khémaïs Khayati. 1977. *La Palestine et le cinéma*. Paris: E. 100.
Kanafani, Ghassan. 1999. *Men in the Sun and Other Palestinian Stories*. Translated by Hilary Kilpatrick. Boulder, CO: Lynne Rienner.
McLarney, Ellen. 2009. "Empire of the Machine: The Oil Industry in the Arabic Novel." *boundary 2* 36 (2): 177–198.
Rosen, Miriam. 1989. "The Uprooted Cinema: Arab Filmmakers Abroad," *Middle East Report* 159 (July–August): 34–37.
Saleh, Tawfik. 2006a. Personal letter to Josef Gugler, March 21.
———. 2006b. Personal letter to Josef Gugler, May 16.
Shafik, Viola. 2007. *Arab Cinema: History and Cultural Identity*. Revised edition. Cairo: American University in Cairo Press.
Shammut, Ismail. 1989. *al-Fann at-tashkili fi filastin*. Kuwait: Matba al-Quds.
Zalman, Amy. 2006. "Gender and the Palestinian Narrative of Return in Two Novels by Ghassan Kanafani." In *Literature and Nation in the Middle East*, ed. Yasir Suleiman and Ibrahim Muhawi, 48–78. Edinburgh: Edinburgh University Press.

*The Extras**
Lovers Suffer the Twin Repressions of a Patriarchal Culture and a Police State

JOSEF GUGLER

Syrian cinema distinguishes itself, among all the cinemas of the Middle East and the Maghreb, by the critical stance its directors have taken time and again vis-à-vis the regime—the very regime that tightly controls film production. Usually the attacks on the regime take the form of allegories. While their significance is readily apparent to Syrians, it commonly remains hidden from most foreign viewers. *The Extras* stands apart in its quite explicit denunciation of the Syrian police state. Nabil Maleh tells of illicit love in a patriarchal culture and of illicit discourse under a tyranny.[1] In an interplay of reality and fantasies, daydreams, and hallucinations, *The Extras* effectively conveys the fears that haunt those who break cultural taboos and just about anybody living in a police state. This moving love story would be all gloom were it not that the lovers bring laughter as well as tears to the troubles they face, and viewers get to smile in turn.

The Extras presents an apparently simple story. Salem is a gas-station attendant who performs at the National Theater as an extra and aspires to become an actor. He has met with Nada, a young widow who works in a factory, for eight months. An apartment borrowed from his friend Adel will allow them to get together in privacy for the first time. Their rendezvous is interrupted by the arrival of Adel's fiancée, Wafa, and the intrusion of a stranger. *The Extras* resembles a play: the entire action takes place within the confines of Adel's small apartment but for stills and shots accompanying the opening credits and the final sequences; the story is tightly integrated around five actors; and it proceeds in

---

* *The Extras/al-Kompars.* 1993. Film written and directed by Nabil Maleh. Produced by the National Film Organization (Syria). Distributed in the United States by Arab Film Distribution. 100 minutes.

Design by Nabil Maleh. Yale University Library

real time. Ghanam suggests that it is this very economy that allowed Maleh "to penetrate deeply into the landscape of everyday life in Syria" (2006, 73).

The specific cultural context of *The Extras* comes across in several ways. In eight months of courtship Salem has not seen Nada's hair. Even though Nada has been married before, she is wracked by fear that her brothers will find out about her illicit relationship with Salem. Salem and Nada appear ready to get married but cannot afford to. Adel and his fiancée strikingly demonstrate that quite different sexual mores coexist in contemporary Syria.

If the fear of being found out hangs over Salem and Nada, they themselves remain bound by traditions that put them ill at ease as they feel their way to becoming intimate. Salem eventually sets out to realize his macho fantasies, but Nada rejects his stormy embrace. A transformation to a sensitive sexual relationship ensues as the two lovers get closer and Nada, the widow, comes to take control rather than Salem, who appears to have little sexual experience beyond pornography and his fantasies. As Salem rests at Nada's bosom, she turns melancholic, articulates her feelings in a surprisingly poetic manner, and comes close to crying. The subdued mood is reinforced by the melody that comes through the wall as their neighbor, a blind beggar, plays the *oud*. His music continues to accompany their fumbling moves toward intimacy.[2] The memory of those sounds becomes all the more poignant when the viewer realizes that this is the last time the blind man plays before his *oud* is smashed and he is hauled off by secret-service agents.

When the stranger first appears, he starts out inquiring in peremptory fashion without introducing himself. That this obnoxious intruder is a secret-service agent will be obvious to any viewer familiar with the operations of police states.[3] As Adel puts it, "People like those have their ID's . . . stamped on their faces." The suspicions of the agent are raised because Adel speaks with the accent of Aleppo, a city where the regime has encountered opposition. The stranger wants to know whether Salem also comes from Aleppo. Told that Salem is a Damascene, he inquires further whether Salem has ever lived in Muhajreen, a poor quarter known for fundamentalist sympathies. The stranger's return will not be just another interruption for the hapless couple; he will become a threat.

The film's original title, *al-Kompars*, refers to Salem performing at the National Theater as an extra. The English title, *The Extras*, is a literal translation of the word, except that it is in the plural, which may be taken to refer to the role Salem and Nada, and most citizens, play in Syrian politics. Maleh commented on this condition in an interview in 1994:

[F]or something like twenty years now, we Arabs have been simple extras in our societies where the Arab citizen is not allowed a voice. In our countries there is no equilibrium of political parties . . . no possible revindication, only orders that come down on us and which we endure like extras, which is also the case of our rulers. Because, as in a pyramid, there are several layers, and they are also subject to international commands . . . Two hundred fifty million Arabs are extras. (1996, 112)[4]

Maleh articulates his political message when he has Salem tell Nada about his experiences at the National Theater. He speaks of roles he has played as an extra and of the two best professions:

[W]hen I'm a soldier
I die for my homeland
When I'm a beggar . . . I die of hunger
When I'm a citizen . . . I die of depression
When I'm [a] thief, bigger thieves come and kill me
When I'm a demonstrator
I mean a revolution[ary]
they beat me up
make me a file and deprive me of ever being employed
I've discovered that [the] best profession is that of belly dancers and . . . informers
It is said that they are permanently needed.

When Salem proposes to act out a special play for Nada, she responds enthusiastically. She readily embraces the role of the abusive ruler but then has second thoughts. And when he tells of having moved at the National Theater from extra to talking parts as a prison guard and as an informer, Nada asks why he has taken on such awful roles. His response applies to extras in the theater as well as Syrian society: "It is a chance. To be something better than an extra, you must accept roles you don't like."[5]

Adel and Wafa provide a stark contrast to the "extras" not just in sexual mores. They illustrate the charmed life of the chosen few. They can afford to get married, and Adel expects to move to better housing. Her father was a simple man who found himself suddenly elevated to join the political elite. Her manners convey the character of the *nouveau riche*. Wafa is ordinary, and she and Adel may be seen as corrupted by their connection with the oppressive regime,

Nada questions the role Salem is playing at the National Theater.

but they acknowledge readily that this elite has little legitimacy and enjoys undeserved privileges.

Salem managed to move on to speaking roles at the National Theater. But if he found a voice, it was that of an accomplice in tyranny. Salem cannot raise his voice in opposition to the police state. He had fantasized about knocking out the secret-service agents, but when they return to arrest the blind neighbor and he protests, a hard slap sends him sprawling. Nada pretends that she did not witness the humiliation of her beloved and takes leave as if nothing were amiss, but as soon as she is out the door she cries in shame. The film concludes on the ordinary surface of daily life. First Nada, then Salem walk out the gate, and the camera moves up the ordinary apartment building and across the ordinary city. We have just learned what is going on daily behind those ordinary appearances in Damascus.

The lovers have failed in their effort to break out of the straightjacket of patriarchal norms, just as Salem could not possibly protect the blind beggar. Nothing has changed but that with the beggar another voice has been silenced and that Salem has been humiliated in front of his love. Nada and Salem still cannot afford to marry, and the threat from her brothers to what they would consider an illicit relationship remains. Before Salem confronted the secret-service agents, Nada held out the prospect that they would find intimacy "next time." The director suggests that Salem's humiliation has put their relationship asunder: "They entered the apartment as lovers, they leave as strangers" (in Wright 2006, 62). Such an ending may have been foreshadowed symbolically even before the arrival of Nada, when the glass shattered from a wall decoration Salem had broken accidentally, a decoration Adel had characterized as representing love. Quite a different future for the couple is suggested, however, by Maleh himself when he commented that all the heroes in his films share a similar fate: they lose the battle, but they are victorious on a moral and human register (2006, 89). Surely Nada sees the moral victory in Salem's defeat as well, or will come to see it. As she and Salem walk away from their ill-fated rendezvous, the *oud* is heard once more, ending on a rather up-beat note. The lovers may well continue their relationship and find intimacy, but it will be under the constant threat of Nada's brothers, just as Syrians live in constant fear of the state.

When Salem and Nada were lying under the bed's metal wire, Nada articulated the political symbolism: "Is it possible that there are people imprisoned for years behind such wires?" Salem attempted to deflect the query, but Nada concluded: "Some people are imprisoned without wire or bars." Her response may be taken in terms of both the politics of Syria and the strictures of the patriarchal culture.

Wedeen (1999, 117) sees political and sexual impotence as explicitly linked in *The Extras*. This raises the contentious issue of the relationship between a patriarchal culture and authoritarian political structures. Oussama Mohammad, another Syrian director renowned for distinguished films that denounce the regime, told Wright: "This society is responsible for creating the dictatorship—it's in our culture, our way of believing and thinking. I am trying to expose the authority inside us and the shadow of political authority in front of our doors" (2006, 46). Maleh, on the other hand, holds that the regime's abuse of power and the lack of democratic expression have been replicated in the relationships between authority figures and those without power—women, children, and the poor—and turned Syrian society violent in the past forty years (in Wright 2006, 63).

The Extras tells of an entire society haunted by fear. Maleh eschews high drama and thus all the more effectively conveys the pervasive fear that permeates the everyday lives of all but a privileged few in a police state and the lives of those who break patriarchal norms. The film leaves the viewer to guess what is happening to the musician next door. Neither does the public witness the sufferings of people like director Oussama Mohammad's brother Ali, who was imprisoned for years after he and several university professors had accepted an invitation to share their views on reform with members of the regime. Ali eventually was threatened with being sent to a prison reputed as a torture chamber, presumably to make his brother, the director, change his ways (Wright 2006, 54–55). Viewers of Maleh's film do get to share in the anxious mood of those who live in fear of persecution by long pauses between movements and in the dialogue that express the restlessness of the characters, by close-ups that convey their emotions, and by the effective acting of Samar Sami and Bassam Koussa,[6] who won the top acting awards for their portrayals of Nada and Salem at the Arab Cinema Biennial in Paris.

The Extras was shown commercially in Syria, unlike most of the films more or less explicitly critical of the regime. This was a time when the Hafez Assad regime was liberalizing ever so lightly. According to Maleh, an official from the Cairo International Film Festival—where he won the Best Director award for *The Extras*—asked a key Syrian official why the film was not in general distribution, embarrassing the regime into releasing it. The six government theaters where art films are screened were packed with viewers during its four-month run (Wedeen 1999, 116).

Maleh was studying nuclear physics in Czechoslovakia when he switched to film directing. He returned to Damascus in 1964, a year after the establishment of the National Film Organization. Maleh, who also is known as a poet and painter, did not join any political party or organization and, unlike most of his Syrian peers, never became a civil servant at the National Film Organization. He was among the few Syrians to join with directors from across the Arab world to establish the pan-Arab "Alternative Cinema." Maleh's *The Leopard* (*al-Fahd*, 1972) was one of the two first full-length fiction films produced by members of the group, to international acclaim. A dramatic tale of the lone rebel against the injustice of a feudal system, based on a novel by Haydar Haydar, *The Leopard* draws on elements of the folk ballad in telling its realistic story. Maleh's productive career was interrupted when he left Syria in 1981, spending most of his time in Greece, where he wrote the script for *The Extras*. When he was invited by the National Film Organization to shoot the film under its auspices, he returned to Syria in 1992 (Cinéma Méditerranéen Montpellier, 2000). He commented on his situation:

Nabil Maleh, seated low, on the set. Courtesy Nabil Maleh

> As a Syrian filmmaker, after a thirty-year long career I am still fighting for a life with dignity without having to become a civil servant. Thirty long years where one never knows if another opportunity for work will be granted. As filmmakers we have all become scattered islands, without a shared history or collective concern. The decay that has been gnawing at the Arab world has caused us to drift apart, separating from one another ... The quest for an identity, and individuality, a language or dream has been impeded with the search and begging and pleading for funding from outside the country or the struggle for opportunity from inside. (Maleh 2006, 91–92)

In 2006 Maleh was honored at the Dubai International Film Festival, along with Oliver Stone and Shah Rukh Khan, for his outstanding contribution to cinema.

Maleh was closely involved in the efforts of prominent Syrians to push the regime toward liberalization as Hafez Assad was dying. The inaugural meeting of the movement that came to be called the Committees for the Revival of Civil Society in Syria took place at his home in May 2000. Initial concessions by the regime were soon followed by repression. As Maleh put it in conversation with Lawrence Wright: "We lost the war without ever fighting it" (2006, 61). Maleh had been told that he would never be able to make another film, but in 2004 he shot a British-Syrian co-production, *The Hunt Feast*, in Syria and Lebanon.[7]

NOTES

1. The director's last name is also transliterated as Al-Maleh, Malih, or Al-Malih.
2. This brief moment of bliss is conveyed in the poetic Syrian poster reproduced here. The poster was designed by the director. In the original color version, this moment appears as a magnificent painting.
3. The review in the trade magazine *Variety* (Nesselson 1994), which usually is served by knowledgeable contributors, misses the political dimension of the film altogether.
4. My translation from the French.
5. Such a play denouncing a despotic ruler could be performed at the National Theater under Hafez Assad provided it was set in a different era (Wedeen 2009).
6. Bassam Koussa was one of the few actors to sign the September 2000 statement by ninety-nine prominent Syrians calling for liberalization.
7. The biographical notes on Maleh draw on Maleh 2006 and Wright 2006.

REFERENCES

Cinéma Méditerranéen Montpellier. 2000. "Syrie, métaphores et réalités historiques," in *Actes du 21e Festival International*, 30–34. Montpellier: Festival de Montpellier.
Ghanam, Oussama. 2006. "Tigers on Their Ninth Day: Syrian Cinema in a Quarter Century." In *Insights into Syrian Cinema: Essays and Conversations with Contemporary Filmmakers*, ed. Rasha Salti, 67–77. New York: ArteEast and Rattapallax Press.
Maleh, Nabil. 1996. "L'Insécurité mentale des gens ou la police des rêves." In *Actes du 16e et du 17e Festival International*, 112–113. Montpellier: Festival de Montpellier.
———. 2006. "Scenes from Life and Cinema." In *Insights into Syrian Cinema: Essays and Conversations with Contemporary Filmmakers*, ed. Rasha Salti, 87–94. New York: ArteEast and Rattapallax Press. Translation by Rasha Salti of "Mashahed min al-hayat wa al-sinama," *Alam al-Fikr* 26 (1): 194–201.
Nesselson, Lisa. 1994. "Al-Compars." *Variety*, November 21, 14.
Wedeen, Lisa. 1999. *Ambiguities of Domination: Politics, Rhetoric, and Symbols in Contemporary Syria*. Chicago: University of Chicago Press.
———. 2009. Personal communication to the author, June 12.
Wright, Lawrence. 2006. "Disillusioned." In *Insights into Syrian Cinema: Essays and Conversations With Contemporary Filmmakers*, ed. Rasha Salti, 45–65. New York: ArteEast and Rattapallax Press.

3

Lebanese Cinema and the Representation of War

LINA KHATIB

The first Lebanese film may be dated to 1929, but Lebanese cinema remained in the shadow of the Egyptian film industry for decades. Production increased substantially in the 1960s when, in the wake of the nationalization of the Egyptian film industry, producers and distributors directed their investments to Lebanon. They continued, however, to produce for the market the Egyptian film industry had established in Egypt and elsewhere in the Arab world.[1] Lebanese cinema has come into its own over the past thirty years as it acted as a commentator on the development of sectarian conflict in Lebanon, on the normalization of war, on reconstruction in the postwar period, and on the way the war still lurks in every corner of today's Lebanon. Since the incipience of the civil war in 1975, it has become a central theme for Lebanese filmmakers across generations. This does not simply apply to films representing the civil war; it also applies to films in which the war inhabits their stylistic elements. From the open-endedness of *A Perfect Day* (*Yawm akhar*, Joana Hadji Thomas and Khalil Joreige, 2005) to the darkness of *Falafel* (Michel Kammoun, 2006), the civil war still casts a shadow on later films.

The war films focus on issues of social fragmentation, sectarian animosities, class divisions, and individual devastation. Only *West Beirut* (*West Beyrouth*, Ziad Doueiri, 1998) and *In the Battlefields* (*Maʿarik hubb*, Danielle Arbid, 2004) represent another side to the war, that of the possibility of having fun under difficult conditions. The other films about the civil war, whether made during the war or after, are more concerned with revealing its dark side. The films differ in genre: while some like *In the Shadows of the City* (*Tayf al-madina*, Jean Chamoun, 2000) take a realist angle on the war, others like *The Tornado* (*al-Iʿsar*, Samir Habchi, 1992) and *A Suspended Life* (*Ghazl al-banat 2*, Jocelyne Saab, 1984) choose a more fantasy-based method of addressing it. What the films have in common is that none of them justifies the war, as they all take part in condemning it in different ways.

Beirut, the Wounded City

During the civil war, Beirut was transformed from a "playground" into a "battleground" (S. Khalaf 1993, 107) as the city became the center of militia fighting. Lebanese cinema foregrounded the representation of a wounded Beirut. Most films depicting Beirut were shot on location, and the destroyed city center became "a natural backdrop that filmmakers were keen to exploit before the area is rebuilt" (George Nasr in *an-Nidaʾ*, 1983). A number of Lebanese films depict the fragmentation of Beirut during the civil war as symptomatic of the fragmentation of Lebanese society at large. Films like *West Beirut* deal with the breakdown of Beirut from a whole city into exclusive, homogeneous, sectarian zones.

West Beirut starts with the tranquil life of a Muslim middle-class family, the Noueiris, living in Beirut. That existence is disturbed by the incident that catalyzed the civil war in Lebanon: on April 13, 1975, a bus carrying Palestinian passengers was attacked by right-wing Christian militants; thirty-one people were killed, and another thirty were wounded. The Noueiris are bewildered by the incident, not understanding its causes or its implications. The father's misunderstanding of the situation leads him to distance himself as a Lebanese from the incident, saying it is "between Palestinians and Israelis, nothing to do with us." This statement echoes a sentiment that was prevalent throughout Lebanon, where the war was referred to as "the war of Others on our land." *West Beirut* works to dispel this myth, forcing the Noueiris to accept that the event of April 13 was not a mere "incident" but a massacre.

The civil war brought large numbers of refugees from the south to Beirut. War films highlight their marginalization, their frustration, and their longing to return home. *In the Shadows of the City* depicts the hardship faced by a family of refugees. The father is forced to take his twelve-year-old son out of school and find him a job. The father himself only survives by performing the menial job of collecting and selling scrap metal from the rubble of bombed buildings. Another father from the south is hit by depression in *A Suspended Life* as he is forced to work as a builder in Beirut. The space of Beirut does not seem to belong to these people.

Perhaps the best illustration of this issue is found in *Beirut, the Encounter* (*Beirut, al-liqaʾ*, Borhan Alawiyeh, 1981). The film uses visual and aural clues to comment on the inhospitability of Beirut toward the displaced. The first shot of Beirut shows a pile of garbage on a street corner to the sound of buzzing flies. The camera then goes inside a building where two brothers from the south are sheltering. The apartment they share is bare except for mattresses on the floor, a broom placed against a wall, and prayer beads hanging from a radiator. One of the men, Haydar, goes out onto the balcony. The camera shows his point of view as he stares at destroyed buildings in the city. A loud noise is heard. The camera goes down to the street to show a truck removing rubble. The scene lingers and the noise intensifies, creating a feeling of discomfort that mirrors that felt by Haydar.

War, Religion, and Sectarianism

The war was both a result of and a cause for sectarian divisions. The prewar divisions were consolidated with the progression of national conflict. Each side declared itself right, announced its paranoia about the threat from "others" to its very existence, and in doing so justified its actions against them. Lebanese cinema does not reflect the full spectrum of sectarian divisions in the country, but it remains one of the few public arenas in which the issues of sectarianism and social fragmentation have been addressed. Lebanon in the films emerges as a place ceasing to belong to all its inhabitants; it is imagined differently by different people who are all nevertheless "citizens." Whether in films made during or after the war, wartime Lebanon is depicted as a space where morality is at risk, where sacredness is threatened by profanity, and where religion is a marker of Otherness.

On one hand, Lebanese cinema is affected by sectarianism. It is telling that the first film about the civil war, *The Shelter* (*al-Malja'*, Rafic Hajjar, 1980), was released in two versions, one shown in East Beirut and the other in West Beirut (G. Khalaf, 1994). On the other hand, it is surprising that Lebanese cinema is generally unconcerned with overt representation of sectarian divisions. Only nine films—*In the Battlefields*, *The Civilized* (*Mutahaddirat*, Randa Chahal, 1999), *In the Shadows of the City*, *The Explosion* (*al-Infijar*, Rafic Hajjar, 1982), *Beirut, the Encounter*, *Martyrs* (*Martyrer*, Leyla Assaf, 1988), *A Time Has Come* (*An al-awan*, Jean-Claude Codsi, 1994), *West Beirut*, and *Bosta* (Philippe Aractingi, 2005)—refer to the issue of sectarianism in Lebanon. *In the Battlefields* and *A Time Has Come* balance references to sectarianism with the defense of religion. *The Civilized*, *Beirut, the Encounter*, and *Martyrs* present stories of Christian women in love with Muslim men. These characters are shown having conversations about the necessity of their transcendence of this division. *Bosta* carries the same storyline into present-day Lebanon, showing a Christian woman and a Muslim man struggling with their past but eventually overcoming it. However, this recurring storyline is not the main one in these films, with the exception of *Beirut, the Encounter*, which revolves almost entirely around the attempts by the man and the woman to meet in Beirut at the outbreak of the war.

The only two films commenting overtly on sectarianism are *The Explosion* and *West Beirut*. In *The Explosion*, the popular Lebanese saying *Illi byekhod min gher millto, bimout bi ʿillto* (The one who marries outside his people dies from his faults) is quoted to the Christian Nada, who intends to marry the Muslim Akram. Nada's brother Fadi opposes their marriage because he does not want her "to repeat the mistake of our parents"—their parents were a Muslim-Christian couple who were killed by the mother's brother who disapproved of their marriage.

West Beirut represents the moment at the outbreak of the civil war when people were forced to adhere to their religious groups. The film's two main characters, the teenage boys Tarek and Omar, are introduced as nonpracticing, even nonbelieving, Muslims. They soon find themselves fighting their characterization as Muslims, which would establish an Otherness that is new to them. Omar tells Tarek that his father "wants us to start praying at the mosque on Fridays, and to fast in Ramadan, and wake up at the crack of dawn to pray." He says that his mother has bought a veil and that his father says that "cinema is *haram*, theater is *haram*, and Western music is the work of the devil." Tarek responds by saying he has never read a word of the Quran. Tarek is warned by a shop owner to respond by saying he is Lebanese whenever anyone asks what his religion is. The boys soon realize that the war has a sectarian basis, and Omar reacts with a degree of apprehension when Tarek's new neighbor, the Christian girl May, joins their group. Tarek's other neighbor Azouri calls Tarek "a traitor" for being with May and subsequently chants an obscenity-filled take on "In the name of the father." Doueiri commented in an interview in 2004 that the presentation of religious tension through children is deliberate:

> When you take a child or a teenager and make them say a political statement, it goes down better with the audience. So when Omar in the film is saying those things about Christianity, you accept it because he is a teenager. You can afford to be more risky. I could have taken the same words and put them in an adult's mouth, but it would not have gone down well.

Although those films are more daring in their criticism of sectarianism, they barely scratch the surface of sectarian divisions, reducing the tension between sects in Lebanon to one simply constructed as being between Muslims and Christians.

One exception that goes beyond the Muslim/Christian binary is *The Civilized*. The film presents the war as a profanity—and consequently has been censored for this representation. *The Civilized* juxtaposes the sacred and the profane in a scene when the Muslim call for prayer is heard as a boy hangs a sign advertising a brothel on a gate in Beirut. The film continues its statement by representing the religious motivation behind the war and how it became warped so that violence was directed at oneself, blurring the boundaries defining the Other. This is shown in a scene depicting a sniper surveying a priest trying to cross the road. The sniper shoots the priest dead, then turns around to a picture of Jesus on the wall and starts praying: "He tried to pass behind my back! Now he's gone to earth. This I learned from you. You have to forgive me after all this time I spent for you. I killed and robbed for you. Now you're abandoning me? 'Thou shall not kill'? But you are killing me every day!"

Another exception is *Under the Bombs* (*Taht al-qasf*, Philippe Aractingi, 2007), which depicts the story of Zeina, a Muslim Shiite woman searching for her son, Karim, who disappeared during the 2006 Israeli attack on Lebanon. The only driver who agrees to take Zeina to South Lebanon to look for Karim during the attack is a Christian man named Tony. Instead of playing off the religious difference between Zeina and Tony or constructing the story around them as being representatives of their respective religious groups, the film focuses on them as individuals. In going around different villages in the south looking for Karim, Zeina warms up to Tony's wisecracking manner, while Tony simply sees Zeina as a desirable woman whom he tries to seduce. The film's focus on highlighting the humanitarian crises caused by the war takes it beyond its two main characters to show that religion matters little as people from all backgrounds are affected by the war.

Violence and Masculinity

A central concern of war films is the transformation of "ordinary men" into fighters. This is seen in films like *A Time Has Come*, *Lebanon in Spite of Everything* (*Loubnan rughm kul shai*, André Ged'oun, 1982), *The Tornado*, *In the Shadows of the City*, and *Little Wars* (*Houroub saghira*, Maroun Baghdadi, 1982). Those films not only represent a process of transformation; they also show that involvement in the war is inevitable. The militarized body is not a choice but a matter of fate. René in *A Time Has Come* is characterized as having been an "orphan who joined the family of war," in the words of his widow.

A similar representation is found in *Lebanon in Spite of Everything* in the character Charbel, a young boy who joins a militia because he has a mother and younger sister to take care of and he has no other way of supporting them. Ibrahim Al-Ariss (2000) sees *The Tornado* as being about the war's stripping of innocence among people, even if they are not directly involved in its atrocities.

This is seen through the main character, Akram, a young man who returns from studying in Russia to Lebanon only to be sucked in by the war machine. Akram's nightmares and real life are merged on the screen as he tries to come to terms with his surroundings. Akram starts off as an engaged observer: he witnesses random acts of violence and paranoia yet tries to understand, interrogate, and resist them. But he becomes a participant in the war after his friend is killed by a militiaman, and he avenges him. Akram's stature changes. The bewildered look on his face disappears. He appears bigger. The way he walks gains a new swagger. We see him smoking a cigarette and then furiously throwing it on the ground, in the manner of militiamen. Akram transforms from a victim into a victimizer. A similar process happens to Rami of *In the Shadows of the City* when he abandons his work as a paramedic to become a militiaman after his father is kidnapped.

The process of transformation is most clearly seen across the films of Maroun Baghdadi. There are no silent, solitary heroes in his films. There is no exaggerated masculinity to be admired. There is no good and no evil. Instead, his three films, *Little Wars*, *Land of Honey and Incense* (*Lubnan, ard al-asal w al-bakhour, 1987*), and *Outside Life* (*Kharej al-hayaf, 1991*) present a frustrated masculinity that is both a result of the war and a catalyst for it. The men in *Little Wars* are shown to be lost during the war. They are young people searching for their identities in a country that is falling apart; they do not know where they belong. The war sucks them into its monstrosity despite themselves. One man dies from a drug overdose. Another joins a militia to avenge the death of his father. But throughout this, Baghdadi portrays his characters as fully human: fearful, dreaming, hesitating, and anxious about the present and the future.

Land of Honey and Incense was filmed five years later into the war. The film's characters are not lost like those in *Little Wars*; they have progressed into becoming self-aware about their involvement in the atrocities. The men are full-fledged militia members who engage in killings and kidnappings. They still retain their humanity, however. One of them, Hassan, attempts to rescue two French doctors of Médecins sans frontières who have been kidnapped by his militia. When Baghdadi filmed *Outside Life* in what turned out to be the final period of the civil war, one recognizes the broken males encountered in the previous films. But now they are even more engrossed in the war's madness. It is in this film that we encounter men who take pleasure in terrorizing others and inflicting acts of horror on the helpless, men who define themselves as monsters. One of them creates a persona for himself based on the character Travis in Martin Scorcese's *Taxi Driver*, while another calls himself Frankenstein. Viewed chronologically, Baghdadi's films depict the gradual loss of humanity. The ever more dismal transformation of the men may also reflect the increasing despair of Baghdadi and the public at large as the seemingly interminable war went on year after year and their perceptions of its grim reality changed.

Censorship

Like cinemas throughout the Arab world, Lebanese cinema is subject to government censorship. Censorship is handled by the Sureté Generale (General Security)—a military department within the Ministry of Interior. Lebanese law allows the censorship of "political and religious materials which could harm the national security of the country" (Wettig 2004). Censorship is inconsistent. When *West Beirut* was made, General Security told Doueiri that his film would have to be approved by a Muslim sheik and a Christian priest before it could be distributed in the country (Doueiri 2004). In the case of Chahal's *The Civilized*, the government cut forty-seven minutes, almost half the film, because of "vulgar language and slurs against both Christians and Muslims" (Hoang 2004). This censorship was accompanied by denunciations of the director in some Beirut mosques and death threats against her and her crew (Riding 2000). The film has been screened only once in Lebanon, at the Beirut Film Festival in 1999, though it has gained awards abroad including the UNESCO Award at the Venice Film Festival in 1999 and the Nestor Almendros Award at the Human Rights Watch Film Festival the following year.

In the Battlefields had flirtations with the censors. Arbid recounted in an interview in 2006 that

> the censors wanted to remove the sex in the car and on the stairs, and a sentence where a girl says she doesn't care about God and refuses to go to church. I refused and told the censors that the film is not theirs, but mine. Is the Lebanese society incapable of watching sex when they can see worse on television and on the Internet? This is an insult to the audience! So in the end they gave it an 18 [adult] rating.

Funding

The major problem identified by filmmakers is financial, in the virtual absence of government funding and the increasing difficulty of securing European support. In 1998 the Ministry of Culture launched the long-awaited Cinema Support Fund, which would allow filmmakers to obtain public funding. The announcement indicated that the ministry would fund 25 percent of the budgets of up to seven feature films per year, with a limit of $200,000 per film, in addition to funding up to ten short films with $50,000 each (Soueid 1998). In practice, however, the ministry's financial assistance to filmmakers has been nominal and mainly aimed at guaranteeing a mention of the ministry in the film credits. In 2002 the Ministry of Culture established the Cinematheque, a division of the National Cinema Center devoted to establishing a library of Lebanese films, restoring film prints, and archiving film-related documents. The main form in which the Lebanese government has supported cinema has been through providing military equipment to films that needed them, such as *West Beirut* and *The Tornado*.

Lebanese films have been produced with extremely small budgets compared to European cinema, as shown by a summary of the budgets of some films released since 1981 (see accompanying table). Only a handful of films made during the past three decades were locally funded. *Lebanon in Spite of Everything*, for example, was funded by a Christian church organization, the Uskofiyaa Organization for Media (Soueid 1986). *Maraka* (Roger Assaf 1985) was funded by "well-to-do Shiite people who donated money to the South Support Fund," as the film was regarded as a social project benefiting the people of the south, "but many things did not cost anything: we did not pay extras, or to use people's houses" (Assaf 2006). *When Maryam Spoke Out* (*Lamma hikyit Maryam*, 2001) was produced by its director, Assad Fouladkar, with funding from the Lebanese American University, where he teaches filmmaking. *Bosta* is a local production but relied on a French seed fund.

All the other Lebanese films have been co-productions. *Beirut, the Encounter* was produced with Tunisian and Belgian money. The funding of *In the Battlefields* was mainly French with some Belgian, German, and Lebanese money. *Little Wars* was supported by an American technical team facilitated by Francis Ford Coppola (Soueid 1998). *The Civilized* was funded by French production companies including Arte and Studio Canal+. *West Beirut* was funded by Belgian, Norwegian, and French money, including funding from France's Ministry of Culture. *The Belt of Fire* (*Zinnar al-nar*, Bahij Hojeij, 2003) was produced by Lebanese producers Marwan Tarraf and Wassim Hojeij, with funding from the Agence de Francophonie and the French Foreign Ministry (Hojeij 2005). *The Tornado* is a Russian co-production.

The reliance on foreign funding does present problems. Arbid insists (2006) that she is not affected adversely by relying on French funding: in France "you have to apply for public funds to make films. They don't care what you say about

Budgets of Lebanese Films

Film	Budget[1]	Budget, U.S. dollars[2]	Year
Beirut, the Encounter	3–4 million French francs	710,000–950,000	1981
Ma'raka	400,000 Lebanese lira	60,000	1985
Letter from a Time of Exile	700,000 French francs	120,000	1988
The Tornado	$600,000	600,000	1992
A Time Has Come	$450,000	450,000	1994
The Civilized	2,400,000 French francs	410,000	1998
Beirut Phantoms	$420,000	420,000	1998
Around the Pink House	Just under $1,000,000	Just under 1,000,000	1998
In the Shadows of the City	$450,000	450,000	2000
When Maryam Spoke Out	$15,000	15,000	2001
The Belt of Fire	$350,000	15,000	2003
The Kite	1,000,000 euros	940,000	2003
In the Battlefields	1,000,000 euros	1,100,000	2004
Bosta	$1,100,000	1,100,000	2005
A Perfect Day	400,000 euros	500,000	2005

[1] The budget figures were provided to the author by the filmmakers.
[2] U.S. dollar equivalents are calculated according to the average exchange rate in the year preceding the release of the film.

Lebanon in the films. France is the only country that funds non-French films. That's why people come here to get funding. It's an oasis for getting funding."

But other filmmakers have felt restricted by foreign funding. Rosen has commented on Lebanese filmmakers exiled in Europe (1989, 36):

> The geographical displacement of the Arab filmmaker is not only a mirror of existing dislocations within the society. The cinema itself becomes uprooted. Attentions, if not allegiances, are suddenly divided. The international production implies international distribution, international audiences, international thinking as well. Jocelyne Saab comments, "I don't have any more complexes

about the openness [of Lebanon] to East and West; as filmmakers, we are the synthesis of these two poles, and if that translates itself into the image, it's fantastic. But it's dangerous: when I get financing of five million francs from France, I run the risk of having to change my scenario."

Not always, but frequently enough, changes are made. The Western viewer becomes a major factor in the filmic equation. In the worst instances, the director-as-guide is suddenly conducting an audience of tourists through his or her culture.

Aractingi (2006) spoke of the difficulty of dealing with these pressures when making *Bosta*:

> I decided to write something that presents a different image from the one we're used to. The French refused it and told me it's far from the reality of the Lebanese society. It was humiliating. Cinéma du Sud refused to fund it because it is not a "serious" film. When you go to festivals showing films from the South, you will see that they have the same language. But I have my own language ... I felt I needed to go beyond the themes normally addressed in Southern films.

Chahal has noted (2006) that French public funding often comes with restrictions on the use of language:

> The French used to say, to get funding, you have to have 50% of the dialogue in French. Now they say it should be 70%. Why should they fund a film in Arabic? The situation is becoming more difficult. My film *The Kite* (2003) had less funding than *The Civilized* because it is in Arabic.

Saab has said that the dialogue in her films *A Suspended Life* and *Once upon a Time, Beirut* (*Kan ya ma kan, Beirut*, 1994) is part-French, part-Arabic "because it's an obligation from the National Fund for Cinema [in France] who funded the film: we can give you a lot of money if all the language is in French. It's a choice, but that's not my case" (2006). Both of Saab's films—as well as Chahal's *The Civilized*—get around this limitation by presenting either French characters or Lebanese characters who come from a French-speaking background. A similar situation could be seen in a number of films by Maroun Baghdadi. While *The Veiled Man* (*al-Rajul al-muhajjab*, 1987) is completely in French and is marketed as a French film, *Outside Life* and *Land of Honey and Incense* merge French and Arabic. In these two films, Baghdadi succeeds in manipulating the use of the French language by the Lebanese characters, especially the militiamen, by giving them strong Lebanese accents in their dealings with the Frenchmen they encounter or kidnap and by peppering their use of French with Lebanese slang.

Codsi presents another problem with foreign funding. He explains (2004) that the European audience is more used to watching experimental and art house films, especially when it comes to what is characterized as world cinema. European producers tend to prefer projects for films that would appeal to this European audience. But this means the films that are produced are not always well received in Lebanon, where the audience is not used to this particular cinema language. Films that might appeal to a mass audience in Lebanon, therefore, are marginalized. But, Ghassan Salhab explains, even art house films encounter problems when they rely on European funding: "Our co-productions are not really 'co.' We go to the French funders having secured $20,000 in local funding, which is nothing. So those funders feel they can dictate what we do" (2004).

The Renaissance of Lebanese Cinema

Lebanese cinema made significant leaps in the 2000s. More Lebanese films are being made, and more are being screened in cinemas in Lebanon. The Lebanese audience is relearning to accept watching Lebanese films. The funding remains largely European, but the films are becoming more sophisticated cinematically: scripts are getting better, and the writers are molding the Lebanese dialect perfectly. An example of this is the film *Falafel*. It is peppered with local expressions and succeeds in using this to create a sense of cultural intimacy with the audience. Film festivals around the world screen Lebanese films. Lebanese cinema is still haunted by the civil war, and with ongoing tension in Lebanon it is difficult to imagine Lebanese cinema not alluding to these conflicts any time soon—as seen in *Under the Bombs*.

Lebanese cinema has extended its subject matter to confront social taboos. *The Civilized* addresses racism. *When Maryam Spoke Out* addresses the pressure put on women in Lebanese society to procreate. *In the Battlefields* confronts class divisions; it and *West Beirut* are about growing up. *Caramel* (*Sukkar Banat*, Nadine Labaki, 2007) addresses women's issues. Still, Lebanese cinema is not an industry; it remains a collection of films made by disparate filmmakers. They struggle to secure funding; they confront the demands of government censors, funding agencies, and foreign co-producers; and they want to get their films distributed.

NOTES

This essay draws on Khatib 2008.
1. On Lebanese cinema prior to the civil war see Chapter 2 in Khatib 2008.

REFERENCES

Al-Ariss, Ibrahim. 2000. "A Look into Lebanese War Cinema on the Civil War's Twenty-Fifth Anniversary" (in Arabic). *Al-Hayat*, April 14.
Al-Nida'. 1983. "Lebanese Cinema in its New Season" (in Arabic). August 9.
Aractingi, Philippe. 2006. Interview by the author. Beirut, April.
Arbid, Danielle. 2006. Interview by the author. Paris, April.
Assaf, Roger. 2006. Interview by the author. Beirut, April.
Chahal, Randa. 2006. Interview by the author. Paris, April.
Codsi, Jean-Claude. 2004. Interview by the author. Beirut, April.
Doueiri, Ziad. 2004. Interview by the author. London, April.
Hoang, Mai. 2004. "Lebanese Filmmaker: Randa Chahal Sabbag." *World Press Review* 51, no. 3 (March). http://www.worldpress.org/Mideast/1803.cfm.
Hojeij, Bahij. 2005. Interview by the author. Beirut, April.
Khalaf, Ghazi. 1994. "Documentary Cinema: A True Human Testimony to the Harshness of War" (in Arabic). *Ad-Diyar*, October 18.
Khalaf, Samir. 1993. *Beirut Reclaimed: Reflections on Urban Design and the Restoration of Civility*. Beirut: Dar An-Nahar.
Khatib, Lina. 2008. *Lebanese Cinema: Imagining the Civil War and Beyond*. London: I. B. Tauris.
Riding, Alan. 2000. "A Filmmaker without Honor or Outlets in Her Own Land." *New York Times*, June 14. http://www.library.cornell.edu/colldev/mideast/chahal.htm.
Rosen, Miriam. 1989. "The Uprooted Cinema: Arab Filmmakers Abroad." *Middle East Report* 159:34–37.
Saab, Jocelyne. 2006. Interview by the author. Paris, April.
Salhab, Ghassan. 2004. Interview by the author. Beirut, April.
Soueid, Mohamad. 1986. *The Postponed Cinema: Films of the Lebanese Civil War* (in Arabic). Beirut: Arab Research Organization.
———. 1998. "Lebanese Cinema: The Migrant Image" (in Arabic). *An-Nahar*, Culture Supplement, October 3.
Wettig, Hannah. 2004. "Lebanese Authorities Ban 'The Da Vinci Code,'" (Lebanon) *Daily Star*, September 16. http://www.dailystar.com.lb/article.asp?edition_ID=1&article_ID=8424&categ_id=2

Design by Obeida Sidami. Courtesy Jean Khalil Chamoun

*In the Shadows of the City**
Reconciling the Diverse Legacies of a Collective Memory

EDWARD GIBEAU

In the Shadows of the City exemplifies many aspects of Lebanon's postwar cinema and the artistic and intellectual challenges of responding to the trauma of civil war. The film demonstrates that fiction can be situated within an authentic historical context and still retain a rich storyline and thematic complexity. Jean Khalil Chamoun tells the poignant story of a twelve-year-old boy growing up as a witness to civil war. While centering the film on early love and family, he effectively renders the grim reality of those years. As Rami grows up, the film bears witness to deepening sectarian divisions within Lebanese society, along with widening physical destruction. Rami lives in what soon becomes a separate Muslim community, but the significant relationships he establishes beyond the sectarian boundaries give a human face to The Other.

Chamoun, like a number of other Lebanese filmmakers, wanted to break the amnesia about the civil war that had engulfed Lebanon and to mitigate the continuing social tensions there:

> The civil war arose from the Lebanese malady. If you try to forget the malady or pretend it never happened you may end up reliving it again . . . Remembering is the only antidote to relapse. But remembering isn't enough. Something must be done to change the condition of Lebanon. Sectarianism is stronger now than it ever was before the war, and nothing is being done to change the way the young are being educated, so they can challenge that. There is no time to waste. (In Quilty 2000)

---

* *In the Shadows of the City/Taif al-Madina.* 2000. Film written and directed by Jean Khalil Chamoun. Produced by Nour Productions (Lebanon). Distributed in the United States by Arab Film Distribution. 102 minutes.

In the Shadows of the City articulates this argument in an exchange between a militia commander and the leader of a group of women agitating for information about the disappeared. Responding to the women's appeals, Abou Samir argues that their demands "are bound to trigger things off and open up old wounds" and that they should "go home, bring up their young, and forget the past." Siham offers an irate retort. "Those who forget," she says, "are the ones preparing for a new war." Minutes later Samir will condemn a hostage to death.

The deconstruction of the logic of sectarianism may be taken as the principal objective of *In the Shadows of the City*. That deconstruction requires the identification of the sectarian affiliations of the principal characters. Chamoun goes about this identification in a sensitive way; he avoids stereotypes and uses discreet indicators such as Muslim women wearing the *hijab* or Yasmin's family being forced to leave the Muslim neighborhood.[1] Central to the film are characters who transcend sectarian bounds. Foremost among them is Rami, but the rejection of sectarianism is more commonly the province of women, most notably Salwa. Unlike Rami, she is unwavering in her identification with a national conscience. Rami works at her café, which offers a haven beyond the sectarian communities, and Rami comes to see Salwa and her customers as "the soul of Beirut."[2]

In the Shadows of the City is set in West Beirut, which will become an exclusively Muslim community in the early days of the war. But when Rami and his family first arrive there from southern Lebanon, they come to know Christian neighbors. Chamoun introduces viewers to the intimacy of Yasmin's family. The religious differences between that family and Rami's own do not appear salient and in any case are altogether distinct from the sectarian divide starkly demonstrated by the militias. The warmth and kindness between the two families stands in stark contrast to the violence and mayhem of the war, highlighting the collective victimization of both sides. This point is dramatized later on when Rami, in search of his father taken hostage by the other side, encounters a hostage taken by his own. Since he knows Yasmin's brother, Nadeem, Rami will be able to support him in a rescue effort across the frontline.

Documentary footage anchors *In the Shadows of the City* firmly in its historical context and serves as a transitional element within the time frames of the story. It gives some sense of the scale of violence and destruction but remains at a distance, sparing the viewer. Though the danger is often palpable, the film refrains from dwelling on the death and injury wrought by fifteen years of war, instead appealing to tender sentiments. With his two child protagonists, Rami and Yasmin, Chamoun draws on the symbolic implications of two children in love, the effect all the more dramatic in the context of war.[3] Their inevitable

Rami, Salwa, and Nabil at Salwa's café

separation suggests the kind of human loss that remains unnoticed by history. The innocence of the children highlights the collective loss of innocence of society as a whole. While the number of lives lost and damaged can be estimated and the destruction of buildings quantified, the corruption and demoralization that permeate an entire society ever more profoundly evade ready measures.

The killing of the musician Nabil at Salwa's café is the one instance when *In the Shadows of the City* does confront viewers with the death of a character they know. Nabil had employed *zajal* to call for leadership to stand up to the militias, exposing himself to their wrath.[4] With his death a voice of the people denouncing the war is silenced, Salwa's café is shut down, and Salwa, who had nurtured this nonsectarian oasis, goes into exile. The iconic dimension of the café and its two principal characters is underscored for Arab viewers, who translate Salwa as "Peace" and Nabil as "Noble." Left behind is Nabil's *oud*, a symbol of Lebanese culture and joy, pierced by a bullet.[5]

Rami and Yasmin defy gender stereotypes. Yasmin is a veritable tomboy. She confounds the prejudice of the boys by joining a soccer game and scoring right away. And Rami distinguishes himself from his peers. From childhood to adulthood, his sensitivity and compassion stand in contrast to the pride and chauvinism of other male characters. The twelve-year-old demonstrates his courage by standing up to the Hyena, the militia leader. As a grownup, he joins an ambulance team rather than the militiamen—this would appear to be a matter of conviction, but his affection for Yasmin, now on the other side, may well have played a role. When little children need to be saved from an unexploded bomb, it is Rami who takes the initiative, and his old friend Walid, now a militiaman, who follows. Rami eventually feels compelled to join the militia in an effort to rescue his kidnapped father, and he demonstrates his heroism afresh not in fighting but in breaking ranks when a hostage faces execution. As Rami assists Siham and her daughter, he appears selfless and sincere rather than pursuing a romantic prospect.

Chamoun does not blame the common people who become caught up on one side or the other. And while he has denounced Lebanon's neighbors that were bent on destroying the unique model of Christian-Muslim coexistence (Barak 2007, 61), they barely figure in the film. Israeli bombardments make Rami's family abandon their home in southern Lebanon, and documentary footage shows Israeli planes bombing Beirut, but the Israeli invasion and the Sabra and Shatila massacre are only alluded to when Rami tells of saving many lives in 1982. Neither the involvement of Syria nor that of the U.S.-led Western force is ever mentioned. The few people who denounce foreigners as responsible for the conflict are referring to Palestinian refugees in Lebanon. Had Chamoun placed culpability for the war outside of Lebanon's borders, that would have been antithetical to his purpose. As Mark Westmoreland puts it (2002, 36), blaming outsiders is part of the "official rhetoric of amnesia," a rhetoric the film seeks to deconstruct.

Lina Khatib argues that "the film's main weakness lies in the way ... it blames the war on mysterious Others" (2008, 177). Such criticism is perhaps not altogether deserved. While Chamoun presents ordinary people as more or less innocent, if overly passive, characters such as the Hyena point to corruption within Lebanese society itself. Chamoun is especially critical of Lebanese politicians who raised popular passions and manipulated the masses for their own political and economic ends. Before armed conflict breaks out, Abou Samir appears surprised to discover arms being unloaded at the docks and comments that the worsening conflict made him sick. But he becomes a militia leader, and toward the end of the war his brother is buying up real estate. By the time peace is restored, Samir and the Hyena have established themselves as successful profiteers; those who once led opposing militias now salute each other as power brokers. Chamoun commented in an interview in 2000 with Mustafa:

> Those are the individuals who used people during the war, who destroyed so much, who put up barriers and forced people to pay before letting them through. They played the part of the state but in a terrible way, because where the state has services and institutions to offer they had only debris.

The nature of sectarianism as depicted in *In the Shadows of the City* frames the principal conflict of the film. That conflict is not between sects of Muslims and Christians but rather between the collective ideals inherent in the interpersonal relationships of characters—in families and among friends—and the untenable realities imposed by the civil war. The film focuses on the moral conflict being fought at the individual level as the war confronts people with difficult choices. Yasmin's brother, Nadeem, leaves home to join a militia as his family's house shakes from nearby explosions. Rami takes up arms only after his father is abducted, and he enables a Christian man to escape captivity and death. While these young men have to make choices about how to act, their families remain passive participants in the war, coping with it as best they can. Yasmin's family flees West Beirut, and Rami's family remains, trying to subsist.[6]

Chamoun shows multidimensional characters who represent a broad spectrum of responses to the war. Their story is well integrated into the historical context, but the line between fact and fiction is readily discernible. Historical reality is conveyed in date captions, interspersed documentary footage, historical details within the narrative, and the authentic Beirut setting, some of its destruction still to be seen when the film was shot (Mustafa 2000).

In the Shadows of the City was Chamoun's first narrative film, its $450,000 budget similar to that of most postwar Lebanese films (Khatib, in this volume). His intended audience was the Lebanese people, many of whom had experienced the war firsthand. Verisimilitude was essential to effectively connect with Lebanese viewers. Here lay Chamoun's particular strength. Unlike filmmakers who went into exile, he experienced the civil war himself, staying on in Lebanon to film the war. Not only could Chamoun draw on his own experience, but some 80 percent of the documentary footage he used was film he and Mai Masri shot together (Human Rights Watch 2002).[7] Furthermore, Chamoun selected actors whose life experiences reflected the film's characters. Majdi Machmouchi, in the role of the adult Rami, experienced the civil war. Christine Choueiri, in the role of Siham, saw her uncle kidnapped during the war. Widdad Hilwani, who inspired the character of Siham, participated in the scenes of women demonstrating, parading photographs of real abducted people (Human Rights Watch 2002, Mustafa 2000).

The film escaped censorship, unlike *A Civilized People* (*Civilisées/Les autres*, 1999), Randa Chahal Sabag's prize-winning take on the civil war. The censors disagreed among themselves about *In the Shadows of the City*. While some demanded cuts, the argument that the screenplay had been approved, as stipulated by law, prevailed (Barak 2007, 60). The film was released in four Beirut

Jean Khalil Chamoun on the set. Courtesy Jean Khalil Chamoun

cinemas, showed there for eleven weeks, and toured other cities and villages (Human Rights Watch 2002). *In the Shadows of the City* went on to win the prize as the Best Lebanese Feature Film at the Beirut Media Festival.

Some have argued that in reviving painful memories of the past, films like *In the Shadows of the City* may have the unintended consequence of reigniting old tensions (Haugbølle 2002, 7). Chamoun, for his part, has suggested: "Shadows express the contingency of what is real, as well as the gap between reality and our fantasies. Although we may try to escape our shadows, it is not possible" (France-Diplomatie n.d.). The film concludes with Rami in his studio decorated with his childhood art, teaching children art, art dealing with the trauma of war.

NOTES

1. Khatib argues (2008, 177) that making religious affiliation ambiguous is among several ways Chamoun undermines the process of remembering, contrary to his intentions.
2. The world-famous singer Fairouz is commonly referred to as "The Soul of Lebanon." She continued to live in Beirut throughout the civil war and became the living symbol of a shared Lebanese culture. We hear her voice in the homes of Rami and Yasmin as well as in Salwa's café (Brandano 2007).

3. Editor's note: The French poster, reproduced here, foregrounds the children: Rami, Walid, and Yasmin. It thus engages the public, while an image of the war fades away in the background.
4. *Zajal* is a semi-improvised, semi-sung form of colloquial poetry that enjoys great popularity in Lebanon.
5. A musician and his *oud* are also silenced in the Syrian film *The Extras* (Tawfik Saleh, 1993), featured in this volume.
6. The fate of Rami's mother and siblings is unclear, as the film does not return to them once Rami has grown up.
7. Four prize-winning documentaries by Jean Khalil Chamoun and Mai Masri on the civil war and the Israeli invasion are distributed in the United States by Arab Film Distribution.

REFERENCES

Barak, Oren. 2007. "'Don't Mention the War?' The Politics of Remembrance and Forgetfulness in Postwar Lebanon." *Middle East Journal* 61 (1): 49–70.

Brandano, Nicole. 2007. Personal communication to Josef Gugler. October.

France-Diplomatie. n.d. "L'Ombre de la ville by Jean Khalil Chamoun." French Ministry of Foreign and European Affairs. http://www.diplomatie.gouv.fr/en/france-priorities_1/cinema_2/cinematographic-cooperation_9/production-support-funding_10/films-benefiting-from-aid_13/film-list-by-country_15/lebanon_657/ombre-ville_691/by-jean-khalil-chamoun_382.html?var_recherche=enseignement.

Haugbølle, Sune. 2002. "Looking the Beast in the Eye: Collective Memory of the Civil War in Lebanon." Master's thesis, Oxford University.

Human Rights Watch. 2002. "Interview with Jean Khalil Chamoun, Director of *In the Shadows of the City*." Human Rights Watch Film Festival 2002. http://www.hrw.org/iff/2002/traveling/shadows-interview.html.

Khatib, Lina. 2008. *Lebanese Cinema: Imagining the Civil War and Beyond*. London: I. B. Tauris.

Mustafa, Hani. 2000. "The Militant Strain." *Al-Ahram Weekly*, November 2–8. http://weekly.ahram.org.eg/2000/506/cu2.htm.

Quilty, Jim. 2000. "Chamoun's Film 'a Modest Effort to Promote Healing.'" (Lebanon) *Daily Star*, November 16.

Westmoreland, Mark. 2002. "Cinematic Dreaming: On Phantom Poetics and the Longing for a Lebanese National Cinema." *Text, Practice, Performance* 4:33–50.

4

Israeli Cinema Engaging the Conflict

NURITH GERTZ AND YAEL MUNK

The relationship between cinema and politics in Israel is a long and tumultuous one. It began with propaganda films in the 1930s, developed into heroic tales of Jewish settlers during the state's first decades, turned to the individual in order to question the price of one's sacrifice in periods of doubts; especially after the Yom Kippur War, it evolved into a popular cinema known as *bourekas* films focusing on social and economic gaps between Western (Ashkenzim) and Oriental (Mizrahim) Jews while intentionally avoiding national issues;[1] and finally it turned back to the sources of Israeli identity to reconsider the inevitability of sacrifice, a demarche that can be identified as the subtext of many recent Israeli films (Loshitzky 2001, 25). More than fifty years after its first appearance, Israeli cinema is still dealing with the challenge of taking a significant part in the politics of the Middle East, a challenge that has yet to be met.

The first Zionist films shared a common hero: the New Jew. As opposed to the diasporic Jew, whose contours were drawn by the anti-Semitic rhetoric as physically weak and effeminate, the New Jew's image was designed according to the Zionist credo. A man of action and deeds, he was eager to work his piece of land, ready to sacrifice in order to achieve the Zionist metamorphosis, that is, to turn the persecuted diasporic Jew into the laborious Zionist (Gertz 2004, 34–39).

In the name of his ideology and the world it promised, the New Jew sacrificed his privacy, his family, and sometimes his life. This demarche was reflected in the first cinematic narratives after the establishment of the state of Israel in 1948. As in any ideological discourse, the protagonist in these films was defined not only by his deeds but also by the contrast to another dweller of this same land, the Palestinian. While the first Zionist settlers arrived from Europe and embodied in their way of life ideas of modernity and progress, the original Palestinian inhabitants demonstrated a traditional way of life.

Influenced by European colonialism, the first Zionist settlers were convinced of the importance of their mission as bearers of modernity and sought to share their culture with the local Arab population. However, they did not consider themselves like the typical Western colonialists who "earned" their land by means of invasion and conquest; instead, the Zionists preferred to see Palestine as the natural shelter for the persecuted Jewish people, the incarnation of the biblical promise according to which the people of Israel were to return to their historical home. From the beginning, Israeli cinema emphasized this dramatic difference that was to wear various configurations throughout the decades. The dramatic change that took place in the cinematic representation of the Palestinians and of the land of Israel/Palestine over the past fifty years reflects the different attitudes Israelis have developed toward their neighbors, attitudes that did not always follow the hegemonic voice (Gertz and Munk, forthcoming).

From the very first days of Hebrew cinema in pre-state Palestine, the land has figured as a major issue. Thus the early Zionist propaganda films, made by Jewish filmmakers from Europe and intended mainly to raise funds from Europe and the United States for the establishment of the new Jewish settlements, depicted the settlers' efforts to adapt to rural life, emphasizing their determination to renew their link with the land of their biblical forefathers. Inspired by the nineteenth-century romantic fantasy of a return to nature, these early films revealed the settlers' ambivalent approach to their Palestinian peasant neighbors: on the one hand the latter embodied their romantic dream regarding the fusion between man and his land and therefore inspired the settlers' admiration and envy; but on the other hand their way of cultivating the soil, ignoring all the progress achieved by modernity, as well as their superstitious beliefs concerning the fertility of the land, were seen to establish the incontestable superiority of the settlers. These films follow a recurrent narrative pattern, beginning with the Palestinians' suspicious approach toward the newcomers and ending with their recognition of the Jews' contribution to the improvement of life in Palestine.

Settlers (*Tzabar*, Alexander Ford, 1933) and *Avoda* (Helmar Lerski, 1935) trace the efforts of a small group of Jewish settlers to adapt to their new way of living. Both films focus on the groups' internal need to coalesce as well as on their effort to create a common understanding with the Palestinians. In *Settlers*, a relatively short film imitating documentary style, a group of Jewish settlers reaches the Promised Land from the sea and looks for ways to accommodate themselves in this Oriental space that differs so much from the place they have left (Shohat 1989, 89). At first they encounter a docile image of the Palestinians—the famous Oriental hospitality—as they are being offered food and drink. But the more they get acquainted with their new land, the less the Arabs cooperate with them.

The prevalent myth of the few against the many becomes most vivid as this alienation reaches its peak in a parallel editing sequence juxtaposing the Jewish settlers, who after much digging finally find a water source, and the Palestinians, who, confronted with the drought, stop praying to Allah and decide to attack the Jews. A close-up shows a sword being pulled out, and the camera withdraws to emphasize the large number of attackers. The editing of this scene establishes the visual representation of one of the leading myths of the Zionist ethos: the few against the many, or in biblical terms, David against Goliath.

What could have ended in a massacre is avoided thanks to the intervention of a Palestinian child who reveals to the attackers' leader that the sheik has closed the well, indicating that the Jews are not responsible for the drought. The narrative closure of the plot shows the rhetoric and iconographic manipulation of the Palestinian Other, depicted as irrational and prone to unexpected reactions. And it illustrates how the first Jewish filmmakers in Palestine built the settlers' image as courageous, in contrast to the Palestinians, establishing the superiority of the Western Jews over the Oriental natives.

Unlike *Settlers*, *Avoda* uses symbolism to tell in a didactic way the metamorphosis of an anonymous passive Jewish settler, revealed at first by the camera only by his footsteps on the sand, into an active New Jew the moment he becomes part of the Zionist enterprise. *Avoda* graphically illustrates the roles Zionism attributed to the two sides. The Palestinians are shown in horizontal compositions, sometimes featuring the traditional Oriental attribute of a convoy of camels, emphasizing their passiveness as opposed to the settlers' determined attitude to change the nature of the place. In this film, the Palestinians' passivity is also revealed in their relation to water: before the settlers' arrival, they considered drought a divine retribution. In the course of the story, their attitude changes as they witness the Jewish newcomers' refusal to passively accept the hardships of the land, which finally leads to the discovery of a hidden source. The iconographic representation of the Palestinian in *Avoda* demonstrates the approach of the Zionist cinema of the time. At the beginning of the film, the Palestinian Arabs are presented as part of the background landscape, but as the narrative progresses, they gradually disappear from the landscape, leaving the entire frame to the Zionist workers.

One of the first feature films made after the establishment of the state of Israel, *They Were Ten* (*Em a'yu assarah*, Baruch Dinar, 1960), returned more or less to this same premise, hardships encountered by a group of settlers, this time in the first decade of the twentieth century. This film, which is representative of the Israeli national cinema genre, begins by retracing the naïve and mostly passive approach of the settlers to the land: they ask the local inhabitants for water and are expelled by a Palestinian mob. This incident leads to a radical change in their attitude: they become active and go to the well without anyone's permission. This scene, revolving around the crucial elements of land and water, functions as a turning point in the film's narrative. The passive and effeminate diasporic Jew abandons his previous self and becomes a New Jew. The Palestinian's opposition to the Jew's presence on his land and the settlers' resistance were to become central themes of Israeli national cinema, not only in its revision of the past but also in its representation of the present (Gertz 1993, 204).

They Were Ten provides an accurate portrayal of the role the Jewish settlers took for themselves and how Zionism, after the establishment of the state of Israel, wanted to remember it: surmounting endless hardships and proposing to the local Arab population a form of coexistence. Indeed, in this film, both sides seem very much concerned with the eventual coexistence imposed by the arrival of the Zionists (Avisar 2005, 131). Contrary to actual developments, this coexistence is realized in the film.

But national cinema did not last long, as ideology weakened and Western influences engendered a certain embourgeoisement of Israeli society. Israeli cinema began to withdraw from the thematic of the Israeli-Palestinian conflict. The late national cinema that appeared just after the Six Day War (Gertz 1993, 95–142), exemplified in Joseph Millo's *He Walked in the Fields* (*Hu halach b'sadot*, 1967) and Uri Zohar's *Every Bastard Is a King* (*Kol mamzer melech*, 1968), depicted a new kind of Israeli hero, torn between his aspirations as an individual and his national duty. Though set at different times, the war of 1948 and the days preceding the Six Day War in 1967, respectively, both films reflected a particular form of national cinema in which the heroes set out on purely individual or existential journeys but are led to recognize their commitment to the country as war breaks out.

Neither filmmaker chose to represent the Palestinians as enemies. In *He Walked in the Field*, the enemy is embodied by the British authorities who seek to stop Jewish emigrants from landing illegally, and the Zionists attack British guards. In *Every Bastard Is a King*, the Egyptian soldiers are the enemy, and just like the Palestinians in the first days of national cinema, they are shown at a distance. Both narratives affirm that in spite of strong Western, individualistic, non-nationalistic influences, even the most nihilist heroes in Israeli cinema will convert to nationalism when the moment comes.

In the late 1960s Israeli cinema abandoned the dominant issues arising from the conflict in favor of more introspective narratives, leaving no room for Palestinian representation. This trend began with the popular cinema often referred to as *bourekas* films, low-budget melodramas depicting the hardships Oriental Jews endured on their way to realize the melting-pot ideology of the time, to marry upper-class Ashkenazi Jews. Parallel to the *bourekas* films, Israeli cinema evolved in a more modernistic form, "personal cinema," also known as the "new sensibility" (Ne'eman 1995, 125–132).

Though very different from the *bourekas* tradition, the personal cinema likewise told the story of alienated and disillusioned Israeli characters. In this case young native-born Israelis, just like their peers in the West, underwent an existentialist crisis. New Sensibility films like Judd Ne'eman's *The Dress* (*Ha-simla*, 1968) and Uri Zohar's *Three Days and a Child* (*Shlosha yamim veyeled*, 1968) formulated narratives mainly set in urban backgrounds, far from the battlefield and the conflict in general. Focusing on universal existentialist questions, these films expressed their Israeli character only through the language they used and the urban landscapes they revealed. In retrospect one may conclude that during this short period—from 1967 to 1974—the *bourekas* films and the personal cinema expressed the same wish: to withdraw from the representation of the Israeli-Palestinian conflict and to reevaluate the image of the New Jew.

The Yom Kippur War in 1973 put an end to both the New Sensibility cinema and the *bourekas* films, and Israeli filmmakers turned to revise the basic Zionist assumptions. One of the first films that announced this tendency was *Hirbet Hizeh* (Ram Loevy, 1976), adapted from a 1950s novel by Smilansky Iz'har. This television adaptation aroused a violent polemic. Set during the last days of Israel's independence war, it centers on a small unit of Israeli soldiers whose mission is to conquer the Arab village of Hirbet Hizeh. At first sight it seems that the place has been deserted, but as the soldiers enter deeper they discover elders, women, and children. The film's plot, narrated by Micha, one of the Israeli soldiers, tells how this mission that initially seemed relatively simple—they just had to put the villagers on a truck and expel them beyond the Israeli border—came to pose a moral dilemma for the Israeli soldier.

Hirbet Hizeh can be considered the trigger for a new thematic approach to the conflict. In 1977, as the Likkud party reached power for the first time since the establishment of the state, Israeli filmmakers, who mostly belonged to the dethroned elite, elaborated a political-critical discourse that covered a large number of issues relating to Zionism's Others. Films like Ne'eman's *Paratroopers* (*Masa alunkot*, 1977), Ilan Moshinson's *Wooden Gun* (*Roveh huliot*, 1979), and Dan Wolman's *Hide and Seek* (*Machboim*, 1980) denounced the way Israeli society excluded the nation's Others: women, homosexuals, Oriental Jews, and Jews from the diaspora in general. *Hamsin* (Daniel Waxman, 1980) and *The Smile of the Lamb* (*Hiuch hagdi*, Shimon Dotan, 1987, based on a novel by David Grossman) dealt with the inevitable consequences of the unsolved Israeli-Palestinian conflict and pointed at the victims on both sides. Rafi Bukaee's *Avanti Popolo* (1986) offered a story of Israeli and Egyptian soldiers sharing a moment of human solidarity.

The Israeli cinema of the 1980s thus reopened the debate about the conflict (Ne'eman 2001). Often accused of not providing any solution, these films provided at least one crucial element to the demystification of the traditional animosity between the two peoples: it openly adopted the Other's point of view (Friedman 2005, 187–196). Varying from empathy to complete interchangeability of self and other, this Israeli cinema demonstrates how far cinema can go in seeking to change political convictions. *Once We Were Dreamers* (*Ha-holmim*, Uri Barabash, 1988) is of particular interest in this respect.

Set at the time of the arrival of the first settlers in Palestine, the film presents an alternative version of the story told in *They Were Ten*. As a small group of enthusiastic European Jews reaches the desolate land of Palestine, the prospective settlers encounter a local Oriental Jew, Amnon, who introduces himself as a kind of coordinator with the Arab population. But the group's leader refuses to accept him, showing in this refusal one of the unspoken "sins" of the first settlers—their European arrogance, feeling superior toward both Oriental Jews and Palestinian Arabs. The Israeli-Palestinian conflict to which the film relates by analogy serves as the background of the plot: these ideologically motivated young men and women had to accept the existence of Others—Jews or Arabs—in order to survive.

While the plot appears to follow Amnon's efforts to accompany the group in its adventurous confrontations with local Palestinians, a closer reading suggests the high price the settlers had to pay to accept the differences between Jews and Arabs and between Jews and Jews. In one of the most dramatic scenes, one of the group's women, feeling that she cannot renounce her past for the sake of the creation of the commune, commits suicide. Her burial becomes the site of confrontation between traditional Jews, represented by Amnon, and modern secular ones, represented by Zeev. As the burial goes on, an intercut shows Palestinian women standing on a hill, watching the disintegration of the Jewish group either by death or by discord.

This burial scene echoes a similar one in *They Were Ten* in which a woman's death miraculously brings an end to the drought and thus contributes to the implementation of the settlers' mission. But in *Once We Were Dreamers*, the woman's death brings no miracle and marks only one more step in the growing divergences inside the group, divergences that lead to the death of the peacemakers on the other side—the Oriental Jew and the son of the sheik, his Arab friend. This pessimistic ending reveals the director's vision of the conflict. As in *Hirbet Hizeh*, the return to the past becomes a way to criticize the present and reveal the sources of its problems (Ben-Shaul 1997, 2–10).

The difference between *They Were Ten* and *Once We Were Dreamers* resides in their attitudes toward the conflict. While the former seems to claim that by paying a high price, this land of conflict could become a land of mutual understanding and peaceful coexistence, the latter rejects this interpretation, suggesting that any understanding has to begin at home, that only a group (and by extension, a nation) that has already solved its own conflicts can address its counterpart and open a dialogue. The film may be taken to suggest that one of the issues that remained unsolved in the Zionist discourse relates to the Jewish religion, which was brutally repelled from the ideological discourse.

Thus the religion of the "dreamers" of the film's title is not emphasized in the narrative except for a monologue by Zeev: he tells how the assassination of his father by Cossacks made him realize that God is dead and a man should take his faith into his own hands; for him this meant beginning a new life in the land of Palestine. At the same time films like *Once We Were Dreamers* emphasized the similarities between Israelis and Palestinians. This interchangeability came to be demonstrated by the choice of actors in political cinema. In *The Smile of the Lamb* the Palestinian actor Makram Khouri plays the role of the Israeli officer whose responsibility it is to implement the occupation of a small village. This approach was used even more strikingly in Bukaee's antiwar film *Avanti Popolo*.

Set in the aftermath of the Six Day War of 1967, *Avanti Popolo* is a road movie about two Egyptian soldiers, Haled and Gassan, trying to make their way home through the desert. As the journey progresses they get to know each other: one, Haled, is an actor at Cairo Theater who has just been cast for the role of Shylock the Jew in Shakespeare's *Merchant of Venice*, a role about which he remains ambivalent; and the other, Gassan, is a simple farmer. Without the war they would not have met, but soon they share the same goal—to return home as soon as possible.

Following the tradition of road movies, the two protagonists experience various encounters with the Israeli enemy, varying from complete ignorance to highest intimacy. The story's climax provides the most powerful iconography of the entire film: the Israeli and Palestinian soldiers march together into the sunset chanting "Avanti Popolo," the renowned song of the Italian left. This scene creates the illusion of a common ground on which these soldiers can share, even if only momentarily, their beliefs and hopes.[2]

During the 1980s, other important films such as *Noa Is 17* (Itzhak Yeshuron, 1982), *Rage and Glory* (Avi Nesher, 1984), *Late Summer Blues* (Renen Shor, 1987), and *Himo, King of Jerusalem* (*Himmo melech Yerushalaim*, Amos Gutman, 1987) turned to the past and just like *Once We Were Dreamers* revealed a crisis in Zionist ideology. Adopting the Other's point of view, these films emphasized the changing roles of the parties involved: in the first years of the state, national cinema offered a picture of Israelis as willing to sacrifice themselves for the birth of their nation, but now the same heroic role with the same motivation was attributed to the Palestinian. Ne'eman's *Fellow Travelers* (*Magash hakesef*, 1983) and *Streets of Yesterday* (*Rehovot haetmol*, 1989) and Barabash's *Beyond the Walls* (*Me'ahorei hasoragim*, 1984), among others, all told of the encounter between Israelis and Palestinians leading to the crystallization of a more humanistic attitude vis-à-vis those who once were enemies (Gertz 1993, 204).

Political opposition transformed in terms of interchangeability between Israelis and Palestinians also can be found in Haim Buzaglo's first feature film, *Fictitious Marriage* (*Nisuim fictiveem*, 1988). Shot during the first Intifada, *Fictitious Marriage* tells the story of a Jewish high school teacher from Jerusalem who, after serving in Gaza during the Intifada, decides to leave his peaceful existence and to elucidate the mysteries of his Israeli identity. Pretending to be flying to the United States for a vacation, he checks into a small and empty hotel in Tel Aviv. He adopts two fake identities, that of an Israeli living in the States who has come to visit his old mother and that of a mute Palestinian construction worker from Gaza. While the Palestinian hotel employee explains to him that unlike the Israelis, as a Palestinian he cannot leave his land, the Palestinian workers show him the basic values that so many Israelis have lost in their race to modernization and capitalism. His visit to the Palestinian refugee camp in Gaza becomes his journey's climax as he realizes the human face of those referred to as "Israel's enemies"—warm families with respect for the elders and for religion, hospitality, and generosity.

But he has not surmounted the anxiety and fear of the Other that characterized Israelis at that point of the Intifada. His journey suddenly ends when his Israeli paranoia is aroused: as he recognizes a tire left by his Palestinian friends in a children's playground, the "mute Palestinian" shouts in Hebrew: "Watch the bomb!" revealing his true identity. Our protagonist returns to his old self, to his home and family, with a better understanding of his Palestinian neighbors.

The director ends his film with a close-up on the protagonist's son opening his presents. The camera shows the child sitting with his legs bent in the same way as the father's Palestinian friends sit. This image summarizes the new understanding of the protagonist: the masquerade hides the many similarities between people who used to share the same behaviors, the same culinary choices, and the same manners.

The interchangeability between Palestinian Arabs and Israeli Jews appears as an important feature of the Israeli political cinema in the 1980s. However, the films' subtext often revealed these efforts to be vain, as such an understanding could only lead to a sense of siege (Ben-Shaul 1997). Moreover, the perspective remains an Israeli one, and the switching of roles, whether by the film's cast or by the protagonist's masquerade, fails to achieve the expected recognition of the similarities between people (Shohat 1989, 202–212). Instead, the Israeli protagonist projects his dreams onto the Palestinian (Gertz 1993, 336–342). Thus in *The Smile of the Lamb* the Palestinian voice embodies all that the Israeli side has abandoned: the beauty of the fields, the magic of nature, the story of origins. The Palestinian becomes the figure through which Israelis express their longing for their own dreams about becoming part of the land and its history (ibid., 209–217).

While Israeli filmmakers in the 1980s chose to depict the Palestinian Arab as a reflection of the first settlers' endeavor to work the land, the few politically engaged Israeli feature films in the 1990s offered a more complex Palestinian image. Set against the background of the first Lebanon war in 1982, *Cup Final* (*Gmar gavia*, Eran Riklis, 1991) follows the journey of a group of Palestinians and their Israeli prisoner in southern Lebanon. The film shows the guerrillas' ambivalence toward their prisoner, some of them wishing to get rid of him before they encounter the Israeli army, others trying to save his life. The dilemma ends suddenly when the Israeli army approaches their refuge and the Israeli prisoner runs toward his compatriots, abandoning his Palestinian captors to die. As in *The Smile of the Lamb*, *Cup Final* concludes on the impossibility of creating solid bonds between the two sides.

Look-Out (*Nekudat tatzpit*, Dina Zvi-Riklis, 1992) offers another representation of this issue. An Israeli soldier posted on a roof in a refugee camp in the occupied territories observes the daily life of a Palestinian village. The naïve voyeur gets emotionally involved in a family's daily life and becomes aware of their tragedy, which derives in part from the unbearable situation the Israeli occupation has created. His remote position, iconographically expressed by the point-of-view shots of the Palestinian family, and the Israeli radio sound track he listens to as he stands at his lookout post become a metaphor of the limited Israeli gaze in general and the cinematic Israeli gaze in particular, both of which fail to communicate an authentic image of Palestinian Arabs (Lubin 2005, 305–308).

At the turn of the twenty-first century, after a long period of silence during which Israeli cinema adopted a more introspective mood of inquiring into the repressed roots of Israeli identity, Israeli films have turned again to meditate on the conflict. However, the films dedicated to the subject are different from those of the 1980s. The political situation has changed, and the Intifadat el-Aksa that erupted in 2000 does not resemble the first Intifada. Israeli filmmakers have become more daring in engaging a critical reflection on the harm the occupation inflicts on occupiers as well as occupied. Amos Gitai's *Kedma* (2002) has refugees from both sides, Jews who fled an anti-Semitic Europe and Palestinians expelled from their home by the Jews, confront each other. Jews are both victims and perpetrators at this decisive political moment when the cards were distributed.[3]

The same message is offered by Udi Aloni in *Forgiveness* (*Mechilot*, 2006) in a completely different context.[4] The film's actual plot takes place on the site of the 1948 massacre in the Palestinian village of Dir Yassin, where an Israeli psychiatric hospital has been established. On this multilayered site, Holocaust survivors continue to live their nightmares, and a young Israeli soldier, haunted by the memory of his killing a Palestinian child, plunges into his soul's depths, deconstructing the teleological Zionist narrative—embodied in the famous phrase "from Holocaust to resurrection"—and finally sinks into his own madness.

Where *Kedma* and *Forgiveness* openly deal with the conflict, relating to it in terms of trauma and irreversible historical wounds that have condemned future generations to live with a sense of guilt, Eran Kolorin in his acclaimed debut film, *The Band's Visit* (*Bikur ha-tizmoret*, 2007), pursues yet another option for the representation of the conflict. Telling the fantastic story of an Egyptian police band that gets lost in Israel, this bittersweet comedy succeeds in pointing at the similarities between Jews and Arabs: Israelis living in a remote development and their Egyptian visitors.

Alongside *The Band's Visit*, another Israeli film that left an impact on international festivals is Joseph Cedar's *Beaufort* (2007). Based on real events that took place when the Israel Defense Forces left southern Lebanon in 2000, the film focuses on a small number of soldiers left in the ancient Crusader fortress Beaufort that has become a synonym for Israel's presence in southern Lebanon. An antiwar film, *Beaufort* asks pertinent questions that challenge some of the basic assumptions of the Israeli security policy and its responsibility for superfluous casualties.

Ari Folman's *Waltz with Bashir* (*Vals im Bashir*, 2008) took Israeli guilt one step further, relating the first Lebanon war trauma as it was experienced by the director, who was then an eighteen-year-old soldier. Folman took a radical artistic decision: he chose animation over reconstruction of the sites and events. But Folman's animated world abruptly ends with documentary footage of the massacre in the Sabra and Shatila Palestinian camps, which, though Israeli soldiers—and Folman himself—were not directly implicated in it, was enabled by the very Israeli presence in this war. Eran Riklis addressed the Israeli-Palestinian conflict in a more traditional way in *Lemon Tree* (*Etz limon*, 2008). The film shares the political perspective Riklis expressed in his remarkable earlier film, *The Syrian Bride* (*Hakala hasurit*, 2004). In both films Riklis chooses Palestinian women as protagonists, hinting that the change in Israeli and Palestinian attitudes will come only from a different approach, a feminine one. Finally, Guy Nativ and Erez Tadmor in their first feature, *Strangers* (*Zarim*, 2007), attempt to show a different aspect of the conflict. It deals with the love affair between an Israeli man and a Palestinian woman who accidentally meet in Berlin and decide to surmount the national barriers. Nativ and Tadmor chose an unrealistic ending, just like Judd Ne'eman did in *Promenade of the Heart* (*Nuzhat al-Fuad*, 2007) and Aloni in *Forgiveness*, reinforcing the tendency of these recent films to withhold any suggestion as to a solution to the traumatic existence lived by both sides.

NOTES

This essay is based on research that was supported by the Israeli Science Foundation (grant No. 786/03) and by the Israeli-Palestinian Science Organization (IPSO).

1. The term *bourekas* originally indicated a cheap Oriental pastry. This designation of the films, popular in the mid-1970s, expresses the mainstream attitude to this genre.
2. On *Avanti Popolo* see the essay devoted to the film in this volume.
3. On *Kedma* see the essay devoted to the film in this volume.
4. The Hebrew title, *Mehilot*, means both forgiveness and underground tunnels.

REFERENCES

Avisar, Ilan. 2005. "The National and the Popular in Israeli Cinema," *Shofar: An Interdisciplinary Journal of Jewish Studies* 24 (1): 125–143.

Ben-Shaul, Nitzan. 1997. *Mythical Expressions of Siege in Israeli Films*. Lewiston, NY: Edwin Mellen.

Friedman, Regine Mihal. 2005. "De l'arabe au palestinien: Le nouveau regard Israelien." In *Israeliens, Palestiniens: Que peut le cinéma?*, ed. J. Halbreich-Euvrard, 187–196. Paris: Editions Michalon.

Gertz, Nurith. 1993. *Motion Fiction: Israeli Fiction in Film* (in Hebrew). Tel-Aviv: Open University.

———. 2004. *Another Choir: Holocaust Survivors, Foreigners, and Others in Israeli Film and Literature* (in Hebrew). Tel-Aviv: Open University and Am Oved.

Gertz, Nurith, and Yael Munk. Forthcoming. "The Representation of the Israeli-Palestinian Conflict in Israeli Cinema." In *Encyclopedia of the Israeli-Palestinian Conflict*, ed. Cheryl Rubenberg. Boulder, CO: Lynne Rienner.

Loshitzky, Yosefa. 2001. *Identity Politics on the Israel Screen*. Austin: University of Texas Press.

Lubin, Orly. 2005. "The Woman as Other in Israeli Cinema." In *Israeli Women's Studies*, ed. Esther Fuchs, 301–316. New Brunswick, NJ: Rutgers University Press.

Ne'eman, Judd. 1995. "The Empty Tomb in the Postmodern Pyramid: Israeli Cinema in the 1980s and the 1990s." In *Documenting Israel*, ed. Charles Berlin, 117–151. Cambridge: Harvard College Library.

———. 2001. "Israeli Cinema." In *Companion Encyclopedia of Middle Eastern and North Africa Film*, ed. Oliver Leaman, 100–128. London: Routledge.

Shohat, Ella. 1989. *Israeli Cinema: East/West and the Politics of Representation*. Austin: University of Texas Press.

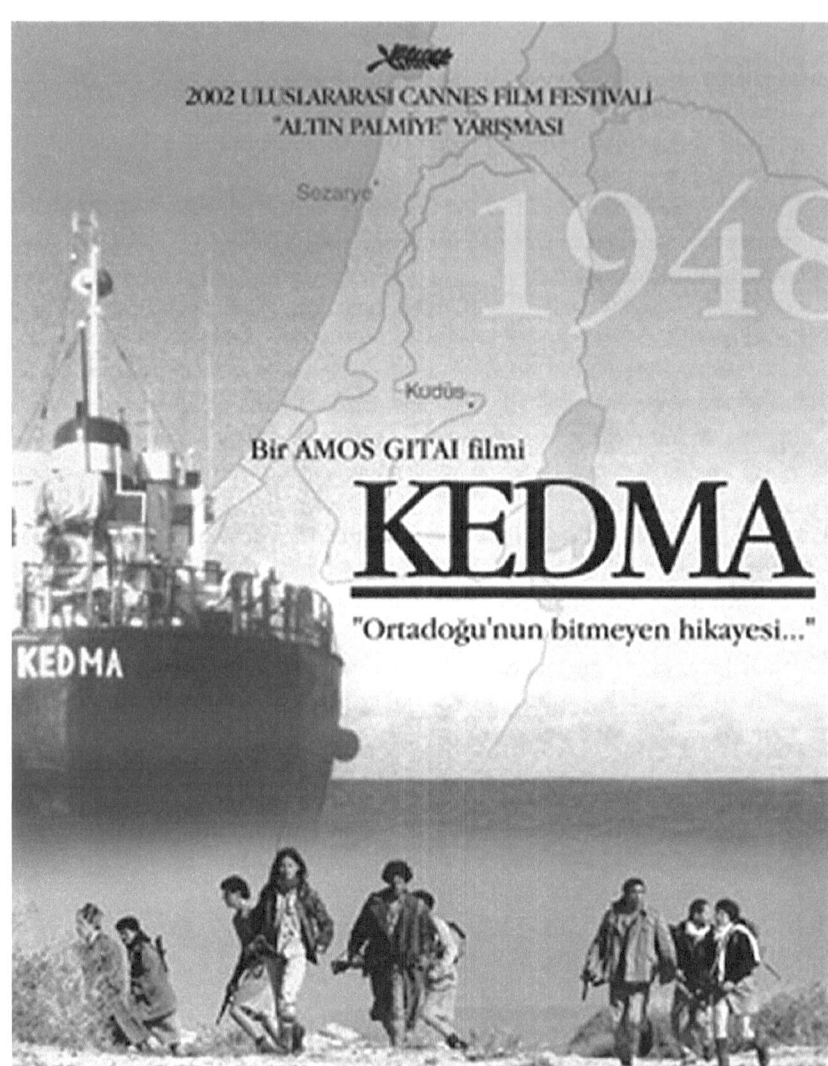

*Kedma**
The Birth of Two Nations at War

NURITH GERTZ, GAL HERMONI, AND YAEL MUNK

Kedma (2002) is one the more recent films in the long and highly acclaimed career of Amos Gitai. Gitai's films engage a broad range of topics including relations between Arabs and Jews, occupation and war (*Yom Yom, Day after Day*, 1998; *Esther*, 1985; *Kippur*, 2000; *Free Zone*, 2005); revealed life in an Orthodox Jewish setting (*Kadosh*, 1999); and incisively analyzed the history of Israel's society and culture (*Devarim*, 1995; *Eden*, 2001). This list of eight films represents only part of Gitai's work, which includes many feature films alongside a considerable documentary *œuvre*. All his films have garnered praise, been screened at festivals, and generated dispute among Israel's general public. To a great extent, *Kedma* is a summing-up of Gitai's filmography.

The film follows the movement of Jewish Holocaust survivors from the ship that brings them to the shores of the Promised Land. The cinematic plot epitomizes the Zionist narrative:[1] the survivors are meant to forget the traumatic events of the past, to overcome the memories of the diaspora, to shed the Jewish characteristics of their identity, to partake in a battle on the road to Jerusalem, and to be transformed from passive Jews to Hebrew fighters who engage in an active war over their lives and fates.

The plot of the film allows it to address movement in space and time in a reflective manner. It is the progression from the ship toward Jerusalem as well as a shift from the diasporic past to the Zionist present. It is both a cinematic narrative movement and an ideological one.[2] Yet, in contrast with the original definition of a journey as an advance from a point of departure to a destination,

---

* *Kedma*. 2002. Film directed by Amos Gitai; written by Amos Gitai and Marie Jose Sanselme. Produced by Agav Hafakot (Israel), Arte France Cinéma (France), Agav Films (Israel), M.P. Productions, and BIM Distribuzione (Italy). Distributed in the United States by Kino International. 100 minutes.

Amos Gitai and Yussef Abu Warda. Stills Gallery on U.S. DVD.

this is a deconstructed, directionless journey flooded by characters moving "to" and "from" aimlessly. This journey falls apart and is obstructed because of a post-traumatic condition that has not yet been worked through and cannot be worked through as long as the survivors are forced to move forward and relinquish their past. It is a paralyzed journey.

The initial indication that *Kedma* is a film about movement and thus allows an examination of its failure is in its title. *Kedma* is a word alluding to progression in both the geographical and ideological spheres: forward, toward the future, toward the east, which bears with it a memory of an ancient past. *Kedma* is of course also the name of an illegal immigrant ship where the story's protagonists begin their movement in time and space in the Zionist as well as in the cinematic narrative. Some of the first scenes in the film enable *Kedma* to expose, from the onset, the aesthetics of paralysis that will characterize it throughout. An example is the scene showing the survivors' descent to shore—a scene that reverses the relationship between subject matter and the way it is shot.

The depicted event is one of hectic activity: hosts of immigrants descend to shore, running in panic every which way, trying to escape the British soldiers chasing them. Some get away; others are arrested. This event invites intensive cinematic delineation to match and cater to the vigor of the activity. But this does not happen. The intensive and crowded scene is filmed in a wide-lens long shot, as a long take, accompanied by a slow and consistent tracking movement.[3] Willemen describes such shots by Gitai as a "courageous (left) intellectual at work with cinema. He does not tell us what to think but leaves us in no doubt as to what he thinks while providing a complex representation of a situation for us to argue with" (1993, 11). In this specific case there is a sharp discord between this shot's content and form. The distance from the objects, the width of the cinematic space, and the speed in which the camera moves seem to neutralize the movement that floods the screen, draining it of the intensiveness of the actions, thus interrupting the movement in space.[4]

During this scene, the camera pauses on the face of a woman, capturing her in close-up as she gazes at the space in front of her. She seems to continue to weave the memories that have begun unfolding aboard the ship while her image is superimposed onto a shot of the British attack on the immigrants. The notion of the past, which is felt through the reminiscing refugee's eyes, blends in this way with the future—the struggle against the British—and the two tenses flood the present.[5]

The flooding of time frames is paralleled in the film by the overlapping of historical periods. Willemen has described (1993) the way *Kedma* retreats to a certain point in the past in order to leave the historical options open. But, in fact, the intersecting of time frames in the film does not allow such options. When the battle described in the film takes place, the future is still wide open. The mass movement of Palestinian refugees has not yet occurred, the British have not yet left Palestine, and the Israelis have not won major victories. And yet the film makes the unknown future present within current events. It does so through the details of the landscape displayed in the film:[6] ruins, land terraces, and unkempt prickly pear bushes (*sabra*). The action of the film is set at a time when the Arab villages, even those that had been deserted, were still intact and prickly pear bushes surrounded them like a hedge. In 2001, when the film was shot, only ruins were left of the deserted villages, and prickly pear bushes were scattered around the landscape as mere tokens of the villages' past existence.[7] In 1948 a prickly pear bush and an Arab house built of stone signaled the existence of a village; in 2001 these same landmarks denoted the destruction of a village. The camera lingers on them, thus inserting the future—the results of the battle and the exodus—into a point in the past when they had not yet occurred.

In a similar manner, the future is incorporated in the present in the words of an Arab refugee confronting the Israeli soldiers who have just won the battle:

[W]e shall remain
like a wall upon your chest,
and in your throat...
We shall remain
a wall upon your chest,

clean dishes in your restaurants,
serve drinks in your bars,
sweep the floors of your kitchens
to snatch a bite for our children from your blue fangs.
Here we shall stay,
... we shall remain,
guard the shade of the fig
and olive trees,
ferment rebellion in our children
as yeast in the dough.

The words are from Tawfik Ziad's 1966 poem and describe a future that was still unknown at the time when the events of the film were taking place. At that period the Palestinian Arabs had not been abused as cheap laborers in Israeli towns, and the extent of the suffering and opposition that would characterize their lives in subsequent years was unknown. Such permeation of times creates a *temporal paralysis*. It disturbs the unfolding of *linear time*, arresting its movement and turning the past, the present, and the future into simultaneous tenses.

Tesson refers to the journey taken by the film as a journey into history. However, he says, at the end of the film "we have the impression of a country comprised of people without a place" (2002a, 27). *Kedma*'s journey into history is indeed problematic and complex. Gitai himself alluded to this complexity in an interview in 2007:

> I wished to seek in the fate of these characters in the past some answers that trouble me today. The entire project of the film relies on condensation, on the principle of compression. It also relates to the characters' time. [I wished] to show their journey and to insert that journey to a polyphony of languages—Hebrew, Yiddish, Polish, Russian, Arabic—and into different forms of narration.

The various narrative structures flooding the film are paralleled by a flooding of contradictory historiographic narratives, stories, arguments, and myths that are assembled and condensed into the fictitious narrative, serving as signifiers to the familiar texts that are absent from it.

The claims concerning the Jewish victim turned victimizer when settling in Palestine are suggested in two consecutive episodes. In one, the survivor recounts the tale of his orphanhood, the loss of his parents, and his distress during

The teacher, the cantor, and the cantor's wife encounter Arab refugees.

World War II. In the other, he attacks an Arab refugee with curses and threats. The historical analysis that had already been processed in countless books and films, describing the lack of willingness to listen to a Holocaust survivor's story by the Israeli public in general and the Israeli-born (*sabra*) in particular, are presented in one episode in which Menahem is asked to sing and begins a song related to Purim: "Yaacov's rose was joyful and merry seeing Mordechai's sapphire blue." The song, sung in a diasporic tune unfamiliar to the *sabra* Palmach fighters, is immediately hushed.[8] The historical and literary analysis arguing that repairing the wrong done to one people has created a wrong to another and suggesting that the Palestinians have paid the price of the Jewish Holocaust are alluded to in the film in an episode describing an encounter between a group of Jewish survivors traveling toward a new settlement and a party of Arab refugees who have abandoned their old settlement. In these cases and others, the myths, the recounted histories, the texts are condensed into one or two episodes that signify them without an attempt to elaborate, to develop, to establish a relationship of cause and effect or historical logic. The text is flooded with signifiers that cross each other and intertwine, creating an overload and density, halting the film's narrative, ideological, and cinematic movement, and veiling its referents. The most interesting example of such a polyphonic flooding of signifiers is the use Gitai makes of literary texts.

While they are still on the ship anticipating their arrival at the shores of the country, some passengers converse about the events of the past that continue to haunt them. At the same time, a woman sings to herself Haim Nahman Bialik's song-poem "To the Bird." Bialik published it in 1912, when he was still a young boy in Russia, in the diaspora, expressing his longing for the faraway, unreachable land of Israel. The poem has become an emotional signifier of the Zionist ideology, of yearning by the diasporic for the land of Israel, from the past to the future, from the static place the poet is in onward to the Promised Land. Its citation at the opening of the film indicates unequivocally the direction of the passengers' journey: yearning for Zion.

Yet, the contexts into which this poem is inserted annul its original meaning, presenting it as an element in a complex configuration of contradictions. It is situated within a tapestry of dialogues in Russian, the language of the diaspora, about the events of the past that occurred in the diaspora. These dialogues occur on the ship—a vehicle moving toward the future, toward the land yearned for. As mentioned earlier, the word *kedma* itself signifies this bidirectional movement. One might say that the signifier of longing for Zion receives in the film, among other complexities and contradictions, an additional but opposite meaning of longing for the past, for the diaspora, to the place where the Holocaust occurred and which the survivors have just left.

At the end of the film, Gitai uses a quote taken from a story written in 1941 by Haim Hazaz, "The Sermon." After a bloody battle in the film, Yanosh, one of the immigrants, walks among the dead and the wounded. Shocked, he gives a speech that is composed of sections of "The Sermon." As in the bird poem, these segments are set in a context that contradicts them: "We have no history!" claims the protagonist of *Kedma*, following Yudke, Hazaz's character. "From the day we exiled from our country we are a people without a history ... We did not create our history, the gentiles did that ... They created history as they wished it and in their shape, while we only accepted it from their hands. But this history is not ours, not ours at all!" Yanosh, like Yudke, goes on: "I protest, I don't recognize it and it does not exist for me! Moreover, I don't respect it ... I oppose it." (Hazaz 1941/2005, 223).

Originally this text by Hazaz prompted military activism among the 1948 fighting youth (Laor 2001). It served as a basis for their demand to take history into their hands and transform themselves from a group of passive victims to an active fighting people. Yet at the time it is presented in *Kedma*, the text cannot support this meaning any longer. The call to transcend passivity and act within history does not fit the end of a battle in which the diasporic survivors emerged out of their passivity and took action in history—fighting for their new country. As at the beginning of the film with "To the Bird," here too the text is taken out of its original context. And in its new context, within a system of contradictions, it also receives a new meaning: instead of negation of the diaspora, the text now expresses, among other meanings, negation of Zionist activism.[9]

This approach was seen by Israeli reviewers and critics as evidence of the film's failure. Raveh lists *Kedma* in the "respectable" rank as number 19 among the "20 Worst Israeli Films of all Time" because Gitai

> overloads a single frame with icons from the pages of Israel's national struggle. A Holocaust survivor, an illegal immigrant, the wandering Jew, the Palestinian driven out of his home—all of them become under his hands battered clichés. Even Sandi Bar, in the role of the courageous fighter, manages to evoke longings for the character role she played in a catalogue for a fashion company. (2007, 5–7)

Kedma was marked by the list's compilers as a cinematic failure, as they identify cinematic success with mimetic success in the belief that an art creation should offer an impression of reality as accurately as possible. What they refer to as "clichés" are in fact those signifiers disconnected from what they signified. What they call "an overload" is in fact the flooding of the film with these signifiers, as described above.

The international criticism, which appeared unfamiliar with the details of Israeli history and the Zionist narrative, was more tolerant toward the film. The prevalent suppositions in these reviews were that *Kedma* was not a spectacle intended to delineate historically familiar images, events, or episodes. Rather, "it began from the legend and myth of this history . . . Gitai sees in cinema . . . a sensitive means of recording not history but its echoes" (Toubiana 2003, 179–180). Or, as Tesson put it: "Gitai expresses the ability of cinema to create through characters a semblance of realism in order to understand better where reality stems from" (2002b, 31). Gitai himself explained this approach as one that "de-mythicizes the Israeli":

> Cinema is very strong. It can mythicize the experience, but it can also do the opposite. Israel today is in a state of dialectic complexity. It is a country that needs to create a mythic image in order to create solidarity with the international Jewish community; yet in order to live it needs to de-mythicize the image of the Israeli. (In Toubiana 2003, 101)

We might say, then, that decoding the Zionist myths in *Kedma* relies on flooding of times, narratives, and ideologies. Such flooding deters, even halts, the film's movement, thus expressing a quintessential post-traumatic condition.

The post-traumatic condition, as suggested by Freud (1901/1951, 1909/1974), is characterized by repeated re-experiencing of symptoms related to a traumatic event and resurfacing a long time after the fact. Thus the original event is displaced and becomes another experience that both signifies and conceals it. Many studies that were based on Freud's writings have made clear the place of the post-traumatic condition in the history of societies and cultures (Caruth 1991, Elsaesser 2001, Greenberg 1998, Kaes 1992). In this respect, the post-traumatic condition is a state of narrative failure: the deconstruction of the sequence of events. We might say that the rhetoric of narrative failure that we have discussed is a post-traumatic, post-Holocaust rhetoric—it displaces events, disconnecting them from their referents and from the temporal sequence in which they occurred, thus creating a sense of impasse and paralysis in both cinematic and ideological narratives that it recounts.

NOTES

1. For discussions concerning the cinematic representation of the Zionist narrative see Ben-Shaul 1997 (103–107) and Shohat 1989 (7–12).
2. Bhabha (1990) views the linear, teleological-casual narrative movement as hegemony's ideological apparatus.
3. For a recent discussion of the long take see Kashales and Sagi forthcoming.
4. See Deleuze and Guattari (1986, 16–27) on flooding major language as a mode of resistance to dominant culture.
5. This survivor's gaze can also be read as a manifestation of the Deleuzean sensormotoric crisis (Deleuze 1986, 197–216, and 1989, 103–107). The character's inability to respond with action is a result of shock.
6. On the politics of the landscape in Israeli cinema see Munk 2006 and Zanger 2004, forthcoming.
7. For a discussion on temporality in ruins as allegory see Benjamin 1928/1988, 103–107.
8. The Palmach (Strike Company) was the enlisted brigade of the Haganah, constituting the military defense force of the Jewish Yishur and Zionist movement until the establishment of the state of Israel. http://www.palmach.org.il.
9. Editor's note: The Israeli, French, and U.S. posters depict the cantor's wife delight when he shows her how to use a rifle. They thus promote *Kedma* with a militaristic

stance altogether foreign to the film. They also misrepresent her: she is distressed at her husband's newfound militancy and tries to hold him back as he joins the fighters. *Kedma* was released in Turkey and is in distribution there on DVD, but the Turkish poster, reproduced here, is altogether different. It establishes the context in a matter-of-fact way, showing the ship *Kedma*, Palmach fighters on the beach, and in the background a map of Palestine and the year; and it addresses its Muslim public with the laconic comment "The never-ending story of the Middle East."

REFERENCES

Benjamin, Walter. 1928/1988. *The Origins of German Tragic Drama*. London. Verso.

Ben-Shaul, Nitzan. 1997. *Mythical Expressions of Siege in Israeli Films*. Lewiston, NY: Edwin Mellen.

Bhabha, Homi K. 1990. "Dissemination: Time, Narrative, and the Margins of the Modern Nation." In *Nation and Narration*, 291–323, ed. Homi K. Bhabha. London: Routledge.

Bialik, Haim Nachman. 1912/1952. "To the Bird" (in Hebrew). In *All Poems of H. N. Bialik*, 1–4. Tel Aviv: Dvir.

Caruth, Cathy. 1991. "Unclaimed Experience: Trauma and the Possibility of History." *Yale French Studies* 79:181–192.

Deleuze, Gilles. 1986. *Cinema 1: The Movement-Image*. Minneapolis: University of Minnesota Press. Translation by Hugh Tomlinson and Barbara Habberjam of *L'Image-mouvement*. Paris: Editions de Minuit.

———. 1989. *Cinema 2: The Time Image*. Minneapolis: University of Minnesota Press. Translation by Hugh Tomlinson and Robert Galeta of *L'Image temps*. Paris: Editions de Minuit.

Deleuze, Gilles, and Felix Guattari. 1986. *Kafka: Toward a Minor Literature*. Minneapolis: University of Minnesota Press. Translation by Dana Polan of *Kafka: Pour une littérature mineure*. Paris: Editions de Minuit.

Elsaesser, Thomas. 2001. "Postmodernism as Mourning Work." *Screen* 42 (2): 193–201.

Freud, Sigmund. 1901/1951. *Psychopathology of Everyday Life*. New York: New American Library. Translation by A. A. Brill of *Zur Psychopathologie des Alltagslebens (Über Vergessen, Versprechen, Vergreifen, Aberglaube und Irrtum)*. Berlin: Karger.

———. 1909/1974. "Remembering, Repeating, and Working Through." In *Standard Edition of the Complete Psychological Works of Sigmund Freud*, vol. 12, 147–156. Translated from German. London: Hogarth Press and Institute of Psychoanalysis.

Gitai, Amos. 2007. Interview by Nurith Gertz, Tel Aviv, August.

Greenberg, Judith. 1998. "The Echo of the Trauma and the Trauma of Echo." *American Imago* 55 (3): 319–347.

Hazaz, Haim. 1941/2005. "The Sermon." In *The Sermon and Other Stories*, 219–237. Translated from Hebrew. New Milford, CT: Toby Press.

Kaes, Anton, 1992. "Holocaust and the End of History: Postmodern Historiography in Cinema." In *Probing the Limits of Representation*, ed. Friedlander Saul, 206–222. Cambridge: Harvard University Press.

Kashales, Aharon, and Eran Sagi. Forthcoming. "On the PCS or 'The Fear of the Cut.'" *New Views on Film Philosophy*, Thesis.

Laor, Dan. 2001. "From the 'Drasha' to 'The Appeal to the Israeli Youth': Some Comments to the Notion of 'the Negation of the Diaspora.'" *Alpaim* 21:171–187.

Munk, Yael. 2006. "The City Space of Accre as the Sick Body's Space: On Judd Ne'eman's Film *Observation on Accre*" (in Hebrew). *Southern Cinema Notebooks* 1:85–90 (Pardes Editors with Sapir College).

Raveh, Yair. 2007. "Top 20 Worst Israeli Films of All Time." *7 Leylot, Yedioth Aharonot*, April 5, 5–7.

Shohat, Ella. 1989. *Israeli Cinema: East/West and the Politics of Representation*. Austin: University of Texas Press.

Tesson, Charles. 2002a. "Amos Gitaï: Mon cinéma, forcément subversive." *Cahiers du Cinema*. 568:24–29.

———. 2002b. "Le Chemin de Jerusalem." *Cahiers du Cinema* 568:30–31.

Toubiana, Serge. 2003. *Exils et territoir: Le Cinéma d'Amos Gitai*. Arte and Editions Cahiers du Cinema.

Willemen, Paul. 1993. "Bangkok-Bahrain-Berlin-Jerusalem." In *The Films of Amos Gitay: A Montage*, ed. Paul Willemen, 5–16. London: British Film Institute.

Zanger, Anat. 2004. "Zionism and the Detective: Imaginary Territories in Israeli Popular Cinema." *Journal of Modern Jewish Studies* 3, no. 3:307–318.

———. Forthcoming. "Landscapes and Maps in *Mezizim* and in *Te'alat Blaumlich*" (in Hebrew). In *Peeping Toms, Cocks, and Other Israelis*, ed. Miri Talmon and Moshe Tzimerman. Tel Aviv: Keter and Open University.

Ziad, Tawfik. 1966. "Here We Will Stay." http://www.statemaster.com/encyclopedia/Tawfiq-Ziad#Poetry.

Avanti Popolo
Battle Cry of the Fallen

JUDD NE'EMAN AND YAEL MUNK

> Don't try to read the desert. There you will find all
> books buried in the dust of their words.
> EDMOND JABES (1978, 178)

In their seminal essay "Nomadology: The War Machine," French philosophers Gilles Deleuze and Felix Guattari (1987) describe two kinds of war machines: the state war machine and the nomadic war machine. The state war machine, whose troops and vehicles advance through a gridded space, has combat for its objective, targeting the enemy to destroy its body and conquer its land. The nomadic war machine moves on a smooth space, and its true objective is survival. The nomadic war machine engages the enemy in combat only as a last resort. The transformation of combatants from state warriors to nomadic warriors and its consequences may account for the canonic status of Rafi Bukaee's *Avanti Popolo* in Israeli cinema, and it informs our interpretation of the film.[1]

Avanti Popolo is set in the aftermath of the Six Day War in 1967. Following the cease-fire, the war machines stopped when the Israeli armed forces occupied the entire Sinai Peninsula, driving the Egyptian army beyond the Suez Canal. In the incommensurable space of the Sinai Desert, thousands of troops are left, straying and trying against all odds to reach the Suez Canal and cross it to go home; among them are the film's protagonists. But can the war machine ever stop? *Avanti Popolo* tells a surrealistic reenactment of these two war machines'

**Avanti Popolo. 1986. Written and directed by Rafi Bukaee. Produced by Kastel Communications (Israel). The Hebrew version is distributed in Israel by Gilgamesh. 83 minutes. For a Hebrew script see Bukaee (1990); for an English translation of that script see Ellenson (2008).

Courtesy Farkash Gallery

clash: an Israeli, representative of the state war machine seeking further victories, confronting the straying troops, representative of a newly formed nomadic war machine, that of the defeated, seeking survival.

The narrative follows the story of two Egyptian soldiers on the run, Gassan and Haled, who strive to reach the Suez Canal and cross to the other side, to home and safety. The film's narrative spans less than forty-eight hours. Mostly on the surreal side, the soldiers' journey does not resemble the traditional representations of war, as there is hardly any combat in the film. Their way home progresses along two parallel and contradicting trajectories: survival and death. While they do everything they can to survive, a point-of-view shot that in one scene can be attributed to a diegetic dead U.N. soldier becomes their companion and foreshadows death right from the opening scene. In our reading of the film we suggest attributing this mysterious point of view to the notion of death. The film's narrative is actually framed by two scenes of dying and killing.

The first takes place at the film's opening when a fatally wounded Egyptian soldier is dying. Following his death and the burial of his body in the sand, the Egyptian commanding officer orders Gassan and Haled to assault an Israeli infantry patrol even though a cease-fire has been announced. The two remaining soldiers refuse to obey the suicidal order; in self-defense Gassan kills his officer. The other framing scene takes place at the very ending of the film, when all the Israeli soldiers but one as well as the two Egyptians get killed on the banks of the Suez Canal. This framing of the film narrative is quite unlike the heroic contrivances of many war movies, although it may suit the configuration of some antiwar films.

In between the two dramatic events Gassan and Haled experience a fantastic journey in the desert, the no-man's-land that the war has turned into a battlefield. The seemingly empty desert not only does bear traces of human existence but also leads to unexpected encounters. In the course of the carnivalesque journey of the two soldiers, their imminent death is continuously suspended. In the film's climactic scene, Israeli soldiers join the Egyptians in singing "Avanti Popolo," the renowned song of the Italian left that spread among labor movements across Europe. The song expresses a strong anti-nationalistic motif and calls for human solidarity. This postnationalist propensity, substituting human solidarity for an automatic allegiance to the nation-state, may explain how *Avanti Popolo* has retained its political relevance more than twenty years after its release. The film powerfully resists the obsession with nationalism and militarism that continues to occupy the Israeli mind no less than the mindset of Israel's neighboring Arab states.

The first point-of-view shot of death appears right after the two Egyptian soldiers have buried their comrade. On top of the grave they fix a marker made of two combat shovels and a helmet. As they and their officer walk away from the grave, the marker, which faintly resembles a scaffold, frames the distancing figures. The shot is repeated when, in an abandoned Egyptian military post, the two exhausted soldiers enter a cabin. Looking for drinking water, they suddenly hear the sound of a jeep and realize that an Israeli army patrol force is approaching. One of them hides behind a window pane and the camera frames him from the side revealing beads of sweat on his forehead, as if death were getting one step closer. As they progress on their journey toward the canal, the two are seen from behind a United Nations jeep as if filmed through the eyes of the dead U.N. soldier sitting immobile. This shot provides a retrospective for the previous frames in which the soldiers are looked at by actually no one. To quench their extreme thirst, they cannot resist drinking from the bottle of whisky they find in the jeep, breaking Islamic law. Their dialogue conveys their twofold trajectory of survival and death. As Haled asks his friend what this Swedish soldier is doing in the middle of the Sinai Desert, Gassan responds twice, "He's dead." Then Haled responds, "The main thing is we're alive," and Gassan retorts, "I'm not so sure." These lines coming from drunken soldiers mark them as "the living dead," those whose death has been suspended for a short while. They proceed driving the dead U.N. soldier's jeep while the radio is playing a typical Israeli military march song—an ironic comment on their being in harm's way but alive.

A further example of such a point-of-view shot appears in a scene toward the end of the film's main segment, when the two Egyptian soldiers and an Israeli patrol march together, singing in unison "Avanti Popolo." Here too an external point-of-view suggests the disaster awaiting them eventually.

If the Sinai Desert constitutes the context of the Egyptian-Israeli Six Day War, the rich symbolism of the desert itself helps create a story that could not have taken place anywhere else. "The desert refers to a complex locus of experience and reflection," writes Klemm (2004, xii). "It is simultaneously an interior space in the mind; an exterior place where pilgrims, adventurers and travellers can visit and dwell . . . [the desert] is a space where humans go to encounter themselves, the demons and their god. The desert is at once an oasis, a paradise, where humans renew themselves and are transformed." In the same vein, Laura Marks suggests that in Arab cinema the landscape has no teleology:

Blowing sand effaces markers, erasing time and memory. A landscape that pre-exists us, outlives us, and unlike other landscapes, forgets us, the desert makes us aware of the limitations of human perception and memory. The desert is not empty, but it can only be navigated by close attention to the wind, the dunes, the oases, and plant life. The desert is not chaotic, but it is best understood locally; it asks for embodied presence, not abstract order. (2006, 125–126)

In *Avanti Popolo* the absence of hegemonic order in the desert can be construed as a striking feature of the film's visual aspect. A space devoid of traces of human existence, the desert brings to mind the Deleuzean notion of deterritorialization. Because of its vast expanse it is not subject to the panopticon gaze and therefore represents a site outside the hegemonic order, a site where the non-hegemonic resides. Moreover, the desert represents the abject space of transgression. The landscape of the desert at different hours of the day and through various angles reflects a sense of stark reality and at the same time a sense of the unreal.

When at the very end of the film Haled arrives at the Suez Canal, he is trapped in crossfire from the two banks, from both Israeli and Egyptian army positions. Thus his transgressive, liminal nature sinks in and becomes inscribed on his body. Killing Haled, both armies, Israelis and Egyptians alike, reject the message of human solidarity that his hyperbolic moves in the film represent. His killing on the banks of the canal also signals the edge of the desert where it touches the domain of civilization. While transgressions were possible and enacted in the wilderness of the Sinai Desert, they end where borders and nation-states begin. The Egyptian soldiers' quest comes to its end exactly where the liminal space ends.

Making their journey home, Gassan and Haled become part of what Deleuze and Guattari define as the nomadic war machine (1987, 351). After killing their officer, they get rid of their infantry gear and weapons and set out on a journey in which they will experience the desert as a space of transgression. Their journey takes place in the "smooth space" of the desert, the space where, according to Deleuze and Guattari, deterritorialization occurs—namely, getting lost and losing ground as well as losing one's footing on the ground. Not only are they disoriented and wandering in the desert, but their attempt to reach home is frustrated time and again as they almost die from thirst. They then get drunk on the dead U.N. soldier's bottle of whiskey and inadvertently come across a small Israeli army patrol. An Israeli soldier spots them with his binoculars, in a frame whose shape is made of two circular areas in which the two soldiers are caught. From this "binocular" shot onward, a surreal situation develops in which the enemy soldiers befriend each other. This situation holds until the following morning, when the same Israeli soldier who had spotted the Egyptian soldiers is seen waking up from deep sleep. These two shots of the same Israeli soldier, ill at ease with the Egyptian soldiers, bracket a long sequence that brings to mind the hypnagogic state of blurred consciousness between being awake and falling asleep. The encounter between enemy soldiers who for a short time become friends emanates from a transformation that occurs as the combatants' consciousness becomes slightly numb by thirst, alcohol, fatigue, and heat.[2]

The mystic aura of the desert and its intoxicating scenery project onto this bracketed sequence and make it surreal, in the vein of the Deleuzean notion of *ligne de fuite*. It expresses timelessness in which one becomes "imperceptible and clandestine" when one's territories are out of grasp, not because they are imaginary but because they are in the process of being drafted by the subject (Deleuze and Guattari 1987, 199). This *ligne de fuite* becomes a strategy designed to avoid what Zizek calls the "obscene supplement" (1997, 26–27), the violent propensity inherent in nationalism, the murderous and cruel impulse to kill human beings simply because they belong to another ethnic group or hold a different religious creed or just because they are on the other side of the frontline. The "frontline" enables one to forcefully exercise one's political power over the other. Zizek argues that the obscene supplement constitutes the way power and law function in society. The law, be it that of the state or of a religion, requires the acceptance of the use of violence and the submission to relations of subordination.

The film's hypnagogic sequence starts out with the Israeli soldiers, to escape the desert ennui, allowing Haled to play the role of entertainer. A theater actor in civilian life, he recites the renowned lines from *The Merchant of Venice* "I am a Jew!" The playful recitation leads the film into a new configuration of power relations between the Israelis, who have won the war, and the Egyptians, who have lost it. The Shakespearean lines relocate the narrative tensions to a distant past when the Jewish ancestors of the Israelis, a minority in Christendom, were persecuted.

Very soon the two Egyptian soldiers become part of the Israeli patrol. The climax of the hypnagogic sequence takes place when the enemies chant "Avanti

Haled leads the Israeli soldiers and his comrade in chanting "Avanti Popolo."

Popolo" together. As they march into the setting sun, the visual difference between Egyptians and Israelis becomes blurred, even imperceptible. For a very short time a true solidarity inhabits this small group of human beings in the loneliness of the desert. At this point, the scene echoes Bakhtin's concept of the carnival that, according to Stam (1989, 86), "abolishes hierarchies, levels social restrictions and creates another life free from conventional rules and restrictions. In carnival, all that is marginalized and excluded—the mad, the scandalous, and the aleatory—takes over the center in a liberating explosion of otherness." For a short moment, the carnival mask liberates the combatants from the obscene supplement of nationalism, and they become what they have been—human beings.

As long as the hypnogogic state lasts, it functions as a *ligne de fuite*, and the defeated Egyptian soldiers are not sent in harm's way. However, on the following morning, as soon as the Israeli soldiers wake up, the nationalistic violent drive re-emerges, and the *ligne de fuite* is arrested. When, early in the morning, the Israelis move on, they leave behind the two Egyptian soldiers, knowing very well that the two may soon die from thirst under the desert sun. As the

Egyptian soldiers get up, they follow the Israelis only to end up facing another sort of *ligne de fuite*, this time under more morbid circumstances. As they approach the Israeli patrol that has walked away, they hear the sound of explosions and soon realize what has just happened. The Israeli soldiers had entered a minefield, and all but one got killed. Lying wounded in the minefield when another Israeli patrol arrives and rescues him, the surviving leader of the Israeli patrol, shell-shocked, mumbles fragmented words about his Egyptians comrades. His condition now spares him from experiencing the nationalistic violence that commands the soldiers' minds on the two sides of the Suez Canal. It is the return in the film of the obscene supplement that decrees death to the two escaping Egyptian soldiers.

Avanti Popolo resists the obscene supplement that dominates nationalistic and religious ideologies and calls for the alternative of human solidarity. The Shakespearean monologue "I am a Jew!" expressing a universal aspiration for survival, on the one hand, and the shell shock that stands for the soldier's withdrawal from the dictate to sacrifice his body, on the other, constitute two *lignes de fuite* that *Avanti Popolo* puts forward. *Avanti Popolo* does not allow such a transformation to happen. Instead the film focuses on the plight of the Egyptian soldiers and through their encounter with the Israeli soldiers articulates a call for universal solidarity that transcends the dictates of the nation-state.

The Egyptian soldiers do not see the Israelis as enemies and invest their efforts in survival, going beyond the national paradigm that defines their identity as warriors. In this sense, the story of the two Egyptians struggling to return home from the war foreshadows the emergence of a new wave of war films in Israeli cinema, such as *Kippur* (Gitai, 2000), *Beaufort* (Joseph Cedar, 2007), *Waltz with Bashir* (*Vals im Bashir*, Ari Folman, 2008), and *Lebanon* (*Levanon*, Samuel Maoz, 2009). These films bring to the screen young men whose lives were disrupted by war and whose experiences on the battleground become a nightmare from which they cannot awaken. While the recent war films tell about the moment when the trauma is inscribed in the bodies and minds of the combatants, in *Avanti Popolo* the soldiers' journey and the film end at the very moment when the trauma is inscribed on their bodies. But they themselves will not read it. "As man lies dying on the battleground, it is the state for whose sake [man] performs the role of the fighter as best he can, that he holds responsible for his humiliation [in death] and for annihilating him" (Ne'eman 1995, 139). In *Avanti Popolo*, both war machines seem to stop, and yet the soldiers' song of human solidarity reverberates high and low in the desert, a new sound, the battle cry of the fallen.

Rafi Bukaee with Salim Daw, members of the crew, and
Suheil Haddad at the rear. Courtesy Mayaan Milo.

Avanti Popolo started out as Rafi Bukaee's forty-minute graduation film project at Tel Aviv University. It grew into a full-length feature that won the Golden Leopard's Eye at the Locarno Film Festival and, against strong political opposition, became the Israeli submission for the Academy Awards. In a public discussion at the 1988 Montpellier Film Festival, Bukaee related how he had gone as cameraman with his teacher Amos Gitai to Beirut to shoot Gitai's documentary *Field Diary* (*Yoman Sadeh*, 1982):

> For the first time, in the course of this war, I saw Israeli planes bombing cities, civilian populations. I saw Palestinians and Israelis suffering all the misery of war, and I understood that Israel's strength for continuing to exist lies in its humanity and justice.[3] (Cinéma Méditerranéen Montpellier 1989, 101)

Bukaee's next feature, *Marco Polo, the Missing Chapter* (*Marco Polo: Haperek ha'aharon*, 1996), retraces the adventures of the legendary Marco Polo in the desert on his way back to fifteenth-century Venice. The film was completed about the time of the assassination of Prime Minister Yitzhak Rabin, and the situation in Israel was so tense that the present-day implications of the "historical" film went unnoticed. The film was hardly screened in Israel and remains a jewel yet to be discovered. Bukaee spent much of his short professional life as a producer. *Life According to Agfa* (*Ha-chavim al-pi agfa*, Assi Dayan, 1992) became one of the most important films of 1990s Israeli cinema; *Ushpizin* (*Ha-ushpizin*, Giddi Dar and Shuli Rand, 2004), his greatest success, was released the year after his untimely death.

NOTES

1. The director's last name is also transliterated as Bukai or Boukai.
2. Editor's note: The Israeli poster, reproduced here, draws on various elements in this surreal part of *Avanti Popolo*, adding the Golden Leopard's Eye trophy Rafi Bukaee won at Locarno.
3. Translated from the French by Yael Munk.

REFERENCES

Bukaee, Rafi. 1990. Avanti Popolo: *The Script*. Ed. Renen Schorr and Orly Lubin. Tel-Aviv: Kineret.
Cinéma Méditerranéen Montpellier. 1989. "Rafi Bukaee: Shylock du désert." In *Actes des 10e rencontres*, 101–107. Montpellier: Fédération des Œuvres Laïques de l'Hérault.
Deleuze, Gilles, and Felix Guattari. 1987. *A Thousand Plateaus: Capitalism and Schizophrenia*. Minneapolis: University of Minnesota Press. Translation by Brian Massumi of *Mille plateaux*. Paris: Editions de Minuit.
Ellenson, Hannah Miriam. 2008. Avanti Popolo: *An Exploration of the Relationship between Politics and Cinema in Israel*. With English translation of Hebrew script. Honors thesis in Jewish Studies, Wellesley College.
Jabes, Edmond. 1978. *Le soupçon, le désert*. Paris: Gallimard.
Klemm, David E. 2004. Preface to *The Sacred Desert: Religion, Literature, Art, and Culture*, ed. David Jasper, xi–xiv. London: Blackwell.
Marks, Laura U. 2006. "Asphalt Nomadism: The New Desert in Arab Independent Cinema." In *Landscape in Films*, ed. Martin Lefebvre, 125–147. London: Routledge.
Ne'eman, Judd. 1995. "The Empty Tomb in the Postmodern Pyramid: Israeli Cinema in the 1980s and the 1990s." In *Documenting Israel*, ed. Charles Berlin, 117–151. Cambridge: Harvard College Library.
Stam, Robert. 1989. *Subversive Pleasures: Bakhtin, Cultural Criticism, and Film*. Baltimore, MD: Johns Hopkins University Press.
Zizek, Slavoj. 1997. *The Plague of Fantasies*. London: Verso. Translation of *Kuga fantazem*. Ljubljana, Slovenia: Drustvo za teoretsko psihoanalizo.

5

A Chronicle of Palestinian Cinema

NURITH GERTZ AND GEORGE KHLEIFI

In its creators' endeavor to invent, document, and consolidate Palestinian history, Palestinian cinema deals with the momentous crisis experienced by Palestinian society in 1948 as a result of the establishment of the state of Israel and the expulsion of a substantial proportion of the Palestinian people from the land. On the one hand, Palestinian films have undertaken the creation of a historical sequence that leads from the past to the present and on to the future. On the other hand, they have frozen history either in a utopian, idyllic past or in the experiences of exile and uprooting that severed that past. Such pasts are habitually revived in films as if they were a part of the present. Freud found that such stagnation characterizes post-traumatic situations in which the traumatic memory is reactivated again and again in the present. To a large extent, historical processes dictate which historical memory Palestinian cinema foregrounds—freezing the past in the present or constructing a historical sequence, even obscuring the past and facing the future in recent years, albeit a future of death and desperation.[1]

During the 1970s Palestinian cinema operated under the patronage of Palestinian organizations and documented the events of the period, whether they were bombardments of refugee camps by the Israeli air force or the civil war between Christians and Muslims in southern Lebanon. The films compiled footage of battles, air assaults, ruins, and victims. They also teemed with militant voice-overs and interviews with warriors, eyewitness civilians, and political as well as military leaders. These films offered a cinematic representation of the Palestinian traumatic history through a plot structure that revived the story of the past in an abstract, symbolic manner through the documentation of present events.

Thus life in the refugee camps in Lebanon, in the days prior to the destruction wrought by Israeli air strikes, is linked by various techniques to the peaceful life in the homeland lost in 1948. The violence of the present is also associated with the violence experienced in the 1948 occupation. In addition to constituting a structure typical of trauma by simulating the past in the present, this pattern served to establish a national identity. At the time, Palestinian society was fractured into various diasporas, classes, generations, and religious groups. The memory of the common past and shared place, along with the revival of that past in the present, functioned to foreground unity rather than dwelling on differences and controversies. Palestinian cinema generated one history revolving around a single, crystallizing memory shared by all. That memory established a national identity and created collective symbols to replace the diverse reality of Palestinian society.[2]

Palestinian cinema shifted in the 1980s. At that time the Palestinian struggle escalated, and the escalation determined the agenda of Palestinian film directors. Filmmakers of that era sought to establish Palestinian narrative on the basis of the actual land, the real place and the life in it, rather than by reviving the past in the present. This change, which reflected the growing significance of land as a symbol of Palestinian identity and nationality, was initially made possible in the films of directors based in Israel and able to shoot there, in particular Michel Khleifi. He was born and raised in Nazareth but spent most of his life in Belgium. His first film, *Fertile Memory* (*al-Dhakira al-khasba*, 1980), was considered innovative not only in terms of Palestinian films but in the framework of Arab documentary films in general. While Khleifi too sought to revive the past in the present and recreate the lost unity of the landscape and the nation, the depiction of real, diverse lives situated new structures alongside the old. In subsequent films, *Wedding in Galilee* (ʿ*Urs al-Jalil*, 1987), *Canticle of the Stone* (*Nashid al-hajar*, 1990), and *Tale of the Three Jewels* (*Hikayat al-jawahir thalath*, 1994), Khleifi continued to document contemporary Palestinian life as well as the trauma affecting it.[3]

Khleifi was the most prominent director of the new Palestinian cinema in the 1980s. But soon others began making films, among them some of the major directors of Palestinian cinema to date—Rashid Masharawi, Elia Suleiman, Nizar Hassan, Hany Abu-Assad. The cinema they have created has been referred to as "Independent Cinema,"[4] "Palestinian Cinema from the Occupied Lands" (Farid n.d., Mdanat 1990), "Post-Revolution Cinema," and "Personal Cinema" (Shafik 2001). All of these titles allude to the nature of the cinema that originated, developed, and gained international acclaim as a result of the efforts of individual filmmakers. These directors operated without the support of either Palestinian public institutions or private Palestinian production companies.

Palestinian directors learned their craft in a variety of institutions around the world—when they enjoyed such training at all: Omar al Quattan, Michel

Khleifi, and George Khleifi studied in Belgium; Subhi a-Zubeidi, Hana Elias, Mai Masri, and Najwa Najar in the United States; Azza al-Hassan in Britain; and Ali Nassar in the Soviet Union. Hany Abu-Assad, Abed el-Salam Shehada, Nizar Hassan, Rashid Masharawi, and Elia Suleiman did not study cinema at all. Hanna Misleh arrived at it from anthropology, Muhammad Bakri and Salim Daw from acting.

Palestinian directors have been working in a context in which the basic conditions for cinema are lacking: they are in want of national institutions for the advancement of cinema, of production companies, of companies supplying equipment, of film laboratories, and of skilled crew members. As an industry, Palestinian cinema does not exist. A Palestinian filmmaker who wishes to produce a film is compelled to use foreign crews or to make do with unqualified local teams. The post-production has to be done elsewhere. The development of digital technology has allowed a number of directors to produce exceptional films with very low budgets—up to $20,000—using small cameras, working with local crews, occasionally acting as cinematographers themselves. Several celebrated directors have adopted this technique, and for some directors at the beginning of their careers it is the only option.[5] But even video productions have to be processed elsewhere.

The better-known directors have found a variety of sources to finance their films. Some have received international funding, mostly from European countries. Michel Khleifi's films were financed by Belgian, Dutch, French, and German sources;[6] Rashid Masharawi and Hany Abu-Assad found funding in the Netherlands.[7] Elia Suleiman drew on sponsors in the United States, Britain, and France.[8] Nizar Hassan was supported by sources in Sweden, Finland, and the United States.[9] Some directors were assisted by Israeli financial funds. They include Masharawi, Suleiman, Nassar, and Hassan, who were severely criticized in Arab countries for accepting such support.[10] Very few films enjoyed Palestinian funding,[11] and only one Palestinian film received financial aid nearly entirely from Arab money—Abu-Assad's film *Rana's Wedding* (*al-Quds fi yom akhar*, 2002), which was produced by the Palestinian Ministry of Culture with the help of funds secured from the Gulf states.

Even for these established directors the work cycle extends over many years, from the initial stage of the idea for a film through the development of the script to securing financial support to completing the production. Between 1980 and 2003 Palestinian directors made only twelve full-length fiction films and a few dozen documentaries, practically all of them on very small budgets.

Subhi a-Zubeidi and Azza al-Hassan produced their first films on altogether minuscule budgets. a-Zubeidi's *The Light at the End of the Tunnel* (*al-Daw' fi nihayat al-nafaq*, 2000), about Palestinian prisoners, was commissioned by a representative of the International Red Cross. The Red Cross imposed upon the director restrictions that are part of the organization's policies, which preclude a political approach. a-Zubeidi eventually reached an agreement with the representatives of the Red Cross: he produced two versions of the film, one compatible with the criteria of the organization that commissioned it, the other more personal and political. al-Hassan's *She, the Sindibad* (*Hiya al-Sindibad*, 1999) went through a similar process.

Palestinian cinema has faced great difficulty reaching its primary audience, the Palestinian public. Since the late 1970s, film theaters in the West Bank and Gaza have shut down one after the other. The two principal causes are television programs broadcast from Arab countries or from Israel and the deterioration in the state of security. But even if film theaters had not shut down, Israeli censors and the military government probably would have put deliberate obstacles in the way of screening Palestinian films in the West Bank and Gaza. Cultural and artistic events that gave expression to Palestinian nationalism were perceived by the Israeli military government as acts of incitement. For every fine arts exhibition or poetry and theatrical event, special permission from the Israeli government was required. Usually such requests were denied. While Palestinian films stirred up considerable interest at international festivals and were shown commercially around the world, they had difficulty reaching their target audience in the West Bank, Gaza, and Israel proper.

Palestinian films did not reach their natural audiences in the Arab countries, either. Arab authorities treated Palestinian films with the same mistrust as the Israelis did. It seems they were afraid of the nationalistic contents and the "instigating" messages. When Palestinian films were allowed to be shown in Arab countries, the screenings were limited to special occasions such as festivals and cultural events. Commercial screenings of Khleifi's *Wedding in Galilee* were permitted only in Tunisia. Another of his films, *Tale of the Three Jewels*, was commercially released in Tunisia and Jordan. As far as we know, only very few Palestinian films circulated commercially in Arab countries.

Major efforts to acquaint Palestinian audiences with their cinema started in the early 1990s. In 1992 the Jerusalem Film Institute in East Jerusalem organized the first festival dedicated to Palestinian films. Thirty-two films produced since 1980 participated. The festival hosted ten filmmakers, some of whom met their Palestinian audience for the first time. The films were screened in East Jerusalem and in Nazareth, and some were shown in Nablus and Gaza as well. The second festival, in 1993, dedicated the Jerusalem Film Institute to alternative Arab cinema and showed additional Palestinian films. After the Palestinian

Authority was established in 1994 following the Oslo Accords and until the second Intifada erupted in October 2000, similar festivals were held in the West Bank. A few were held in Gaza as well.

At the same time, attempts were made to launch mobile cinema units to bring films to villages and the refugee camps. The first unit was initiated by the Jerusalem Film Institute and operated from 1992 to 1995. A second unit was set up by the Cinematic Production and Distribution Center in Ramallah, headed by Rashid Masharawi. It functioned from 1997 until 2000, when it was closed upon the outbreak of the second Intifada.

After the Oslo Accords, cinemas reopened in the cities of the West Bank and Gaza, but they were closed again in 2000 during the second Intifadah. Now two theaters in Ramallah screen films on a daily basis; they show mainly commercial films but some Palestinian films as well. In Nazareth a cinematheque was established, and films are screened in Beit Leham and Jerusalem. In Gaza, fundamentalist Muslims set the local theater on fire, and it has not reopened since.

In recent years, Arab satellite television channels have begun to show more interest in screening Palestinian films. They air Khleifi's and Masharawi's films from time to time. The satellite-broadcasting network Orbit, owned by Saudi Arabian media tycoons, even participated in the funding of Muhammad Bakri's *Jenin, Jenin* (2002). Suleiman's film *Divine Intervention* (*Yad ilahiya*) is rarely broadcast to the general public on Arab television networks, yet it has appeared on the pay-per-view film list of home cinema in the Gulf area.

Khleifi established himself as a director in the 1980s, and other important directors like Rashid Masharawi, Ali Nassar, and Elia Suleiman soon followed. More recently filmmakers including Hany Abu-Assad, Tawfiq Abu Wael, Juliano Mer, and Subhi a-Zubeidi joined them. Abu-Assad has described the evolution of Palestinian cinema thus: "Michel Khleifi cleared a path that had not existed before, Rashid Masharawi scattered the gravel, Elia Suleiman paved it, and I drive on it at 120 kilometers per hour" (2003).

All of these directors endeavor to tell the Palestinian historical narrative from a personal angle, thus escaping the image of an enchanted past frozen in the present. In that way, they attempt to create a flow of vivid experience-based memory connecting daily life with what preceded it and what will follow it. Yet, maintaining the normal historical sequence became ever more difficult with the two waves of uprising—the first Intifada in 1987 and the second in 2000; the attempts at reconciliation, Oslo Accords A and B, and their failure; the expansion of the settlements; the large number of roadblocks; and the intensification of terrorist attacks.

When mundane life becomes an ongoing torment, when it is characterized less by diversity and more by a static, passive, and irremediable nature, time stops and the historical sequence is interrupted. This interruption, the experience of being stuck in the present, is what revives and recreates the lost idyllic past and particularly the trauma that disturbed that idyll. If there is "no direct line from the home to the place of birth, to school" and if "all events are accidental, all progression is a regression" (Said and Mohr 1999), the imaginary past remains the only vital and enduring time.

Generally, one might say the new films start out from the ambivalence in Khleifi's films. But even when they endeavor to replace the interrupted traumatic time with the mundane everyday and shape a private diverse life in the present, within a historical flow, in many cases they eventually establish the frozen national past. Historical events clarify why it is so difficult for Palestinian cinema to disengage from past traumas and create a time sequence in which there is a place for memory and where life in the present is a basis for the creation of the future.

This difficulty intensified in the context of the problematic dialogue with the political establishments as well as with critics and audiences who demanded that their cinema "close ranks" during a trying phase of the national struggle. On the one hand, films created during those years were attempts to shape a coherent history, beginning in the past and progressing toward the future. They even succeeded in carving histories out of authentic personal memories. But in many films the mythic images that revive the past and its loss in the present dominate.

Time standing still is the time in Tawfiq Abu Wael's *Waiting for Salah al-Din (Fi intizar Salah al-Din,* 2001) of the people waiting hours upon hours at the Erez roadblock, dragging their feet on winding roads detouring around Israeli army checkpoints, or waiting in line at the Ministry of the Interior on Ibn Shadad Street. Abu Wael presents five separate tales set in Jerusalem. These episodes are not concerned with heroic events or major disasters; instead they concentrate on the minor, ubiquitous grievances of everyday life. Everything in this film contributes to the sense of distress experienced by people who are caught in static time in which the same meaningless actions are repeated over and over again—endless job hunts, houses rebuilt and demolished repeatedly, Sisyphean efforts to operate fruit stands opposite the city walls even as police officers confiscate the merchandise. This is not merely a static time but also a "marginal" one—it flows in a place where there are no occurrences or plots, leading nowhere toward no goal. Out of this barren time, people attempt to find hope, to find a story and a purpose. And they find them in the distant time appearing as currently present—beyond all the aimless expectations, there is one great anticipation reflected by the title, the anticipation of Salah al-Din, a hero in battling the Crusaders.

Palestinian cinema has endeavored to discard the notion of being stuck in the present by attaching itself to subjective, private memory. Subhi a-Zubeidi's *My Private Map* (*Kharitati al-khassa jiddan*, 1998), for example, marks the distance between the present and the past through a journey in time. The film recounts two histories. The first is the chronicle of the Jilazun refugee camp, where the director grew up, from the establishment of the camp to the time of filming. The second is the earlier story of life in Palestine and the people's expulsion from it. The film does not revive the past in the present in a manner typical of the documentaries of the 1970s. It emphasizes the process of remembering the past rather than the past itself.

The films of Rashid Masharawi serve as an example for both tendencies, the construction of a living historical sequence and the freezing of the past in the present. Masharawi's protagonists live and struggle in a dead-end present without any prospect of a better future. Aspirations to change the present situation invariably turn to hopelessness as calamity is followed by catastrophe. This fate, described exclusively in the present, evokes the initial crisis, the distant defeat, echoing it as the traumatic return of the repressed. Masharawi's films have enjoyed critical acclaim. *Curfew* (*Hatta ish'ar akhar*, 1993) was screened during Critics' Week at the Cannes Festival and won several prizes, among them first place at the 1994 Cairo International Film Festival. *Haifa* (1995) was screened as a 1995 Cannes Festival Official Choice,[12] and *Waiting* (*Attente*, 2005) was broadcast by Arte France and screened in many festivals, including Venice, Toronto, London, Dubai, and Jerusalem.[13]

The artistic success of Masharawi's films stems from the realistic and vibrant manner in which they describe Palestinian life under the occupation. It is a result of the way they delineate the refugees' here-and-now daily struggle for survival within a space that has been gradually diminishing from the time Palestinians were driven out of their native villages and gathered in refugee camps up to the period of siege that they endured during the second Intifada. Yet, the more the past in these films is portrayed in a vivacious and detailed way, the more it is experienced as a static past. The ideal past is not Khleifi's creation, but as for him it is the past before 1948, the traumatic point in time when the disengagement from that ideal occurred.

Perhaps the difference between Khleifi's films, which reconstruct the country's idyllic past, and Masharawi's films, which resurrect its loss, is rooted in the different backgrounds of the two directors. While Khleifi grew up in Israel in the landscapes of pre-1948 Palestine, Masharawi matured in a refugee camp and spent most of his youth as a poor laborer in Israel. The landscapes of the past also permeate the films of other directors such as Nizar Hassan (*Independence*) and Ali Nassar (*The Milky Way* and *In the Ninth Month*) who grew up in Israel.

The difference between Elia Suleiman's two feature films, *Chronicle of a Disappearance* and *Divine Intervention*, best illustrates what transpired in Palestinian society and its cinema in the time between the peace accords and the outbreak of the second Intifadah, between the "calm before the storm" and the period of "total destruction and disintegration" (Suleiman in Prokhoris and Wavelet 1999, n.p.).[14] In *Chronicle of a Disappearance* various spaces appear. The early part of the film focuses on Nazareth, on a local coffee shop, the street, a souvenir shop, and the home of Suleiman's parents. The living room is presented, the kitchen, the father playing backgammon, the mother conversing with her neighbors. From this house, from this town, the film sets sail and wanders around the country. It reaches the Acre shore, the Sea of Galilee, the road to Jericho, and the Tel Aviv promenade. The second part of the film is set in Jerusalem. Different locations in the city are represented: East Jerusalem and the American Colony hotel, the office of a real estate agent, the director's house, and the road leading from the Mount of Olives to the Wall and the Al Aqsa mosque. These spaces are congested and threatened, always shot through a car window, but it is possible to reside there, even if life is fraught with violence.

In *Divine Intervention*, in contrast, we find almost no open spaces and no past times. All we see is a small grove to which Santa Claus flees from those attempting to kill him; a private yard into which one of the neighbors discards his rubbish while another repeatedly cleans the yard, piling the garbage up to a single heap; a narrow street leading to the house of the director's father, filmed through the car window; a street with an abandoned bus stop where no bus will arrive; a house roof where one of the neighbors collects bottles while two elderly men observe him. The father's house is reduced mainly to the kitchen, and instead of the Jerusalem sights, the A-Ram roadblock separating Jerusalem and Ramallah appears. Daily life has deteriorated into a routine full of hate, rage, and friction. In this disturbed present life, the past gradually vanishes and is replaced by fantastic plans for exploits that would change this unbearable situation: the bombardment of a tank with a peach pit, a balloon adorned with Arafat's image sailing beyond roadblocks, ninja combat against Israeli agents.

Abu-Assad's *Paradise Now* (*al-Janna al-an*, 2005) was the first Palestinian film to reach an international audience. It won the European Film Academy Award for Best Script and the Golden Globe's Best Foreign Film award and was nominated for Best Foreign Film at the Academy Awards. *Paradise Now* was a German, Dutch, and French co-production presented at the Oscars as a Palestinian film. From the onset, the film was highly controversial in Israel, since it was the first Palestinian feature film to directly address the issue of suicide attackers. Abu-Assad and producer Amir Harel applied in 2003 for a public grant from the Israeli Film Fund. Several lectors denied their request, and one, the writer Irit Linor, harshly criticized the work as "a moving and high-brow Nazi film" (2006). After *Paradise Now* won the Golden Globe award, no Israeli distributor agreed to acquire the film. It was only screened at the Jerusalem cinematheque, enjoying little success.

Some of the debate concerning the film was unnecessary. The real topic of *Paradise Now* is not the "Paradise" but the "Now." The film does not deal so much with the eternal life promised suicide bombers as with the present in which they are living, the life of Palestinians in the West Bank and Gaza, the subject of all the Palestinian films produced in recent years. It is a distressed time, frozen, repeating itself, halting, and threatening to burst, explode, burn, or overflow. From this perspective the film may be understood as an attempt to replace the time of desperation and all that appeared in earlier films with eternity in heaven, after the terrorist act, and with a time of action and pursuit. Thus the first part of the film is constructed as a long anticipation and preparation for the terrorist act, while its second part is set up as a Hollywood chase after one of the protagonists. This structure is probably what was responsible for the film's success where better, more important films failed.[15]

Several other films demonstrate the tendency of Palestinian cinema, after the second Intifadah, to transcend the boundaries that fixed it within the historical and geographical trauma, within a state of distress caused by a seemingly endless occupation. Juliano Mer's *Arna's Children* (2003), Tawfiq Abu Wael's first feature film, *Thirst* (ʿ*Atash*, 2004), Annemarie Jacir's *Salt of This Sea* (*Milh hadha al-bahr*, 2008), Masharawi's *Laila's Birthday* (*Eid milad Layla*, 2008), and Suleiman's *The Time that Remains* (*al-Waqt al-baqi/Le temps qu'il reste*, 2009) may be understood in these terms. They move beyond trauma and distress to rebellion or to desperation begetting death and destruction.

NOTES

This essay is based on research that was supported by the Israeli Science Foundation (grant No. 786/03) and the Israeli-Palestinian Science Organization (IPSO). It draws on Gertz and Khleifi 2007.

1. For analyses of Palestinian cinema see Bresheeth 2002a,b; Hennebelle and Khayati 1977; Shafik 2007; and Shohat and Stam 1994.
2. See, for example, Mustafa Abu Ali's film *Zionist Aggression* (*'Udwan sihyuni*, 1973).
3. On *Tale of the Three Jewels* see the essay devoted to the film in this volume.
4. This is not to be confused with the "Revolutionary Cinema," which operated in the framework of the PLO during the Beirut period.
5. Subhi a-Zubeidi, Azza al-Hassan, Najwa Najar, and Ghada Tirawai began their careers with video productions.
6. *Fertile Memory* (1980) was prefinanced by the German television channel ZDF, the Dutch network IKON, and the Netherlands Organization for International Development Cooperation. *The An-Naim Route* (1981) was produced by the Belgian network RTBF. *Maloul Celebrates Its Destruction* (*Malul tahtafil bi-damariha*, 1984) was mainly financed by the Brussels Foundation for Audio-Visual Arts. *Wedding in Galilee* (1987) was a joint Belgian-French-German production that drew on the Belgian and French departments of culture, the German network ZDF, and other sources; its budget of $1,250,000 was about one-fifth the cost of a European film of the same scale. Most of the financing for *Tale of the Three Jewels* (1994) came from the BBC. *Canticle of the Stone* (1990) was largely financed by the Franco-German television network ARTE.
7. Rashid Masharawi failed in his attempt to avoid the problems of foreign financial support by founding a production company comprised exclusively of Palestinians. Abu-Assad's *Nazareth 2000* (*al-Nasira 2000*, 2000) and *Ford Transit* (2002) were produced mainly with Dutch funding.
8. Suleiman's *Introduction to the End of an Argument* (*Muqaddima li-nihayat jidal*, 1990) was produced with the aid of U.S. funds, and his *Divine Intervention* (*Yad ilahiya*, 2002) was financed in France.
9. Hassan's *Invasion* (*Ijtiyah*, 2003) was financed by Swedish television, the Finnish Department of Foreign Affairs Fund, the American Sundance Institute, and the Lebanese company ash-Shahed, in addition to private financial support.
10. Masharawi's *Passport* (*Jawaz safar*, 1986), *The Shelter* (*al-Malja'*, 1989), *The Magician* (*al-Sahir*, 1992), and *Tension* (*Tawattur*, 1998) were financed by Israeli funds. Suleiman's *Chronicle of a Disappearance* (*Sijill ikhtifa'*, 1996) was financed mostly by the Israeli Fund for Quality Films. Nassar's *The Milky Way* (*Darb al-tabana*, 1997) and *In the Ninth Month* (*Fi al-shahr al-tasi'*, 2002) were chiefly funded by the Israeli Film Fund. Hassan's first major film, *Independence* (*Istiqlal*, 1994), was funded by the Israeli Channel Two, *Jasmine* (*Yasmin*, 1996) by Channel One and the New Israeli Fund, and *Cut* (2000) mostly by an anonymous European source and the New Israeli Fund.
11. *Myth* (*Ostura*, 1998) was almost entirely funded by the director, Nizar Hassan, with additional help from an anonymous Palestinian source and the Nazareth touring

company Nazarine Tours. *His Defiance* (*Tahaddi*, 2001) was financed mostly by Palestinian sources.
12. The category allows the film the privilege of using the title Official Choice of the Cannes Film Festival but does not bestow the right to compete for the Golden Palm award.
13. On *Waiting* see the essay devoted to the film in this volume.
14. See also Brooks 2003.
15. On *Paradise Now* see the essay devoted to the film in this volume.

REFERENCES

Abu-Assad, Hany. 2003. Interview by George Khleifi, Jerusalem.
Bresheeth, Haim. 2002a. "Telling the Stories of Heim and Heimat, Home and Exile: Recent Palestinian Films and the Iconic Parable of the Invisible Palestine." *Intellect* 1 (1): 24–39.
———. 2002b. "A Symphony of Absence: Borders and Liminality in Elia Suleiman's *Chronicle of a Disappearance*." *Framework*, 43, no. 2 (Fall): 71–84.
Brooks, Xan. 2003. "When We Started Shooting, So Did They." Interview with Elia Suleiman, *The Guardian*, January 13.
Farid, Samir. n.d. *Palestinian Cinema in the Occupied Land* (in Arabic). Cairo: Film Collection, Public Authority for Cultural Institutions.
Gertz, Nurith, and George Khleifi. 2007. *Space and Memory in Palestinian Cinema*. Edinburgh: Edinburgh University Press; Bloomington: Indiana University Press.
Hennebelle, Guy, and Khémaïs Khayati. 1977. *La Palestine et le cinéma*. Paris: E. 100.
Linor, Irit, 2006. "Anti Semitism Now." www.ynet.co.il, February 7.
Mdanat, Adnan, ed. 1990. *The Palestinian Encyclopedia*, vol. 4 (in Arabic).
Prokhoris, Sabine, and Christophe Wavelet. 1999. Interview with Elia Suleiman, *Vacarme*, May. www.vacarme.eu.org.
Said, Edward, and Jean Mohr. 1999. *After the Last Sky: Palestinian Lives*, 2d edition. New York: Columbia University Press.
Shafik, Viola. 2001. "Cinema in Palestine." In *Companion Encyclopedia of Middle Eastern and North African Film*, ed. Oliver Leaman, 509–532. London: Routledge.
———. 2007. *Arab Cinema: History and Cultural Identity*. Revised edition. Cairo: American University in Cairo Press.
Shohat, Ella, and Robert Stam. 1994. *Unthinking Eurocentrism: Multiculturalism and the Media*. New York: Routledge.

Composite from http://www.moviecovers.com/film/titre_ATTENTE.html and http://www.sudplanete.net/_uploads/images/films/MASHARAWI_Rachid_2005_Attente_poster.jpg

*Waiting**
A Scattered People Waiting for a Shared Future

NADIA YAQUB

The plot of *Waiting* is simple—three Palestinians from the Gaza Strip—Ahmad, a filmmaker and reluctant director of the project; Bissan, a television journalist; and Lumière, a cameraman—travel to refugee camps in Jordan, Syria, and Lebanon to audition actors for a new national theater under construction in Gaza. The film chronicles their interactions with Palestinians they meet during their journey. As they travel, they receive periodic updates from Abu Jamil, the director of the national theater, about construction progress in Gaza. The film ends on a somber note: stranded in Lebanon, they hear that the theater has been bombed, borders are closed, and they cannot return to Gaza. Within this simple structure, however, director Rashid Masharawi addresses questions surrounding Palestinian identity and its relationship to time and place that Palestinians are treating with increasing urgency. Masharawi's work is particularly important because he is the only contemporary director of feature films from Gaza and the only one born and raised as a refugee. This background is evident in both his perspective and subject matter; Masharawi takes Palestinian refugees outside Israel/Palestine as a major theme and explores what binds them culturally and experientially with their compatriots within the borders of the homeland.

How to define a collective identity for Palestinians whose historical experiences since 1948 have been widely divergent—in exile, under occupation, and as citizens of the state of Israel—is a central challenge of Palestinian intellectuals and artists. The challenge has been not just to imagine a Palestinian community but to imagine one that can be sustained while the geographic

---

* *Waiting/Intizar.* 2005. Directed by Rashid Masharawi; written by Rashid Masharawi and Oscar Kronop. Produced by Silkroad Production (France), Cinema Production Center (Occupied Territories), and 2M Télévision (Morocco). Distributed by Les Films du Losange. 88 minutes.

and temporal site to which it refers, pre-1948 Palestine, recedes into history. *Waiting* directly addresses this challenge. The project of staffing the theater that frames this film is inherently inclusive. Abu Jamil's decision to audition refugees residing outside of Palestine/Israel is an attempt to bridge the political and geographical factors that separate Gazans from the diaspora. However, his insistence on inclusiveness signals the very divisions he seeks to bridge. Thus, the fissures that Abu Jamil wants to heal are, paradoxically, brought to the fore by his efforts. The paradox is not lost on Masharawi, who mirrored Abu Jamil's efforts in the making of his own film. "It was important for me to bring together these Palestinian actors living in various countries into one film," he says. "Most are unable to return to Palestine. In a way, their participation in *Waiting* is their way of travelling back" (n.d.).

As the film's title suggests, Ahmad eventually identifies waiting as the quintessential Palestinian experience.[1] Much of the film records the types of waiting that Palestinians do. On a national level there is the waiting for return and for statehood that Palestinians have endured for sixty years. The film asks, provocatively, whether that is a long or short time. At the film's start, Ahmad is tired of waiting and ready to relinquish the idea of Palestine, but it is he who later convinces Bissan that their waiting is but a brief moment within the context of cosmic history. In contrast, the urgency of time passing is expressed in talk about European Union deadlines and audition timetables. It emerges that waiting is what Palestinians do most of the time. They are, in Masharawi's words, "professional waiters" (in Bedarida 2006). They wait at checkpoints and borders, for hotel rooms, for a turn to audition, and for orders from the film director. Bissan has waited ten years to be reunited with her father. Her stepmother has waited seven months for him to return from Syria. At a demonstration, Palestinians wait through a moment of silence commemorating their martyrs. Palestinian women wait in line to fill water jugs from a communal spigot. A disabled man awaits a visa to emigrate to Canada. Palestinians wait with or without patience, quietly or noisily. They wait standing, sitting, lying down, and pacing. They wait in private and public spaces.

While Masharawi has identified the liminal act of waiting as the experience that binds Palestinians together, he identifies the spaces of that waiting as liminal as well. Ironically, to find the best actors for this nationalist project, Abu Jamil sends the crew *outside* the borders of historic Palestine. Thus the project itself suggests that contemporary Palestinian-ness may not lie within a geographically defined Palestine. To be Palestinian means to live apart from one's homeland, for even those who reside in their ancestral homes do not live within

Lumière films Palestinian refugees in Jordan waiting to audition.

a Palestinian state. If the quintessential Palestinian experience is waiting for the return, waiting for statehood, and all the waiting—at borders, water spigots, theater auditions—that results from dispossession, then it follows that contemporary Palestine, that is, the locus of contemporary Palestinian-ness, must exist "betwixt and between" *spatially* as well.

That contemporary imagined Palestine exists outside of historical Palestine is informed as much by the Palestine that was left in 1948 as it is by the Palestine that Palestinians hope for in a future state. At one point Lumière tells Bissan that the refugees remember a Palestine that is more beautiful than the one he lives in. Here the character is voicing Masharawi's own thoughts: "For most refugees in other countries, Palestine is remembered as a paradise of sun and olive trees. Those who were forced to leave fifty years ago can't imagine today's settlements, checkpoints, curfews" (n.d.). Significantly, *Waiting* portrays neither the Palestine of checkpoints, settlements, and curfews that Masharawi has shot in other films nor the idyllic Palestine of the refugees' memories. Rather, he depicts the fixed desire of the refugees to return and the effect that desire has on Ahmad's cynicism. By igniting Ahmad's belief in the theater project, the refugees' imagined Palestine proves stronger than Ahmad's own experience with violence and confinement there.

Powerful though this imagined Palestine may be, it is not a physical space in which Palestinian bodies can exist in the present. Physical spaces occupied by Palestinians in *Waiting* are defined by claustrophobia and travel. As in his earlier films, the cinematography in *Waiting* is characterized by cramped spaces (Gertz 2004). Landscape shots are brief and always followed by contrasting shots of the limited view characters have from their taxi windows. They see the crowded hills of Amman, the billboard-lined highways that connect Amman, Damascus, and Beirut, and, of course, borders. They are caught in traffic jams and navigate the narrow alleyways of refugee camps. Panning shots are tightly focused on shops and busy sidewalks and rarely show any sky. Even a scene of Ahmad and Bissan's meeting at a beachfront café is shot such that the characters are hemmed in rather than released by the open sea. Ahmad sits with his back to the water, his body position belying his plan to leave the country. His head is framed by the sea such that his desire to travel is evoked, but the high horizon and lack of deep focus suggest he is trapped rather than liberated by the water.

Although much of the film is shot in enclosed spaces, it shows little of Palestinian domestic life. The three main characters are never depicted in their homes. Scenes shot within the home of Abu Ziyad, the crew's host in Jordan, are so tightly framed around people that we do not get a sense of its layout, and the décor reveals little if any personal details about the family. There are no scenes of cooking, cleaning, or eating family meals. Masharawi's earlier film *Curfew* (*Hatta ish'ar akhar*, 1993) focuses almost entirely on the domestic spaces of a Palestinian refugee camp, which suggests he consciously chose to avoid the private sphere in *Waiting*. He is not concerned here with depicting Palestinians' homes outside the homeland, and his avoidance of such spaces reinforces the film's sense of limbo.

One of the recurring cramped spaces in *Waiting* is the interior of the taxis in which the crew members ride through Jordan and Syria to Lebanon. Masharawi's use of this international journey as a structuring device for his film is ironic, for such mobility is impossible for most Palestinians (Roy 2006). The ease with which these Gazans cross borders is unrealistic, coding the journey as a symbolic rather than mimetic depiction of Palestinian lived reality. In this regard *Waiting* is not a roadblock movie, a genre that treats the social significance of the political impediments to Palestinian mobility (Gertz and Khleifi 2005). The distinction is suggested in the opening scene when Ahmad passes through the Eretz crossing. His bag is searched, and he does speak later of having been detained for hours, but the scene lacks the crowds, potential for violence, and abuse of power that one finds in films that thematize impediments to Palestinian mobility.

However, Masharawi does exploit features of the road-movie genre in *Waiting*. In road movies characters' relationship to the vehicles in which they travel are indices of the ability to move and/or communicate quickly across space that is important to functioning independently in the modern world. In this regard it is significant that Ahmad and his crew do not drive but rather rely on public transportation. The crew is mobile, but their mobility does not connote the independence, control, or agency, either actual or illusory, that is suggested when characters drive themselves.

Road movies often explore their characters' journeys into or out of society. Jordan, Syria, and Lebanon are given short shrift in the film, however, and the characters have little interaction with anyone outside the Palestinian refugee camps. This lack of interaction with a larger Arab environment is directly related to Masharawi's treatment of space. While his earlier films eloquently depict the claustrophobia of Palestinian spaces under occupation, *Waiting* illustrates that exile does not relieve Palestinians from this condition; claustrophobia, like waiting, is a defining feature of contemporary Palestinian existence.

Masharawi also exploits the ironic distance inherent within the road-movie genre. By filming the camps through the eyes of the traveling crew, he depicts simultaneously the refugees and the effect on the Gazans of their encounters with them. As the film progresses, this ironic distance is paradoxically shortened even as the crew's experiences grow ever more alien. In Jordan Ahmad is annoyed with the refugees' insistence on using his video to communicate with the homeland. In Damascus he cannot bear the celebration of Palestinian identity that is performed in Palestinian folk dancing. In Lebanon all three crew members are stunned by the deprivation and violence that characterize camp life. And yet it is in Lebanon, an utterly alienating and dystopic space, that they realize the similarities between their own condition and that of the refugees.[2]

Their ironic perspective makes road movies ideal vehicles for diasporic filmmakers who bring to their subjects a critical eye born of their experiences abroad (Naficy 2001). In this regard Masharawi's position is unusual in that he is not returning to his homeland but exploring Palestinian identity in places he has never lived. The protagonist, an *alter ego* for Masharawi, bears the added burden of the experiential and geographic difference that separates him and his film crew from the Palestinian refugees they meet. Living on Palestinian soil, the crew members do not know the refugees' yearning to return until they find themselves stranded in Lebanon, where they are surrounded by people who do not look like themselves (maimed men and veiled women) and who engage in practices they do not share (a political demonstration). The sense of alienation at the end of the film is not an expression of Masharawi's exile from Palestine but rather a graphic representation of the diaspora that all Palestinians share. In other words, the quest to find what binds all Palestinians has been successful, but the shared experience that has been discovered is a bitter one indeed.

Rashid Masharawi (second from right) with actors and crew.
Courtesy Eurozoom, © Eurozoom

Waiting, like most Palestinian feature films, is funded largely by European sources, a circumstance that Masharawi addresses obliquely in the running motif of European Union support for the theater project. He does not directly criticize the role of the E.U. in Palestinian affairs, but its support—and Palestinian dependence on it—are explicitly tied to the deformed nature of authority in the film. Palestinian reliance on international support is ubiquitous; the United Nations Relief and Works Agency (UNRWA) feeds Palestinian children. E.U. documents, not Palestinian passports, get the crew across international borders. Palestinian institutional authority is embodied in Abu Jamil, who not only is inaccessible—throughout most of the film he exists only as a voice on Bissan's cell phone—but also is bizarrely beholden to the European Union. He refers to the E.U., its funding, and the constraints it imposes on him whenever he speaks. Thus, Abu Jamil is less a Palestinian authority figure than a conduit for international attempts to manipulate Palestinian behavior. Ahmad's relationship with authority is different. He participates in the project against his will and better judgment. Lumière flouts his authority with silence, while Bissan scolds him at every turn. Actors argue with him and mostly get their own way. As an artist, he finds his voice, so to speak, not within the framework of this foreign-funded project but in the behavior of ordinary Palestinians.

Ahmad's imperfect authority contrasts with that of Bissan, who at first seems more adept than Ahmad. Bissan's femininity is overdetermined; she wears flowing dresses and pants that accentuate the lines of her body, and she changes her hairstyle frequently and conspicuously. As the crew crosses the border into Jordan, the contents of her bag spill out while it is being checked, revealing cosmetics and a frilly velvet bag. Despite her femininity, Bissan is emphatically confident in the public sphere. When she and Ahmad meet for the first time, it is at a café that she frequents, and she, not he, places their order. Moreover, as a news anchor for Palestinian television, she is a celebrity and frequently recognized as such by the refugees she meets. Because of her skills as a communicator and networker she appears more effective than Ahmad. She gets Lumière hired onto the project over Ahmad's protests and can talk to both men, although they fail to communicate with each other. One sympathizes with her when she chides Ahmad for his rude behavior. However, in the end she does not succeed in bridging the gaps dividing Palestinian characters. She is an impediment to true, two-way communication between Ahmad and Abu Jamil and never mends the rift between Ahmad and Lumière. She fails to locate her father and, despite her better access to Palestinian institutional authority, finds herself in the same predicament as her male companions in the end. In *Waiting*, women bring important skills to the national project and have a role to play in the public sphere, but like men, they are stymied by the circumstances that keep all Palestinians in a state of limbo.

Bissan also embodies a feistiness that Masharawi identifies as a particularly Palestinian trait. The refugees may be leaderless victims of international politics and economically reliant on the handouts of international institutions, but they have individual perspectives and desires and are not afraid to express them. This spirit is part of an underlying humanism that counters the film's dark message. As is true of Masharawi's earlier films (Gertz 2004), the movement in *Waiting* is toward ever narrower spaces and diminishing opportunities. However, the film insists on the humanity of all its characters, major and minor; they are fully formed, with individual quirks and interests.

The film suggests alternative avenues for Palestinian motility. Most important are the possibilities inherent in film itself, a theme Masharawi also addresses in *Ticket to Jerusalem* (*Tadhkira ila al-quds*, 2002).[3] In that film the protagonist's drive to screen movies impels him to travel to Jerusalem, where he overcomes the physical obstacles thrown up by politics and creates a shared Palestinian experience. In *Waiting* viewers are first alerted to the motility inherent in film when the first "actor" in Jordan uses his audition to communicate with relatives in the West Bank. By the time the crew reaches Damascus, Ahmad reluctantly recognizes the communicative power of film when he allows a young mother and her daughter to send a video message to the girl's father "inside."

Film, which is ever present in the scenes of Lumière shooting video and in the clips of his footage that are interspersed throughout, contrasts with the national theater project it is supposed to serve. While the theater project is distant and ineffective, film is intimate and transformative. Lumière's camera work is loving and respectful; his subjects look into the camera with quiet dignity. Most importantly, this footage allows Ahmad to finally "see" the Palestinian people and through that vision reengage with the Palestinian idea.

Near the end of the film there is a telling exchange between the crew and a refugee in Lebanon. As they watch the bombing of the theater on television, twice Ahmad and Bissan ask the older man about the theater, and twice he answers them with a statement about the human casualties. In this deceptively simple film that turns notions of time and place on their heads and interrogates the roles of art, exile, and institutions in society, there is also a deceptively simple message: in the end, however bad the politics, it is people, ordinary Palestinians, who matter. People, not ideologies and institutions, give meaning to struggle and inspiration to artists. It is this message and Masharawi's ability to convey it visually through his film portraits of refugees that save *Waiting*, despite its realism, from paralyzing pessimism.

NOTES

1. Editor's note: The French poster, reproduced here, emphasizes the Palestinian condition of waiting, contrasts a scene of the protagonists watching a dance performance with the destruction wrought in Gaza, and calls the film "the first road movie that doesn't lead anywhere."
2. The crew's alienation in Lebanon is best captured when their driver takes them to the inadequate memorial for the 1982 massacre of Sabra and Shatila. For more on the memorial see Khalili 2005, 41–44.
3. Masharawi says that "cinema has created a strong Palestinian homeland that revives geographic memory. Practically speaking, Palestinian cinema has been able to bring into being a Palestinian homeland that politicians and negotiations have not been able to realize. Even the Intifada has not been able to bring into being the homeland that exists in cinema" (in al-Jazeera 2006; my translation).

REFERENCES

Bedarida, Catherine. 2006. "Israël-Palestine, mémoires plurielles." *Le Monde,* January 29.

Gertz, Nurith. 2004. "The Stone at the Top of the Mountain: The Films of Rashid Masharawi." *Journal of Palestine Studies* 34 (1): 23–36.

Gertz, Nurith, and George Khleifi. 2005. "Palestinian 'Roadblock Movies.'" *Geopolitics* 10:316–334.

al-Jazeera. 2006. "Rashid Masharawi . . . al-sinima al-filastiniya." October 2. http://www.aljazeera.net/NR/exeres/F78C7121-652F-46AC-91E4-EEA88CF27C8F.htm (accessed December 7, 2007).

Khalili, Laleh. 2005. "Places of Memory and Mourning: Palestinian Commemoration in the Refugee Camps of Lebanon." *Comparative Studies of South Asia, Africa and the Middle East* 25 (1): 30–45.

Masharawi, Rashid. n.d. "Comments from the Director." Silkroad Production press kit. http://www.silkroadproduction.com/waiting/WAITING-Flyer-Text.doc (accessed December 7, 2007).

Naficy, Hamid. 2001. *An Accented Cinema: Exilic and Diasporic Filmmaking.* Princeton, NJ: Princeton University Press.

Roy, Anne. 2006. "Temps palestinien." *L'Humanité,* January 28. http://www.humanite.fr/2006-01-28_Medias_Temps-palestinien (accessed December 7, 2007).

Design by Yves Prince

Tale of the Three Jewels*
Children Living and Dreaming amid Violence in Gaza

NURITH GERTZ AND GEORGE KHLEIFI

Khleifi's film *Tale of the Three Jewels* (*Hikayat al-jawahir thalath*, 1994) is set in a refugee camp in Gaza, a nonplace where people live for the moment, remembering and yearning for the places from which they were deported or dreaming about other places. This is the liminal space in Homi Bhabha's terms (1990), existing in the territory of not belonging (Rogoff 2000) in an area of exiles who were displaced and lost their roots. This is a place where one does not wish to live and where one dreams about other places, in particular about Palestine. Even shooting in such a place was impossible, as Michel Khleifi has recounted (in SFJFF n.d.):

> We shot *Tale of the Three Jewels* after the Oslo accords and before the Israeli army pulled out of Gaza. There were areas in Gaza where the army did not enter. The day after we arrived with the film crew there was an explosion in Jerusalem. We started shooting on a Thursday and on Friday the Hebron Massacre took place. The country was in uproar; curfews, demonstration, deaths. The film schedule was cancelled and for 3 weeks I doubted our ability to shoot at all. Just to travel 2 or 3 miles was an adventure. Little by little we decided to stay and make the film in Gaza because it could be made ONLY in Gaza. By then we were considered mad and known by the locals as "The Fools."
>
> It is impossible to shoot a film like this with a crew of 30–40 people in secret. So the film script was submitted to the Israeli army from the start. The army said we can't film any scenes including weapons or demonstrations. I would have liked to shoot some scenes differently. For example, we filmed one

---

* *Tale of the Three Jewels/ Hikayat al-jawahir thalath*. 1994. Film written and directed by Michel Khleifi. Produced by Sindibad Films (Britain) and Sourat Films (Belgium). Distributed in the United States by Arab Film Distribution. 107 minutes.

scene with weapons anyway, when the four young men are killed, and we had to "steal" the images; that is why the camera in that scene is running.

In this respect, Michel Khleifi's second fiction film is entirely different from his first and his other early films, which were shot in Israel. *Tale of the Three Jewels* follows the daily life of the twelve-year-old protagonist, Yusef (Mohammed Nahhal), his mother (Bushra Qaraman), and his sister (Raida Adon). Yusef's father is in prison; his brother, wanted by the Israeli army, has gone into hiding; and the family manages life as best it can in the shadow of the Israeli army, of fences and watchtowers, under curfew orders. The boy attempts to escape from this nonplace into other spaces, and the camera accompanies and supports him.

The "other spaces" consist mainly of the idyllic Palestine of days gone by. These spaces usually resurface as part of the traumatic memories of the occupation and the expulsion. A blind old man (Makram Khouri), Yusef's friend, remembers how the man's father had clung to the soil and refused to abandon it and escape with the rest of his family. Yusef's mother recalls how their land was occupied while she was on the beach. His girlfriend's father (Muhammad Bakri) tells of how jewels in his mother's necklace were lost when the family fled from Jaffa. The film reports the memories of this trauma but also holds onto the time and place that preceded it. It thus materializes the absence in the presence and transfers what has occurred in Palestine, in the past, to the wrong time and place—to the camp in the present.

What is missing now is the landscape of Palestine, but it is reflected as though a reality in spaces around the refugee camp: in an oasis, in the sea, and in an orange grove. The blind old man speaks longingly of the land from which he escaped and recites a poem about a date palm.[1] From his recitation the camera cuts to a date palm in the Gaza oasis under which Yusef is walking. Yusef's father, when released from prison in a deranged state, rants about the oranges that surround him on all sides. These oranges, symbols of the country that the refugees have left, appear in the present, in the grove where the boy hides after he has decided to run away to South America.

As the camera follows the boy's wanderings along sandy landscapes of a desert oasis, on the seashore, and in other spaces around the refugee camp, it weaves a fantasy of a large space. It is not a real space but a post-traumatic reflection, a representation of the past in the present. The narrow, obstructed place of the camp is opened up. Shots of a barbed-wire fence, of a soldier in a watchtower, and of military vehicles are replaced with shots of the oasis, the sky

Yusef meets Saladin in a dream.

and the palm trees, the sea and the beach, the moon and the birds, seagulls on the waves. The camera and the poetic editing of the film hurdle the obstacles, burst into open nature, and construct a large space in lieu of the cloistered and cramped one where the characters live.

While the film expands the bordered space, it also deconstructs the borders, creating a fantasy of a border-free world. Yusef aspires to obliterate all borders. He wanders beyond the refugee camp to the oasis, the seashore, the orange grove, the town proper, where his girlfriend, Aida (Hana' Ne'meh), lives. Neither Gaza's internal borders nor the external borders constructed by the Israelis seem to hinder him. The map delineated by Yusef's endless roaming not only expands the national space; it also defines an open and wide area where a love story, a story that has nothing to do with nationhood, can take place. The film moves beyond the limits of Palestinian culture as well when Aida, a gypsy, spins tales of demons, spirits, and fairies. Her stories, including "The Tale of the Three Jewels," are based on folk stories from various cultures and religions.[2]

For Yusef, however, it is not enough to escape the cramped confines of the camp, of its memories and traditions. He wants to venture far away. According to the story that Aida's grandmother told her, three jewels from a precious necklace were lost in South America. Aida promises to marry Yusef if he recovers them. To accomplish this task, he tries to cross the border into Israel and find work there. When he fails, he hides in an orange crate in the hope of reaching Europe, where the oranges are exported, and from there to proceed to South America. Khleifi has set out the significance of breaching national borders of time and space:

> I based the script upon the prevalent, cultural, and religions traditions of the region: legends, folklore, belief in spirits, and so on. A historical space cannot be divided into community and religious segments—Jewish, Christian, Muslim—and I would add atheist, as well. I believe that everyone is entitled to inherit the legacy of the region, including the pre-monotheistic legacy of yesterday and the secularism of today. (1997, 12)

Crossing borders, Yusef embodies the complexity of Palestinian society, with its diverse classes, regions, and ideologies—a complexity that is not confined to national identity alone but recognizes an intermingling of perpetually changing identities, exiles, and borderless cultures that intertwine with each other.[3] This heterogeneity is linked to that of the different time sequences, replacing the uniform national time that reconstructs the static paradise of the past in the present.

In addition to the time sequences, different identities are linked in the film to national and gender issues. The occupation has damaged the adult men in Yusef's family: his brother is a fugitive in hiding, and when he comes home, he does so to bring a wounded friend; the head of the household is imprisoned, and when he returns home he is deranged. Against this defeated masculinity, Yusef, the film's protagonist, wishes to pave a path for himself that will lead him to a different kind of manhood. But for that to happen he must distance himself from his surroundings—the camp, the first Intifada, the prison—and find a place removed from the national struggle: "I must grow up; I must marry you," he tells Aida. With that cause in mind, he wishes to travel to South America to retrieve the lost jewels. The association of an alternative notion of masculinity with a new idea of space emerges from a picture that Yusef draws in school. The drawing shows a man in a woman's form, an androgynous creature of sorts, surrounded by the word "borders" repeated over and over again. The borders Yusef attempts to obliterate in his wanderings are not only those of space, class, and race but also the gender boundaries between the feminine and the masculine. These boundaries are blurred by the women around him, as well—his mother, his sister, his friend Aida. They dominate the world that Yusef inhabits at home and outside. They reflect the position of women at the time the film was shot.

In all his films Khleifi links masculinity to domination over the land and the homeland, with manliness as an expression of patriarchal rule over the family. In *Tale of the Three Jewels*, when women join the national struggle, it is still presented as a purely masculine matter. This is why many Arab critics regard the image of the women in Khleifi's films as a symbolic one. Abed al-Wahab al-Moadeb suggests a reason: "It is not surprising that Michel Khleifi chose to present a world of women. He did it in order to represent Palestine. He listened to the otherness of the oppressed women in his own society in order to embody his oppressed, helpless nation struggling to survive" (in Farid n.d., 54).

The role of women in *Tale of the Three Jewels* and in other films of Khleifi is not limited to a national one. Women in these films represent the voice of the oppressed in Palestinian society, the voice of those living in a patriarchal society. They offer an alternative that is based not on an "us/them" dichotomy but on hybridity, difference, and a variety of identities and loyalties. Khleifi explains:

> Back then, we thought simplistically that the whole world is against us and that the Zionists are everywhere. It may be so, but since childhood I've had my own outlook on the matter and I wanted to place it at the core of my cinematic expression. This outlook consisted of the belief that the Israelis derive their strength from our weakness and that our weakness, in turn, is not derived from Israeli strength but from the archaic structure of our Arab society: tribalism, patriarchy, religion, and community life. A person isn't recognized as an individual: men, women, and above all, women's rights [are disregarded]. (1979)

He later expands on this theme:

> The Palestinians, while being victims of oppression are also guilty of oppressing others: the rural population, the laborers, and the women. I have attempted to make a film about zero oppression... The oppressing Jews, who are they? They are themselves the victims of inhuman persecution. However, they still oppress another people, the Palestinians. And the Palestinians, are they merely victims, or are they victimizers as well? The answer is that they are both. Their society oppresses women and children... Things should be taken at all levels, there is no point in merely discussing the wrong done. This will not determine who the victim and who the oppressor is. We must unveil the systems and the logic that cause us to become potential oppressors and victims. In order to reach the depths, there was a need to penetrate the characters'

inner world, and for this purpose, one needed to disregard the borders between the documentary and the fictional. (2003)

The film particularly relates to the role of women in the first Intifada, when it was shot. Shohat and Stam suggest (1994) that the women in Khleifi's early films foreshadow processes that were to become more apparent after the first Intifada, when women went into the streets and took an active role in the uprising. This, they claim, led toward symbolic liberation and a change in the role of women. However, it should not be forgotten that the voices of Islamic forces grew louder during the Intifada, including those of Islamic resistance movements such as Hamas and the Islamic Jihad, which rose in opposition to the leadership of the PLO and Fatah. About a year after the outbreak of the Intifada, nearly all the women in Gaza were wearing the traditional head scarf, the *hijab* (Kimerling and Migdal 1993). Khleifi reflected on these contradictory facets of women's status in his film. On several occasions the women, and especially Yusef's sister, complain about the constraints of tradition and lack of freedom. At the same time, they hold the family together, control life in the camp, and offer an alternative to the national, masculine regime. Their power becomes very clear when Yusef creates a sort of symbiosis with them, with Aida in particular. He seems to unite with her in nature, among the animals, against the background of the fables that she tells him.

At the end of the film, its themes of the national and the personal, of the political and the fantastic resurface together. Israeli soldiers shoot Yusef after he emerges from a crate in the orange grove and turns to run toward the bird that his mother had released from its cage. *Tale of the Three Jewels* thus appears to conclude on the national narrative of repression and occupation that leads Yusef back to his national identity. However, the film has a second ending. After Yusef is shot, he rises up as if nothing had happened, the film reaffirming its fantastic dimension.

Michel Khleifi was born in Nazareth in 1950. In the mid-1960s he cultivated an interest in theater, like many other youngsters who perceived the theater as a means of sublime national cultural activity. Never thinking of cinema as an option, he dreamed of studying theater and television abroad. His flight was set for September 1970, the month that came to be known as Black September. Egyptian President Nasser had just been assassinated. Anticipating his departure, Khleifi visited East Jerusalem and purchased portraits of the adored president, such as were sold at every street corner there. On his way back to Nazareth, he was stopped and searched by a police officer when he changed buses in Afula.

Michel Khleifi with Mohammad Nahhal. Courtesy Sindibad Films

The officer found Nasser's portrait, ripped it apart, and beat Khleifi severely, to the encouraging cheers of Jewish boys of Khleifi's age. The bruise marks and the taste of the blatant insult followed him when, a few days later, he flew to Belgium to commence his theater and television studies.

The circumstances of his life—being born and raised in Nazareth, living many years in Belgium, his freedom of movement between his native home and Belgium—have fed the ambivalence in his films, which utilize Eastern as well as Western models of home and exile. This ambivalence became possible, among other reasons, because his production and distribution sources were varied. *Tale of the Three Jewels* was funded by the BBC, the One World Group of Broadcasters (an association of several European public broadcasters), and Televisión Española. The film was screened in numerous festivals worldwide to high critical acclaim.[4] In Palestine and Israel, however, it was shown in only a few limited settings: semi-private screenings in Jerusalem, Ramallah, and Nazareth and two screenings in Gaza, completely closed off by Israel at the time.[5]

NOTES

This essay is based on research supported by the Israeli Science Foundation (grant No. 786/03) and by the Israeli-Palestinian Science Organization (IPSO). It draws on Gertz and Khleifi 2008.

1. Here, blindness is related to the disconnection with the land and with losing the possibility to see it. On the connection between blindness and castration see Boyarin 1997, following Freud.
2. Editor's note: The French poster reproduced here conveys the poetics of a film in which childhood dreams and prepubescent love overcome an ever-threatening reality. Another French poster foregrounds Aida and Yusef dominating the reality of Israeli occupation and smiling to themselves.
3. See Khalidi 1997 for a description of the Palestinian identity as a mixture of region, family, clan, village, and pan-Arab components, including the identities of Palestinians in the diaspora. See also Bhabha 1990.
4. *Tale of the Three Jewels* was an official selection of the Cannes Film Festival, the Human Rights Watch International Film Festival, and the San Francisco Jewish Film Festival. The film won the Golden Butterfly at the Isfahan International Festival of Films for Children and Young Adults, the Grand prix des lycèens at the Nantes Film Festival, the Prix des elèves francophones at the Film Festival Ragazzi, Bellinzona, and the Silver Olive Tree and the Critics Prize at the Festival of Mediterranean Culture, Bastia.
5. On Michel Khleifi and his *œuvre* see "A Chronicle of Palestinian Cinema" in this volume; Gertz and Khleifi 2008, 74–100 and passim; and Khleifi 2006.

REFERENCES

Bhabha, Homi K. 1990. "Dissemination: Time, Narrative, and the Margins of the Modern Nation." In *Nation and Narration*, ed. Homi K. Bhabha, 291–320, London: Routledge.

Boyarin, Daniel. 1997. *Unheroic Conduct: The Rise of Heterosexuality and the Invention of the Jewish Man*. Berkeley: University of California Press.

Farid, Samir. n.d. *Palestinian Cinema in the Occupied Land* (in Arabic). Cairo: Film Collection, Public Authority for Cultural Institutions.

Gertz, Nurith, and George Khleifi. 2008. *Palestinian Cinema: Landscape, Trauma, and Memory*. Edinburgh: Edinburgh University Press; Bloomington: Indiana University Press.

Khalidi, Rashid, 1997. *Palestinian Identity*. New York: Columbia University Press.

Khleifi, Michel. 1997. "From Reality to Fiction, from Poverty to Expression." *El Pais* (Madrid), 12–13. n.d.

———. 2003. Interview by Nurith Gertz in Paris, September.
———. 2006. "From Reality to Fiction—From Poverty to Expression." In *Dreams of a Nation*, ed. Hamid Dabashi, 43–57. London: Verso.
Kimerling, Baruch, and Joel Migdal. 1993. *Palestinians: The Making of a People*. Cambridge, MA: Harvard University Press.
Rogoff, Irit. 2000. *Terra Infirma: Geography's Visual Culture*. London: Routledge.
San Francisco Jewish Film Festival (SFJFF). n.d. "Michel Kleifi—Biography." http://www.sfjff.org/film/biography?id=746&last=Khleifi&first=Michel&role=Director.
Shohat, Ella, and Robert Stam. 1994. *Unthinking Eurocentrism: Multiculturalism and the Media*. London: Routledge.

Courtesy Haut et Court

*Paradise Now**
Narrating a Failed Politics

NADIA YAQUB

Distributed by Warner Brothers Independent Pictures and recipient of numerous awards—including the Golden Globe Best Foreign Film award and an Oscar nomination—*Paradise Now* is probably the best-known Palestinian film in the United States. Much has been written about the film's controversial subject matter: Palestinian suicide bombings.[1] It has been praised for intelligently portraying the social, political, and psychological conditions that give rise to such acts of violence and panned for giving voice to what many find to be a repugnant moral point of view.[2] While this debate is important, it does not do justice to the complexities of the film itself. *Paradise Now* is a film not only about suicide bombers but also about the social and cultural conditions of contemporary Palestinian society. In it director Hany Abu-Assad raises important questions that connect gender, geography, politics, and culture in the West Bank.

While there are many ways to approach *Paradise Now* as a cultural text, one fruitful method of analysis is to situate the film within the context of film genre. Genre films, by addressing well-known themes in conventional ways, present defined perspectives and raise specific expectations in their audiences. By playing with these expectations, a filmmaker can explore, confirm, or confound cultural and social assumptions inherent in these genres. In *Paradise Now*, Abu-Assad plays with two film genres, the wedding and the road movie, to contextualize his characters' actions within a richly textured social environment. In addition, through self-reflexive references to film and video, he questions the transformational power of art within the context of social and political failure.

---

* *Paradise Now/al-Janna al-an*. 2005. Directed by Hany Abu-Assad; written by Hany Abu-Assad and Bero Beyer. Produced by Augustus Film (Netherlands) with Lama Films (Israel), Razor Film (Germany), Lumen Films (France), Hazazah Film (Netherlands), and Arte France Cinema (France). Distributed in the United States by Warner Independent Pictures. 90 minutes.

Hany Abu-Assad brandishes the Golden Globe, alongside co-writer Bero Beyer and the presenter, Sarah Jessica Parker. © Hollywood Foreign Press Association

As a commentary on current Palestinian politics, *Paradise Now* can be read as an anti–wedding film. Wedding films play on the potent symbolism of community and continuity inherent in the wedding itself. Weddings contribute to the construction of selves, particularly gendered selves; define the limits and extent of communities; and play important roles in the construction of abstract identities of belonging by fictionally extending familial and personal ties outward to ethnic groups and nations. They provide a context through which states can control their citizens and citizens can question and resist their states. Abu-Assad's earlier feature film *Rana's Wedding* (*al-Quds fi yawm akhar*, 2002) is a classic example of the genre. The film, made after the outbreak of the second Intifada, focuses on the role culture plays for Palestinian steadfastness in the face of occupation. Rana's father has served her with an ultimatum: she must marry by the end of the day or travel with him to Egypt to complete her studies. Overcoming various obstacles that result from Israeli occupation, including military patrols, house demolition, a street fight, a martyr's funeral, and roadblocks, Rana locates her lover, Khalil, and brings him to her father to obtain consent for the marriage. The film ends with Rana's triumphant wedding at an Israeli checkpoint where the magistrate who is to perform the ceremony has been detained.

The political ramifications of Rana and Khalil's decision to marry are multiple. By marrying and remaining in Palestine, Rana performs *sumud*, or steadfastness. Moreover, Rana's and Khalil's efforts to bring their wedding into being are acts of resistance, for it is the apparatus of occupation that impedes them; every step toward the realization of the wedding is a successful circumvention of Israeli authority.

Paradise Now, on the other hand, uses a planned suicide bombing to explore not the nature of Palestinian *sumud* but rather the division and sterility that characterize post-Intifada Palestinian society. Two friends, Said and Khaled, have been selected to carry out a suicide mission in Israel. Khaled, after a botched first attempt and reconnection with family and friends, decides not to carry out the attack, while Said becomes increasingly determined to blow himself up as he contemplates his humiliating past, alienating present, and bleak future. Throughout the tense day and a half that elapse between the recruitment of the men for this operation and Said's final act, the lives of the two men are constantly juxtaposed against a background of weddings. When Said visits a photography shop to have his portrait taken, a wedding video plays in the background. Said and Khaled are given a wedding alibi by their handlers, and as they search for each other after their first bungled mission, newly barbered and dressed in natty suits, they are asked by everyone they meet if they are going to a wedding. The wedding references code the film as the dark underbelly of *Rana's Wedding*. Indeed, Abu-Assad's shift in perspective is signaled by

Khaled and Said relaxing

the eventual erasure of the wedding motif from the film itself; when Said and Suha, a potential love interest, return to the photography shop, the wedding video that had played earlier has been replaced with a martyr's video similar to the one Said and Khaled taped earlier that day.

Both *Rana's Wedding* and *Paradise Now* were made after the outbreak of the second Intifada. This conflict differed fundamentally from the first Intifada in that it was conducted at roadblocks and borders rather than within Palestinian communities (Johnson and Kuttab 2001, 30–31). Indeed, the recurrence of roadblocks throughout the film and the final location of Rana's wedding ceremony at a checkpoint suggest the importance of these spaces—as opposed to the Palestinian village—as the loci of conflict and contestation. However, positioning Rana and her wedding in these spaces is at odds with Palestinian lived experience at that time. During the first Intifada, women, through their informal networks and presence at the site of the conflict, played crucial roles in the uprising. Johnson and Kuttab argue that structural changes in Palestinian communities, the movement of the conflict outside villages and towns, and its militarization minimized women's participation in the second Intifada. The reclamation of the checkpoint as a Palestinian communal space in which women play a pivotal role that is celebrated in *Rana's Wedding* does not reflect what was happening on the ground. Thus, the film must be read prescriptively as a call to action that recognizes the need for women's presence in these contested public spaces.

Women play markedly different roles in *Paradise Now*. They are bearers of culture and sustainers of life; both Said's and Khaled's mothers, Umm Said and Umm Khaled, are shown lovingly preparing food for their families and busy with the chores that keep a home functional. Suha brings to the film the experience of exile and a love of cinema. However, women's efforts are only marginally effective. Khaled gives the sandwiches his mother has prepared for him to Jamal, one of the suicide mission recruiters, who ostentatiously eats them while Khaled records his martyr's video. The powerful connection between the sandwiches as physical sustenance and mothers as communal sustainers is evident in the effect this act has on Khaled, for it is when he sees Jamal begin to eat that he thinks to include a message to his mother in his video. However, what the eating and message from Khaled to his mother emphasize is not Umm Khaled's participation but her distance from the act of nihilistic violence in which Khaled is about to engage. Unlike the mothers of the first Intifada who protected and sustained children and young men as they fought Israeli soldiers before their eyes, Umm Khaled is absent, unaware of what is unfolding. She and Umm Said are realistic portraits of the marginalization of women and inadequacies of maternal protection that characterized the second Intifada (Johnson and Kuttab 2001, 37).

Unlike Umm Khaled and Umm Said, who are seen only within the confines of their own homes, Suha is conspicuously present in public spaces. Bareheaded and stylishly dressed, she crosses checkpoints alone, talks to mechanics, and engages in political discussions. But we know from the film's opening that Suha's experience in the public sphere will not be easy. The film begins as she approaches a checkpoint at the entrance to Nablus. No words pass between Suha and the soldier who checks her belongings. While she refuses to lower her gaze, he rifles through her bag, insolently moves her passport beyond her reach, and signals her right to pass with a silent tilting of his head. Rana's wedding at a checkpoint signifies the appropriation of contested spaces as Palestinian, while Suha's encounter with this soldier suggests a challenge to the rights of women to occupy such spaces.

Suha is ineffective in her relationship with Said as well. She is assertive but ultimately fails to build a connection with him. Suha is the daughter of a respected martyr to the Palestinian cause, but she has grown up abroad. Her Arabic is inflected, and her cultural frames of reference are alien to Said. She speaks of Japanese minimalism, while Said's film experiences consist of martyrs' and collaborators' videos and his own participation in the destruction of the Nablus cinema. Suha is a privileged Palestinian, economically well off and endowed with the choice of leaving or staying that other characters lack. She chooses to stay in Palestine for idealistic reasons, but that choice is not rewarded; her relationship with Said does not develop, and viewers last see her crying over Said's photograph as he carries out his suicide mission. Moreover, the cross-gender camaraderie of Rana and Khalil in *Rana's Wedding* is missing in *Paradise Now*; men and women are utterly divided in their roles, concerns, and values. If Rana's wedding represents the successful transfer of Palestinian culture from the private to the public sphere, Suha and Said's failed relationship is a manifestation of the sterility of the community from which Palestinian culture and politics should (but cannot) arise.

While reading *Paradise Now* as wedding film reveals the failure of culture and community in Abu-Assad's post-Intifada Palestine, analyzing it as an anti–road movie offers us insights into his representation of Palestinian modernity. Through his depictions of cars and movement through space, Abu-Assad raises questions about the nature of that modernity and the Palestinian individual.

As an anti–road movie *Paradise Now* is again more fully understood in conjunction with *Rana's Wedding*. In their friend Ramzi's VW bug, Rana and

Khalil successfully pass through Israeli obstacles to bring about their wedding. Ramzi's car is old, signifying the limited nature of the tools with which Palestinians must navigate the modern world. Nonetheless, it gets the couple where they need to go. The limitations of Ramzi's car only add to the triumphant nature of Rana and Khalil's success, for it is through their resourcefulness and determination that they bring about the performance of their Palestinian-hood at the public site most associated with Israeli control and Palestinian immobility: the roadblock.

A closer examination of the film, however, reveals a darker subtext. Abu-Assad alludes to Palestinian fragmentation in the landscapes through which the characters travel. Jerusalem is portrayed as a stunningly beautiful city. The West Bank, on the other hand, is another world. Rana, Khalil, and Ramzi pass destroyed neighborhoods, desert, and piles of junked cars. The proliferation of roadblocks pushes the protagonists' car off paved and serviced roads onto dirt tracks and through inhospitable landscapes. These scenes point to the dependence of drivers on the state control that brings a country's road system into being. In other words, motorists are not truly autonomous but dependent on both the services provided by the state and on their own willingness to follow the rules of the road. Driving, then, is an act not only of independence but of citizenship. Forcing Palestinians off the road becomes a metaphor for their forced removal from structured, civilized society and by extension the disenfranchisement of occupation and exile.

Significantly, Ramzi's car is used as a container to control Rana. In Palestinian films the car is often a mobile Palestinian private space that moves along Israeli public roads. To a limited degree, Palestinian-ness can be performed within the car at a remove from the violence of Israeli-controlled roads. For Khalil and Ramzi, this is certainly the case. They choose the itinerary and discuss how best to drive. Rana is relegated to the back seat and is always left behind when there is business to tend. Most strikingly, she is left in the car as Khalil, the magistrate, and her father discuss the terms of her marriage. The car, then, while transporting Palestinian-hood through public roads also transports the problematics of gender relations inherent in Palestinian society. As such, it has a role to play in disciplining Rana, who at the beginning of the film defies her father and proposes marriage to her lover but who in the end sits silently in the vehicle as five men determine the terms of her marriage.

Despite the emphasis on the disciplining of the feminine inherent in *Rana's Wedding*, the film suggests a limited autonomy for Palestinian men. In *Paradise Now*, even this is called into question. The prevalence of broken cars in the film suggests that the entire social and economic fabric of Palestinian society is in trouble. We first encounter Said and Khaled at the garage where they work when a customer complains of a crooked bumper, and it is through her constant car trouble that Suha meets Said. Taxis are decrepit; the window in one taxi cannot close, and the door in another is jammed. Early in the film Said and Khaled sit on a Nablus hillside surrounded by the abandoned chassis of old cars. The entrance to Khaled's house is partially blocked by a wall of old tires. While searching for Said after the botched first mission, Khaled drives through streets lined with piles of immobile cars. The plethora of malfunctioning vehicles in *Paradise Now* suggests the ineffectiveness of the Palestinian presence in the public sphere. They are on public roads but with a weariness that belies the spunk with which Palestinian vehicles inhabit these spaces in Abu-Assad's earlier films.

Said walks, runs, and rides but never drives. Ironically, although he works as an auto mechanic, ensuring the mobility of others, he spends most of the movie on foot. In road movies, private car travel rather than travel by foot or public transport often communicates an ironic distance between protagonists and the societies through which they move. Although Said moves on foot, he is largely disengaged from the society through which he passes. Viewers see him walking through the bustling streets of downtown Nablus but never see those streets through his eyes. In contrast, they are shown Khaled's perspective as he drives through these streets in search of Said. Thus a distinction is drawn between Said's solitude—the result of a politically induced social breakdown—and the autonomy that is beyond his reach. Even in his final act, as he alone and of his own will carries out his suicide mission, he is driven, not driving, first by the Israeli collaborator and then by the driver of the bus that he ultimately blows up. Significantly, it is after his limited stint as a driver while searching for Said that Khaled changes his mind about carrying out the suicide attack. Driving, then, signifies the autonomy that is a psychological necessity for the modern individual.

By invoking the road and wedding movie in *Paradise Now*, Abu-Assad critically addresses the breakdown of the social and political in contemporary Palestinian society. Through a self-reflexive turn he raises questions about the power of his art within this difficult context. Although there are many references to moving pictures in the film, it is the character of Suha who best embodies the filmmaker's perspective. Suha's choice during a 4 a.m. conversation with Said to talk about film encourages the viewer to see her as the self-reflexive representation of the filmmaker that is typical of exilic filmmakers (Naficy 2001,

276). Like Suha, Abu-Assad is a privileged Palestinian who has returned from abroad to participate—through his filmmaking—in Palestinian society in the homeland. Suha's failure to influence Said can be read as a commentary on the limitation of film or art in general to influence politics.

The inexorable connection between moving pictures and violence in *Paradise Now*—martyrs' and collaborators' videos, the burning down of the Nablus cinema, and, in Khaled's words, the moment of death when one's life flashes before one's eyes "like a video"—suggest a reflexive questioning by Abu-Assad himself of the efficacy of this project and his own limited ability to speak to and for a Palestinian audience. In this regard *Paradise Now* reflects the need, inherent in other diasporic filmmakers' work, to address national questions that continue to be critical to Palestinians struggling with communal fragmentation and failed political aspirations while answering to a transnational system of financing and marketing that encourages directors to address the personal and universal (Alexander 2005, 153–155).

In its assessment of the power of art to affect the contexts in which it is created, *Paradise Now* is more pessimistic than Rashid Masharawi's *Waiting*. While in *Waiting* Lumière's videos are transformative, within *Paradise Now* film can only reflect and at times reinforce the desperation of the Palestinian politics depicted. Both films convey the intense pessimism that prevailed in the face of increased Israeli oppression and internal Palestinian conflicts following the second Intifada. What is perhaps most surprising is that while the state of Palestinian politics has steadily declined since 2005, five years later Palestinians are in the midst of a new and highly productive period for the arts in general and cinema in particular.

NOTES

1. Editor's note: In the French poster, reproduced here, an image dominated by Khaled's torso strapped with explosives confronts the viewer with the grim reality of suicide bombing. The German, Spanish, and Swiss posters employ similar motives. The French, Italian, and Spanish posters comment "24 hours in the mind of a Kamikaze." The U.S. poster, in contrast, avoids such confrontation by showing the two men from the back in what may be taken as business attire, hinting at the deception involved.
2. Chahine (2005, 73–74), Georgakas and Saltz (2005, 16–9), and Ruby (2006, 28–30) address the political controversy that has surrounded the film.

REFERENCES

Alexander, Livia. 2005. "Is There a Palestinian Cinema? The National and Transnational in Palestinian Film Production." In *Palestine, Israel, and the Politics of Popular Culture*, ed. Rebecca Stein and Ted Swedenburg, 150–174. Durham, NC: Duke University Press.

Chahine, Joumane. 2005. Paradise Now. *Film Comment* 41 (5): 73–74.

Georgakas, Dan, and Barbara Saltz. 2005. "This Is a Film You Should See Twice: An Interview with Hany Abu-Assad." *Cineaste* 31 (Winter): 16–19.

Johnson, Penny, and Eileen Kuttab. 2001. "Where Have All the Women (and Men) Gone? Reflections on Gender and the Second Intifada." *Feminist Review* 69 (Winter): 21–43.

Naficy, Hamid. 2001. *An Accented Cinema: Exilic and Diasporic Filmmaking*. Princeton, NJ: Princeton University Press.

Ruby, Rich B. 2006. "Bomb Culture." *Sight and Sound* 16 (4): 28–30.

—6—

Political Film in Egypt

WALTER ARMBRUST

Egyptian political cinema builds on a film industry dating to the late 1920s and comprised of more than three thousand films, most of them financed without European involvement and screened to mass audiences in Egypt and the Arabic-speaking world. Egyptian cinema presents thematic breadth, historical depth, and a scale of distribution far beyond any other national cinema of the Arabic-speaking world. Consequently, while political films made over the past two decades are the main focus of this chapter, they must be contextualized within a more expansive history of Egyptian political films.

Films that address social themes relevant to politics, if not necessarily politics *per se*, have been ubiquitous in Egyptian cinema over the decades. Nationalism, for example, is one of the über-themes of Egyptian political cinema.[1] Films sometimes treat nationalism in ways that articulate with conventional politics, but the line between overtly political nationalist films and films that are uninterpretable outside a national context is not always clear. Likewise, many Egyptian films from the 1930s to the present address the role of women in modern society, and such representations are often richly evocative of politics. Gender is one of the organizing themes of Shafik's 2006 book on popular cinema. She notes numerous social and symbolic issues connected to representations of women and also that female directors in Egyptian cinema have tended to eschew promoting feminism (189–196). In many ways the huge proportion of Egyptian films that focus on love can be seen as a long-running discussion of the tension between patriarchy, depicted as control of marriage by the parents, and individualism in the younger generation, elaborated as various forms of love match or companionate marriage. Patriarchy, in turn, is linked to constructions of political authority (Armbrust 2008). The approach to gender, like deeply embedded representations of nationalism, is not necessarily elaborated as specifically political. But there are instances in which gender politics are specifically addressed by films, for instance as sociolegal issues in *I Want a Solution* (*Uridu hallan*, Sʿaid Marzuq, 1975) and *Pardon Me, Law!* (*ʿAfwan ayyuha al-qanun*, Inas al-Dighidi, 1985). At least one film, *The Open Door* (*al-Bab al-maftuh*, Henri Barakat, 1963), an adaptation of an important feminist novel of 1960 by Latifa Zayyat (2000 in translation), directly links the liberation of women to the achievement of true national sovereignty.

Class is another political theme not easily reducible to "political cinema." Social class is, to be sure, a hugely complex phenomenon anywhere. Very briefly, the myriad ways of giving narrative form to social class in Egyptian cinema are structured by a concern with the emergence of a "middle" class that for many has historically been more an aspiration than a material reality. The bulk of Egyptian films are incomprehensible without giving due attention to this phenomenon. The socioeconomic extremes, nominally "rich and poor," have themselves been constantly renegotiated through their relationship to colonialism, nationalism, and more recently globalization, and all these metaprocesses may be converted in films to various idioms of cultural authenticity or indeed its absence.[2] Shafik gives an excellent survey (2006) of a number of ways of looking at class in Egyptian cinema. Of course, in the end all films can be viewed through the lens of class; hence one is compelled to specify what role it plays in a particular kind of film.

Colonialism and the Rise of Nasser

Colonialism powerfully shaped early Egyptian films but was not itself a central narrative preoccupation of the cinema. Instead, hundreds of films from the 1930s through the 1950s focused on characters, practices, or situations that straddled a contested and often shifting boundary between what was Egyptian and what was foreign. "Westernized" Egyptians or Westernizing practices depicted in films demanded resolution of boundary-straddling ambiguities. This animated narratives far more than a political imperative to dramatize European domination. Hence close readings of musicals, dance films, and melodramas can easily yield greater insight into the politics of colonialism than films about colonialism.[3]

After the Free Officers came to power in 1952, mainstream films gradually began to reflect the new political landscape.[4] The first full-scale cinematic attempt to assess the meaning of the Free Officers' ascent to power was *God Is with Us* (*Allah maʿna*, Ahmad Badrakhan, 1955). It was by no means a harbinger of an extensive "mobilization cinema."⁵ Given the military backgrounds of the Free Officers, the institutional centrality of the military to a newly independent nation-state, and the impact wars had on Egyptian society between 1948 and 1973, one might expect the military to have been a focus of political mobilization. It was, but only to a limited extent in cinema. For example, a short series of military recruitment films was made in the latter half of the 1950s. The films were hardly heavy-handed propaganda but rather light-hearted vehicles for Isma'il Yasin, the most popular comedian of the 1950s (Armbrust 2007b). Actors including Farid Shauqi, Ahmad Mazhar, and Shukri Sarhan began to take on heroic military roles—and it must be remembered that such roles were impossible under colonial rule.⁶ But even in the 1960s, when the cinema was nationalized, films glorifying the military were not numerous.

The newly independent state's military experiences were ambiguous at best. The 1948 war in Palestine was a catastrophe, though even that could form the backdrop for heroism in a film, as Kamal al-Shaykh's *Land of Peace* (*Ard al-salam*, 1957) shows, albeit at a distance of several years from the war. By contrast, the Suez War of 1956 was a triumph for Nasser. British and French troops reclaimed the Suez Canal, but American pressure forced the invading powers to withdraw, making it clear that the age of European colonialism was over and that Nasser had stepped boldly into the space left by European retreat. One blockbuster depiction of Egyptian resistance to the Anglo-French invasion was made: *Port Said* (*Bur Sa'id*, 'Izz al-Din Zulficar, 1957). Given the importance of Suez for Nasser's reputation, surprisingly few other films focused specifically on the conflict.⁷ Less surprisingly, Egypt's substantial but far more ambiguous involvement in the Yemeni civil war between 1962 and 1972 went almost unnoticed in the cinema.⁸ The film that most clearly glorified Nasser and armed struggle against imperialism was a historical allegory—Youssef Chahine's *Saladin* (*al-Nasir Salah al-Din*, 1963), which projected contemporary Egyptian and Arab conflicts with Europe and, by implication, Israel onto the war between Salah al-Din al-Ayubi and the Crusaders.⁹

Cinema was nationalized in 1963, and public-sector productions began to reach the market by 1964.¹⁰ Although the public sector was and remains controversial,¹¹ critics readily acknowledge that most of the significant films of the 1960s were public-sector productions. The seven years of the public-sector era were bisected by the Six Day War in 1967, and the most politically interesting films were made after the war.

The Decline of Nasser and the Post-Public-Sector Cinema

The Six Day War in 1967 and the October War in 1973 were crucial events in Egyptian history, and they were vital for the trajectory of political cinema, though not in a straightforward way. Eventually the Six Day War and, more importantly, its aftermath brought Israel squarely onto center stage in the Egyptian political imaginary, but this was not widely reflected in the cinema of the late 1960s. Instead, some of the key political films of the era interrogated the flaws of the Nasser regime. Dubbed the "green light" cinema, the period from the 1967 debacle to slightly after the death of Nasser on September 28, 1970, witnessed a degree of regime and social criticism that had not been possible earlier in the 1960s, when the state's repression of its political opponents was quite fierce.

Gordon (2002, 209–210) attributes the phrase "green light cinema" to the film scholar Duriya Sharaf al-Din (1992). The idea was that filmmakers were given a green light to criticize the regime and society. Sharaf al-Din did not intend to coin a positive label; her point was rather that an apparent liberalization of cinema was part of regime management—a tactic to let off political steam. Whether or not the liberalization of censorship in the late 1960s was managed by the state for its own purposes, it was unquestionably tied to Egypt's disastrous defeat by Israel, so shocking that it was nearly unrepresentable. The immediate reaction in the cinema was stunned silence. Criticism in these films was indirect—aimed at society rather than at the regime—or allegorical.[12] Only one film made between 1967 and 1973 actually depicted the war. This was *Song on the Pass* (*Ughniya ʿala al-mamarr*, ʿAli ʿAbd al-Khaliq, 1972), a grim tale of five soldiers holding a pass in the Sinai after the rest of their unit has been wiped out by the Israelis. As their provisions and ammunition run low, the narrative tacks between their current predicament and flashbacks to their previous lives, which were largely defined by futile struggles against authority and social convention. The unsuccessful civilian lives of the soldiers underscore their heroism in holding the pass. But ultimately *Song on the Pass*, like most of the green-light films of the late 1960s, suggests that successful resistance to an external threat (here, the Israelis) can only come through social reform at home. There is little direct political discussion. *Song on the Pass* was screened in 1972, early in the Sadat years, but actually was written in the late Nasser era.[13] The avoidance of direct representation of the war applies to several other Sadat-era films screened or in production before the 1973 October War.[14] Most of these were public-sector films; thus, the "green light" label spans the late Nasser and early Sadat years—and the argument that such films are artifacts of state management rather than unfettered political expression applies to both regimes.

It was only after the October War in 1973 that the Six Day War of 1967 could be represented. The first attempt to do so was veteran filmmaker Husam al-Din Mustafa's *The Bullet Is Still in My Pocket* (*al-Rasasa la tazal fi jaybi*, 1974). Like its predecessors, it located the cause of the defeat in social corruption rather than directly in the political leadership. But *The Bullet* depicted the defeat of 1967 graphically—much more so than *Song on the Pass*—showing the massacre of unarmed and helpless Egyptian soldiers. Most importantly, *The Bullet* ended on a triumphant note, with the crossing of the Bar Lev Line at the beginning of the October War in 1973. Redemption afforded by the October War unlocked a steady trickle of reevaluations of the Six Day War, some of which directly condemned the human rights abuses of the Nasser era.[15] However, they did so from beyond the boundary created by the October War, which Egyptians saw as a victory, contrary to American and Israeli narratives on the war. The reestablishment of Egyptian military credibility made criticism of the Nasser era less difficult because it was now possible to be *for* something and not simply *against* Nasser, who for many was still seen in light of his avowed goals of economic independence, social equity, and modernist progress rather than for the political repression that marked his rule, particularly in the 1960s.

The post–October War context of filmmaking was dominated by *infitah*—the "open door" economic policies of Sadat, which were continued and in many ways intensified by the Mubarak regime in the 1980s. The social distortions and materialist excesses of *infitah* became the primary political preoccupation of the latter half of the 1970s and the decade of the 1980s. Some of these films qualify as political cinema implicitly by contrasting the present with the social equity ideals of the Nasser era. For example, *Police Station in the Street* (*Karakon fi al-shariʿ*, Ahmad Yahya, 1986) and *Love on the Pyramids Plateau* (*al-Hubb fawqa hadbat al-haram*, Atif al-Tayyib, 1986) dramatized a postwar housing crisis that for many became a *de facto* "marriage crisis."

An image of *infitahi* vulgarians flourishing at the expense of hard-working citizens—the "myth of the fat cats," as Shafik puts it (2006, 275)—was a staple of a critical *infitah* film genre. *Infitah* films deployed visual and thematic styles that overlap with "new realism" (Shafik 2001a, 62–64; 2006, 275–280). The core group of directors associated with the neorealist movement included ʿAtif al-Tayyib, Khayri Bishara, Daud Abd al-Sayyid, and Muhammad Khan. Although their work spans a number of genres and periods, it was unified in certain respects. Their approach to location shooting acknowledged urban decay—many of their films foregrounded class conflict—and they all exhibited a degree of social commitment. Frank portrayal of an increasingly decrepit Cairo was itself a political statement because it raised implicit contrasts between a disappointing present and a modernist project spanning a century and a half that located progress in an urban middle class. The core new realists were critically acclaimed, but many less critically successful—and more commercially prominent—films of this period also shared their blunt commitment to showing the city, and a previously valorized middle class, in decline.[16]

Of the core new realists, Atif al-Tayyib was the most directly concerned with politics. In *The Bus Driver* (*Sawwaq al-utubis*, 1983) he portrayed an October War veteran struggling to adapt to the *infitah*; *The Innocent* (*al-Bari*', 1986) focused on the torture of political prisoners by state security forces but also on the wretched conditions of the Central Security Forces themselves; and *A File in Vice* (*Milaff fi al-adab*, 1986) depicted the corruption of the police, the decline of the middle class, and double standards applied to women's propriety. They were some of the sharpest political films of the 1980s.[17] Nonetheless, the most important political story of the 1980s was the rise of Islamist movements. al-Tayyib made more reference to it in his films than most directors, but it cannot be said that any of the core new realists attempted to address the phenomenon of Islamism head-on in the 1980s. Undoubtedly tensions within the middle class were connected to the rise of Islamism. But filmmakers of the 1980s overwhelmingly approached decline as a problem that was specific to a middle class defined by older criteria. The rise of Islamism precisely *in* a middle class that was formerly linked to secularism occurred in a blind spot for cinema.

Globalization, Regional Conflicts, and Politicsploitation

New realism ran its course by the early 1990s. Directors and critics often alluded to audiences no longer interested in relentless exposure to depressing depictions of their own decline. If audiences were indeed searching for something new, no doubt dramatic changes in the mediascape had something to do with it. Satellite broadcasting was introduced to Egypt during the 1991 Gulf War, and commercial satellite broadcasting began shortly thereafter. The al-Jazeera news network began broadcasting in 1996, and there can be no doubt that it heightened awareness of politics and particularly of such regional political issues as the Israeli occupation of Palestine and American sanctions against Iraq.

The Internet made its debut also in the early 1990s, and by the end of the decade both new media were sufficiently widespread in Egypt that no account of politics can ignore them.

Concurrent with the rise of new media, awareness of globalization expanded. Certainly by the mid-1990s, if not earlier, the Arabic term for globalization—al-ʿawlama—was a commonplace in Egypt. The salience of "globalization" as an objective reality was less important than the use of the term by Egyptian filmmakers as an idiom to frame local issues. An early harbinger of this idiom was a minor trend of films evaluating "the American dream." These were connected to rhetoric about an American-dominated "new world order" in the wake of the 1991 Gulf War. Such films were all political to some degree, but they ranged from thoughtful meditations on what it means to leave Egypt to overt anti-Americanism.[18]

These films signaled a reframing of metanarratives: from Egypt seen in national terms to Egypt thrust into a suddenly accessible global order. Some films created a sense of the larger stage upon which "Egypt" acted without leaving the country. For example, Tariq al-ʿAryan's *The Pasha Nightclub* (*al-Basha*, 1993) features a music-video pace in some scenes, together with slick interiors in an international style that was new to Egyptian audiences.[19] Since the mid-1990s, this globalized music-video style has been increasingly emulated by other directors. Some films were set partially or entirely abroad. This was by no means unprecedented in Egyptian cinema, but in earlier films travel was exceptional; films of the past two decades suggest a diffusion of the problematics of being Egyptian in a globalized world to the entire nation.[20]

The theme of defining Egypt's place in a globalized world lends itself readily to politics. Abroad, the most keenly observed of these "Egypt in the world" films are undoubtedly the ones featuring depictions of the United States and Israel. Relatively few films before the 1990s—before globalization became a consciously discussed issue in Egypt—depicted Israel, Israelis, or Jews. Some war films depicted Israeli soldiers in predictably narrow terms, as enemies in uniforms, and a few films featured Israeli spies. But the process of reframing Egypt in a global context compelled consideration of the question of Israel because the global stage was not closed to Israelis. If Egyptians were to play on this stage, how should they interact with their former adversaries? Egypt had formal diplomatic relations with Israel since 1979, but for the citizenry it was a cold peace. By the early 1990s, cold peace or not, the larger cinematic engagement with globalization invited narratives dealing with Israel in contexts other than outright warfare.

Egyptian films about Israel—and generally about the United States as well—suggest three observations. First, all representations of Israel and Israelis in Egyptian cinema are antagonistic. Jews are largely conflated with Israel, and representation of Jews in Egyptian cinema ranges from unfriendly to openly disparaging and hostile. Second, the politics of representing Israel as a belligerent entity are not controversial in Egypt—the films operate through a politics of consensus, not contestation. Third, representation of the political consensus on Israel is marketable. The number of films that enter this market niche is small but steady.

Egyptian treatments of Israel are often denounced in Israel and the United States as anti-Semitic. Such criticism is expressed both officially and through quasi-official channels.[21] In some cases the criticisms are nominally justified. *Friends or Business* (*Ashab wala bizniz*, Ali Idris, 2001), for example, extols suicide bombing as a Palestinian tactic for resisting brutal Israeli occupation of the West Bank and presents it as an action aimed strictly at uniformed military targets rather than at civilians. The Israeli occupation of the West Bank *does* brutalize Palestinian civilians every day, often causing immense hardship for all and many deaths from Israeli military actions. However, it is false and utterly propagandistic to suggest that Palestinian suicide bombings—many of which have slaughtered non-uniformed civilians within the pre-1967 borders of Israel—are a neat military response to violent Israeli oppression of civilians. But such propagandizing is more typical of the vilification seen in war films than of the insidious European-style anti-Semitism that Americans and Israelis often claim has been adopted in Middle Eastern discourse about Israel.

The antagonism of other films, such as *The Embassy Is in the Building* (*al-Sifara fi al-'imara*, Amru 'Arafa, 2005), is expressed less stridently. *The Embassy* depicts an Egyptian petroleum engineer returning from the Gulf to find that his flat in a highrise apartment building is next door to the Israeli embassy. His neighbors make his flat worthless, since nobody would knowingly live next to the Israelis, and the Israelis themselves eventually occupy his flat, more through pushiness than through conquest. This and other films do obliquely criticize the Egyptian government for its official stance on normalizing relations between Egypt and Israel. *The Embassy* argues against normalization; no Egyptian film could do otherwise and remain marketable. The film is aggressive and insulting toward Israelis but by no means anti-Semitic. A review in *The New York Times* even interpreted *The Embassy* as a small step in favor of normalization (Slackman 2005). But as many outside observers have noted, the Egyptian government has little trouble deflecting criticisms from the public by permitting anti-Israeli discourse in all media. The official position toward Israel can easily be rationalized as a product of American pressure, and few people inside or outside the government are eager to be seen publicly defending normalization.

The Egyptian experience of Israel is of a nation-state and moreover one that consciously and very loudly conflates the distinction between religious faith and national *raison d'être*—Israel as a Jewish state. While the vilification of Israel in Egyptian cinema is undeniable, it is vilification of a nation-state and its people against whom Egypt has fought several costly wars. Much Egyptian discourse about Israel routinely characterized as anti-Semitic by American and Israeli standards appears in a very different light when put in the context of what citizens of a nation-state say about nation-states they have fought against. Americans continue to make films about Nazi Germany more than sixty years after the end of hostilities against Germany; hence it should be unsurprising that Egyptians make films about their conflicts with Israel. It is worth noting that the conclusion of World War II was considerably more decisive than the conclusion of Egypt's wars against Israel. Germany has not fought since 1945, while continuing Israeli occupation of the West Bank underpinned by violence makes, for many Egyptians, a mockery of the sacrifices they made in the October War. The same is true of repeated incursions into Lebanon as recently as 2006 and the blockade of Gaza since 2007, compounded by an invasion in 2009. Egyptian preoccupation with Israel is an expression of alarm at local events.

In this light, Egyptian cinematic vilification of Israel seems unremarkable. Most Egyptians would find it exceedingly odd to make pro-Israeli films or indeed to simply treat Israel as a neutral subject. Egypt's close-range experience of Israel through fighting wars and observation of recent local conflicts is now being augmented by an increasingly firsthand experience of the United States. As a subject of popular culture, the United States entered Egyptian consciousness after 1973, which is to say after the United States intervened in Egypt's conflict with Israel by initiating jaw-droppingly generous foreign aid programs to a former enemy—and one with whom hostilities could easily have resumed throughout the 1970s, for all anyone knew. None of the rationales for the American presence in the region are accepted in Egypt, including the U.S. sanctions against Iraq throughout the 1990s, the American invasion of Iraq in 2003 on the now-discredited pretext of eliminating weapons of mass destruction,[22] and massive U.S. support for Israel after the 1973 October War for both ideological and nominally strategic reasons. Approval of these actions would make an Egyptian film unmarketable, and no representation of the United States would be possible without evoking them.

Egyptian films about Israel are expressions of conflict between nation-states. Nation-states in conflict vilify each other. Given that the films in question express consensual attitudes, one must be careful not to misinterpret their political content. This does not mean that one should feel compelled to deny the phenomenon of reprehensible discourse, but rather that one should put it in context. The Israel/America genre has to be understood historically, and much of what I have described serves to highlight this point. War and peace are among the most powerful forces structuring Egyptian political cinema, and these films cannot be understood outside those forces.

The consensual politics of these films points in another direction, toward marketing. They are "exploitation" films that function through sensationalism. In the United States exploitation films appeal to the public's more prurient interests in sex, violence, drug abuse, and nudity. These are not necessarily part of "politicsploitation" films, but the essence of exploitation—driven by a marketing logic—is sensationalism, and this certainly is an aspect of the Egyptian films that address the role of the United States in the region and the world. This does not mean that exploitation films cannot express politics. American cinema is again instructive. The "blaxploitation" subgenre of exploitation films produced in the 1970s eventually gained a degree of critical respectability. In many respects they were conventional exploitation films, with the key difference that they featured all-black casts, though not necessarily black directors. Blaxploitation films reversed the polarity on whites' stereotypes of blacks. Pimps, gangsters, or criminals became the heroes. Such films have been condemned as racist, as have many of the Egyptian films addressing Israel as a central theme. Blaxploitation cinema makes a good analogy for thinking about much Egyptian popular culture that comments on the United States and Israel—not just films but also songs and videos. Politicsploitation functions through crude national stereotypes but is predicated on *reversing* their usual forms of representation in foreign media. The most relevant form of media in this context is not cinema but news. One of the reasons al-Jazeera was an instant hit in the Arab world is that it reversed the polarity that Arabs were accustomed to seeing and hearing in international reporting on such issues as Palestine. It is no coincidence that the rise of the Israel/America genre in Egyptian cinema came almost simultaneously with al-Jazeera's news broadcasting—or that al-Jazeera has been accused of sensationalism.

Crucially, politicsploitation, like blaxploitation, does not mean to discuss issues or engage in debate. The point rather is to make viewers feel good about themselves. The white hero becomes the white villain in blaxploitation;

American moral posturing becomes American hypocrisy in politicsploitation. Who is right is irrelevant because most who watch these films *know* who is right. Egyptian Israel/America films, by this logic, do not try to convince anyone of anything; they reflect a consensus back to their audiences. The self-appointed anti-American police, Zionist anti-Semitism police, and anti-Israelism police disingenuously counsel vigilance against a spreading hate virus. But Israel/America films and other politicsploitation productions do not spread a virus—they reflect a consensus. What is the origin of this consensus? To locate it in media discourse is implausible. For politicsploitation to exist in media, the origin must *already be there*—in wars that one's fathers and uncles fought, in fraudulent rationales for invading Arab states, in preaching human rights while practicing torture, or in talking peace while occupying, bombing, and invading neighbor states.

Islam and Islamism

The hand of the censor is easily discerned in portrayals of Islamism in Egyptian cinema. Egyptian filmmakers can criticize Islamism as a political movement, but they cannot make an overtly *pro*-Islamist film. No endorsement of Islam as a political alternative is allowed in cinema or in public-sector media, and Islamic social signifiers, specifically the *hijab*—the neo-Islamic head covering worn by women, are severely circumscribed in print and broadcast media. Public-sector broadcast media include practically all terrestrial television and radio broadcasting. Suppression of the *hijab* is not achieved through formal state censorship but is rather a reflection of the worldview of media producers who work within state-controlled institutions. However, the growth of a relatively free private-sector press since the 1980s and of transnational satellite television broadcasting since the mid-1990s has eroded the state's ability to control discourse on Islamic practices. Since the mid-2000s, terrestrial television broadcasting has been made almost irrelevant by the burgeoning access to satellite dishes and technology. The transnational media in turn exert pressure on Egyptian cinema to diversify its portrayals of Islam. The success of religious programming funded privately or by other states and of music videos broadcast on satellite television suggests that there could be a market for openly Islamic films. It requires no great stretch of the imagination to suppose that this could extend to Islamist films if the censors were inclined to permit their production. And while film production in Egypt is still largely national, the sources of both financing and exhibiting films are increasingly complex—tied to the Arab Gulf states in the case of commercial films and Europe for art-house films.

Historically, Egyptian films have been concerned with secular narratives. Depictions of Islam have been made, but they are compartmentalized within a film industry that historically furthers a secular worldview.[23] Films that depict Islam are distinct from those that depict contemporary political Islamism or the diacritica of contemporary Islamic social movements.[24] Islamism as a political movement began in earnest with the founding of the Muslim Brotherhood by Hasan al-Banna in 1928. The movement attracted a mass following in the 1930s and by the late 1940s was an active agent in a violent period of Egyptian history. Both Islamism and, for the most part, the tumultuousness of the period were absent from the screen.[25]

Later Nasser severely repressed the Muslim Brotherhood, but when Sadat came to power he used Islam both as a counterweight to the left and as a motivational force in Egypt's conflict with Israel. This was done initially through building up state-run religious institutions. However, the government failed spectacularly in containing the resurgence of Islamist groups outside the state and opposed to it, including the Muslim Brotherhood as well as other, more radical groups, one of which eventually assassinated Sadat in 1981. From the 1970s to the mid-1990s Islamism grew steadily as a social movement, particularly in ramshackle quasi-legal new neighborhoods growing on the edges of an ever-expanding Cairo. In such neighborhoods the state failed to meet demands for social services and basic amenities. A loose network of Islamist mosque-based and voluntary organizations filled the gap, forming an Islamic sector that paralleled the state.

Up to the mid-1990s the Islamist movement proclaimed sweeping political goals that were often promoted violently through assassinations and acts of terrorism. From the mid-1990s the political campaign of the Muslim Brotherhood and other groups became less violent, while the social agenda of Islamism evolved into an increasingly widespread and complex phenomenon. It is difficult to make clear-cut distinctions between such analytical abstractions as the state, business interests structured by globalized neoliberalism, and the wave of Islamization that washed over society during the past four decades. All have been treated separately in social and historical writing, but they can no longer be considered mutually exclusive.

Between the early 1970s and the mid-1990s the growth of Islamism as a political and social movement was staggering. No person in any part of the country was unaffected by it. In cinema and television at the beginning of the period, this vast social transformation with its associated turbulent politics was all but invisible. The exceptions are so few that they only serve to emphasize the rule. One such film was *Pay Attention to Zuzu* (*Khalli balak min Zuzu*, Hasan al-Imam, 1972), a popular film about a college student who works secretly in a family wedding-dance trade, a profession stereotypically connected with prostitution. *Zuzu* depicted Islamist politics in the university. The story culminates in a brawl between an Islamist student group that objects to her profession on moral grounds and the dancer-student's secular group. Universities were, in fact, on the cutting edge of the Islamist revival in the 1970s—a product of Sadat's efforts to build up alternatives to the left. However, *Zuzu* was a musical romance by a director known for melodrama and hence gave only a faint echo of the violent student politics of the period. If one could have seen the future of the Islamist movement and its rapidly growing influence among college students from the perspective of 1972, it would have been difficult to imagine that *Zuzu*'s depiction of the very real and crucially important phenomenon of Islamism on campus would be almost the only such film for the next thirty years.[26]

In the 1970s and 1980s a few films mocked Islamists and an even smaller number took them seriously, but none made Islamists or Islamist activities their central focus. A favorable invocation of Islamism came in Saʿad ʿArafa's *Love before Bread Sometimes* (*al-Hubb qabla al-khubz ahyanan*, 1977), which ends with an open call for women to wear the *hijab*. This was a time when the *hijab* was a more ideologically loaded symbol than it became in the late 1990s and 2000s, when motivations for wearing it could rarely be reduced to either an individual's wish to express piety or to mere social conformity.[27] The "new realist" director Atif al-Tayyib pushed the boundaries of censorship but also of social representation. For example, his *A File in Vice* has a minor female office worker who wears a *hijab* but is conspicuous by her sensible refusal to jump to conclusions about allegations of immoral behavior made against her colleagues, unlike more secular characters. His *Sons and Murderers* (*Abnaʿ wa qatala*, 1988) depicts an Islamist student as the only sympathetic character in a narrative about social corruption in the post-Nasserist period. And *Uncovering the Hidden* (*Kashf al-mastur*, 1994) features an ex-prostitute who becomes an Islamist. She is blackmailed by the government into carrying out sexual espionage to locate her former handler. To get to him she looks up her old colleagues, one of whom has become an Islamist. The Islamist former colleague is shown now organizing Islamic outreach (*daʿwa*) for repentant actresses and other well-off women.[28] It is not a flattering portrait of an Islamist, but it was well-observed sociologically.

Uncovering the Hidden is more perceptive than most films of the period, but it still treats the phenomenon of Islamism obliquely. In 1994 reservations about Islamism were finally overcome by *The Terrorist* (*al-Irhabi*, Nadir Galal).[29] It was released in a coordinated government campaign against terrorism. Prior to the campaign, Islamists had committed terrorist acts that killed or injured Egyptian and foreign civilians as well as political and security personnel. The state's campaign aimed to firmly link Islamists with violence. Such a conflation does not at all capture the complex realities of Islamism in Egyptian society. In any event, for various reasons, politically organized Islamism did in fact abandon its most violent tactics after the mid-1990s.

The Terrorist was a conversion narrative structured around an injured Islamist assassin hiding from the police. The circumstances of his injury enable him to hide in a sumptuous villa inhabited by a modern Muslim family that does not know his true identity. In the course of the film the family converts the terrorist to secularism by unwittingly exposing him to a series of implicit comparisons between his harsh Islamist ideology and their enlightened worldview.

The Terrorist was inspired by the 1961 film *In Our House There Is a Man*. That film revolved around the 1945 assassination of Ahmad Mahir Pasha, a collaborator with the British, by a man suspected to have been a member of the Muslim Brotherhood. It is a conversion narrative, but it is the fugitive who converts his hosts. The host family is middle class and apolitical, and the point of the film is the assassin's success in making nationalists of his hosts, who are well aware of who he is and what he has done. Where *In Our House* argues that violence in the nationalist cause is acceptable, *The Terrorist* paints violence in the Islamist cause as illegitimate. Conversion to secularism in *The Terrorist* happens during a soccer match between the Egyptian national team and Zimbabwe in the qualifying rounds for the World Cup; nationalism is the common thread in the two films.

Since *The Terrorist*, a small but steady number of films have addressed political and social aspects of post-1970s Islamism. Three films by Youssef Chahine were prominent in this trend: *Destiny* (*al-Masir*, 1997), an allegorical defense of *tanwir* (enlightenment) against Islamist dogmatism set in Arab Andalusia; *The Emigrant* (*al-Muhajir*, 1994), based on the story of Joseph in the Bible and the Quran and expressing skepticism toward organized religion; and *The Other* (*al-Akhir*, 1999), a contemporary story about an Egyptian-American man who falls in love with a woman whose brother is an Islamist terrorist. Chahine's films of this period are co-productions made with an eye on European art-house cinema and hence somewhat peripheral to my discussion. Such films have an ardent following among some intellectuals, and Chahine's activities, if not necessarily the films themselves, are an important part of public culture.[30] Another significant work is Daud ʿAbd al-Sayyid's *Citizen, Detective, Thief* (*Muwatin wa mukhbir wa harami*, 2001), a brilliant allegorical argument that Islamists, the state, and intellectuals have made an implicit agreement to trade freedom for security, with all three parties gaining material comfort as a result.[31] The film stands alone; it is more or less a mainstream production starring marketable commercial actors, but it does not articulate with trends in Egyptian cinema of this period.[32]

Some post-*Terrorist* films were head-on polemics against Islamism, such as *Closed Doors* (*al-Abwab al-mughlaqa*, Atef Hetata, 1999), which shows the tragic recruitment of a vulnerable youth into the Islamist movement by a schoolteacher.[33] *Birds of Darkness* (*Tuyur al-zalam*, Sharif ʿArafa, 1995) depicts a corrupt lawyer working for the Islamists. Other films made more oblique reference to Islamism, but such references were still striking by the standards of the 1970s and 1980s. The 1988 comedy *An Upper Egyptian in the American University* features a secondary character who elopes with his girlfriend. This is unremarkable by the standards of Egyptian cinema, but in this film the girl is a *muhajjaba* (veiled woman) with a pious and overprotective brother. The film makes little direct comment on the girl's wearing the *hijab*, and this is nominally a bid to normalize it. However, *muhajjabat* characters in films remain conspicuous. The *hijab* is still a social diacritic that must be explained; depictions of the *hijab* in most cases are *about* the *hijab*.

The representational stakes are clear in two more recent films. One is *The Yacoubian Building* (*ʿImarat Yaʿqubyan*, Marwan Hamid, 2006), based on the best-selling novel by Alaa Al-Aswany (2004). The film was lauded for breaking taboos, including the depiction of police brutality and torture of suspected Islamists. The significance of *Yacoubian*'s political intervention was somewhat overstated. There was no taboo against depicting state-sponsored torture; it was shown in films such as *The Karnak Café*, *Behind the Sun*, and *We Are the Bus People*. Crucially, *Yacoubian* depicts the abuse as the responsibility of the ruling regime at the time the film was made, while the other films depict it as taking place during the previous regime. Atif al-Tayyib's *The Innocent* (1986), however, sets a precedent for indicting a sitting regime with the crime of torture. Aside from the matter of precedent, a more important question is whether the depiction of the state's human rights abuses led to a structural change in censorship. The answer is: Probably not.[34] *Yacoubian*, though, is a recent film, and perhaps the jury is still out on its legacy. More hopefully, one might plausibly argue that mainstream cinema, a "big" medium requiring much capital and infrastructure, is simply the wrong place to look for the sort of political interventions that have been attributed to *Yacoubian*. In many ways *Yacoubian* is a pale reflection—or less charitably, a commercialized defanging—of much fiercer critiques regularly carried in print media.

The way Islamists look in films is a strand of political discourse tailor-made for the cinema. In this regard *Yacoubian* says one thing through its narrative—Islamists are produced through social injustice, and the state oppresses them—and a different thing through the way it controls space visually. *Yacoubian* is utterly conventional in its deliberate erasure of the *hijab* in normative space and pointed inclusion of it only in scenes connected to the film's Islamist characters. In reality, all public space in Cairo is populated with Islamically marked people, particularly women. They may or may not be Islamists, but the cinema consistently has treated them as if they all were. *Yacoubian* is set in downtown Cairo, which is a relatively familiar urban setting for Egyptian films and a place where the appearance of women in *hijab* is unremarkable. And yet the film erases women in *hijab* from its visual field in three ways: through physical crowd control by cordoning off locations so filmmakers can strictly determine who appears in them; by manipulating depth of field so people in uncontrolled backgrounds are a blur, making it impossible to tell what they are wearing; and by filming uncontrolled street scenes at night and from a distance so no details of people in the frame are apparent.

Crowd control is a part of most location filming, and it always demands a social engineering of who goes into the frame. Like *Yacoubian*, almost all Egyptian films have engineered a removal of women in *hijab*. But *Yacoubian*'s use of depth of field and nocturnal distancing to such effect are more novel, if not without precedent. Thus a film that potentially ventures into risky territory, arguing that Islamism stems from social and state-sponsored injustice—rather than an ignorant refusal of modernity, as depicted in *The Terrorist*—and that the state exacerbates violence through torture, also contradicts itself by adhering to a conventional cinematic visual code prevalent in almost all films from the 1970s through the 1990s that conflates Islamism with the ubiquitous everyday display of piety through dress.

The visual codes of *Yacoubian* go beyond its conventional tactics of excluding pious dress. Its techniques for removing "incorrectly" dressed people from society extend to removing all warts from the urban fabric. *Yacoubian* is set in exactly the same urban space as many gritty "new realist" films of the 1980s but to a diametrically opposite effect. It visually gentrifies urban space in ways that articulate with precisely the neoliberal capitalist order that underpins the Mubarak regime it is perceived to have criticized. Decrepit, unsightly buildings remain out of sight. *Yacoubian* carefully disposes of urban "problems," including the *hijab*, by engineering their removal from the camera frame.

I Am Not with Them (*Ana mish maʿahum*, Ahmad al-Badri, 2007) addresses both Islamism and the phenomenon of pious dress. The comedy is set in the new suburbs of Cairo, which are often marketed in an aggressively un-*hijab*ed manner. This is evident, for example, in the television advertisements for the Dreamland gated housing development on the outskirts of Cairo about eight kilometers from the Pyramids. The advertisements show sleek, thin women with long, straight hair wearing form-fitting clothes. They appear in gardens barbecuing, on golf courses, and in giant mansions. The advertisements leave no doubt that Dreamland is a no-*hijab* zone. *I Am Not with Them* is set in such a dreamland, but it firmly rejects the marketing strategy of making such places *hijab*less. In fact the film is bluntly about the *hijab*. A secular male college student falls in love with a *muhajjaba* colleague, and the bulk of the narrative deals with how they negotiate their choices in how to appear in public.

I Am Not with Them makes an intriguing standard by which to measure the development of mainstream films about Islamism. When *The Terrorist* was released in 1994, symbolically opening the gates to further discussion of religion in the cinema, Islamists were depicted as violent and crazy—the antithesis of modern society and fundamentally *outside* modern society. *I Am Not with Them*, by contrast, acknowledges that a debate over the place of religion in society has occurred right at the center of modern life: certainly in the universities as key sites for ideological debate over the role of religion in modern society, though one would never have guessed this from even the "new realist" films of earlier decades; and in the new suburban dreamlands that are secular and Westernized, at least in the marketing visions of the developers who build them. *Yacoubian* suggests that the state produces Islamists through political and social repression; at the same time the film presents Islamism as the only formulation of religion while displaying a *hijab*less world where Islamism does not belong. *I Am Not with Them* maintains that people choose their own ways of practicing piety and that these are separate from Islamism. *I Am Not with Them* does carry a subplot about Islamists. They are shown to be a front for Egypt's foreign enemies—probably Israel, though it is not specifically named. The subplot serves the purpose of clearly delineating Islamism from the personal choice to be pious. The reduction of politics to personal choice can easily be read as an expression of neoliberal ideology; hence one can by no means say that this film distances itself from the ideological undertones that *Yacoubian* conveys through its visual codes. Nonetheless, the blunt treatment of the *hijab* in *I Am Not with Them* contrasts strongly with *Yacoubian*'s normative cinematic tactic of visually eliminating signs of public piety that everyone knows have become ubiquitous over the past forty years. Whatever its faults, *I Am Not with Them*, a light, low-budget comedy, does qualify as a political intervention.

Conclusion

Two political themes are salient in recent Egyptian cinema: first, Islamism, and second, criticism of the United States and Israel. The latter is an extension of a long-running political discourse shaped by nationalism, independence, and conflict; the former is a new departure for Egyptian cinema. These themes have been palpable for roughly two decades, but the innovations and continuities of these general trends are only apparent in a larger historical context.

Criticism and often vilification of Israel and the United States is linked to long-standing concerns about national identity, but it is also largely a reiteration of consensual politics. As long as a social and political consensus on opposing Israel and the United States stays in place, it is likely that sensationalism will be intrinsic to the genre. Egyptians have maintained that rejection of Israel and America is rooted in events rather than in discourse, while Israelis and many Americans argue the opposite. The films themselves do seem to generate new narratives based on events, and it must be said that Israeli and American campaigns against such films on the basis of their anti-Semitism are disingenuous. Ultimately whether Egyptian films on Israel would look different if Israel had not continued to occupy the West Bank, repeatedly bombed and invaded Lebanon, and blockaded Gaza is a counterfactual question to which we will never know the answer.

Islamism, the other salient theme of recent years, is of great significance socially, very amenable to representation in visual terms, but less easy to convert to a manifestly political idiom—or at least less easy to discuss in politically subtle ways. Indeed, Egyptian cinematic discussions of Islam have for the most part been quite strident. Nonetheless, the theme of Islamism does have the virtue of articulating with the most important sociopolitical dynamic of the past three decades, namely the relation between Islamically inspired movements and the state. Representations of this dynamic were largely absent from the cinema before the mid-1990s, even though Islamist movements thrived throughout the 1970s and 1980s.

The insertion of religion into the representational field of Egyptian cinema therefore has the potential of enabling a kind of discussion that does not occur in consensus-driven "politicsploitation" films. The proliferation of public forms of piety in Egypt over the past forty years, particularly the wearing of the *hijab* by women, suggests that if there is a social consensus on the importance of religion in modern Egyptian society, then the cinema has mostly reflected its diametric opposite. Recent films have begun to negotiate a place for representing public Islamic piety in Egyptian cinema. Whether or not such displays of piety constitute Islamism or, alternatively, a *de facto* secularization of Islam as religion consigned to the realm of personal choice, is ambiguous. Egyptian films will surely have more to say on this matter in the future.

NOTES

1. The number of nationalist-themed Egyptian films is immense. Analyses of nationalism in Egyptian cinema can be found in Armbrust 2004, Gordon 2002, and Shafik 2006, among others.
2. For a discussion of the performance of authenticity and its role in the social construction of class in cinema and various other forms of mass culture see Armbrust 1996.
3. This is not to say that no films directly portrayed colonialism. Some examples are *Mustafa Kamil* (Ahmad Badrakhan, 1952), *In Our House There Is a Man* (*Fi baytina rajul*, Henri Barakat, 1961), *Almaz and ʿAbduh al-Hamuli* (*Almaz wa Abduh al-Hamuli*, Hilmi Rafla, 1962), *Down with Colonialism* (*Yasqut al-istiʿmar*, Husayn Sidqi, 1952), and *Return My Heart* (*Rudd qalbi*, ʿIzz al-Din Zulficar, 1957).
4. See, for example, *The Inspector General* (*al-Mufattish al-ʿamm*, Hilmi Rafla, 1956), an adaptation of Gogol's *The Inspector-General*. Released at the height of the Suez crisis, it contained a tacked-on ending in which corrupt small-town officials are swept from power by a heroic military coup.
5. I borrow the term from Rugh 2004. Gordon examines (2002) the broader politics of the entire Nasser era—not "political cinema" but rather politics of the period as refracted in a wide variety of films.
6. On the development of tough, heroic masculinity in the career of Farid Shauqi see Armbrust 2002b.
7. *The Prisoner of Abu Zabal* (*Sajin Abu Zabal*, Niyazi Mustafa, 1957) was a melodrama set partly around the discovery of a spy in Port Said during the invasion. After that, the depiction of Suez was relatively muted for almost forty years, until Muhammad Fadil's *Nasser 56* (*Nasir 56*, 1996), a meticulous historical recreation of the events leading to the crisis. For more on the two films see Gordon 2002, 72–79.
8. Only two public-sector productions, *The Ultimate Wedding* (*Muntaha al-farah*, Muhammad Salim, 1963) and *The Revolution of Yemen* (*Thawrat al-Yaman*, ʿAtif Salim, 1966), commented on the war.

9. See also Chahine's *Jamila* (*Jamila bu harid*, 1958). It dramatizes the Algerian war of liberation against French colonialism, using many of the same tropes later featured in Gillo Pontecorvo's *The Battle of Algiers* (1966). Nasser is not depicted directly in *Jamila*, but support for the Algerian cause was popular in Egypt and Nasser's aid to the Algerian FLN well known.
10. Nationalization was not total. Most of the films produced between 1962 and 1972 were privately funded (Gordon 2002, 208).
11. Sharaf al-Din (1992), for example, gives an unfavorable assessment of the public-sector era.
12. A notable exception is *Chatter on the Nile* (*Tharthara fawqa al-Nil*, Husayn Kamal, 1969), which bluntly depicts despair and decadence in the late Nasser years. The film was released after Nasser's death. It is based on a novel by Naguib Mahfouz that was published in 1965, before the Six Day War.
13. *Song on the Pass* was an adaptation of a 1969 play by ʿAli Salim.
14. These films are *The Bath House of Malatili* (*Hamam al-Malatili*, Salah Abu Seif, 1973), *Fear* (*al-Khawf*, Saiʿd Marzuq, 1973), *Wildflowers* (*Zuhur barriyya*, Yusuf Francis, 1973), and *The Back Stairs* (*al-Silim al-khalfi*, Atif Salim, 1973).
15. These include *Children of Silence* (*Abnaʾ al-samt*, Muhammad Radi, 1974), *The Sparrow* (*al-ʿUsfur*, Youssef Chahine, 1974), *The Karnak Café* (*al-Karnak*, Ali Badrakhan, 1975), *Return of the Prodigal Son* (*Awdat al-ibn al-dal*, Youssef Chahine, 1976), *Ascent to the Abyss* (*al-Suʿud ila al-hawiya*, Kamal al-Shaykh, 1978), *Behind the Sun* (*Waraʾ al-shams*, Muhammad Radi, 1978), and *We Are the Bus People* (*Ihna bituʿ al-atubis*, Husayn Kamal, 1979). Badrakhan's, Kamal's, and Radi's films all include scenes of explicit torture, mainly of leftist university students. Kamal's torture scenes are less graphic and include Islamists among the victims. Two other films that deserve mention here are *The Guilty* (*al-Mudhnibun*, Saʿid Marzuq, 1976), and *On Whom Do We Open Fire?* (*ʿAla man nutliq ar-rasas*, Kamal al-Shaykh, 1975), which do not depict the wars but are harshly critical of the social legacy of Nasserism.
16. See Armbrust 1996 on actor ʿAdil Imam's antimodernist trilogy: *Rajab on a Hot Tin Roof* (*Rajab ʿala safih sakhin*, Ahmad Fuad, 1979), *Shaʿban below Zero* (*Shaban taht al-sifr*, Henri Barakat, 1980), and *Ramadan on the Volcano* (*Ramadan fawqa al-burkan*, Ahmad al-Sabʿawi, 1985).
17. Other signature works of new realism are *Vagabonds* (*al-Saʿalik*, Daud ʿAbd al-Sayyid, 1985), *Return of a Citizen* (*ʿAwdat muwatin*, Muhammad Khan, 1986), and *Bitter Day, Sweet Day* (*Yawm murr, yawm hilw*, Khairy Bishara, 1988).
18. In Daud ʿAbd al-Sayyid's *Land of Dreams* (*Ard al-ahlam*, 1993), a woman loses her passport the night before she is to emigrate to America; her frantic search for the missing passport gives her cause to rethink the move. In Khairy Bishara's *America Abracadabra* (*Amrika shika bika*, 1993), members of a group of Egyptians have been told that they can get visas to America if they travel to Romania; again the experience causes them to consider whether they really want to emigrate. Among

the anti-American films, *The Toughest People* (*Agdaʿ nas*, Midhat al-Sharif, 1993) depicts a visit of the American national karate team to Egypt. An apparently outgunned Egyptian team triumphs over them. The decisive last match pits Egypt's best fighter against a sinister American Jew who cheats. Other films made America into a central narrative device, enabling meditations on Egyptian national character. See, for example, *An Upper Egyptian in the American University* (*Saʿidi fi al-Jamiʿa al-Amirikiya*, Saʿid Hamid, 1998), *Hello America* (*Allu Amrika*, Nadir Galal, 2000), and *Alexandria ... New York* (*Iskandiriya ... New York*, Youssef Chahine, 2004). One might also mention *The Visit of Mr. President* (*Ziyarat al-Sayyid al-Raʾis*, Munir Radi, 1994), which revolves around the visit of Richard Nixon to Egypt in 1974, just after America had restored Israeli military superiority in the October War. Rumors of Nixon's train stopping in a delta town causes a frenzy of greed, as the townspeople assume that Nixon's brief stop will bring them vast quantities of American aid.

19. Al-ʿAryan is Palestinian American, not Egyptian, but all his media work has been in the Middle East. The five films he has directed thus far are mainstream Egyptian productions.

20. Examples include comedies such as *Haman in Amsterdam* (*Hamam fi Amstirdam*, Saʿid Hamid, 1999), *Hello America*, *Africano* (Amru ʿArafa, 2001), set in South Africa, and *Great Beans of China* (*Ful al-Sin al-aʿzim*, Sharif ʿArafa, 2004); action films such as *Mafia* (Sharif Arafa, 2002), set in Europe; and co-produced art-house films by Chahine, *Alexandria ... New York* (2004), and Yousry Nasrallah, *The City* (*al-Madina*, 1999), set in Paris.

21. For details on official and quasi-official American and Israeli global campaigns against anti-Semitism see Armbrust 2007a.

22. Egyptian films have begun to address America's Iraqi experience. *An Upper Egyptian in the American University* depicts campus protests against American sanctions in the 1990s. *The Night Baghdad Fell* (*Laylat suqut Baghdad*, Muhammad Amin, 2005), *Excuse Us, We're Being Humiliated* (*Maʿalish ihna binitbahdal*, Sharif Mandur, 2005), and *Night of the Baby Doll* (*Laylat al-baby doll*, Adil Adib, 2008) make reference to the invasion and to American torture in Abu Ghrayb prison.

23. Narratives set in "classical" Islamic history, the seventh to tenth centuries, include *Lashin* (Fritz Kramp, 1938) and the Umm Kulthum vehicles *Widad* (Fritz Kramp, 1936), *Dinanir* (Ahmad Badrakhan, 1940), and *Salama* (Togo Mizrahi, 1945). None is about religion per se. Their invocation of classical Islamic civilization stems from nationalist before Islamic imperatives. Films depict Islamic history in narratives that focus on religion directly, though not necessarily to the complete exclusion of nationalism; such films include *The Victory of Islam* (*Intisar al-Islam*, Ahmad al-Tukhi, 1952), *Rabiʿa al-ʿAdawiya* (Niyazi Mustafa, 1963), Chahine's *Saladin* (1963), *The Dawn of Islam* (*Fajr al-Islam*, Salah Abu Seif, 1971), and *Al-Shaymaʾ* (Husam al-Din Mustafa, 1972). Other films portray religious characters

in modern society; among them are *Faith* (*al-Iman*, Ahmad Badrakhan, 1952), *The Night of Fate* (*Laylat al-qadr*, Husayn Sidqi, 1952), and *They Made Me a Criminal* (*Jaʿaluni mujriman*, Atif Salim, 1954). For more on religion in Egyptian cinema see Qasim 1997.

24. Diacritica are marks used to distinguish in the performance of the self. They index selves in a social field. Examples in contemporary Egyptian society are, for women, the neo-Islamic *hijab* along with a wide range of modest clothes worn in increasingly diverse ways, and for men, beards and the *zabiba*, a callus on the forehead cultivated (only by men) from touching the head on the ground in prostrations during prayer. Diacritica can consist of bodily dispositions, such as deferential body language that conveys modesty aside from elements of dress, and linguistic registers. Religion is only one social characteristic that can be conveyed indexically. Class, seniority, education, and modernity are others.

25. A few films from the period address social conditions of the times obliquely: Yusuf Wahbi's *The Blacksmith's Son* (*Ibn al-haddad*, 1944), Kamil al-Tilmisani's *Black Market* (*al-Suq al-suda'*, 1945), and actor Husayn Sidqi vehicle *Al-Misri the Efendi* (*al-Misri Efendi*, Husayn Fauzi, 1949). Sidqi was a sympathizer or perhaps outright member of the Muslim Brotherhood. His films did not overtly depict the Brotherhood, which by 1944 was estimated to have anywhere from 100,000 to 500,000 members. No films of the period allude to the widespread political violence: assassinations, demonstrations—often put down violently by the authorities—and strikes.

26. *Pay Attention to Zuzu* is the only one I have seen; possibly there are others. For more on *Zuzu* see Armbrust 1996, 117–125.

27. Arafa's *The Strangers* (*Ghuraba'*, 1973) was another pro-Islamist anomaly. *Al-Shayma'*, a historical film structured around the Prophet Muhammad's foster sister al-Shayma', and Salah Abu Seif's *The Dawn of Islam* can be seen as part of a state strategy to enlist Islamists against the left while mobilizing the country to fight Israel.

28. Actresses taking the veil were often interpreted as having repented, understood as leaving the profession. See Abu-Lughod 1995, Shafik 2001b.

29. *The Terrorist* was credited with breaking the ice on the subject of Islamism in cinema, but the ice was cracking around that time anyway. In addition to al-Tayyib's *Uncovering the Hidden*, Sharif ʿArafa's *Terrorism and Kabab* (*al-Irhab wa al-Kabab*, 1992) features open mocking of an Islamist character (see Armbrust 1998). Such mocking also occurs in Inas Al-Dighidi's *Disco, Disco* (*Disku disku*, 1993), which denigrates a form of Islamist literature also prominent in *The Terrorist* (see Armbrust 2002a). *Ramadan on the Volcano, Mercedes* (*Mirsaydis*, Yousry Nasrallah, 1994), and *We Are the Bus People* likewise launched broadsides at Islamists.

30. For more on Chahine's films see Fawal 2001.

31. It is, in my opinion, the best Egyptian political film ever made. Shafik provides an excellent analysis (2006, 294–301).

32. Another superb stand-alone film that should be mentioned is *I Love Cinema* (*Bahibb al-sima*, Usama Fawzi, 2004), which critically depicts Coptic religious zealotry. Few Egyptian films depict Copts at all, and historically most that have included reference to Copts do so to explicitly endorse Coptic-Muslim unity within Egyptian nationalism. A parallel sector of Coptic film and television production exists, but as yet there is no academic literature on it.
33. *Closed Doors* was quite controversial in Egypt and has never been shown widely. A more extensive analysis of the film can be found in Armbrust 2002a.
34. Youssef Chahine's final film, *Chaos* (*Heya fawda*, 2007), did follow up *Yacoubian* with another critical discussion of police brutality.

REFERENCES

Abu-Lughod, Lila. 1995. "Movie Stars and Islamic Moralism in Egypt." *Social Text* 42 (1): 53–67.

Armbrust, Walter. 1996. *Mass Culture and Modernism in Egypt*. Cambridge, England: Cambridge University Press.

———. 1998. "Terrorism and Kabab: A Capra-esque View of Modern Egypt." In *Images of Enchantment: Performance, Art, and Image of the Middle East*, ed. Sherifa Zuhur, 283–299. Cairo: American University in Cairo Press.

———. 2002a. "Islamists in Egyptian Cinema." *American Anthropologist* 104 (3): 922–931.

———. 2002b. "Manly Men on the National Stage (and the Women Who Make Them Stars)." In *Histories of the Modern Middle East: New Directions*, ed. Ursula Wokoeck, Hakan Erdem, and Israel Gershoni, 247–278. Boulder, CO: Lynne Rienner.

———. 2004. "Egyptian Cinema On Stage and Off." In *Off Stage/On Display: Intimacy and Ethnography in the Age of Public Culture*, ed. Andrew Shryock, 69–100. Stanford, CA: Stanford University Press.

———. 2007a. "Bravely Stating the Obvious: Egyptian Humor and the Anti-American Consensus." *Arab Media and Society* (Fall). http://www.arabmediasociety.org/?article=413 (accessed July 14, 2009).

———. 2007b. "Ismail Yasin in the Coloring Book." *ARTE News*, October 1. http://www.arteeast.dreamhosters.com/pages/artenews/nostalgias/128/.

———. 2008. "Long Live Patriarchy: Love in the Time of Muhammad Abd al-Wahhab." *History Compass* 6 (December). http://www.blackwell-compass.com/subject/history/article_view?article_id=hico_articles_bpl575.

Aswany, Alaa Al-. 2004. *The Yacoubian Building*. Cairo: American University in Cairo Press. Translation by Humphrey Davies of ʿImarat Yaʿqubyan, Cairo: Maktabat Madbuli, 2003.

Fawal, Ibrahim. 2001. *Youssef Chahine*. London: bfi.

Gordon, Joel. 2002. *Revolutionary Melodrama: Popular Film and Civic Identity in Nasser's Egypt*. Chicago: Middle East Documentation Center.

Mahfouz, Naguib. 1999. *Adrift on the Nile*. Cairo: American University in Cairo Press. Translation by Frances Liardet of *Tharthara fawqa al-Nil*, Cairo: Maktabat Misr, 1965.

Qasim, Mahmud. 1997. *Surat al-Adyan fi al-sinima al-misriyah*. Cairo: Markaz al-Qawmi lil-Sinima.

Rugh, William. 2004. *The Arab Mass Media: Newspapers, Radio, and Television in Arab Politics*. Westport, CT: Greenwood Press.

Salim, ʿAli. 1969. *Thalath masrahiyat: Bir al-qamh; ughniya ʿala al-mamarr; al-mubawwaqiyya*. Cairo: Dar al-Thaqafa al-Jadida.

Shafik, Viola. 2001a. "Egyptian Cinema." In *Companion Encyclopedia of Middle Eastern and North African Film*, ed. Oliver Leaman, 23–129. London: Routledge.

———. 2001b. "Prostitute for a Good Reason: Stars and Morality in Egypt." *Women's Studies International Forum* 24 (6): 711–725.

———. 2006. *Popular Egyptian Cinema: Gender, Class, and Nation*. Cairo: American University in Cairo Press.

Sharaf al-Din, Duriyya. 1992. *al-Siyasa wa al-sinima fi misr, 1961–1981*. Cairo: Dar al-Shuruq.

Slackman, Michael. 2005. "Egyptian Comedy Takes Peace Seriously." *New York Times*, September 21. http://www.nytimes.com/2005/09/20/world/africa/20iht-egypt.html (accessed July 16, 2009).

Zayyat, Latifa. 2000. *The Open Door*. Cairo: American University in Cairo Press. Translation by Marilyn Booth of *al-Bab al-Maftuh*, Cairo: Maktabat al-Anjlu al-Misriya, 1960.

Courtesy Marianne Khoury

*Destiny**
Liberal and Fundamentalist Islam Clash amid the Splendor of Twelfth-Century Andalusia

JOSEF GUGLER

Youssef Chahine is one of the very few Egyptian filmmakers to enjoy international recognition. In 1997 at the fiftieth Cannes Film Festival, where *Destiny* was screened, he received the Lifetime Achievement Award. In Egypt Chahine has been attacked over several of his films, but he is also highly respected. When in 1996 the Egyptian film community named the top one hundred films in the history of Egyptian cinema, he came first with thirteen listings (Fawal 2001, 199). The descendant of immigrants from present-day Lebanon, Syria, and Greece, Chahine grew up in a family in which four languages were spoken. Educated at a prestigious British-style school, he subsequently trained in the United States at Pasadena Playhouse. Born into Egypt's small Catholic community, he represents a cosmopolitan tradition based on Alexandria. He married a Frenchwoman born and raised in Alexandria as well.[1]

Chahine was prompted to produce *Destiny*, his thirty-third film by one count, by his clash with Egyptian fundamentalists who had attacked him over his preceding film, *The Emigrant* (*al-Mohager*, 1994). *The Emigrant* had been banned for blasphemy, Chahine had received personal threats, and he was taken to court, where he won eventually. He proceeded to resurrect "an old dream, to make a film about the Golden Age of Islam, about Arab Andalusia and true Islam which is extraordinarily tolerant" (Chahine 1997b).

Destiny, released when Chahine was seventy-one, is perhaps his finest film.[2] While recalling the achievements of Islamic civilization and its philosophical

---

* *Destiny/al-Masir.* 1997. Film directed by Youssef Chahine; written by Youssef Chahine with the collaboration of Khaled Youssef. Produced by Ognon Pictures (France), France 2 Cinéma (France), and Misr International Films (Egypt). Distributed in the United States by New Yorker Films and Leisure Time Features. 135 minutes.

Youssef Chahine and lead actress Laila Eloui celebrate his Cannes Lifetime Achievement Award. Courtesy Marianne Khoury

and scientific contributions to the rise of the West, the film gives historical depth to the conflict between liberals and fundamentalists. Chahine presents a twofold critique of fundamentalist ideology. The anti-fundamentalist teachings of a renowned twelfth-century Muslim philosopher are complemented by Chahine's own anti-fundamentalist philosophy of life—that life is to be lived and enjoyed to the fullest. *Destiny* is the story of a sage and lovers of life confronting life-denying fundamentalists hungry for power.

Destiny revolves around the life and teachings of Averroës, also known as Ibn Rushd, who was influential in Jewish and Christian thought and played a key role in the transmission of classical scholarship to Western Christianity.[3] The film shows a humanist Averroës confronting the fundamentalists of his day. The film was released just in time for the eight-hundredth anniversary of the death of Averroës (1126–1198).

A film about a philosopher may suggest a soporific, but *Destiny* partakes of passionate romance and melodrama;[4] the film features song, dance, and revelry; it is spiced with intrigue, suspense, and derring-do; and it is leavened with humor. If Chahine draws on the traditions of Egyptian cinema and Hollywood to provide thrilling entertainment, he also transcends them. The song and dance sequences, seamlessly integrated into the action, serve to complement the philosopher's teachings with Chahine's philosophy of *joie de vivre*. It is conveyed by music and dance at the tavern of Manuella, the gypsy woman, and most especially by Marwan's songs. The first song we hear defies Borhan, the fundamentalist hit man, enjoining his listeners: "Hear me, lovers of life." Marwan's second song, after he has recovered from his wound, calls for resistance to the fundamentalist threat:

> Sing your song to your heart's content
> for we can still sing.
> And we will keep on singing
> day in, day out, for the rest of our lives.

Muslims had established control over most of present-day Spain and Portugal within a few years of crossing over from North Africa in 711. Their flourishing civilization presented a stark contrast to the Dark Ages of Western Christianity. *Destiny* brings to life the splendor of Muslim Andalusia. The epic film is set at the end of the twelfth century in Córdoba, which by 1000 CE had become the world's third-largest city, with a population estimated at 450,000, surpassed only by Baghdad and Constantinople (Modelski 2003). Chahine introduces viewers to the city with a sequence at a market overflowing with books, every one of them produced by scribes in long hours of painstaking work. *Destiny*

Joseph arrives in Córdoba.

features the impressive architecture of classic Arab palaces and mosques. They are, however, not located in Andalusia, but in Syria and Lebanon. Chahine had explored shooting in southern Spain (1997b). But while he found the locations amazing, they were flooded with tourists, and, apart from the monuments, the cities had changed beyond recognition from what they had been in Arab times.[5]

The film shows what the screenplay can only describe, and it adds glimpses of Arab achievements in physics such as Averroës's telescope and the caliph's shipyard. Marwan makes the music and poetry of Andalusia come alive. Eventually a visit to the world-famous library of Alexandria reinforces our appreciation that Islam represented the region's preeminent civilization. Averroës stood at the pinnacle of this learned civilization.

Destiny reminds us that the conflict between liberals and fundamentalists is nothing new in Islam; in fact, they have confronted each other time and again in each of the monotheistic religions. *Destiny* is set in the twelfth century, but it is a comment on the present. Fundamentalists then instigated the burning of Averroës's books; their spiritual descendants sought to have *The Emigrant* banned. Fundamentalists have Marwan stabbed in *Destiny*; they had Nobel laureate Naguib Mahfouz stabbed in 1994. Caliph Al Mansur feels that he has to accommodate the fundamentalists, and so do rulers in many Muslim countries today.

Given his background, it is not surprising that Chahine is opposed to fundamentalism of any stripe, to all fundamentalisms. This rejection is emotionally charged by what happened to Mahfouz and by Chahine's own experiences. Even before the attack on *The Emigrant*, Chahine had seen young actors he had nurtured renounce acting as incompatible with their newfound fundamentalist beliefs (Chahine 1997d, 47). Mohsen Mohiedine, for one, had appeared in several Chahine films and was to have played Abdallah in *Destiny*, but he joined a fundamentalist sect as the shooting was about to begin. Chahine tells of another actor he had recruited for one of his major films, *The Sixth Day* (*al-Yawm al-sadis*, 1986), who joined the fundamentalists in the middle of the shoot and within three weeks became "a zombie" (1997a).[6] Eventually Chahine succeeded, with the help of friends, to extract the actor from the sway of fundamentalism. The script of *Destiny* is based on that experience.[7]

In *Destiny* the twelfth-century philosopher appears quite like Chahine's alter ego. In an interview (1997d, 58), Chahine acknowledges the resemblance between Averroës and himself. The philosopher certainly represents Chahine's humanist ideas. And neither man flinches from confronting unjust rulers and intolerant religious leaders. The historical Averroës is unlikely, though, to have been such a jolly fellow, appreciative of song and dance, but that portrayal fits

Chahine well. Chahine composed a little song for *Destiny* (ibid.), and he confided in another interview (1997c): "When I am writing and a good idea comes my way, I begin to dance all alone like a fool." The humor and laughter of the film's Averroës echoes in Chahine's interviews.

Chahine invented a great deal, with little regard for historical accuracy, as Meddeb spells out (1997).[8] Aiming for a mass audience, Chahine created the implausible character of an eminent twelfth-century philosopher partaking of popular entertainment. Averroës's friendship with Marwan is pure fantasy, even if the character of Marwan recalls the famous twelfth-century poet Ibn Quzman. The historical Averroës likely was cloistered in his library, moving within a small elite. After all, his was an elitist philosophy that sought to restrict the interpretation of the Quran to philosophers like himself. We hear very little philosophy from the protagonist—philosophical discourse a popular film does not make. Still, *Destiny* conveys key elements of Averroës's writing: the affirmation of the importance of reason alongside revelation; the homage rendered to the Hellenic tradition—the pre-Islamic era of ignorance, according to Islamic interpretation—and with it the acceptance of the Other; the Platonic affirmation of the equality of the sexes.

Destiny has Averroës confronting the fundamentalists with the affirmation "No one can claim to know the whole truth." In his writings, Averroës advanced a more far-reaching claim for philosophy. He argued that demonstrative reasoning cannot clash with the principles of religion, that philosophy and theology are compatible—and he claimed for philosophers the final word in disputes:

> We affirm definitely that whenever the conclusion of a demonstration is in conflict with the apparent meaning of Scripture [or Religious Law], that apparent meaning admits of allegorical interpretation according to the rules for such interpretation in Arabic. This proposition is questioned by no Muslim and doubted by no believer. But its certainty is immensely increased for those who have had close dealing with this idea and put it to the test, and made it their aim to reconcile assertions of intellect and tradition. (In Taylor 2005, 186)

Chahine adopts a Manichean perspective of good liberals against evil fundamentalists. His story leaves out the conservative philosophers who proposed a fundamentalist interpretation of Islam; it does not acknowledge that the proponents of fundamentalism were seen by many as men of God. Chahine only allows for power-hungry subversives who do not shrink from murder. The simplistic characterization of fundamentalists is matched by a refusal to explore their appeal. Abdallah, the prince who is treated by his father as a wayward child, is drawn into the fundamentalists' arms by flattery, and so was the brother of one of Marwan's attackers. As for that attacker, he is an unemployed youth, and his mother appears to agree with what everybody says about her son: that he is a good-for-nothing who talks about making her and all her neighbors rich.[9] In sharp contrast, Atef Hetata's *Closed Doors* (*al-Abwab al-moghlaka*, 1999) grounds the fundamentalist mass appeal in contemporary Egypt in the failure of a political class intent on enriching itself and the Muslim Brotherhood's message of purity.[10] Chahine's Al Mansur is not corrupt, but when challenged by his brother, he proclaims: "I am Andalusia!"—quite like contemporary rulers in nearly all Arab countries who have usurped absolute power.

The film concludes with Averroës and his followers being banished from Córdoba and his books being burned at the instigation of Muslim fundamentalists.[11] But Chahine ends *Destiny* with a coda of hope. As the flames devour Averroës's books, we hear Marwan sing once more and eventually read, "Ideas have wings. No one can stop their flight." This affirmation, previously enunciated by the caliph's brother, is now signed "Youssef Chahine." Viewers may appreciate such an uplifting ending, but, of course, fundamentalist ideas do not lack for wings. Nor does the historical record support such an optimistic conclusion. Averroës was rehabilitated within a year or so, but philosophy itself fell into something of a disgrace in the Muslim community. Only at the end of the nineteenth century, with the modernist movement in Islam, was interest in Averroës rekindled (Leaman 1998, 163–178). "Averroes' philosophy marks the climactic point in the development of Arab-Islamic philosophy and the conclusion of four centuries of philosophical warfare in Islam," Fakhry has observed (2001, xv); the conservative philosophers had won the war. In Western Christianity, Averroës had a profound influence, but the Catholic Church, like the Islamic establishment, rejected his views of the relationship between reason and revelation.

The film starts out with another burning, this one in Languedoc, across the Pyrenees, the *auto-da-fé* of Joseph's father and his works, translations of treatises written by Averroës; the first wave of Inquisitions by the Catholic Church had just begun. Asked by a French interviewer about this prologue, Chahine did not mince words:

> You have forgotten your own history. As I said in one of my earlier movies, when my ancestors were building the pyramids, your granny was eating grampa's forearm. Mathematics, medicine, algebra, astronomy, cartography all started with the Arabs. Now you treat us like baboons. You're in the wrong.

A few centuries ago, you were pretty brutal. Of course, there were some [enlightened] people in Europe, they were the ones you prosecuted. And today, the torture, the lies, the obsession with racial distinctions are still going on. It's not nice. It's time to speak up about it. (Chahine 1997b)

NOTES

1. Malek Khouri's 2010 study of Chahine was published too late for me to consult.
2. The DVD issued in France, which offers English subtitles and a glossary, has both an Arabic and a French version. The spoken French is more expansive and refined than the French subtitles, which closely follow the published French screenplay (Chahine 1997d). That script appears somewhat like a draft, one of twenty-one successive versions (Chahine 1997a). The film drops several characters, avoids some implausibilities, and gains in cinematic quality.
3. Averroës commented at length on nearly all the writings of Aristotle. Translations of his commentaries played the principal role in introducing the philosopher to Catholic Europe, where the Greek heritage had been all but lost. Averroës was commonly referred to as "The Commentator" in medieval Europe. For an introduction to his writings and their impact on Western Christianity see Leaman 1998.
4. The melodrama reaches an extreme when the dying Marwan addresses his final words to Abdallah: "I wish it had been you who delivered the deadly blow. To die by your hand ... what bliss."
5. *Destiny* was one of Chahine's most expensive films (Chahine 1997d, 53). The film was shot on location in Syria, Lebanon, Egypt, and France, where the *auto-da-fé* is set in Carcassone. Chahine recruited stars such as Nour El Cherif, Mohamed Mounir, and Laila Eloui while nurturing young actors, as was his wont. Chahine was able to produce the epic film because he co-produced it with French partners, received additional financing from a French television channel and public agencies, and enjoyed generous material support from the authorities in Syria and Lebanon as well as from Walid Jumblatt, the Lebanese politician.
6. Translations from the French are mine.
7. The parallels in Chahine's experience with the actor from *The Sixth Day* are obvious, but the transcript of Jean-Michel Frodon's interview with Chahine (1997a) is misleading when it suggests that the same actor took on the role of Abdallah.
8. *Destiny* avoids the use of classical Arabic except for several short passages from Averroës's writing (Meddeb 1997). Chahine has argued (1997d) that an effective delivery of classic Arabic would have required highly accomplished professionals such as are rare to find, especially when it comes to representing young characters. He tells of working hard at making an extremely simplified language as poetical as possible. *Destiny* thus brings the dialogue into the viewers' present.

9. Unlike other Chahine films, Destiny found distribution in the United States straight away. Massad addresses the distributor's interest in *Destiny*: "Given Chahine's depiction of the Islamists as a fantastic mix of Protestant puritans, ruthless assassins, evil mafiosi, and obscurantist cultists—an image that does not fit the most extreme among them, much less the majority—it seems hardly coincidental that this is the only film of Chahine's that has ever been picked up by a U.S. distributor" (1999, 82). Several other Chahine films have found U.S. distribution since.
10. On *Closed Doors* see the essay in this volume.
11. The Egyptian poster reproduced here highlights the burning of Averroës's books and conveys the epic character of the film with a crowd scene. Another Egyptian poster promotes the film with portraits of actors complementing the book burning, giving major play to Nour El Cherif. The French poster is entirely devoted to the book burning; a variation superimposes Chahine brandishing the scroll of his Lifetime Achievement Award.

REFERENCES

Chahine, Youssef. 1997a. "Entretien avec le réalisateur." Interview by Jean-Michel Frodon. *Le Monde*, May 17.

———. 1997b. "Interview." In *Le destin*, press book. Paris: Pyramide.

———. 1997c. "La leçon de la tolérance." Interview by Sophie Grassin. *L'Express*, October 16, 13.

———. 1997d. *Scénario Le destin. Traduit de l'arabe par Marie-Pierre Müller et Yousry Nasrallah. Précédé d'un entretien avec le cinéaste sur l'ensemble de son œuvre*. Paris: Petite Bibliothèque des Cahiers du Cinéma. The interviews, by Thierry Jousse, were first published in 1996 and 1997 in *Cahiers du Cinéma* 506:9–30 and 517:35–39.

Fakhry, Majid. 2001. *Averroes (Ibn Rushd): His Life, Works and Influence*. Oxford, England: Oneworld.

Fawal, Ibrahim. 2001. *Youssef Chahine*. World Directors. London: British Film Institute.

Khouri, Malek. 2010. *The Arab National Project in Youssef Chahine's Cinema*. Cairo: American University in Cairo Press.

Leaman, Oliver. 1998. *Averroes and His Philosophy*. Revised edition. Richmond, Surrey, England: Curzon.

Massad, Joseph. 1999. "Art and Politics in the Cinema of Youssef Chahine." *Journal of Palestine Studies* 28 (2): 77–93.

Meddeb, Abdelwahab, 1997. "Réplique à l'intégrisme: Entretien avec Abdelwahab Meddeb." Interview by Antonio de Baecque. *Cahiers du Cinéma* 517:40–43.

Modelski, George. 2003. *World Cities: -3000 to 2000*. Washington, DC: Faros 2000.

Taylor, Richard C. 2005. "Averroes: Religious Dialectic and Aristotelian Philosophical Thought." In *The Cambridge Companion to Arabic Philosophy*, ed. Peter Adamson and Richard C. Taylor, 180–200. Cambridge, England: Cambridge University Press.

Closed Doors*
The Attractions of Fundamentalism

JOSEF GUGLER AND KIM JENSEN

Closed Doors (1999),[1] a social-realist depiction of life in Cairo during the 1991 Gulf War, tells a compelling story of male adolescence while condemning an array of social, economic, and political ills in modern-day Egypt. This vivid exploration of the disastrous effects of poverty, repressive moral codes, and the rise of religious fundamentalism is one of the strongest political films to emerge from Egypt since the late 1990s. In his debut feature, director Atef Hetata attacks fundamentalism, as did Chahine two years earlier, but *Closed Doors* does what *Destiny* failed to do: it purposefully depicts the attractions of religious extremism. While some viewers might wish for a more differentiated picture of fundamentalist leaders and a less dramatic ending, the film effectively conveys the seductive qualities of the fundamentalist creed and community.

The film is the coming-of-age tale of an adolescent, Mohamed, also known as Hamada. His father has deserted the family for a younger wife, and Hamada and his hard-working mother, Fatma, live in poverty in a small apartment on a rooftop. Meanwhile, the Gulf War has exacerbated an economic and moral crisis in Egypt, making life even more difficult for the family of two. Faced with a life of poverty, a repressive atmosphere at school, and a turbulent sexual awakening, Mohamed, a likable young dreamer, is slowly drawn toward radical Islam as a convincing solution for his many dilemmas.[2]

Closed Doors is filled with details of working-class life and a boy's adolescence, some heartbreaking, others humorous, details that give the film a memorable humane quality. Hetata's finely nuanced characters have psychological

---

* *Closed Doors/al-Abwab al-moghlaka*. 1999. Film written and directed by Atef Hetata. Produced by Misr International Films (Egypt), Médiane Production (France), and Arte France Cinéma (France). Distributed in the United States by Arab Film Distribution. 110 minutes.

Courtesy Marianne Khoury

depth; the actors' performances are compelling; and a politically astute camera suggests that these eminently likable characters' troubles are rooted primarily in economic difficulties and a repressive social climate.

The doors of proper education and occupational opportunity are effectively closed for an adolescent of Hamada's background. In school he finds himself in a large, crowded class with authoritarian teachers who routinely cane students and who are known to be corrupt. Even with tutoring, there is little prospect that Hamada will be able to go to college, let alone realize his dream of becoming a pilot. Hamada's callous father offers him nothing more than emigration to one of the oil-rich countries; but his older brother, Salah, who has already taken this route, vanished after being drafted into the Iraqi army during the war with Iran.

A more promising future seems to open up when a teacher, Hassan, persuades Hamada to take Arabic tutorials in the tranquil, comforting environment of the local mosque. One of the clerics, Sheik Khaled, soon becomes a surrogate father figure for Hamada, offering much-needed guidance and support. When Hamada's mother loses her job as a maid for a wealthy, lecherous boss and his bitter, alcoholic wife, the mosque steps in to provide Hamada with financial help. As Hamada's adolescent body and mind are wracked by sexual urges, the sheik helps to channel the boy's natural lust into a more legitimate yearning for the hereafter. And while the Egyptian government is shown to be collaborating with Western powers by participating in the U.S. attack on Iraq during the Gulf War, Sheik Khaled passionately advocates Muslim brotherhood and solidarity.

The benefits of religious fundamentalism—sustenance, guidance, moral certainty—are persuasive, at least to the teenage protagonist, who lacks any adult male support outside the mosque. Hamada's emotional floundering leads him to embrace the comprehensive personal and social salvation that radical Islam represents. The adolescent, who early in the film acts out the role of a jilted lover in front of his bedroom mirror, now rehearses a sermon:

> We live in a society of heretics. They take no heed of God's word. Morality no longer exists. Sin and corruption are rife. Some people make millions. They hoard gold and silver while today's youth live in poverty. Poverty and despair.

The tension in the film is created by the contrast between Hamada's trust of the religious leaders and most viewers' essential distrust of their fundamentalist worldview. This distrust is cultivated by Hetata's camera. Hassan may appear kindly, but the solemn way the camera rests on Hassan's pensive face, blazoned with a dark "prayer scar" on his forehead, when he recruits Hamada catalyzes the viewer's suspicions. Sheik Khaled, the man who becomes Hamada's mentor, can readily be seen as sinister in appearance and demeanor. While the religious leaders depicted here are never categorically vilified, the film portrays them as opportunists who seduce Egypt's most vulnerable youth.

Hamada's panic and confusion only increase with his religious indoctrination as he is torn in opposite directions. The clerics' strict doctrines contradict not only his body and his desires but also his mother's somewhat liberal, nonjudgmental outlook. The conflict escalates when Sheik Khaled begins to press Hamada to control his mother's life, advising him to not let her work, to keep her inside the house, and to make sure she covers her head. Eventually Sheik Khaled offers to help protect Fatma's honor by arranging a marriage for her with his own spiritual leader, Sheik Aziz, an unpleasant-looking older man who is already married. This prospect is firmly and angrily rejected by Fatma.

Complementary to the political and social dimension of *Closed Doors*, the internal family dynamic is central to the development of the story. As a divorced single mother, Fatma's relationship with her son is loving and intimate. This intimacy, however, becomes problematic as Hamada's adolescent sexual drive transforms into an occasional incestuous impulse. In addition to this dilemma, Hamada's budding patriarchal aspirations exacerbate the tension between the two. As the film unfolds, Hamada increasingly wants to assume the authoritarian role of "the man of the house." He sets out to establish himself as the family provider and insists that his mother stay at home. As he becomes more deeply influenced by the fundamentalists, their teachings further expand the restrictions he seeks to impose on Fatma.[3]

If a sexual element emerges in the relationship between Hamada and his mother, the appearance of his teacher Mansour triggers an Oedipal reaction. Mansour agrees to tutor Hamada in their home free of charge, but Hamada realizes that Mansour's seemingly generous offer is a ploy to get closer to his mother. Hamada has additional reasons for disliking and mistrusting this "intruder" beyond Oedipal reactions. Mansour is the very teacher who has beaten and humiliated Hamada at school.[4]

Hamada's rejection of Mansour is further reinforced by religious teachings that condemn the courtship developing between Mansour and Fatma.[5] Thus Hamada continues to lack a strong educational role model as well as a worthy father figure. The Islamic community, however, is able to fill these particular gaps and many more. Sheik Khaled and Hassan have an answer to every social, political, spiritual, and emotional crisis faced by the confused, unhappy protagonist. In their warm embrace, Hamada believes that he will flourish.

Sheik Khaled urges a morsel on Hamada.

In one pivotal scene, we see Hamada radiant at a meal hosted by Sheik Khaled. Sitting between the sheik and Hassan, he relishes the friendly banter between the two and feels part of the community. Sheik Khaled feeds Hamada a morsel of food by hand, further reinforcing the notion that religious communities nourish the whole person, body and soul. In another important scene, Mohamed and other young recruits sit with Sheik Khaled in a circle, basking in his attention. Their faces are ablaze, enraptured, by the sheik's intoxicating descriptions of the virgins of paradise. This scene of spiritual entrancement conveys how effectively Hamada has been drawn into the fundamentalist orbit.

While Hamada is told that the doors to paradise are opening toward him, the viewer perceives a different truth: the doors of reality are actually slamming all around him. The clerics are turning him against his own natural urges and feelings, against his mother, against their neighbor Zeinab, and against Mansour, his teacher, tutor, and potential father. Hamada himself closes up the peep hole in his high school classroom through which he used to eye the girls at the school next door.

In the midst of this indoctrination, Hamada still has two last two secular influences in his life—his lawless new friend Awadin and his neighbor, a prostitute named Zeinab. The free-spirited Awadin invites Hamada to join him in becoming a street vendor. Together they hawk cheap goods to motorists in downtown Cairo. Hamada grows to care deeply about Awadin, who is anything but devout. Awadin curses, speaks freely of his incestuous experiences, and takes Hamada to visit a brothel.

While that mission fails, the kind-hearted, "loose" neighbor Zeinab, confidante of Fatma, is willing to initiate Hamada sexually. Zeinab's character is emblematic of all that Hamada finds corrupt—she wears lipstick, smokes, listens to romantic popular music—yet he is drawn to her. But each time he lurches toward her with sexual fervor, he withdraws precipitously, ever conscious of his moral transgression. Awadin ironically pinpoints the adolescent's conflict when he asks Hamada: "Are you Romeo or a fundamentalist?"

Awadin's perceptive query underscores Hamada's dilemma: he is tortured by his attraction to two opposing forces, his sexual desires and his emotional need for religious purity and community. Hamada is tempted by the libertine lifestyle Awadin represents, and their friendship appears as a final escape route from the fundamentalist leaders who are interfering more and more in his private life. But when Awadin dies a sudden accidental death, this last door is closed abruptly as well.

Awadin's death marks the critical turning point in the film. Overcome by grief, Hamada seeks succor. He runs home to his mother, but she is away—presumably with Mansour. Distraught, he dashes off to the mosque, but Sheik Khaled is said to be at his village preaching. Hamada hitches a ride to the village, just missing the sheik's fiery speech condemning corruption, Western decadence, and Egypt's alignment with the United States in the 1991 Gulf War.

The Arab regimes that condoned and even participated in the 1991 attack on Iraq were widely denounced across the Arab world. And many viewers will have no reservations about the sheik's moral teachings, either. However, most will likely part company when he invokes the necessity of holy war:

> Pagan communism has died in Eastern Europe. In the West the system has given way to decadence, promiscuity, homosexuality, and corruption. Humanity needs a new direction. The Islamic nation must strive to take the helm. It was, and always has been, the best of nations . . . He who sees wrongs must set them right. The Holy War is necessary to wipe out corruption and to pave the way for Islam.

It is this aggressive and dogmatic certitude that genuinely assuages Hamada's tormented spirit. Later, when an army deserter at the assembly exclaims, "I have no country. My homeland is Islam," Hamada finally collapses in tears. It is a form of baptism; he has forever broken with his past. Hamada finds solace with the sheik, and he is now entirely committed to the fundamentalist creed. It is from this climactic moment onward that the film moves quickly to its tragic conclusion. Hamada's indoctrination leads him to commit an act of extreme violence from which there is no return.

Because *Closed Doors* offers a subtle story with nuanced characters, its dramatic conclusion shocks viewers all the more. The tragic ending may appear overwrought to some, but it may also be seen as a wake-up call for fundamentalist fellow travelers. When asked about the dramatic ending, Hetata responded: "I think it was important to take things all the way. Extreme circumstances call for extreme actions, if we are to avoid trivializing the issues" (2000a).[6]

It comes as no surprise that Hetata's film takes such a critical stance toward the influence of fundamentalists in Egypt in the 1990s. Hetata has experienced their menace from close by. His parents, Nawal el-Saadawi, the world-famous Egyptian medical doctor, novelist, and women's right activist, and Sherif Hetata, a novelist and civil rights activist, have both been placed on death lists by fundamentalists.[7] Hetata's film gives voice to their secular, progressive, feminist viewpoints.[8]

Hetata was born in New York in 1965 but grew up in Cairo. He was working on the screenplay for *Closed Doors* while studying communications in the engineering school at Cairo University. In 1988 he graduated with honors and immediately moved into filmmaking (Farzanefar 2005, 50). Hetata assisted several directors, including Youssef Chahine and Spike Lee, and directed three

Atef Hetata (right) on the set. Courtesy Atef Hetata

short films of his own.[9] Two of them won international awards; the Grand Jury Prize at the Montpellier Film Festival for *Bride of the Nile* allowed Hetata to begin work on *Closed Doors*, his first feature. Additional support came from Chahine's company, Misr International Films, which co-produced it.

Hetata, like Chahine with *Destiny*, chose to present an undifferentiated picture of fundamentalist leaders. The clerics appear manipulative, their motives suspect. Neither director seems prepared to consider the fundamentalist faith at face value. *Closed Doors* features no characters representing a moderate, tolerant Islam with the exception of Hamada's mother. Fatma is not overtly religious; she does not pray or go to the mosque, but she seems to be a believer. She has raised a religious son and often makes references to God. At one point she asks her prostitute neighbor Zeinab if she is scared of God's judgment. Fatma exhibits a combination of both faith and tolerance when Hamada begs her to stop working as a maid for people who are not pious. "Why should we bear their sins?" he demands angrily. She responds: "Who are we to judge them? Let God do that!"

As for the other characters, they exhibit purely secular tendencies. There are no indications as to Mansour's religiosity, and Awadin and Zeinab both appear untroubled about transgressing major Islamic injunctions. *Closed Doors* thus presents an almost perfect binary opposition of quite secular characters confronting fundamentalists. That may suit Hetata and Western viewers, but it does not provide an alternative to the surge of fundamentalism in an overwhelmingly Muslim country.[10]

According to Hetata, his film did not elicit any reactions from fundamentalist organizations, no phone calls, no journal articles. In the official press, however, some writers accused Hetata of spreading a negative image of Islam and Egypt (Farzanefar 2005, 48). *Closed Doors* remains substantially unknown in Egypt. If the film's social realism limits its appeal to mass audiences, the suspicion of the imprint of foreign funding on a depiction of Islamic politics may well have precluded a general release. In the West, *Closed Doors* garnered prizes at several film festivals. Among Egyptian expatriate and diaspora audiences, however, the film was the object of ambivalent reception or even suspicion (Armbrust 2002).

Closed Doors exposes some of Egypt's political, economic, and social problems while categorically rejecting Islamic extremism as a solution. The film raises important questions: What are the attractions of fundamentalism in a country where much of the population is economically and politically marginalized? What are the consequences of restrictive social traditions? What does it take to transform an appealing adolescent into a bewildered extremist? As the film poses these questions, it responds with a compelling, persuasive story.

NOTES

1. The title *The Closed Doors* is commonly used. However, *Closed Doors* is the title given in the film, and it more accurately reflects the thrust of the film
2. Ahmed Azmi, in the role of Hamada, succeeds in conveying the wide range of emotions of the sensitive adolescent.
3. Sawsan Badr's remarkable performance in the role of Fatma earned her the Best Actress award at the Thessaloniki Film Festival. Early in her distinguished career in theater, film, and television she was blacklisted for four years by the Saudi authorities because she played the lead in *Death of a Princess* (Antony Thomas, 1980), a docudrama of the execution of a Saudi princess and her adulterous lover (Rakha 2001).
4. Viewers eventually get a different appreciation of Mansour. Initially they have little reason to trust the dour teacher, and his request that Hamada's father come to see him is readily interpreted as part of a familiar racket of pressuring parents to pay teachers personally for out-of-class tutoring. As it turns out, Mansour at first refuses to give Hamada private lessons and later provides them for free. And when he tells Fatma of the abject humiliation he has experienced in his own love life, he appears in a new light. His sensitive character is strikingly displayed when he and Fatma eventually approach each other. Mansour is played by Mahmoud Hemeida, whom we have encountered already in *Destiny* as Al Mansur, the caliph. Hemeida's performances in the two very different roles are remarkable. He subsequently took on an altogether different leading role in *Alexandria . . . New York* (*Iskanderija . . . New York*, 2004), the last installment in Chahine's autobiographical series, as Yehia, Chahine's alter ego.
5. The Egyptian poster, reproduced here, promotes the film by giving play to the romance of the established actors, eclipsing the film's protagonist and his troubles. The focus of the sleeve of the DVD issued in the United States is on Hamada, showing him in a rather anxious mood. The French poster shows Hamada's eye at the peep hole in his classroom where he used to watch the girls at the school next door.
6. Our translation from the French.
7. Atef Hetata's parents are not popular in Washington, D.C., either: they served on the Commission of Inquiry for the International War Crimes Tribunal, which investigated U.S. war crimes against Iraq during the 1991 Gulf War and issued a highly critical report (Dembrow 2003).

8. Hetata has said he intended to make a film about adolescence; he points out that the subject is avoided in Egyptian cinema because it is sensitive and touches on taboos and because adolescents are not established stars who can promote a film. According to Hetata, the few films that do portray adolescence are extremely moralistic. A concern with adolescence necessarily led him to the issue of fundamentalism, especially in the context of the 1991 Gulf War (Barlet 2000; Farzanefar 2005, 46–47; Hetata 2000a,b).
9. *Salut Barbès* (1989), made during Hetata's internship at the French film school FEMIS, is set in a Paris neighborhood that has attracted a large number of Arab immigrants. *Violin* (1991) explores the way a musician's work transforms as he becomes a fundamentalist. *Bride of the Nile* (1993) denounces the financial motives for arranged marriages, which often violate the wishes of the young people (Barlet 2000).
10. Merzak Allouache's *Bab el-Oued City* (*Bab al-wad al-humah*, 1994), set in Algiers, features a moderate cleric who, in the face of the rise of fundamentalists, returns to his village.

REFERENCES

Armbrust, Walter. 2002. "Islamists in Egyptian Cinema." *American Anthropologist* 104 (3): 922–931.

Barlet, Olivier. 2000. "Interview with Atef Hetata." Translated by Michael Dembrow. http://www.africultures.com/php/index.php?nav=article&no=5472. First published as "'Le meilleur moyen d'éviter l'intégrisme est d'être le plus libéral possible' entretien d'Olivier Barlet avec Atef Hetata," http://www.africultures.com/php/index.php?nav=article&no=1603.

Dembrow, Michael. 2003. "*The Closed Doors/Al Abwab al Moghlaka*." *Cascade Festival of African Films No. 13, Program Notes and Resources.* http://spot.pcc.edu/~mdembrow/closeddoors.htm.

Farzanefar, Amin. 2005. *Kino des Orient: Stimmen aus einer Region*. Marburg, Germany: Schüren.

Hetata, Atef. 2000a. "Entretien avec Atef Hetata." *Les portes fermées*, press book, Paris: Tadrart Films. http://www.tadrart.com/fr/films/portes_fermees/dpresse2.html#.

———. 2000b. "Propos de compétiteurs: Atef Hetata." In *Actes du 21e Festival International*, 43–47. Montpellier: Festival de Montpellier.

Rakha, Youssef. 2001. "Sawsan Badr: Mundane Propositions." *Al-Ahram Weekly Online* 556. http://weekly.ahram.org.eg/2001/556/profile.htm.

7

Cinema and State in Tunisia

FLORENCE MARTIN

Tunisian cinema cannot be understood without investigating the history of its complex relationship with a state eager to promote a national filmic discourse and with a diverse audience at home and abroad. While a thorough account of this cinema would need to address the range of documentaries, short films, and feature films produced in Tunisia, this essay will focus mostly on the latter.

State-Sponsored Cinema

On March 20, 1956, when from a French protectorate Tunisia became an independent developing country, cinema was not a national priority: information was. Newsreels were shot in Tunisia, sent to France to be developed, and then finally shown before the feature film at the various *ciné-clubs* scattered throughout the country. When Habib Bourguiba became president of the newly established Republic of Tunisia on July 27, 1957, there was no Tunisian film laboratory, just as there was no Tunisian television.

Then, in 1961, the "Bizerte incidents"—in which Tunisians were subject to French military aggression—changed everything. During the Algerian war, Franco-Tunisian relations deteriorated to the point of armed confrontations. Tunisian villages along the border often provided shelter to Algerian nationalists. On February 8, 1958, French army planes took off from Algeria and bombed the Tunisian village of Sakiet-Sidi-Youssef, killing sixty-eight Tunisians and injuring a hundred more. On July 19, 1961, Tunisian troops surrounded the naval base of Bizerte that the French had refused to evacuate. Two days later the French army besieged the city and killed 1,300 Tunisians.

It took a U.N. resolution to reach a cease-fire on July 22. The "events" were shot by a local camera crew and the film sent to a French laboratory, as was customary. This time, however, the French did not return the processed film, thus imposing censorship from abroad. This prompted Bourguiba to ensure greater freedom of information by subsequently founding Tunisian Radio and Television (ERTT, Etablissement de la radiodiffusion télévision tunisienne) in 1961, to be inaugurated in 1966. He also created the Tunisian Production and Cinematographical Expansion Company (SATPEC, Société anonyme tunisienne de production et d'expansion cinématographique) in 1964, and it was inaugurated in 1968 after technicians were trained and the facilities built. In the 1970s SATPEC was an importation and distribution company, with a monopoly on foreign film until 1981, and a state production company that co-produced local or foreign films shot in Tunisia.

The creation of SATPEC was only the first step of many undertaken by a state aware of the potential impact of film as a propaganda tool at home and an advertising agent abroad. During Bourguiba's presidency and since 1987 to a somewhat lesser degree under Ben Ali's leadership, the Tunisian government developed various cultural policies meant to support cinema, and a department devoted entirely to the audio-visual arts still exists within the Ministère de la culture et de la sauvegarde du patrimoine (Ministry of Culture and Heritage Preservation). This department has played a particularly crucial role in supporting three institutions:

- Journées cinématographiques de Carthage (JCC), the Carthage Film Festival, for Arab and African cinema. Founded in 1966, this biannual event alternates with FESPACO, the Pan-African Film and Television Festival in Ouagadougou, Burkina Faso.
- The Tunisian Cinémathèque. Created in 1954 and later closed, the Cinémathèque was reopened in 1973 under the management of SATPEC.
- The Museum of Cinema, created in 1998.

The Tunisian government has issued a series of decrees designed to foster film production and diffusion, including a regime of tax breaks: for instance, the materials imported to make a film are exonerated of all import taxes, which otherwise are particularly high in Tunisia; the national production of films in Tunisia is exempt from the value-added tax (VAT). The March 19, 2001, decree structures how state aid for film production is dispensed in the form of support grants (*primes d'encouragement*) intended to help finance writing and revising feature-film scripts and the production or post-production costs of a short or feature-length film. Each grant represents up to 35 per cent of the total production cost of a feature film and 70 per cent of the total production cost of a short film, up to 400,000 Tunisian dinars (about $300,000) for a feature film at the time of writing. The Ministry of Culture funds two or three feature films annually. That aid is disbursed in increments over the production process, effectively ensuring state control at all stages of the process.

Furthermore, in a nation where tourism is a major economic priority, the Ministry of Tourism has a vested interest in cinema's potential as an advertising agent in promoting the image of Tunisia abroad. Cinema intersects with tourism through another state institution created in 1998: the Museum of Cinema, located right next to the Ministry of Culture and Heritage Preservation in Tunis. The museum houses a permanent exhibition tracing the national history of cinema from its perceived cultural roots—in, for instance, the popular, itinerant Theater of Shadows—to the advent of the first Tunisian films. The pioneering Tunisian filmmaker Albert Samama, also known as Chickli, is hailed here as the first Maghrebi director; he produced a short, *Zohra*, in 1922, and a full-length feature film, *The Girl from Carthage* (*Aïn al-ghazal/La fille de Carthage*), in 1924. Didactic in its approach, the museum presents cinema as deeply ensconced in Tunisian culture.

The state-controlled broadcaster, ERTT, regularly co-produces Tunisian films through its own production company: the National Agency for the Promotion of Audio-Visual Material (ANPA, Agence nationale de la promotion audiovisuelle). The ANPA co-subsidizes and buys films and television series for the ERTT. In its function as a production company, the ANPA can award 100,000 dinars (about $75,000) to a filmmaker who in return cedes Tunisian TV broadcast rights to the ERTT but retains the rights for foreign TV channels. Most importantly, this funding comes with the promise that the film will be broadcast on Tunisian television—although the latter may later decide not to broadcast it.

Finally, an intragovernmental commission issues the licenses under which films may be screened in Tunisian cinemas. The commission consists of a panel of "film experts and intellectuals," one representative from the Ministry of Culture, and another from the Ministry of Religion. The government created the Ministry of Religion at a time when Islamic fundamentalist movements were ravaging neighboring Algeria, and it effectively enabled the Tunisian government to oversee what was said in the various mosques while giving some representation to religious affairs in what had hitherto been a secular state. However, this negotiation has led to predictable side effects, including censoring particular scenes and banning some films deemed inappropriate to the cultural landscape of pious Islam.

The ERTT commission has a representative of the Ministry of Religion with the power to stop a film from being broadcast. Raja Aman's *Red Satin* (*al-Sitar al-asmar/Satin rouge*, 2002) was co-produced by the ANPA but denied broadcasting ostensibly because of a fairly modest sex scene between a woman and her daughter's boyfriend. Ibrahim Letaïef's *Visa* (2004), also co-produced by ANPA, was denied broadcasting—a day before its projected date and after the filmmaker had been interviewed on television to promote his film—on the grounds that the short comedy poked fun at the government-controlled daily *La Presse*. These two levels of cultural, religious, and political censorship determine the more insidious phenomenon of self-censorship in Tunisian authors of written, cinematic, and other texts who end up silencing what they want to say, anticipating the rejection of their work.

The state thus plays a multifaceted role as it promotes and controls, supports and silences. And yet, Tunisia is the most tolerant of Arab countries in the way it treats cinema, whose directors do not shy away from topics often deemed taboo in other Muslim cultures, such as male homosexuality, sex before marriage, and adultery.

Close-Up on the Individual

Tunisian filmic narratives have a rich local history upon which to reflect. At the dawn of independence there was, as in other liberated countries, an urgent need to create and portray a distinct, collective identity that could promote pride in the newly founded nation. In 1966 Omar Khlifi directed the first bona fide Tunisian feature film, *The Dawn* (*al Fajr/L'aube*), the inaugural work in a trilogy about the nationalist struggle; his trilogy was completed in the 1970s. This tragic story of three nationalists sacrificing their lives in the struggle for independence in 1954 ends on a hopeful note: Habib Bourguiba's return from exile in June 1955.

The focus on individual characters as national emblems recurs in another 1966 feature film, Hamouda Ben Halima's *Scabby Khlifa* (*Khalifa al aqraʿ/ Khélifa le teigneux*). In contrast with the Orientalist colonial films that framed the Tunisian countryside as an exotic, voiceless landscape awaiting the values of the West (Benali 2005, 113), *Scabby Khlifa* offers a refreshing look at the *medina*, the old Arab city, through the eyes of its protagonist. Khlifa, a young orphan on the eve of manhood, is a messenger who earns a living by running errands. The camera follows him from a man's shop to a woman's home, a palatial dwelling to a humble abode, and all the spaces in between including the connecting terraces of the rooftops, the meandering alleys, and the inner courtyards, thus revealing the complex network of relationships and the people inhabiting the *medina*. He is a character in transition from childhood to adulthood; soon he will lose his freedom of movement and be unable to enter the houses where women are. Eventually Khlifa has to occupy a fixed space. Khlifa and his story can be read as embodying the *Zeitgeist* of a nation in search for its own identity as seen through a representation of the daily interactions of humble people.

Khlifa prefigured a trend in 1970s cinema of focusing on social issues rather than yielding to the state's desire for a national grand narrative. Tunisian filmmakers, like their Moroccan and Algerian counterparts, perhaps trapped by the state's eagerness to educate and inform through the careful yet not necessarily artistic construction of a national image (Chikhaoui 2004, 25), did not immediately turn to the immense reservoir of their own rich popular culture, with its ethnic roots that include Arabic, Berber, French, and Italian ones. However, unlike their counterparts south of the Sahara who were preoccupied with achieving new national filmic representation, Tunisian filmmakers had access to an alternative filmic tradition besides the Western one: Egyptian cinema, which in the 1950s and 1960s, along with numerous musicals, produced Youssef Chahine's political narratives steeped in popular culture. Consequently, in the 1970s Tunisian filmmakers began to turn from a national(ist) discourse to (neo)realist filming of the bitter starkness of social issues. Thus Brahim Babaï depicted rural migration and unemployment in *What about Tomorrow?* (*Wa ghadan?/Et demain?*, 1971), while Naceur Ktari described emigration in *The Ambassadors* (*as-Sufara'/Les ambassadors*, 1976), and Ridha Béhi cast a critical eye on tourism in a poor country in *Sun of the Hyenas* (*Shams al-dîba/Soleil des hyènes*, 1977), the story of a fishing village transformed into a resort that profits a handful and leaves the poor in the dust. Here, tourism illustrates the neocolonialism imposed by the developed world on the developing one.

The fate of *Fatma 75* (1976) by Selma Baccar, the first woman director in Tunisia, indicates some of the contradictions inherent in the circumstances of film production in the country at the time. Produced to celebrate the Year of the Woman, this film focused on the history of women in Tunisia since the Carthaginian era through a montage of evocations including Kahena, the Berber queen who successfully led her troops against Muslim invaders in the seventh century, and Jelejel, Ibrahim Ihn el Aghleb's wife, who founded the first

Quranic school for girls in the holy city of Kairouan. *Fatma 75* features interviews with key figures such as Bchira Ben Mrad, a famous leader of the Tunisian women's movement.

The film credits acknowledged Habib Bourguiba for his role in promoting women's equality through the *Code du statut personnel*. The statute adopted on August 13, 1956, guaranteed women's rights while respecting the spirit of Islamic Law. It outlawed polygamy; abolished men's renouncement of their wives and replaced it with judicial divorce giving equal right to men and women; and gave women the right to vote. Yet, Baccar demonstrated that relatively progressive 1975 Tunisia still had room for improvement: for example, women did not earn equal pay, and when applying for a passport a woman still required her husband's authorization. Bourguiba was not amused by the criticism, and *Fatma 75* was effectively banned. The official reason given by the Secretary of Information was that some of its content—a sequence on sex education in school—was unfit to be shown to the public (Chikhaoui 1994, 9). *Fatma 75* was shown in the Netherlands, where it was co-produced, but the original French-subtitled version was to remain in the Ministry of Culture's archives until April 2006, when Baccar was invited to show the film in France.

The 1980s was a decade in which Tunisian *auteurs* produced a number of films articulating what Tahar Chikhaoui (2004, 28) calls "the wounded or forgotten memory" to be stitched together and/or healed by filming individual stories "re-membering" a trauma in flashbacks.[1] In these films the sense of the nation recedes into the background, with the camera focused more prominently on the individual and his or her relationship to the community. Thus Nejia Ben Mabrouk's *The Trace* (*As-sama/La trace*, 1985) depicts a poor young woman about to go study in Tunis who remembers her childhood and denounces the unfair treatment of little girls from birth to their wedding nights: "On men no trace can be detected, so they do not forgive a trace." As with *Fatma 75*, this film did not promote a positive image of women's condition in Tunisia, and it met with a similar response from the government.

Tunisian Filmic Discourse

Political authorities changed, but Zine el-Abidine Ben Ali's coup in 1987 simply replaced one dictator with another and apparently recycled the same people from Bourguiba's regime. Filmmakers could still obtain government funding, albeit with little freedom of expression if their work presented even a remotely unfavorable image of the Tunisian government. While on the surface the past two decades suggest an apparent lack of censorship, political expression remains covert, buried in the films. Often the image of Tunisia that directors want to explore is not what is shown to tourists. For example, the Tunisian "forgotten memory" was an aspect of what Taïeb Louhichi wished to address in his film *Shadow of the Earth* (*Dhil el-ardh*/*L'ombre de la terre*, 1982), the story of a small community of nomads living on the edge of the desert in isolation and poverty that is harassed by the central government (Ben Brik 2000, 82–84). Louhichi's film can be viewed as the urgent recording of a moribund culture and, as such, an attempt to "re-member" it, in Toni Morrison's sense of the term: to re-attach to the memory (Morrison 2007). It is a matter, more specifically, of both recalling and re-attaching that memory to a larger narrative—here the narrative of the nomads—that has hitherto been given insufficient attention. *Shadow of the Earth* can be seen as an emblematic narrative about certain social realities that have been systematically excised from the official discourse in Tunisia.

While perfecting their skills in expressing the repressed via subtle detours, Tunisian filmmakers in the 1980s created a unique cinematic language, at once highly referential and elliptical. Nouri Bouzid's films remain the most salient examplars of this cinematic language. In *Man of Ashes* (*Rih essed*/*L'homme de cendres*, 1986), he tells the story of a young man about to get married who remembers being raped as a teenager by his carpenter employer. Bouzid suggests the repressed forced-sex scene by filming around it, recording the muted isolation of the protagonist. Thus, as the young man is unearthing his individual trauma, the director brings to the screen the hidden practice of male homosexuality that a Muslim culture has trouble publicly acknowledging. In *The Golden Horseshoes* (*Safaih min dhahab*/*Les sabots en or*, 1986), Bouzid depicts a political prisoner upon his release from jail, traumatized by the torture he has endured and now unable to fit into life outside. An intellectual trying to re-attach himself to his various former communities—his family, his circle of friends, Tunis, and the town of Sidi Bou Said—he seems condemned to exclusion. He remains on the periphery of society as he wanders the streets at night, no longer recognizing his own country, which is now starting to bear signs of a budding Islamic fundamentalism, and he is finally driven to suicide. Here the corporeal reality of torture invades the entire screen in a close-up on a naked, twisted, bound, male body writhing in pain. The sequence relies entirely on an appeal to a connotative semantic regime as the audience knows that the torture is taking place in one of the prisons in the country.

This mode of construction became frequent in Tunisian films, with directors particularly intent on filming border areas between the inside and the outside, hinting at a space elsewhere, off camera, away from confining spaces. The themes of enclosure and its corollary—a longing for open space—haunt the films of what Sonia Chamkhi has termed "New Tunisian Cinema" (2002), produced between 1980 and the mid-1990s and defined by a particular visual aesthetic and by certain structures. In each film an increasingly claustrophobic protagonist like Youssef in *The Golden Horseshoes*, Ramla in Moncef Dhouib's *Sultan of the Medina* (*Ya soltane al-medina/Le sultan de la médina*, 1991), and Sabra in *The Trace*—is incarcerated in the oppressively constricting space of family and society and desperately looks for an exit, his or her trajectory of desire leading farther and farther away, past the house gate, onto the connecting roofs of the *medina*, away from the village, the city, even the country, to a free space. Yet the dream destination remains out of reach, as illustrated by the close-ups on interstitial spaces such as windows, doors, connecting alleys, and thresholds. Poised on a liminal spot, the camera itself titillates the viewer as it cuts from the walls of the home to the object of desire, including the frequent panning shots of the sky or the image of a bird in flight.

This mode of filming can be seen, Stone McNeece notes, as a Tunisian form of "image writing," that is, "a tendency to exploit the ambiguity of connotation systems by putting on hold what the images and words refer to" (2004, 69). The construction of meaning relies on shared references, patterns of communication, and an imaginary world and implies that the elements off screen are the ones that literally "make sense." It is an astute and effective way to film a taboo or the silence that surrounds it, as Moufida Tlatli's sequence in *Silences of the Palace* (*Samt al qusur/Les silences du palais*, 1994) best illustrates (Martin 2004). The film is set in a Bey palace on the eve of independence and focuses on the world of women servants imprisoned downstairs at the beck and call of their male masters upstairs.

The central protagonists are Alia and her mother, Khedija. Alia, unbeknownst to her mother, sees one of the Beyat, Sidi Bechir, forcing her mother onto her bed. The next shot is a wide-angle view of the entrance to the palace in the background and of the outside wrought-iron gate slowly closing in the foreground. Alia's shadow is coming closer, but by the time she reaches the gate, it is too late. Her hands grab two railings of the gate, she pushes her face in between and screams—the camera zooms in on her face and then on her open mouth, but no sound comes out. Devoid of extradiegetic music, the entire sequence is arrestingly silent. The combination of Alia's averting violation, followed by imaging an impossible flight with no human intervention visible, and the culmination in a scream of pain literally and metaphorically inaudible

(Spaas 2000, 169–170)—all point to a multiple construction of meaning off screen. The traumas unearthed are off screen, literally obscene, and a sober audience fills in the carefully orchestrated rests in the sound track.

In addition to such formal strategies, Tunisian cinema is an open cinema in the sense that it has been distinguished by complex intercultural patterns that have become more visible since the mid-1990s. It has therefore continued to refine its language while relating to its multicultural base and the global audience it attempts to reach. Tunisian filmmakers are often multilingual—Ferid Boughedir, for one, is equally at ease in Arabic, English, French, and Italian; have experienced at least two cultures; and function in a global cinematographic culture. Their films portray some of their own multicultural complexity, not necessarily as a traumatic, painful loss of grounded identity but as the accumulation of riches. Much like Odysseus, the protagonist finally returns to the motherland with either a romanticized vision of home, as Wahid does in Mahmaud Ben Mahmoud's *Pomegranate Siestas* (*Kouaïl er-roummen/Les siestes grenadines*, 1998), or a fresh look at old traditional gender roles, as Jamil does in Saheb-Ettaba's *The Bookshop* (*Al kotbia/La librairie*, 2002). The latest Tunisian films put in motion Tunisian and European or Western elements along "transvergent" shifts (Novak 2002); this time, filmic expression takes on enlarged, multiple referential systems and plays with them. As a result, its kaleidoscopic meanings unfold differently for, say, a French, an American, or a Tunisian audience.

At the turn of the millennium, films by a new wave of young directors like Ibrahim Letaïef, Nadia El Fani, Mohamed Zran, Raja Amari, and Nawfel Saheb-Ettaba aim to address a large Tunisian audience as well as an international one. Under their impulse, a few productions with popular appeal have appeared: Zran's romantic modern fairy tale set in downtown Tunis, *The Prince* (*El emir/Le prince*, 2004); Nawfel Saheb-Ettaba's *The Bookshop* (2002); Ibrahim Letaïef's comic short films *One Laugh Too Many* (*Un rire de trop*, 1999) and *Visa* (*La dictée*, 2004), and his collection of ten shorts, *Ten Shorts, Ten Feature Films* (*Dix courts dix regards*, 2006). Nadia El Fani, in her first feature film, *Bedwin Hacker* (2003)—the first Tunisian feature film to acknowledge female homosexuality and bisexuality—adopts some of the stylistics of the spy thriller, such as high-tech communication devices and hacking that disrupts European TV channels. Reality is not what is shown; the almighty police are everywhere in Tunisia as well as in France. The result is a fast-moving film built along multiple cuts, reminiscent of the virtual realities common on computer screens, such as the ones under the scrutinizing eyes of the hacker and the detective (Martin 2007).

In contrast, Ibrahim Letaïef uses comedy in *Visa* to denounce the plight of Tunisians who want to emigrate and are caught in a maze of adverse bureaucratic rules as well as a general malaise of split identity. In it, Rachid faces the choice between France's Western and Mediterranean culture and Saudi Arabia's Muslim culture, only to be rejected eventually by both.

Since the 1990s Tunisian cinema has diversified its thematic palette considerably, ranging from some of the side effects of present-day globalization and/or social and gender inequities to the uncovering of a mythical past. Nouri Bouzid's *Bezness* (1991) focuses on sex tourism, while his *Clay Dolls* (*Araïs alten/Les poupées d'argile*, 2002, awarded the Silver Tanit at the Carthage Film Festival) describes the exploitation of little girls from the country who become indentured servants to urban families; Mohamed Zran's *Essaïda* (1995) shows poverty and survival in a poor neighborhood. At the other end of the spectrum, a few directors seem to take their inspiration from the oral traditions of the past and create films with a mythical aura. Such is the case for the series of intensely original and poetic films by Nacer Khemir. After *The Wanderers* (*El haitnoune/Les baliseurs du désert*, 1984), Khemir went on to direct *The Dove's Lost Necklace* (*Tawq al-hamama al-mafqud /Le collier perdu de la colombe*, 1991) and *The Prince Who Contemplated His Soul* (*Bab Aziz/Le prince qui contemplait son âme*, 2005), vast frescoes shot in the desert, in keeping with the spirit of Khemir's one-man shows around the world in which he narrates tales from *The Arabian Nights*. In between these two extremes, other films tell the hitherto untold history at mid-distance; one such is Moufida Tlatli's second feature film, *Season of Men* (*Maussim al-riyal/La saison des hommes*, 2000).

Contemporary world politics and their theaters are prominent in some recent films. Ahmed Baha Eddine Attia produced a collection of five shorts, *The Gulf War ... What Next?* (*Harb El Khalij ... wa baad?/La guerre du golfe ... et après?*, 1991), by five Arab filmmakers, Borhan Alawiyeh (Lebanon), Nejia Ben Mabrouk (Tunisia), Nouri Bouzid (Tunisia), Mustapha Derkaoui (Morocco), and Elia Suleiman (Palestine). Ridha Béhi shot *Sparrows Don't Die in Jerusalem* (*Les hirondelles ne meurent pas à Jérusalem*, 1994) on the Israeli-Palestinian conflict. And Nouri Bouzid won the Golden Tanit in 2006 for his *Making Of* (*Making of, le dernier film*) on terrorism.

Finally, focusing on the here and now, Kalthoum Bornaz denounces legal gender inequities such as the inheritance law that privileges sons over daughters in *The Other Half of the Sky* (*Shtar mhaba/L'autre moitié du ciel*, 2008). Khaled Ghorbal, after breaking the silence around virginity in his film *Fatma* (1999), narrates a worker's long return home from France to the Tunisian desert, where he wants to die, in *Such a Long Journey* (*Safra ya ahlaha/Un si long voyage*, 2008). The picture would not be complete without *Cinecittà* (2008), the innovative and successful comedy by Ibrahim Letaïef; it is an action-film parody about the difficulty of making a film in Tunisia, with numerous references to Italian, Tunisian, and Egyptian cinemas.

Yet, paradoxically, given the variety of its production and its increasing visibility abroad, Tunisian cinema continues to struggle to find an audience at home. After a period of renewed interest from the mid-1980s to the mid-1990s—when each of Nouri Bouzid's three films found audiences of more than 200,000 viewers, Ferid Boughedir's *Halfaouine* (*Asfour Stah*) sold 500,000 tickets in 1990, and Tlatli's *Silences of the Palace* sold 300,000 in 1994—the domestic audience for Tunisian films seems to have steadily decreased. *Red Satin*, for example, sold only 35,000 tickets in 2002 (Barlet 2004).

Shoot Locally, Screen Globally?

Globalization has had positive as well as perverse side effects on the funding, the distribution, and to some degree the primary material of cinema in Tunisia. Beyond government funding, filmmakers can apply to various European co-production agencies of great impact, such as the Hubert Bals fund in the Netherlands, Fonds Sud in France, and even European TV-channel film production companies like Arte or Canal+. In each case, the selection occurs at the stage of the script, usually written by the director. A wave of scripts in the 1990s seemed to coincide with prefabricated "neo-Orientalist" images of Tunisia replete with shots of couscous, *hammam* (Moorish baths), sea, sex, and sun, all of which catered to the *a priori* visions of members of the various commissions abroad. The laminated scripts led to a repetition of similar tropes.

Clearly, this may not be the kind of representation that a Tunisian audience craves to see year after year. But other issues affect local audiences. Film piracy via illegal videotapes and now DVDs, burned at home as well as in any cybercafé, has become institutionalized in Tunisia. Although laws prohibit such practices, local feature films, some of them not yet even released commercially, are readily available on the street for 2.5 dinars (about $1.50). Rampant piracy has developed into a parallel economy that serves everybody, and although the police are omnipresent in the urban centers, they rarely raid the places that break global as well as national copyright laws. As a result, film buffs can watch films at home or in a café offering a large screen more cheaply and comfortably than in a film theater.

There is no multiplex in Tunisia, although recently the government has talked about helping to create some; and the state of film theaters is deplorable, with defective sound systems, limping projection devices, antediluvian seats, and old, musty carpeting. As patronage has shrunk, the number of theaters in the country decreased from ninety-two in 1981 to thirty-five in 2004. Furthermore, the forest of satellite dishes on roofs signals another entertainment medium: people now have access to, among other programs, films broadcast by hundreds of TV channels from Europe and the Arab world.

Finally, American blockbusters reign supreme at the box office—and leave little room for domestic films, as Moufida Tlatli has observed: "The cinemas in Tunisia mainly show American, Egyptian, and Bollywood films. It is a paradox that globalization threatens diversity in our cinemas, while international funding helps sustain Tunisian cinema" (in Fallaux, Halasa, and Press 2003, 12). In the end, Tunisian cinema has become increasingly characterized by films that are shot locally but viewed primarily by audiences outside the country, pirated copies excepted.

Still, contemporary Tunisian cinema is healthy and promises to continue to produce a wide assortment of fascinating films. Part of its sense of unease in the global landscape might reside, ironically enough, in Tunisia's own geopolitical and geocultural location, west of the Middle East, of the Arabian Peninsula, but not Western all the way, and south of Europe. Caught between, to simplify, a Western secular world and an Islam-inflected culture, Tunisian cinema has evolved imaginative strategies to create films that avoid various levels of censorship at home through the use of nuances. Through its narrative and visual detours, it has produced aesthetics reminiscent of ancient arabesques, with a rare level of mastery and independence.

NOTES

This essay is an abridged, edited, and updated version of "Tunisia," by Florence Martin, in *The Cinema of Small Nations*, ed. Mette Hjort and Duncan Petrie (Edinburgh: Edinburgh University Press, and Bloomington: Indiana University Press, 2007), 213–228.

1. Translations from the French are mine.

REFERENCES

Barlet, Olivier. 2004. "La crise du cinéma tunisien." *Africultures*, September. http://www.africultures.com/php/index.php?nav=article&no=3568.

Benali, Abdelkader. 1998. *Le cinéma colonial au Maghreb*. Paris: Editions du Cerf.
Ben Brik, Taoufik. 2000. *Une si douce dictature*. Paris: La Découverte.
Chamkhi, Sonia. 2002. *Cinéma tunisien nouveau—Parcours autres*. Tunis: Sud.
Chikhaoui, Tahar. 1994. "Selma, Nejia, Moufida et les autres/Selma, Nejia, Moufida and the Others." *Ecrans d'Afrique* 8:9–10.
———. 2004. "Maghreb: De l'épopée au regard intime." In *Au Sud du cinéma: Films d'Afrique, d'Asie et d'Amérique Latine*, ed. Jean-Michel Frodon, 22–39. Paris: Cahiers du Cinéma/Arte.
Fallaux, Emile, Malu Halasa, and Nupu Press, eds. 2003. *True Variety: Funding the Art of World Cinema*. Rotterdam: International Film Festival Rotterdam.
Martin, Florence. 2004. "Silence and Scream: Moufida Tlatli's Cinematic Suite." *Studies in French Cinema* 4 (3): 175–185.
———. 2007. "Transvergence and Cultural Detours: Nadia El Fani's *Bedwin Hacker* (2002)." *Studies in French Cinema* 7 (2): 119–129.
Morrison, Toni. 2007. "Toni Morrison: The Art of Fiction CXXXIV." Interview by Elissa Schappell and Claudia Brodsky. In Paris Review *Interviews*, vol. 2, 355–394. New York: Picador.
Novak, Marcos. 2002. "Speciation, Transvergence, Allogenesis: Notes on the Production of the Alien." *Architectural Design* 72 (3). http://www.mat.ucsb.edurmarcos/transvergence.pdf.
Stone McNeece, Lucy. 2004. "La lettre envolée: L'image écrite dans le cinéma tunisien." In *CinémAction* 111 (2nd Trimester), *Cinémas du Maghreb*, ed. Michel Serceau, 67–76.
Spaas, Lieve. 2000. *The Francophone Film: A Struggle for Identity*. Manchester, England: Manchester University Press.

http://images.allocine.fr/r_760_x/medias/nmedia/18/35/10/80/affiche.jpg

Bedwin Hacker
A Hacker Challenges Western Domination of the Global Media

JOSEF GUGLER

The modernity of our countries is never perceived, nor is it shown.[1]
NADIA EL FANI (IN ABASSI 2002)

Bedwin Hacker (2002) is an innovative film.[2] Nadia El Fani presents a Tunisia quite different from both Western depictions and most Tunisian films. In particular she offers a new perspective on gender, with women who are very much in control in the world at large—they are not victims, they are not engaged in a struggle against victimization, and they are not enclosed in a domestic world.[3] She brings to the fore a key issue in globalization: Western domination of the global media. And she pioneers a high-tech theme in Arab film. The story of an Arab woman challenging Western domination of the global media in cyberspace, with a French secret-service agent in hot pursuit, has the qualities of a thriller at times. El Fani has commented:

> It's a style of cinema that Arab directors have not yet appropriated. As for me, it was first and foremost a gag to enable me to communicate a political message with humor. Saying things that make people gnash their teeth is easier in a genre film. (In Marsaud 2005, 392)

---

* *Bedwin Hacker.* 2002. Film written and directed by Nadia El Fani. Produced by Z'Yeux Noirs Movies (Tunisia), ANPA (Tunisia), 2M Soread (Morocco), and Sedat Canal+ Horizons (Tunisia). Distributed in the United States by Cinema Libre Studio. 103 minutes.

Bedwin Hacker tells a light-hearted story with a good deal of humor; it does not so much represent reality as react to it. At the same time, the film raises significant issues. Especially salient is the demand that voices and images other than those spread by global media corporations be heard and that conventional images of the Arab world, and of Arab women in particular, be challenged. The film furthermore highlights the problems of emigration to rich countries. A fourth theme, the denunciation of the police state Tunisia has become under the Ben Ali regime, is conveyed in subtle allusions that do not similarly catch the attention of foreign audiences even as they are readily apparent to Tunisian viewers, for whom they are poignant reminders of their political circumstances. The significance of the four themes varies for different audiences. And their implied messages vary as well.

The film addresses three audiences: Tunisians, Western viewers, and, distinct from both, Maghrebi immigrants in the West. Tunisian audiences may see El Fani calling on them to challenge Western dominance of the global media, to embrace the emancipation of women, to resist the lure of emigration, and to reject the authoritarian regime of Ben Ali. That call may be heard by other Arab viewers as well and in many other countries marginalized in the cyberspace era, wherever women struggle for equality, where the best trained abandon their countries, and where people suffer under oppressive regimes.

Western audiences are called upon to understand and support efforts to curb the global domination of Western media corporations, to recognize the modernity of the Arab world and jettison their preconceptions about Arab women, and to extend sympathy to the plight of immigrants. First- and second-generation emigrants from the Maghreb, who make up a large part of the potential audience for Maghrebi films in France, will see the film proffering various forms of resistance, and they will hear a call to return to their roots. El Fani reminds Tunisian, Western, and emigrant viewers alike of the splendors of Tunisia as she takes them from a rather drab Paris to Tunis to El Jem to Midès, an oasis in the desert mountains of southern Tunisia. With limited resources she produced a quality film that was selected for numerous festivals and won several prizes.

The film's protagonist is a Tunisian hacker who interferes with satellite transmissions of European television programs, overlaying their images with cartoons of an anthropomorphic camel and teletexts starting with, "In the third millennium, there are other periods, other places, other lives ... We are not a mirage." The messages, written in Tunisian Arabic, are signed "Bedwin Hacker."[4] Numerous television programs are interrupted, among them a documentary

The camel in action

presenting a speech by President Truman in which he thanks God for having given nuclear power to the United States, a sports show, talk shows, newscasts, nature programs, and films. If ready access to the media allows the DST to resort to disinformation at will, the hacker readily exposes its falsehoods.[5] When the hacker asks viewers to walk in the streets in *babouches*, Arab leather slippers, the mass response demonstrates her impact. Another message launches a call-in at La Défense that makes it necessary to close down the huge office complex to avoid the risk of a circuit overload.

Bedwin Hacker may be seen to end on a conciliatory note in terms of both the personal relationship between Kalt and Julia and the secret-service agent's pursuit of the hacker—instead of a showdown we get a draw: the hacker has been stopped, but Kalt remains free to subvert again. When viewers expressed disappointment that Kalt did not emerge victorious, El Fani responded (2003b) that she had to be realistic but that there can be victory in defeat. She identified herself with Kalt, the "unreasonable" rebel who knows full well that she does not have a chance against the strong and mighty.

Central to El Fani's contemporary Tunisia are women characters who subvert Western stereotypes.[6] Strong women feature in many Tunisian films, whether produced by women or men.[7] They remain, however, largely confined within the family context as clichéd powerful matrons. *Bedwin Hacker*, in distinct contrast, no longer defines the protagonist in terms of her position within the family. In fact, we never learn anything about Kalt's immediate family.[8] At the same time, El Fani shows Kalt to be well integrated in her "gang" of family and friends. The emancipated Tunisian woman, she suggests, lives within a communal pattern, altogether different from Western individualism. And she fully assumes her sexuality, a nonconformist bisexuality in the case of Kalt.[9] El Fani juxtaposes the strength of Kalt and of Julia, aka Agent Marianne, who pursues her, to the weakness of her conventional male characters. The rather hapless journalist Chams is caught between the two women. Julia's annoying boss is an incompetent preoccupied with public relations who readily resorts to a strategy of disinforming the public. A neighborhood informer and a police officer recall the stereotypical fools of Arab cinema. All the while Kalt is training her friends' ten-year-old daughter, Qmar, to become a computer expert and hacker in turn.

Alongside unconventional women, *Bedwin Hacker* conveys a vibrant Tunisian culture of poetry and music. But El Fani does not advocate closure to the outside world. A visit to the Roman Coliseum at El Jem and the reference to the Bedouin heritage serve as reminders that Tunisia's multicultural character has a long history. Her characters are thoroughly cosmopolitan in experience, culture, and language; they enjoy life wherever they are—in an early scene of music and dance we are left guessing for a while whether it is set in France or in Tunisia. El Fani proposes a vision of a multicultural world in opposition to the homogenizing power of a global media industry dominated by the West. That multicultural world is secular. Islam remains invisible but for a call to prayers in Midès, a call none of Kalt's gang answers and that escapes most non-Muslim viewers altogether.

In one of the very first sequences, *Bedwin Hacker* denounces police repression of a peaceful sit-in protesting the deportation of illegal immigrants. At the same time, El Fani problematizes the general desire in Tunisia, as in other poor countries, to emigrate to the El Dorado of the rich. Her heroine graduated top of the class from the prestigious École Polytechnique, but when pressured to join the DST with the prospect of French citizenship, she preferred to return to Tunisia. Chams's weakness is reflected in his unconditional desire to get a French passport.

For those who, unlike Chams, spend part of their lives in Tunisia, a French passport provides a measure of protection from the police state Ben Ali has established. Subtle allusions to the character of his regime are readily apparent to Tunisian viewers. They will take for granted the mandatory Ben Ali poster that can be glimpsed in a shop. The denunciation of the police state is obscured for U.S. viewers when two mentions of a police informer are rendered with the British slang term "grass." After Le Figaro, a prestigious conservative French daily, has not been available in Tunis for two days, El Fani's characters joke that it has become a subversive newspaper. *Bedwin Hacker* humanizes the agents of the state, often poking fun at them: the plump neighborhood "grass" who inquires of the poet about the "girls"; the officious police officers who stop their car when looking for Frida; the police officer who gets all flustered when he recognizes the famous singer.[10]

El Fani's screenplay won prizes at the Carthage Film Festival and from the International Agency of Francophone Countries. Nevertheless, it took her more than four years to secure funding.[11] Most Tunisian film productions rely on initial funding from the Ministry of Culture. But El Fani had to submit four applications until such funding was finally granted. The French public agencies that provide crucial support for many African films refused her their support. Most of the funding was provided from within the Maghreb. Apart from the government funds, finance from Tunisian and Moroccan television and expertise and equipment provided by a Tunisian Internet company were crucial. In the end El Fani produced *Bedwin Hacker* with less than 800,000 euros, some $700,000 at the time (El Fani 2003a). She had to forgo shooting the reactions to the intrusion of Bedwin Hacker's messages on television programs in other countries (El Fani 2003b). And she had to cut back on cinematographic opportunities: forgo filming the desert from a helicopter, using cranes in Midès, and getting proper views of streets in Paris and of the La Défense complex (Amarger n.d.).

Censorship loomed in the difficulties of securing funding for *Bedwin Hacker*. El Fani made some cuts in the screenplay demanded by the Ministry of Culture. We do not hear "This is better than Ramadan" from characters drinking at a party nor a reference to Saddam Hussein that, in those days, offended because it was disrespectful. Where the script had Frida challenge the rude officer at the French police station—"You talk like this to the Saudis who come to buy the Champs Elysées?"—this reference to Saudi nabobs has been dropped (El Fani 2003a).

The ministry wanted further cuts when the film was completed: the two women in bed, Kalt's nudity, but El Fani refused (2003a), threatening that she would raise international protests. She thus managed to take a distinctive feature of Tunisian cinema, a greater freedom in addressing sexuality than found elsewhere in the Arab world, a big step further, pushing the limits of what could be shown on Tunisian screens.

Muriel Solvay, Nadia El Fani, Tomer Sisley, and Lilia Falkat. Courtesy Nadia El Fani

Bedwin Hacker was the opening feature at the Carthage Film Festival in 2002, but the film was not selected for the competition, and El Fani was not invited. The release in Tunisia was delayed until 2006. The Tunisian authorities take pride in the film—outside the country. Tunisia's woman ambassador to France screened it at the French parliament. The Tunisian embassy in the United States showed it when Ben Ali visited President Bush in 2004. The French international television channel TV5 transmitted *Bedwin Hacker* to the Maghreb as part of its Africa programming but did not transmit it to the Arab world beyond (El Fani 2003a,b; 2006a; 2008).

Bedwin Hacker was shot digitally by Tarek Ben Abdallah, who obtained excellent results. In Tunisia, a hand-held camera was used to convey that Tunisian society, unlike France, is not stable (El Fani 2006a). On the other hand, the contrast between light colors in Tunisia and dark colors in France was not intended but came naturally. It is in part El Fani's affection for the beauty of the desert that prompted her to situate a major part of *Bedwin Hacker* in the south of Tunisia.

El Fani has moved back and forth between Tunis and Paris, where she was born, the child of a French mother and a Tunisian father.[12] She was not able to attend film school and learned her craft as an assistant for close to ten years to a string of directors, most notably Alexandre Arcady, Nouri Bouzid, Romain

Goupil, Roman Polanski, and Franco Zeffirelli. In 1990 she produced her first short and established her own production company, Z'Yeux Noirs, which might be rendered as "Them Black Eyes." Several more shorts, videos, and spots for advertising, videos for Tunisian women's organizations, and producer services for foreign film productions followed. *Bedwin Hacker* is El Fani's first narrative feature (Gabous 1998, 115–130, 190–191).

Kalt is played by an amateur. Sonia Hamza, who had lived in France for twelve years, works at the Musée d'Orsay. She took a year to accept the role, discussing the script at length with El Fani (Hamza 2003). El Fani recruited several members of her own family, most prominently her father, Bechir El Fani,[13] in the role of Kalt's uncle Salah, the distracted poet. According to El Fani, her father very much played himself, to the point of providing the appropriate wardrobe (2006b). El Fani's mother and daughter, Allia, put in cameo appearances, along with El Fani herself, as passersby when Frida is arrested. El Fani recruited family for the crew as well: her half-brother, Sofian, as cameraman, her half-sister Ghalia as script intern. Digital filming allowed many takes with the actors, who relaxed little by little (Barlet 2002).

El Fani shall have the final word. Asked whether her film was subversive, she replied (in Amarger n.d.):

> In as much as one can be subversive in Tunisia today.... In a society, when there is no freedom of expression, humor becomes a veritable form of the freedom of expression. The film's major assets are the energy we put into making it and the element of surprise. A Tunisian film like this is unexpected.

NOTES

1. Translations from the French are mine unless indicated otherwise.
2. Martin goes so far as to suggest that the film, "in its play with the self-referential and the alien, as it flashes the familiar within the alien and the alien within the familiar ... might be creating the next stage in film-making" (2007, 120).
3. Shafik observes that "in breaking away from the usual dualism of Tunisian feminist 'women's cinema', *Bedwin Hacker* displays an entirely postmodern vision" (2007, 256).
4. Bedwin sounds like *bédouine*, the female form of "Bedouin" in French. If the camel appears to take us back to a tourist vision of the Arab world, El Fani talks of adopting it because it is arrogant, does not care about time, bears grudges, and above all because it bites when least expected to (Bancal 2003).

5. The French Direction de la Surveillance du Territoire literally translates as Directorate of the Surveillance of the Territory. Historically a counterespionage service, the DST has evolved into a domestic intelligence agency with a broader remit.
6. El Fani dedicated her film to her paternal grandmother, who, denied an education by her father, decided to take evening classes when she was fifty-five and learned to read, write, and do arithmetic (Driguez 2005, 392).
7. In 1956, just a few months after independence, Tunisia promulgated legislation that gave women rights such as they do not enjoy anywhere else in the Arab world to this day. *Inter alia* women gained the right to vote, the minimum legal age of marriage was set at eighteen, polygamy was outlawed, civil marriage was introduced, and divorce became the province of secular courts. The results have been far-reaching in terms of the position of women within the family, their educational opportunities, and their professional achievements. They are reflected in filmmaking, where women exercise a much more important role than their peers in other Arab countries.
8. The French poster, reproduced here, effectively conveys the strength as well as the independence of Kalt, who dominates the screen, the landscape, and her camel, with the El Jem Roman Coliseum in the background.
9. Two women sculpt a man in El Fani's very first short, *Pour le plaisir* (For Pleasure, 1990). He comes alive and joins the two sleeping women.
10. The sound track of the songs was recorded by a Tunisian-French star, Amina Annabi, generally known as Amina. She was to play Frida, with more extended rehearsals, a performance, and dancing. But when it finally came to filming she was not available (El Fani 2006b), and Nadia Saiji took on the role.
11. El Fani expressed her frustration over the difficulty of getting funded in her short *Tant qu'il y aura de la pelloche . . .* (As Long as There Is Film Stock . . ., 1998), in which she repeats a single message, "I would like to film," in various settings.
12. The protagonist of El Fani's short *Fifty-fifty mon amour* (*Qahwa ashtar*, Fifty-Fifty My Love, 1992) lives similarly between the two countries—and two men. But the protagonist of her short *Unissez-vous, il n'est jamais trop tard!* (Never Too Late to Unite!, part of the multidirector *Paris, la métisse*, 2005), who has worked in France for thirty-five years and whose father died "pour la France," wants to be buried in a Paris cemetery, next to a monument for Arabs who died "pour la France" back in 1870, so that his children and his grandchildren will have a reason to love this land as if it were their home.
13. Bechir El Fani is one of the central figures in Nadia El Fani's documentary *Ouled Lénine* (The Children of Lenin, 2008). The film gives voice to Tunisian communists who played major roles in the struggle for independence but were suppressed once Tunisia became independent. El Fani explores their heritage with them and their children.

REFERENCES

Abassi, Hamadi. 2002. "Rencontre avec Nadia El Fani, réalisatrice de 'Bedwin Hacker.'" *Le Temps* (Tunisia), October 25.
Amarger, Michel. n.d. (about 2003). "Bedwin Hacker." Interview with Nadia El Fani. Beurfm.net/article.php3?id_article=273.
Bancal, Damien. 2003. "Bedwin Hacker." Interview with Nadia El Fani. http://zataz.com/interviews-securite/7055/fim-bedwin-hacker-nadia-el-fani.html.
Barlet, Olivier. 2002. "Bedwin Hacker: Interview with Nadia El Fani." http://www.africultures.com/php/index.php?nav=article&no=5624. Translation of "A propos de *Bedwin Hacker*, entretien d'Olivier Barlet avec Nadia El Fani." http://www.africultures.com/php/index.php?nav=article&no=2511.
Driguez, Michèle. 2005. "From a Conversation with Nadia El Fani." In *Encyclopedia of Arab Women Filmmakers*, ed. Rebecca Hillauer, 390–393. Cairo: American University in Cairo Press. Translated from "Nadia el Fani: Le Louvre à Tunis, la mer à Paris!" in *Actes du 14e Festival International*, 65–69, Montpellier: Festival de Montpellier, 1992.
El Fani, Nadia. 2003a. Personal communication to the author, December 13.
———. 2003b. Public discussion after screening of *Bedwin Hacker*, New York University, December 13.
———. 2006a. Public discussions after screening of *Bedwin Hacker*, Five Colleges African Film Festival, Smith College and Amherst College, March 30–31.
———. 2006b. Personal communication to the author, April 3.
———. 2008. Personal communication to the author, April 17.
Gabous, Abdelkrim. 1998. *Silence, elles tournent: Les femmes et le cinéma en Tunisie.* Tunis: Cérès Editions.
Hamza, Sonia. 2003. Personal communication to the author, December 13.
Martin, Florence. 2007. "Transvergence and Cultural Detours: Nadia El Fani's *Bedwin Hacker* (2002)." *Studies in French Cinema* 7 (2): 119–129.
Marsaud, Olivia. 2005. "Speaking with Nadia El Fani." In *Encyclopedia of Arab Women Filmmakers*, ed. Hillauer, 396–398. Cairo: American University in Cairo Press. Translation of "La Tunisie sans tabous," Afrik.com/article6344.html, 2003.
Shafik, Viola. 2007. *Arab Cinema: History and Cultural Identity.* Revised edition. Cairo: American University in Cairo Press.

8

From State Production to *Cinéma d'Auteur* in Algeria

ROY ARMES

Film formed a vital part of the liberation struggle by the army, the Front de libération nationale (FLN), and the Algerian provisional government in exile, the GPRA (Gouvernement provisoire de la République Algérienne). The first production unit, the Groupe Farid, was set up in 1957 by a group of filmmakers led by the French FLN activist René Vautier, who went on to make the major film of the period, *Algeria in Flames* (*Algérie en flammes*, 1959) (Maherzi 1980, 62). A resistance film school was established, but Vautier was to see four of his pupils die in battle. Mouny Berrah notes that "from 1957 to 1962, Algerian cinema was a site of solidarity, exchange, and expression between members of the Algerian *maquis* (the resistance to the French) and French intellectuals who sympathized with the liberation movement" (1996, 64).[1] Among those involved were some of the key figures of the future Algerian cinema, including Mohamed Lakhdar-Hamina and Ahmed Rachedi. But the first post-independence feature, *Such a Young Peace* (*Une si jeune paix*, 1965), was directed by French FLN activist Jacques Charby.

Most of the 1960s generation of Algerian directors had close personal links with the liberation struggle. Ahmed Rachedi, who made the first feature-length film directed by an Algerian, the masterly compilation film *Dawn of the Damned* (*L'aube des damnés/Fajr al-muʿadhdhabin*, 1965), on Third World struggles, had worked with Vautier in the army film unit and then followed him to the production collective CAV (Centre audio-visuel), where the documentary *Algeria in Flames* was made. Mohamed Lakhdar-Hamina, who had worked in the provisional government's film unit in exile in Tunis, made Algeria's first fictional feature, the striking film *The Wind from the Aurès* (*Rih al-Awras/Le vent des Aurès*, 1966), a powerful dramatic tale of a family destroyed by war. Mohamed Slim Riad used his own experiences as a detainee in France as a basis for his first feature, *The Way* (*La voie/al-Tariq*, 1968). Other new directors of the 1960s and early 1970s—such as Mustapha Badie, Tewfik Fares, Amar Laskri, Ahmed Lallem, and Sid Ali Mazif—had to choose similar subjects for their first features, even though they lacked this personal involvement.

In general, Algerian critics have been harsh in their response to these films of the 1960s and 1970s about the liberation struggle, preferring by far the later films dealing with the agrarian revolution. As Mouny Berrah puts it, "If the films about the war convey the image of an ideal nationalism, they are challenged by the films about the land, which put their emphasis on the internal contradictions of the Algerian society of the same period" (1981, 46). Ahmed Bedjaoui found a decade later that "Algerian film, whether in cinema or television, has practically never been able, in the course of the ten years following independence, to make a work of history or to explain, for example, who had chosen to fight and above all why" (1992, 35). As a result, Algerian audiences could not recognize themselves in their cinema's deformed image of the struggle, but the films did serve an ideological function: "The cult of heroes and epics about the liberation struggle, just like commercial cinema, turns the Algerian spectator away from the new realities of his country" (Bedjaoui 1992, 278–279).

Though Algerian filmmakers had every reason to celebrate the success of their struggle for liberation, the context in which they had to work could hardly have been less promising. To a quite surprising degree, the structures chosen for the newly nationalized film industry, the CNCA (Centre national du cinéma algerién) and its successor, ONCIC (Office national du commerce et de l'industrie cinématographiques), took their inspiration from the Centre national du cinéma (CNC) in Paris (Bedjaoui 1992, 83). The immediate censorship context was equally daunting, Monique Gadant explains: "The FLN did not arrive at independence with a really precise political programme," and in the case of culture "they stayed at the level of the slogan, thinking that the subordination of culture to politics went without saying" (1982, 249). In terms of film, this meant productions were "strictly designed for the defence and illustration of the official version of events" (Berrah 1997, 149–150). The year 1965, when the first Algerian feature film appeared, also brought the *coup d'état* by the military led by Houari Boumediene. Benjamin Stora has observed that "for the Algerian military who seized power in 1965, there is a need to rewrite Algerian history, negating the role of the resistance inside the country" (1994, 57–58). The emphasis was therefore on the encouragement of stories from which certain key figures were eliminated and others "projecting the mythical image of a Manichean universe, where roles are clearly defined between the hero and the traitors, the liberators and the oppressors" (ibid.).

In the late 1960s and the 1970s, Rachedi and Lakhdar-Hamina made further significant films about the liberation, this time with big budgets. Rachedi's *Opium and the Stick* (*L'opium et le bâton*/*al-Afyun wa-l-'asa*, 1969), adapted from a novel by Mouloud Mammeri, tells of a Kabyle family divided by the war. Rachedi has admitted to "weaknesses and concessions to the audience" (1981, 72). The effect is to simplify a complex novel, omitting "the anguish, the contradictions and the lucid though desperate commitment of an Algerian intellectual to the war" (Brahimi 1997, 66). The use of the Arabic language for the Berber protagonists further served the state's ideological desire to depict Algeria as a unified, totally Arab entity. Lakhdar-Hamina followed two lesser films about the anticolonial struggle—the comic tale *Hassan Terro* (*Hasan Tiru* 1968) about an insignificant man caught up in the resistance by accident and *December* (*Décembre*/*Dicember*, 1972), told through the eyes of a French officer—with what is generally recognized as his masterpiece, *Chronicle of the Years of Embers* (*Waqa'i' sanawat al-djamr* /*Chronique des années de braise*, 1975). This epic film, the first Arab or African production to win the Golden Palm at Cannes, was made—at a cost estimated to be equivalent to a dozen ordinary Algerian features—to celebrate the anniversary of the beginning of the Algerian War of Liberation on November 1, 1954.

Shot in a 70 mm format, the film is technically remarkable, but the use of a lush Hollywood-style score by Frenchman Philippe Arthuys denies it a specifically national feel. Tracing events in the years up to 1954, the narrative entwines two parallel stories—that of the wise madman (played with enormous gusto by the director himself) and that of Ahmed, a totally mythologized figure who is successively uneducated peasant, skilled craftsman, and legendary swordsman. Lakhdar-Hamina describes the film as a "personal vision," and this characterization of the film allows him to elide awkward historical facts. Oddly for a film aimed to be an epic of the national consciousness, it ends with the parallel deaths of both protagonists just as the struggle for liberation finally gets under way. *Chronicle of the Years of Embers* is a striking, if mystificatory film, more a work of lyrical protest than a lucid historical study.[2] Lakhdar-Hamina was unable to capture the same impact in his subsequent work, though both his 1980s films, *Sand Storm* (*Vent de sable*/*Rih al-raml*, 1982) and *The Last Image* (*La dernière image*/*al-Sura al-akhira*, 1986), showed the desire to find an international audience.

Given that the ONCIC was a state organization, it is hardly surprising that the so-called agrarian revolution of the early 1970s found an immediate reflection in the cinema and formed the second collective focus for Algerian cinema.

Filmmakers adopted two main approaches: documenting the abuses of the colonial past and looking at progress in contemporary rural society. Rural life in the colonial period was explored in *Noua* (*Nua*, 1972), the sole feature made by Abdelaziz Tolbi. It gives an explicit picture of the sufferings endured by the peasantry under French rule but ends with the emergence of *mujahidin*, freedom fighters, who give the people fresh hope. Two features directed by Mohamed Lamine Merbah, *The Plunderers* (*Les spoliateurs/al-Mufsidun*, 1972) and *The Uprooted* (*Les déracinés/Beni hendel*, 1976), took a more analytic perspective on the wretched lives of peasants uprooted from their land under colonialism.

A larger number of films looked at progress in contemporary rural society. In the forefront was Mohamed Bouamari's *The Charcoal Burner* (*Le charbonnier/al-Fahham*, 1972), a contemporary tale about a charcoal burner who loses his livelihood with the introduction of gas to the countryside and his wife, who finds fresh opportunities offered by the new order; the film reached an international audience. Bouamari's later films—*The Inheritance* (*L'héritage/al-Irth*, 1974), *First Step* (*Premier pas/al-Khutwat al-ula*, 1979), and *The Denial* (*Le refus/al-Rafd*, 1982)—were more overtly experimental and structurally complex works that received a muted reception in Algeria. Other studies of rural life include Riad's *Wind from the South* (*Vent du sud/Rih al-janub*, 1975) and Mazif's *The Nomads* (*Les nomades/Masirat al-ruhhal*, 1975). A further hymn to the virtues of collective action was Moussa Haddad's *Near the Poplar Tree* (*Au près du peuplier/Min qurb al-saf-saf*, 1972), while Ghaouti Bendeddouche's *The Fishermen* (*Les pêcheurs/Echebka*, 1976) depicted a group of fishermen who gradually develop political awareness. Works by Ahmed Lallem, Amar Laskri, and Mohamed Nadir Azizi followed the same trends, though in distinctively personal fashion, while the collectively made *So That Algeria May Live* (*Pour que vive l'Algérie*, 1972) drew attention to a whole range of government programs and achievements, of which rural reform was one.

The sense of conformity to a centrally determined set of themes was strong in the 1970s. But Ahmed Rachedi's *Ali in Wonderland* (*Ali au pays des mirages/Alifi bilad al-sarab*, 1979) offers a caustic picture of the situation confronting immigrants in France. Five years later he satirized the FLN post-independence bureaucracy in the wonderfully acerbic satirical comedy *Monsieur Fabre's Mill* (*Le moulin de M. Fabre/Tahunat al-sayyid Fabre*, 1984), his last film for twenty-five years. Other films that depart from the mainstream concern with war and agrarian reform include *The Good Families* (*Les bonnes familles/al-Usar al-tayyibah*, 1973), a deliberately propagandistic feature made independently on behalf of the FLN by a collective headed by Djafar Damardjji; Mohamed

Slim Riad's political thriller *Autopsy of a Plot* (*Autopsie d'un complot/Tachrih mouamara*, 1978); and Sid Ali Mazif's *Leila and the Others* (*Leïla et les autres/ Laila wa akhawatuha*, 1978), a study of women's lives in an urban context.

Several directors established at Radiodiffusion télévision algérienne (RTA) made films for the cinema. Moussa Haddad, for example, directed the comedy *Inspector Tahar's Holiday* (*Les vacances de l'inspecteur Tahar/ʿUtlat al-mufattich Tahar*, 1973). Two highly original 16 mm films directed by the novelist Assia Djebar, the sole female Algerian director of the period, were produced by RTA and shown at international festivals. In *The Nouba of the Women of Mount Chenoua* (*La nouba des femmes du Mont Chenoua/Noubat nissa jabel Chnouwwa*, 1978), the fictional story of Lila is interwoven with the documentary accounts of six older women who recall the events of the war; a section is devoted to the legends and battles of the distant past such as the 1871 revolt in the area of Mount Chenoa.[3] *La Zerda* (*La zerda et les chants de l'oubli/Zerda wa aghani al-nisyan*, 1980) is an equally personal and meditative piece of filmmaking. In general, films by television directors helped shape foreign perceptions of Algerian filmic identity, but they did not create institutional unity between film and television production at home.

Mouny Berrah aptly observes that the real Algerian cinema "is composed of thematic and aesthetic exceptions" (1996, 63). This is borne out by the handful of isolated works of distinctive quality, aside from the prevailing style and mood, and these are the films that have best stood the test of time. In addition to Djebar's work, there is *Tahia ya didou* ("Greetings; Didou," *Alger insolite*, 1971), a portrait of Algiers made by Mohamed Zinet. This is a loosely shaped narrative about the wanderings of two French tourists that begins lightly but takes on a darker tone when memories of the past return to haunt the man. Another isolated but striking work is *Nahla* (1979), directed by Farouk Beloufa. Set in Lebanon in 1975, the film follows the relationships between an Algerian journalist and three women, the singer Nahla, the journalist Maha, and the Palestinian activist Hind. Deftly shot and elliptically narrated, the film captures graphically the confusions of civil conflict. Neither Zinet nor Beloufa was able to make a second feature, but the equally innovative Merzak Allouache did establish himself as one of Algeria's most prolific directors. His debut feature was *Omar Gatlato* (1977), a picture of Algerian youth that has become a key date in the history of Algerian cinema. Formally innovative, it offers an amusing and completely unofficial view of the post-revolutionary generation growing up in Algiers.[4] Allouache made two more highly individual features, *The Adventures of a Hero* (*Les aventures d'un héros/Mughamarat batal*, 1978) and *The Man Who*

Watched Windows (*L'homme qui regardait les fenêtres/Rajulun wa nawafidh*, 1982), before leaving Algeria for France to make *A Paris Love Story* (*Un amour à Paris/Hubbun fi Baris*, 1986).

To the end of the 1970s, Algeria maintained its position of having produced more films than Tunisia and Morocco combined. Then the state monopoly of film production was abolished. ONCIC was dissolved in 1984 and its functions split between two separate organizations for production and for distribution, but state production and distribution were joined afresh three years later when CAAIC (Centre algérien pour l'art et l'industrie cinématographique) was set up to take on all the activities previously undertaken by ONCIC. A parallel step was taken with respect to television production when RTA resources were regrouped in the same year to form ENPA (Entreprise nationale de productions audiovisuelles). The new organization participated in numerous co-productions with CAAIC, so that the boundaries that separated television from cinema at the time of RTA and ONCIC became blurred.

Among the major works of the 1980s is Ghaouti Bendeddouche's *Harvests of Steel* (*Moissons d'acier*, 1982), a tale of peasant resistance as villagers rebuild their lives despite the "harvests of steel" of the title: the landmines laid during the war and still threatening life and limb. Amar Laskri, after a ten-year silence, completed *Gates of Silence* (*Les portes du silence/Abwab al-çoumt*, 1987), the story of a deaf-mute who seeks to avenge the destruction of his village in 1955. Sid Ali Mazif's *I Exist* (*J'existe*, 1982), co-produced with the Arab League, is a three-part compilation film looking at a range of issues concerning women's roles in society. Mazif then returned to fiction with *Houria/Huria* (1986), a story of the unhappy love affair of two students. Among the newcomers of the 1980s, Rabah Laradji made *A Roof, a Family* (*Un toit une famille/Saqat waaila*, 1981), a study of the problems of the homeless, and Sid Ali Fettar made two family dramas, *Rai* (1987) and *Forbidden Love* (*Amour interdit*, 1993). Mohamed Meziane Yala made *Autumn Song* (*Chant d'automne/Angham al-kharif*, 1983), the unhappy love story of a French girl and an Algerian peasant. Jean-Pierre Lledo made his debut with *Empire of Dreams* (*L'empire des rêves/Mamlakkat al-ahlam*, 1982), which looked at the lives of an eccentric body of actors and would-be actors. His second idiosyncratic feature, *Lights* (*Lumières/Adwa'*, 1992), dealt with a forty-year-old filmmaker's enthusiasm for cinema. Abderrahmane Bouguermouh contributed *Cry of Stone* (*Cri de pierre/Surakh al-hajar*, 1986), a story of city dwellers who return to the land.

Beginning in 1982, Okacha Touita made a quartet of films spanning twenty-five years about the divisions within Algerian ranks during and after the War of

Liberation: *The Sacrificed* (*Les sacrifiés*, 1982), *The Survivor* (*Le rescapé*, 1986), *The Cry of Men* (*Le cri des hommes*, 1990), and *Morituri* (2007). Also from a base in Paris, Mahmoud Zemmouri directed the comedy *Take a Thousand Quid and Get Lost* (*Prends dix mille balles et casses-toi*, 1981), in which two French-educated young Algerians attempt to rediscover their "homeland." He followed this with two striking social satires, *The Crazy Years of the Twist* (*Les folles années du twist/Sanawat al-twist al-majnouna*, 1984) and *From Hollywood to Tamanrasset* (*De Hollywood à Tamanrasset*, 1990). One of the most talented of the newcomers, Brahim Tsaki, made two highly original studies of children. *Children of the Wind* (*Les enfants du vent/Abna' al-rih*, 1981) was composed of three episodes, each illustrating a different aspect of childhood. *Story of a Meeting* (*Histoire d'une rencontre/Hikayat liqa'*, 1983) tells the story of the relationship of two deaf-mute children, one American and the other Algerian. His third and final film, *The Neon Children* (*Les enfants des néons*, 1990), was made in France. The equally gifted Mohamed Rachid Benhadj, who had worked for RTA, received wide acclaim for his feature film debut, *Desert Rose* (*Rose des sables/Louss*, 1989), the tale of a crippled youth.

Another director previously active with RTA, Mohamed Chouikh, began his film career with *Breakdown* (*La rupture/al-Inqita'*, 1982), about a prison escape in the colonial era. With his second feature, Chouikh began a loosely linked trio of films looking at Algeria in relation to its past. In *The Citadel* (*La citadelle/al-Qalʿa*, 1988), the love of Kaddour for the shoemaker's wife creates tensions in a village community where men and women keep to their traditional roles: his passion can lead only to disaster.[5] In *Youssef: The Legend of the Seventh Sleeper* (*Youcef, la légende du septième dormant/Youcef kesat dekra sabera*, 1993), an amnesiac travels through the country struggling to understand and failing to find in contemporary Algeria any of the ideals for which he and his colleagues fought during the liberation struggle.[6] In yet another allegory, *The Desert Ark* (*L'arche du désert*, 1997), Chouikh looked at a remote desert community, exploring and questioning the validity of its values and traditions.[7]

The ranks of directors were reinforced in the 1980s by a number of self-taught filmmakers. Ali Ghalem returned from film work in exile in France to make a rather muted version of his own novel, *A Wife for My Son* (*Une femme pour mon fils/Zawja al-ahlam*, 1982). He was followed by Tayeb Mefti directing *Moussa's Wedding* (*Le mariage de Moussa*, 1983), another tale of an emigrant's return, and by two young directors, Mustapha Mengouchi and Rabah Bouchemha, who compiled the episodes of a film on children's roles in the liberation struggle, *We Shall Go onto the Mountain* (*Nous irons sur la montagne*, 1987). The early

1990s also saw new films from a number of established directors, some of them veterans from the 1970s. The new head of ENPA, Mohamed Lamine Merbah, made a 16 mm feature, *Radhia* (1992), the story of a fragmented family. Djafar Damardjji, whose first film dates from 1972, finally completed his second, *Wanderings (Errances)*, based on the travels of the European explorer Isabelle Eberhardt. Another isolated achievement by a veteran was the completion by Amar Laskri—head of CAAIC from 1996—of *Lotus Flower (Fleur de lotus*, 1998), which occupied him through much of the 1990s. This ambitious Algerian-Vietnamese co-production, co-directed by Trân Dàc, chronicles some of the less expected outcomes of colonial occupations and wars.

A new generation emerged, quite literally, at the beginning of the 1990s with the feature debut by Mohamed Lakhdar-Hamina's son, Malik Lakhdar-Hamina. His *Autumn—October in Algiers (Automne—octobre à Alger/ Uktubur fi-l-Jaza'ir*, 1991) is a vivid portrayal of a family caught up in the tumultuous events of October 1988, when young Algerians took to the streets in protest and were confronted by inexperienced and frightened soldiers. Other early 1990s debuts include those of journalist Saïd Ould Khelifa with *White Shadows (Ombres blanches/al-Dhilal al-bidh*, 1991), Rabie Ben Mokhtar with *Marathon Tam* (1992), and the editor-turned-director Rachid Benallal, who directed *Ya ouled* ("Hey Children," 1993), yet another tale of children growing up during the war. Many of those who made their first films for cinema release in the 1990s came—often with considerable experience—from television. These included the television veterans Mohamed Hilmi, Hadj Rahim, Abderrazak Hellal, Rabah Bouberras, Yahia Debboub, and Rachid Benbrahim. Among the most interesting of this group are Benamar Bakhti, who made the highly successful comedy *Moonlighting (Le clandestin*, 1991), and the novelist Hafsa Zinai-Koudil, a woman whose controversial *The Female Devil (Le démon au féminin*, 1993) about fake exorcists led to a dispute with the producers and a delayed release.

The chaos as Islamic fundamentalists continued their war on politicians, intellectuals, and foreigners finds clear reflection in a number of films of 1993–1994. In Mohamed Rachid Benhadj's second film, *Touchia* (1993), a woman trapped in her flat by pro–Islamic Republic demonstrators in 1991 recalls a parallel disillusionment when her 1950s childhood dreams of independence ended in the brutal reality of her own rape and the murder of her closest friend. Mahmoud Zemmouri's *The Honor of the Tribe (L'honneur de la tribu/Charaf al-qabilu*, 1993) is a bleak—if often farcical—look at the impact of twenty-five years of FLN rule, reflecting the confused situation of Algeria in the early 1990s. Perhaps the clearest depiction of the Algerian predicament is Merzak

Allouache's *Bab el-Oued City* (*Bab al-wad al-humah*, 1994), which marks a return to the quarter of Algiers that formed the setting of *Omar Gatlato* but is now totally transformed by the new and violent force of Islamic fundamentalism.

Initially the 1987 reforms seemed to favor Algerian production, and nineteen features were released in 1990–1993. But October 1993 saw yet another radical reorganization of the Algerian film sector, when production was privatized and film directors were given three years' salary and invited to set up their own companies. CAAIC continued in existence to offer production support and to administer a new system whereby filmmakers could receive state support for specific projects on the basis of scripts read by a commission chaired initially by the writer Rachid Mimouni. This reorganization, coinciding with widespread political upheaval, seriously threatened Algerian film output. But worse was to come in 1998 when the government closed down CAAIC, ENPA, and the newsreel organization ANAF without any indication of what new structures—if any—would be put in place. Four feature films were left uncompleted, and CAAIC's 217 employees—the backbone of the Algerian film industry—found themselves unemployed. The abrupt privatization, combined with the increasing political turmoil and waves of mass killings, seriously disrupted Algerian cinema and its links with the outside world. Only five Algerian features were seen abroad in 1995–1999, and many leading filmmakers, actors, and technicians were forced into exile.

A significant development in late 1990s was a retreat from the urban environment and a shift from realistic narratives to fables and allegories. Some filmmakers with Berber connections turned to the Atlas Mountains. Three films in the Berber language were released in 1995–1997.[8] *Once upon a Time* (*Il était une fois/Machaho*, 1995), directed by Belkacem Hadjadj, offers a critical examination of traditional attitudes and beliefs, particularly the male concept of honor, in a simple narrative leading inexorably to confrontation and death. Abderrahmane Bouguermouh's long-delayed *The Forgotten Hillside* (*La colline oubliée*, 1996), based on the novel by Mouloud Mammeri, tells of an isolated mountain community shaken by the forces of colonialism and by its own inner passions. Another film to depict a mountain community and to use the Berber language was *Baya's Mountain* (*La montagne de Baya/Djebel Baya*, 1997), a first fictional film by the documentarist Azzedine Meddour, dealing with a legendary figure in the Berber resistance.[9]

For many other filmmakers who had once worked within the structures of Algerian national production, the only choice in the 1990s was exile. The French- or Italian-funded films of Merzak Allouache, Mahmoud Zemmouri, and Rachid Mohamed Benhadj are shaped by and directed at the European market. More recently several of these exiled filmmakers have returned to work in Algeria. Merzak Allouache followed his fairly conventional drama of a young woman's search for her missing fiancé, *The Other World* (*L'autre monde*, 2001), with *Bab el Web* (2005), a return to the Algiers location of his two finest films, *Omar Gatlato* and *Bab el-Oued City*. Saïd Ould Khelifa offered a very muted study of the pressures of living in 1990s Algeria in *Ania's Tea* (*Le thé d'Ania*, 2004). Several films have been shot in Algeria by long-established members of the Algerian immigrant community in France working from a production base in Paris.[10] These directors include Mehdi Charef, Abdelkrim Bahloul, Nadir Moknèche, Rabah Ameur-Zaïmèche, and Amor Hakkar. Newcomers of Algerian origin but based in Paris include the documentarist Djamila Sahraoui, with her first fictional feature, *Barakat!* (2005); Lyes Salem, who made his debut with the popular comedy *Mascarades* (2008); and Tariq Teguia, who directed two austere studies of isolation and the lure of immigration, *Rome Rather Than You* (*Rome plutôt que vous*, 2007) and *Inland* (*Gabbla*, 2008).

Only a handful of Algerian-based filmmakers were able to release feature films in the 2000s, and there is no sign of production and distribution structures being restored within the country. Bendeddouche's *The Neighbor* (*La voisine/al-Jara*), one of the films left incomplete when the production organizations were shut down in 1998, was finally shown in 2002, while the similarly delayed biographical study *Si Mohand U M'hand*, co-directed by Rachid Benallel and newcomer Liazid Khodja, was not released until 2006. The editor Yamina Bachir-Chouikh made an impressive debut with *Rachida* (2002), a sensitive study of a woman's struggles in a world of violence that offers her no protection, as did the documentarist Nadia Cherabi-Labidi with *The Other Side of the Mirror* (*L'envers du miroir*, 2007), her tale of a taxi driver who finds a newborn baby left in his taxi and sets out to find the mother. Another newcomer, Mohamed Lebcir, completed *My Sister, My Friend* (*Mon amie ma sœur*, 2003). Several established directors managed to relaunch their careers in the new decade. Belkacem Hadjadj made *El Manara* (2004), which traced the impact of the 1988 upheavals on the lives of three young people; and Mohamed Chouikh followed his allegorical trilogy with *Hamlet of Women* (*Douar de femmes*, 2005), the lively study of a group of women who, in the absence of their menfolk, have to take over the defense of their village.[11] Two other veterans making their returns after an absence of more than twenty years are Ahmed Rachedi, with *Ben Boulaid* (2008), and Brahim Tsaki, with *Ayrouen* (2008). At the time of writing, there is some hope for a revival of Algerian film production, but the obstacles are formidable.

NOTES

1. Translations from the French are mine.
2. For a detailed analysis of *Chronicle of the Years of Embers* see Armes 2002.
3. On *The Nouba of the Women of Mount Chenoua* see Agnès Peysson-Zeiss 2004.
4. On *Omar Gatlato* see Armes 1998.
5. On the œuvre of Mohamed Chouikh see Brahimi 2004.
6. On *Youssef: The Legend of the Seventh Sleeper* see Armes 2007.
7. The script of *The Desert Ark* is included in Taboulay 1997 (83–181).
8. See the dossier "L'emergence d'un cinéma berbère," in Serceau 2004 (204–215).
9. Azzedine Meddour published a novel (1999) based on the film.
10. On the immigrant cinema in France see Armes 2005 and Tarr 2005.
11. On *Hamlet of Women* see the essay devoted to the film in this volume.

REFERENCES

———. 1996. *Scenario salut cousin!*, script. (Paris) *L'Avant-Scène du Cinéma* 457:6–64.

———. 1998. *Bab el-Oued*. Boulder, CO: Lynne Rienner. Translation by Angela M. Brewer of *Bab el-Oued*, Paris: Editions du Seuil, 1995.

Armes, Roy. 1998. *Omar Gatlato*. Trowbridge, England: Flicks Books.

———. 1999. *Omar Gatlato de Merzak Allouache: Un nouveau regard sur l'Algérie*. Paris: Editions L'Harmattan.

———. 2002. "History or Myth: *Chronique des années de braise*." In *Celaan 1, Cinéma Maghrébin*, ed. Ida Kummer, 7–17.

———. 2005. *Postcolonial Images: Studies in North African Film*. Bloomington: Indiana University Press.

———. 2006. *African Filmmaking: North and South of the Sahara*. Bloomington: Indiana University Press.

———. 2007. "Youcef ou la légende du septième dormant/Youssef or The Legend of the Seventh Sleeper." In *The Cinema of North Africa and the Middle East*, ed. Gönül Dönmetz-Colin, 135–142. London: Wallflower Press.

———. 2008. *Dictionary of African Filmmakers*, Bloomington: Indiana University Press.

Bedjaoui, Ahmed. 1992. "Silences et balbutiements." In *France-Algérie: Images d'une guerre*, ed. Mouloud Mimoun, 29–41. Paris: Institut du Monde Arabe.

Berrah, Mouny. 1981. "La guerre, la terre, la vie quotidienne." In *Cinémas du Maghreb*, ed. Mouny Berrah, Victor Bachy, Mohand Ben Salama, and Ferid Boughedir, Paris: Editions Papyrus; *CinémAction* 14:46–50.

———. 1996. "Algerian Cinema and National Identity." In *Screens of Life: Critical Film Writing from the Arab World*, ed. Alia Arasoughly, 63–83. Quebec: World Heritage Press.

———. 1997. "Histoire et idéologie du cinéma algérien sur la guerre." In *La guerre d'Algérie à l'écran*, ed. Guy Hennebelle, Mouny Berrah, and Benjamin Stora, Paris: Corlet/Télérama; *CinémAction* 85:144–183.
Brahimi, Denise. 1997. "A propos de Tala ou *L'opium et le bâton*: Du roman au film." (Paris) *Awal* 15:65–73.
———. 2004. "Images, symboles et paraboles dans le cinéma de Mohamed Chouikh." In *Cinémas du Maghreb*, ed. Michel Serceau, Paris: Corlet/Télérama; *CinémAction* 111:154–159.
———. 2009. *50 ans de cinéma maghrébin*. Paris: Minerve.
Gadant, Monique. 1982. "L'apolitique culturelle." In *Algérie*, ed. Georges Châtillon and Edwige Lambert, 242–253. Paris: Autrement.
Ghalem, Ali. 1979. *Une femme pour mon fils*. Paris: Spyros.
Lakhdar Hamina, Mohamed. 1981. "Ecouter l'histoire aux portes de la légende." In *Cinémas du Maghreb*, ed. Mouny Berrah, Victor Bachy, Mohand Ben Salama, and Ferid Boughedir, Paris: Editions Papyrus; *CinémAction* 14:67–72.
Maherzi, Lotfi. 1980. *Le cinéma algérien: Institutions, imaginaire, idéologie*. Algiers: SNED.
Mammeri, Mouloud. 1952. *La colline oubliée*. Paris: Plon.
———. 1965. *Opium et le bâton*. Paris: Plon.
Meddour, Azzedine. 1999. *La Montagne de Baya ou la 'diya'*. Algiers: Editions Marinoor.
Peysson-Zeiss, Agnès. 2004. "*La nouba des femmes du Mont Chénoua*: De l'histoire muette au cinéma parlant." In *Cinémas du Maghreb*, ed. Michel Serceau, Paris: Corlet/Télérama; *CinémAction* 111:81–85.
Rachedi, Ahmed. 1981. "Sans grand public, il n'y a pas de cinéma." Interview in *Cinémas du Maghreb*, ed. Mouny Berrah, Victor Bachy, Mohand Ben Salama, and Ferid Boughedir, Paris: Editions Papyrus; *CinémAction* 14:72–73.
Serceau, Michel, ed. 2004. *Cinémas du Maghreb*, Paris: Corlet/Télérama; *CinémAction* 111.
Stora, Benjamin. 1994. *Histoire de l'Algérie depuis l'indépendance*. Paris: Editions la Découverte.
Taboulay, Camille. 1997. *Mohamed Chouikh*. Interview and script of *L'arche du désert*. Paris: K Films Éditions.
Tarr, Carrie. 2005. *Reframing Difference*: Beur *and* Banlieue *Film*making in France. Manchester: Manchester University Press.

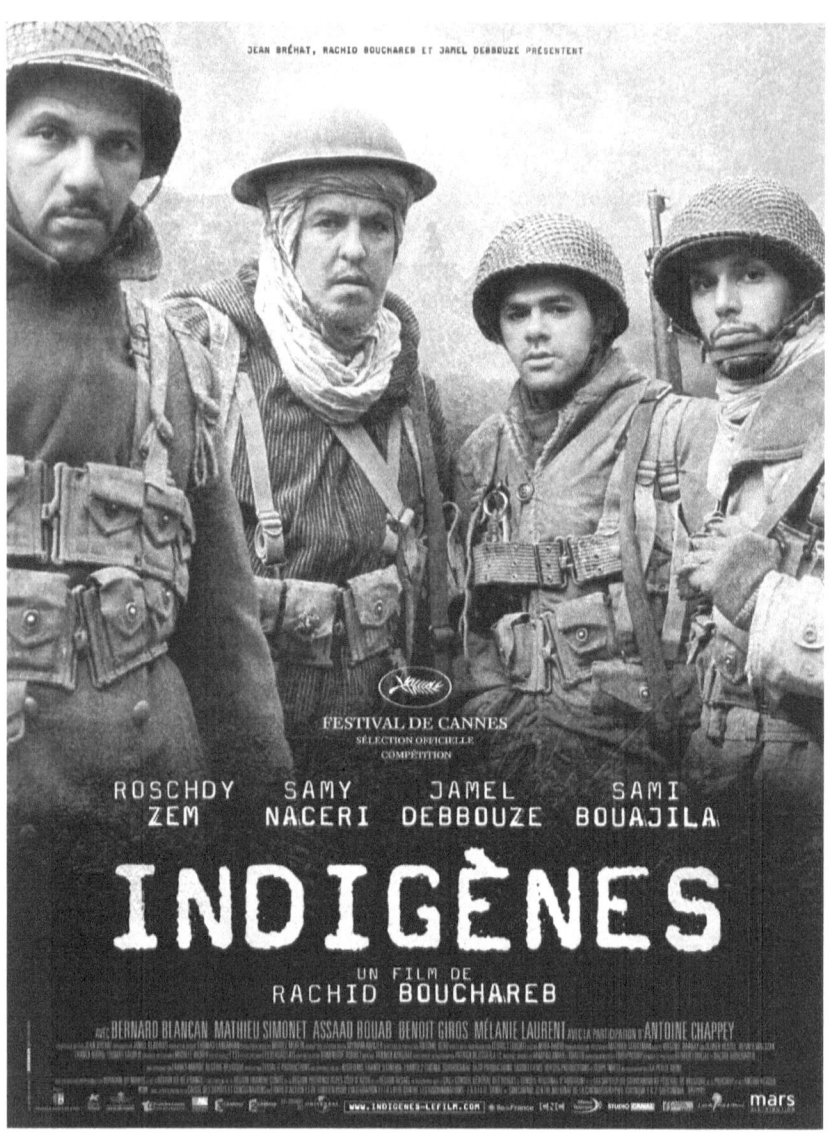

Design by Aussitôt dit/Soazig Petit. Courtesy Jean Brehat

Days of Glory
Another Vision of French History

OLIVIER BARLET

"The film tells our parents' story."¹ That is without a doubt the key to the success of Rachid Bouchareb's film.² But more than just a box-office hit, *Days of Glory* effectively helped to repair the injustice done to Africa's World War II veterans.

When shown for the first time, at Cannes in May 2006, the jury chaired by Wong Kar-Wai awarded Best Male Actor honors to the film's leading actors: Jamel Debbouze (Saïd), Sami Bouajila (Abdelkader), Roschdy Zem (Messaoud), and Samy Naceri (Yassir) in the roles of the four "native" soldiers,³ and Bernard Blancan, who plays the ambiguous and unsettling Sergeant Martinez. At the awards ceremony, the actors and the director broke into the song the colonial infantrymen sing in the film. French President Jacques Chirac subsequently published a statement:

> I warmly congratulate you for this award, which celebrates your talented acting in a film that pays tribute to the soldiers of the Army of Africa during the last war. *Days of Glory* conveys a message full of courage, fraternity, and a common destiny woven on both sides of the Mediterranean between France and the countries that, at a given moment, shared a common hope and history.

But the question of the war veterans' pensions was not settled. At the time of decolonization in 1960, France froze the retirement and disability pensions paid to veterans from its former colonial empire at their 1959 level. This

---

* *Days of Glory/Indigènes*. 2006. A film by Rachid Bouchareb, written by Olivier Lorelle and Rachid Bouchareb. Produced by Tessalit Production (France), Kissfilms (France), France 3 Cinema (France), France 2 Cinema (France), StudioCanal (France), Taza Productions (Morocco), Tassili (Algeria), Versus Production (Belgium), and Scope Invest (Belgium). Distributed in the United States by Genius Products. 120 minutes.

freezing of pensions steadily exacerbated a glaring difference of treatment between war veterans from Africa and French veterans; it was the cause of great bitterness, with the gap ranging up to tenfold. A former colonial infantryman, Amadou Diop, took the French state to court, and in 2001 the Council of State posthumously found in his favor, forcing the French government to pay his full pension. Successive administrations thereafter committed to paying the eighty thousand veterans from the former French Empire the pensions rightfully owed to them, a sum of 1.85 billion euros, but never actually carried out the promise. On August 13, 2004, an official statement from the French Ministry for War Veterans announced that a sum of 120 million euros had been allocated to pay compensation. Two days later, during the commemoration of the Allied landings in Provence, Jacques Chirac paid homage to the African infantrymen, but the question of freezing their pensions was still not settled. After a private screening of Bouchareb's film on September 5, 2006, Chirac decided to put an end to the discrimination toward the African war veterans. This decision was officially announced by the Minister for War Veterans, Hamlaoui Mekachera, after a cabinet meeting on September 27, 2006. The announcement coincided with the film's release in France.[4]

The film's success is also due to its casting. The four lead infantrymen characters are all played by second-generation immigrant actors who have managed to make names for themselves in the French film and entertainment world. Their names and popularity are an important asset, especially the highly popular comedian of Moroccan origin Jamel Debbouze, who, with the director, became personally involved in securing the film's funding.[5] Indeed, he was called to the rescue at a time when the producers were pulling their hair out trying to find the necessary budget. Initial funding had been secured from France 2 Cinéma, France 3 Cinéma, TF1 Vidéo, and the French National Center for Cinematography (CNC) *avance sur recettes* subsidy. But it was far from sufficient. Canal+ producers were unenthused by this tale of four Arabs who liberate France. Finally conceded, the channel's participation was, however, far from the amount needed to complete the estimated $31 million budget.

It was at this point that Jamel Debbouze saved a considerable portion of the budget by getting Morocco to contribute free support for all the battle scenes and the services of Royal Air Maroc. Producer Jean Bréhat, director Rachid Bouchareb, and actor Jamel Debbouze agreed to forgo their salaries, but they were still $1.9 million short of the final $17 million production budget. Canal+, France 2, and France 3 agreed to increase their backing, and the shoot began even though they still did not have the entire budget. At times, it was Debbouze who called the various regional authorities to get their backing. In the

Rashid Bouchareb and Jamel Debbouze. Courtesy Jean Brehat

end, the Ile-de-France region contributed $600,000 in the name of "memory, integration, and culture"; the National Assembly and the senate granted small subsidies, right down to the prime minister, who contributed $25,000; and the French army notably provided a helicopter.

Bouchareb has described the historical significance of the film's subject:

> Our constant work with the actors consisted of talking about the film, every day, and beyond the realm of cinema. We surpassed cinema; it became a simple tool. Our feeling was that, in making this film, we were also learning from the progression of the shoot and our encounters. People came to see us from all over France, not to see a film in the making, but to discuss history.

The enthusiasm generated by the shoot was indeed huge, both in Morocco and in France. In Morocco, the film was shot in Ouarzazate, whose infrastructure has permitted the shooting of numerous international films. During the battle scenes, the Moroccan soldiers playing the bit parts had to charge in flimsy sandals on the rocky ground. The director hesitated to have them redo the shots, as it was getting too painful for them, but they insisted, arguing that the film was about their forefathers and a period that deeply marked their history. Similarly in France, people came from afar to meet the film crew and to recount their memories.

At Cannes, the director and actors "ascended the stairs" in the company of North African war veterans. "When we arrived here with the colonial infantrymen and went up the stairs, it was not to present a film, but to present a chapter of French history," said Bouchareb. This certainty of rewriting history is at the heart of the project and the film's success. Bouchareb added,

> We all share the same history—and that is what unites us—that of our parents' immigration, in the generally hazy family memory of those events. All, or nearly all of us, have a great-grandfather who died in the First World War, and some, like my uncle, fought in Indochina. We have always been closely tied to French history. We are a part of French history. That is why it was important for us to say, "Let's open our own chapter within French history. Let's tell that chapter, which is part of French history, from our point of view."

In the film Bouchareb seeks, in his words, to "unveil this chapter of French history, which is largely unknown in France and even in the North African or African countries." The film came at a time of fierce debate in France over Article 4 of a law passed on February 23, 2005, that invited teachers to highlight the "positive contributions" of colonization; the article was withdrawn in early 2006 to appease tensions. In *Days of Glory* Bouchareb thus seeks through film to restore the memory and the importance of the African colonial infantrymen's role in the liberation of France, despite the fact that they were gradually sidelined as the Army of Africa progressed northward and toward Germany, joining with the Allied forces that landed in Normandy. Aware of the difficulty this would later pose in keeping the colonies under the French yoke, De Gaulle did not want the colonial infantrymen to be associated with the victory. Although they made up half the troops that landed in Provence in 1944, these battalions were "whitened" the further they advanced. De Gaulle chose to integrate resistance groups into the French First Army and, given the shortage of equipment, decided to disarm some of the colonial infantrymen battalions to equip the new soldiers. Despite their military feats, not one African soldier was allowed the honor of parading on the Champs Elysées on the day Paris was liberated.

At the end of the film, Abdelkader (Sami Bouajila), is the sole survivor. We find him sixty years later in the sadness and solitude of his tiny immigrant lodgings. Has he been shortchanged by the ideology he fought to defend? "Yes," Bouchareb replies:

The liberators are feted in France.

It's the situation of hundreds of men still living in France in immigrant hostels in Bordeaux, Nantes, Paris, or Mulhouse. Just like the other survivors back in Africa, at ninety years old, they are still waiting for some recognition. Most incredible of all, however, is that they all told me that, in spite of everything, they would do it again if they had to. Because they experienced an amazing communion with the French people. They were given a wonderful welcome when they arrived here, they shared their food with the French, they slept in their homes, they married French women; for them it was an incredible time, an incredible encounter.

The film thus contributes a positive, humane note to the debate animating French society concerning its relation to its colonial history and its relation to its populations descending from France's former colonies. At the very same moment that the National Museum of the History of Immigration, a project backed by Jacques Chirac, was inaugurated in almost complete silence in the former colonial museum at Porte Dorée in Paris, President Nicolas Sarkozy created a Ministry of National Identity, as if it were possible to fix this identity by decree! *Days of Glory* represents an evolution in films dealing with the immigrant question. While in the 1980s the anti-racist nongovernmental organization SOS-Racisme and its slogan "Don't Touch My Buddy" demanded the right to be different, the ensuing tendency to confine people to this difference drove the immigrant movement to demand the right to "indifference," to be just like anybody else, without being excluded, to be citizens benefiting from the same rights and status as everybody else, without any special attributions.

Rather than portraying the colonial infantrymen as victims, the film positions itself at the start of a shared history that could have been mutually beneficial if the colonial yoke had not immediately relegated all the players again to their place. It is this shared history that Bouchareb chooses to highlight in the film and that determines the timeline:

> I originally wrote a screenplay that ended in Sétif,[6] but that was too far. It will be part of the next film. It's an event that took me much too far, so I stopped before Sétif, even though I wrote all the later scenes of the return to Algeria. I felt that this risked opening up another chapter that would undermine the film's message. The film's message is this old man who ends up in his lodgings waiting. It's the end of his life, and I wanted to entirely inscribe it in the history of France.

A historical period drama, an eighteen-month shoot, twelve months' post-production, with captivating violins and a star cast, *Days of Glory* clearly was meant to reach a wide audience, as Bouchareb acknowledges:

> I did not want to adopt the same approach to this film as I did the others, for example *Little Senegal*, which is cinematographically more sober, stricter. Here, for this story, I absolutely wanted to reach French audiences, audiences in North Africa, in Africa, and in the rest of Europe and the world if possible, but first of all the different partners who contributed to this common history. I knew I was going to make a film where there would be war scenes, pretty heroic characters, and I wanted to go more in this direction of a popular cinema, which isn't something I look down on at all. I love popular cinema; it has produced great works. It was this particular genre I wanted; I did not want to become trapped in an overly naturalistic, realist cinema. I wanted to give the film a different ambition. I want this film to be a film that airs on French TV in five years time, in ten years too.

This approach does not detract from the accuracy of the film's tone. The period photos that scroll past in the credits are of ordinary folk. They are people from all over North Africa—the film does not focus on sub-Saharan Africa—who enlisted in the French army in 1943, motivated by idealism a little but in the main to discover new lands or for the money and an escape from eternal poverty. There were 130,000 of them from all over Africa, whom the military hierarchy wanted to distinguish from the "men" by calling them "natives."[7] In an effective effect, the black and white images progressively give way to color: it is through fiction and emotion that Bouchareb chooses to tell the men's story. This requires skilled actors who truly carry the film. After having situated the different characters, Bouchareb brings them together to cross the sea and land in Italy. The first battles are epic and dramatic, but he focuses on the five protagonists to remain on a human register. Although they are but cannon fodder disposed of by those safely behind the lines, they manage to survive and are given an ovation and welcomed in Marseilles. A series of scenes demonstrates that everything was done to stop Franco-African couples from lasting or colonial infantrymen from rising up the ranks of the army. The integrity of the "motherland" would suffer no interracial relationships, and the colonial hierarchy had to be safeguarded at all costs. Nonetheless, the men Bouchareb portrays are truly heroes—isolated, certainly, but diehards to the point of sacrifice.

Even though its pedagogical ambitions structure the screenplay in layers a little too transparently, this is not annoying, as most viewers' ignorance of the facts justifies it. These simple folks' story is so little known that these four North African heroes are revelatory. The quality of Bouchareb's cinema does the rest. Filmed with extreme precision, each situation is significant and brimming with human density. Several fine lines spell out both the already present anti-colonial resistance and the soldiers' solidarity. The republic's three cardinal values—liberty, equality, fraternity—are constantly put to the test, and the film appeals to our hearts in order to understand what the descendants of these soldiers ultimately confined to oblivion might feel today.

Yet resentment never prevails: "If they had been full of violence or rancor, I would have put it in the film. But that wasn't the case," Bouchareb insists. That is unquestionably where the force of this memorable film also lies: these remarkable men were freedom fighters. They shared the conviction that they were liberating their country from Nazi barbarity, and the injustice inflicted upon them did not diminish that certitude. That is where *Days of Glory* draws its inspiration; this shared history bore the foundations of a great wealth of exchanges. That could still be the case today, if only French society would recognize it before it is too late. This film has effectively contributed to such a recognition.

NOTES

This essay has been translated from the French by Melissa Thackway.

1. Bouchareb's quotations are taken from an interview with the author at the Cannes Film Festival in May 2006 (Barlet 2006).
2. Born in Paris in 1959, Rachid Bouchareb went to film school before becoming a television assistant director. At the same time he continued to make short films.

His first short, *Peut être la mer* (Perhaps the Sea), was selected in competition at the Cannes Film Festival in 1983. Two years later, he made his first feature, *Baton Rouge*, the story of three friends who decide to emigrate to the United States to find work. After *Cheb* (1991), about a deported Algerian who tries to return to France, his 1992 television drama, *Des années déchirées* (The Torn Years), focused on two FLN veterans' disarray as they observe Algeria's changes. *Dust of Life* (*Poussières de vie*), the tale of the son of an African-American officer and a Vietnamese woman, abandoned by his father after the U.S. retreat from Vietnam in 1975, received an Academy Award nomination for Best Foreign-Language Film in 1995. With his associate, Jean Bréhat, Bouchareb set up 3B Production in 1989 and Tadrat Films in 1997, producing numerous films of different nationalities. *Little Senegal* (2001), about a man's voyage from the Gorée Island house of slaves to the United States to find his ancestors' descendants, was a box-office hit.

3. Editor's note: Roschdy Zem, Samy Naceri, Jamel Debbouze, and Sami Bouajila are featured on the French poster reproduced here. Their expressions convey their grim experiences. One U.S. poster uses the same image, while another foregrounds the romance that blossomed as the liberators were welcomed in France. The Chinese and Japanese posters emphasize combat.

4. The adjustment of the pensions was not retroactive. And it was limited to the small pensions of those who served in war or became disabled in combat. The much more substantial retirement pensions of those who served more than fifteen years, which can be claimed by widows and surviving children, were frozen until 2002, when they were indexed to the cost of living in each veteran's country of origin; they remain much lower than those of French-born soldiers.

5. Jamel Debbouze, as a result of a childhood accident, only has the use of one arm; he uses a pistol rather than a rifle in the film. This anachronistic detail seemed to bother no one, evidence of his highly convincing acting and his popularity.

6. On May 8, 1945, the very day of the Allied victory over Nazism, violent riots broke out in Sétif, Algeria. The riots were repressed in an extremely brutal way. Officially, there were 1,500 deaths, but in reality between 8,000 and 20,000 Algerians died.

7. For a historian's account of African recruits in the French army see Echenberg 1991.

REFERENCES

Barlet, Olivier. 2006. "'Le passé nous fait réfléchir sur aujourd'hui et sur notre future' entretien d'Olivier Barlet avec Rachid Bouchareb à propos de *Indigènes*." *Africultures*. http://www.africultures.com/php/index.php?nav=article&no=5749.

Echenberg. Myron. 1991. *Colonial Conscripts: The Tirailleurs Sénégalais in French West Africa, 1857–1960*. Portsmouth, NH: Heinemann; London: James Currey.

*Hamlet of Women**
Village Chronicles from a Time of Terrorism

DENISE BRAHIMI

With *Hamlet of Women*, Mohamed Chouikh undertook to revisit what had come to be known as *les années de violence*, the Years of Violence, when fundamentalists confronted the military regime that had denied them electoral victory in 1991.[1] He shot just after many fundamentalists had laid down their arms in response to a government amnesty, and his film is conciliatory. When Chouikh presented his film at Vues d'Afrique, the Montreal African film festival, he spoke of exorcising the drama, of his desire that viewers, while remembering, reconcile with each other (Chouikh 2006). His film offers a nuanced treatment. His villagers fight off the insurgents—and they fear government. Chouikh has commented on giving voice to the grievances that made a man join the insurgents: "He says that he took up arms in response to an injustice. If there hadn't been grassroots complicity, there would have been no terrorism" (in Barlet 2005).

If one wanted to find a title to designate both the style and the theme of *Hamlet of Women*, it might be "Village Chronicles from a Time of Terrorism," with an emphasis on "chronicles" in the plural. Of what does this plurality consist, and why does it appear to encapsulate the essence of the film? That is the first question it seems important to raise, before looking at the attitude of the women portrayed in the film. Their attitude, which is assuredly courageous, strikes us as being different from heroism. In this respect, the subject of the film is not the reversal of traditional male and female roles; it is not the tale of a temporary inversion in which the women take the men's place, proving themselves to be as heroic as they have been in other situations or other times. The

---

* *Hamlet of Women/Douar nssa/Douar de femmes*. 2005. Film written and directed by Mohamed Chouikh. Produced by Acima Films (Algeria) and Enterprise Nationale de Télévision (Algeria). 100 minutes.

Photo by Louiza Sid-Ammi. Courtesy Yamina Bachir Chouikh

women's hamlet is different from that of the men in both essence and functioning; that is what Chouikh's title highlights.

The notion of heroism is also called into question, differently and nonconceptually, by the wordless images of the village environment. At issue is the question of the reality of Algerian independence and the representation of the conquest of its freedom: the *maquis*, the brushland in which men and women joined guerrilla forces to fight the occupying French army and in which guerrillas are hiding now, is a constant presence in the film.[2] One might be tempted to say that the *maquis* is aesthetically present too, if the term did not seem reductive in relation to the variety of meanings suggested by this incontestable and ambiguous beauty, which ultimately remains a mystery. It is a *maquis* that, if it still signifies resistance and war, is returning to its true nature, which is precisely to be nature—a nature whose unflagging creativity and simmering life are the best response to the Islamic fundamentalists' tragically notorious "culture of death."

Mohamed Chouikh to the left of the camera; on his right Salim Aggar and cinematographer Allel Yahiaoui. Courtesy Salim Aggar

Plurality of Motifs

This plurality signifies that the film is not constructed around a sole theme. Chouikh's film is neither linear nor progressive nor built on suspense followed by combat. *Hamlet of Women* is not driven by a unitary movement as if it were a western or a tragedy—and that is why we cannot accurately define it as a film devoted to the heroic resistance of women who take up arms against terrorism. What, on the contrary, do we find? Not strictly speaking a story, but about a dozen episodes, which take place between a departure and a return. It is true that the anxious anticipation of an ever-possible terrorist attack hovers over this collection of varied scenes, but this does not stop other moments of expectation, like that of waiting for a late and intensely desired fiancé, or events such as the unexpected arrival of a handsome young merchant from the city or the slightly premature but successful delivery of a much-awaited baby. These scenes, which constitute the fabric of village life, are juxtaposed like the patterns on a rug. Intertwined here are the presence and absence of the terrorists, more often than not on the edge of the village, there where the children tend the flock, or in the forest where they drag their victims off to cut the throats. The only time we see them close up, inside the hamlet, there are three of them, one of them wounded, in such a pitiful state that the Madwoman, who showers them with insults and stones, is enough to frighten them off. At their final attempt, it is all the women in the hamlet, a dozen at the most, who force them to beat a retreat and disappear into the woods.

The existence of terrorism and the abominations it perpetuates—decapitations, rape, slit throats—is not at all in question. The film's project, however, is not so much to show that violence but rather the way in which the threat is integrated into daily life. The subject of the film may thus be defined as how the women organize not the armed struggle but the hamlet's survival, which notably takes the form of weddings and births, and a certain day-to-day happiness to be alive in spite of it all.

Of the conditions necessary for marriages, births, and survival, the film gives a significant place to love, whether graceful or sensual, mischievous or tender—the stirrings of teenage love between Amin and Aicha; a more adult love, precociously matured by the adversity of the times, between the beautiful Sabrina, cruelly marked by her family's murder, and Anis from Algiers; the sensual pleasure a buxom, attractive woman finds. This diversity of the juxtaposed episodes makes it artificial to distinguish between the supposedly secondary characters and the central heroes or heroines. Various characters only appear in one or two episodes but are as decisive or significant as Sabrina, who is at the heart of the film through her beauty, her knowledge of guns, and her inexpiable hatred of the terrorists who killed her family.[3] Among these characters who in another film would be called secondary, there is the Woman in Black, a kind of incarnation of vengeance, who appears simply to pass through the village, and the Madwoman, who appears two or three times but remains marginal in the literal sense of the word, living in the cemetery on the outskirts the hamlet. Yet it is clear that these two women are essential to the project of the film. They have their place on the same level as all the others in the exposition of the ensemble of scenes rather than the unfolding of the action. The word "scene" is important because it designates the hamlet as a theatrical setting. The film offers representation rather than realist effect. We are quite close to what the baroque theater was in its time, at least as Pier Paolo Pasolini reinterprets it in his version of *The Canterbury Tales* (*I racconti di Canterbury*, 1972). It is in this direction that we need to look for references, not in the neorealism or naturalism of a cinema that adheres to reality in a documentary style.

The choice of a mode of representation has, as we know, ideological and even metaphysical significance. Here it is Chouikh's position vis-à-vis Algerian history that imposes a choice that breaks away from dominant or readily expected practices. What is signified to the audience is that the heroic age of this story, which corresponds in literary writing to the epic or tragic genre, is now past. History cannot be relived. The Algerians fought heroically against the invader long ago and in more recent times. But it is time to move beyond the age of trumpeted heroism. To survive the murderous madness, the women seek to invent something different from equally murderous heroic combat. How to ensure that life goes on, that is the strength of the women—they have an intimate understanding of daily life.

Against Heroism, Day-to-Day Courage

How can we qualify this female courage that makes no attempt to conform to the heroic model? It is important to immediately nuance what, on the whole, might be a valid affirmation that heroism is a masculine act, at least as a claim and myth. In Algeria, as elsewhere, female heroic figures have been and are still celebrated as such, and the war of independence featured several. Gillo Pontecorvo's *The Battle of Algiers* (*La battaglia di Algeria*, 1966) pays homage to them, and Sabrina recalls some. The Woman in Black, through her physical allure, brings to mind the mother character in Mohamed Lakhdar-Hamina's *The Wind from the Aurès* (*Le Vent des Aurés Rih al-awras*, 1966), for they both roam from place to place with the same distress and unflagging relentlessness.

Chouikh, however, narrates other women, other forms of behavior on the part of female freedom fighters, whose courage is of another order to the mythical heroism of ancient or more recent models. The women are not at all ashamed to admit, as Sabrina does herself, that their courage stems from their fear. The reasons to be afraid are indeed very real, and there is no point in denying them. The only real problem is survival using a range of arms other than Kalashnikovs. And it is these other, far more feminine arms that Chouikh strives to show.

We could start, symbolically, with two highly concrete objects, the pestle and mortar, present in all kitchens in Algeria. Here, they are at the heart of the resistance: they are used to sound the alarm and assemble the dispersed women and children. This symbol brings us back to the tradition of Greek comedy and Aristophanes, who comically showed how women knew to turn the instruments of their daily chores to their advantage to finally win their cause. But here the director does not aim to be funny or farcical; at most, he makes the viewer smile, as happens frequently in this film in which horror is nonetheless one of the sources of inspiration.

The originality of the means the women put into action demonstrates that they do not content themselves with simply taking the men's place; they do not simply substitute—they invent. It does happen that, by force of circumstances, they perform jobs habitually reserved to the men. Taking the men's place may pass for a feminist demand, but the film explains it otherwise, as the sometimes extreme effect of the logic of things and necessity. This is the case with wearing trousers: given that the women tear their dresses when they have to take to the brushland, they demand the right to "wear the pants," as they put it, even if it is thanks to a "temporary *fatwa*" pronounced by the sheik. It is more a triumph of pragmatism and common sense than of feminism, but it just so happens that it is the women who are pragmatic and sensible!

The main difference between the men and the women regarding their overall attitudes toward life consists in the far greater place the women openly accord to love, a love that is not limited to the sexual. It would be more apt to speak of the ability to love, encompassing the concern for protecting the weakest and most fragile, those in whom life is unsteady because it is nascent or deeply traumatized. These include Sabrina's little sister, who barely escaped having her throat cut. It is through tenderness, gentleness, songs, and dance that she finds her voice and the will to live again. These are the remedies with which the women counter the terrorists' culture of death. The women do not partake of a certain heroic tradition that venerates abstinence. It is one of the forms of death with which it has joined forces, a sign of surpassing the self.

The women love joy, and for them any occasion to laugh is welcome, even in the most dire moments. It is thus that Sabrina cannot help but burst out laughing in the middle of the gathering for the deceased Ali. Joy and terror are closely intertwined: just after giving birth right in the middle of a terrorist alert, the elated young woman declares laughingly: "It was terror that made me give birth." Between alerts, the women never lose their taste for joyous chatter. The sensual, buxom woman tells salacious stories that make everybody laugh, and when the long-awaited fiancé finally arrives, the women and children participate in the wedding party, singing and dancing as if there were nothing untoward. Terrorism or not, everybody answers the threat looming over them by enjoying themselves. Consciously or not, the women know that marriage and birth are what the hamlet must preserve at all costs as a guarantee of its future and its survival.

Is this to say that the women do not have a sense of the tragic, or rather that the director resolutely opts for comedy? Assuredly not; that would constitute a reductive or partial vision of the film. The women do not cultivate a cult of death, but they do cultivate a cult of the dead, as one of the first scenes in the film shows: the Madwoman is wiping the graves in the cemetery with a large red veil that, to her, represents the blood it is impossible to stem; never, she says, will she let the dead be forgotten.

Another tragic character is the Woman in Black, who roams the mountains in relentless pursuit of the killers of her son, whose death she wants to avenge. Sabrina herself, in her refusal to abandon the dead to oblivion, is something of an Antigone, and we understand that whatever happens, nothing will make her give in. She has not, for that matter, set herself specifically against terrorists as an officially designated category, as public enemy number one. Right from the start of the film, we understand that her enemy is the inhumanity in man, the violence and the barbarity shown notably in certain men's behavior toward women. Before the men's departure for the factory, one of them, a young man whose face is full of hatred and cruelty, beats his wife so badly that she has to call for help to escape. Sabrina, who comes running with the other women, stands before him, a gun in her hand, and tells him: "Lay another finger on her and I'll blow your brains out." The man realizes that she will indeed do so if he dares continue. He hurls brutal abuse at her but refrains from hitting her.

We notice at this moment that this man has exactly the same expression, words, and attitudes as those attributed to the terrorists: it is clear that he is no better than they and that by chance alone he is not in their ranks. But what matters to Sabrina is not the label this man bears; it is his behavior that outrages her. Here we see the pragmatism and the refusal of formalism that characterize

Sabrina confronts an abusive husband.

female behavior. The women have understood that they must defend themselves on every front and first of all in the little social cosmos in which they live.

It is perfectly clear that this combat will continue beyond terrorism. At the end of the film, when the men are saved from a terrorist attack by their women, there is again an exchange of looks, this time silent, between Sabrina and this man, who is as cowardly as he is violent. Perhaps he feels, at least for the time being, that he does not have the right to speak out. But it is evident that he will want his revenge, and the exchange of looks also says that the story continues. Sabrina will never drop her guard before this dangerous man, for her judgment of him is unrelenting and final. Throughout the film, the women's usually ironic judgments of the men demonstrate their lucidity and lack of illusions. But they have to coexist, which is not any easier than surviving, and this requires great subtlety and inventiveness. The director puts his trust in the joyfully inventive pertinence of female imagination and in the affinity between the women and the natural environment of the hamlet, the *maquis*.

What Is the *Maquis*?

As has already been said, in *Hamlet of Women* all opportunities to laugh are seized and all opportunities to roam the surrounding *maquis*, for us to admire its beauty even though anxiety and anguish are constantly present there. The film's astonishing force—one is tempted to say its lyricism, for it is a force that transports—comes in part from this tension between two contradictory feelings that can quite simply be summed up as, "Isn't the setting beautiful, and how come it nonetheless harbors this death threat?" This contradiction is connected to other contradictions among the events narrated in the film: a wedding and a birth but also two burials. However paradoxical it might be, the *maquis'* beauty is striking, and *Hamlet of Women* can be taken as homage to it.

The first descent into this *maquis* occurs when the women go looking for the children who have not come back to the hamlet with the herd. We know they are worried to death, and yet their run through the wild gives off a powerful, even elated, feeling of freedom. They go beyond the limits imposed by the men's law and paradoxically, in this wild brushland, the quintessential site of the terrorist threat, discover the joy of penetrating an apparently unviolated nature.

When the children come to tell them that they have found a decapitated woman, all the women rush to look for the missing head in the thickets and bushes. It is a new, albeit tragic, vision of the *maquis*, but we do not see the decapitated woman's body or head. When the head does appear, it is in the hands of the Madwoman, who caresses it and fixes its hair. Then she performs the funeral rites to appease the dead woman's spirit. From the poor woman's grave, the Madwoman henceforth watches over the cemetery, presented as a site beyond all boundaries, between the hamlet and the *maquis*, if closer to the latter. The *maquis* is a mysterious place, where something of the presence of the dead floats. It takes us back to an ancient sense of the sacred, before Islam, to which the women have undoubtedly remained more sensitive than the men.

The *maquis*, as a site of unbridled nature, is at the heart of the film, but it is not there as the setting for heroic battles between the two sides. Despite the hidden terrorists and the army helicopters that fly over it, the *maquis* remains a preserved site, a kind of reserve of life—laden with ambiguity certainly, for it pays a high price for the privileges it owes to its isolation.

Hamlet of Women is a far cry from a pamphlet on terrorism or female power. It is not a film of denunciation or a political analysis. The viewer is free at his or her own convenience to appreciate the causes of terrorism, the central authorities' action, and the severity or indulgence that should be accorded to repentant terrorists. What does powerfully emerge from the film is a conviction concerning the response one should try to give the death threat that hovers over the whole country: the only valid and effective response is the affirmation of life and its indestructible permanence. These rural women respond to life not as an idea or a theory but from a practical and instinctive knowledge. That knowledge is so essential and so precious that evil sorts hate those who have it because they stand up to their culture of death. Yet the aim of the film is not to depict their murderous activities or to pit the good against the bad. *Hamlet of Women* shows the fundamental sources of a culture of life that resists the culture of death.

NOTES

This essay has been translated from the French by Melissa Thackway.

1. *Hamlet of Women* won the top prize at Vues d'Afrique, the Montreal African film festival. On Chouikh's *œuvre* see Brahimi 2004; for an extended interview with the directors see Taboulay 1997. Larbi Benchiha has devoted a documentary, *Mohamed Chouikh, cinéaste résistant* ("Mohamed Chouikh, a filmmaker who resists," 2008), to the director.
2. The film was shot in the summer of 2004 between Algiers and Béjaia.
3. Editor's note: The French poster, reproduced here, features Sabrina with the literal translation of the title, *Douar nssa*, inscribed on her hand in Arabic.

REFERENCES

Barlet, Olivier. 2005. "Un film ancré dans la réalité algérienne. Entretien d'Olivier Barlet avec Mohamed Chouikh à propos de 'Douar de femmes.'" *Africultures*. http://www.africultures.com/index.asp?menu=affiche_article&no=4071.

Brahimi, Denise. 2004. "Images, symboles et paraboles dans le cinéma de Mohamed Chouikh." In *Cinémas du Maghreb*, ed. Michel Serceau. Paris: Corlet/Télérama; CinémAction 154–159.

Chouikh, Mohamed. 2006. Remarks, *Hamlet of Women* screening, Vues d'Afrique film festival, Montreal, April. Notes by Josef Gugler.

Taboulay, Camille. 1997. *Mohamed Chouikh*. Paris: K Films Editions.

9

Morocco
A National Cinema with Large Ambitions

KEVIN DWYER

A decade ago I compared the newfound success of Moroccan filmmakers in their nation's cinemas with Odysseus's journey in Homer's eponymous Mediterranean epic. Allegorically, the Moroccan filmmaker was "returning in rags from a long voyage, finally reconciled with his wife Penelope, his privileged [home] audience, after vanquish[ing] other suitors"—in this case "satellite television, video clubs, and big-budget films from the West." The possibility remained, however, in the face of these and other threats, that the filmmaker might, "after reuniting with his audience for a time, . . . set off on a new long voyage." Five years later I wondered whether positive momentum could be maintained, whether "a strengthening of [Moroccan cinema's] independence, creativity, and audience relationship . . . is possible in a country situated as Morocco is with regard to the global marketplace." I went on to suggest that "with Moroccan films' box-office success continuing, and with a political and cultural system rapidly changing in mostly encouraging directions, Morocco is very well positioned to provide an instructive lesson concerning whether this particular national cinema, and Third World cinemas more generally, can grow in their domestic markets and reach international audiences as well."[1] Now, having carried out anthropological research on Moroccan cinema for more than a decade, I would like to return to these questions and try to judge Moroccan cinema's outlook and the current orientation of the Moroccan filmmaker's odyssey.

Moroccan films continue to rank high in Moroccan audience preferences, and there is great vitality in the creative and productive sectors, with contributions from young filmmakers, a growing number of women filmmakers, and a striking variety in film themes and genres—all signs of a very fertile creative environment. Yet, distribution and screening problems are crippling, with theaters rapidly closing, overall movie attendance and box-office receipts plummeting, and piracy rampant. Internationally, there have been some advances in

Moroccan films' exposure and recognition abroad as well as in attracting foreign productions at home. However, it remains very difficult for Moroccan films to break into the international commercial circuits. In this paradoxical situation—dynamic production in the context of grave distribution and screening problems and a mixed outlook internationally—the Centre cinématographique marocain (CCM) and other Moroccan institutions have drawn up expansive plans for the future. One of my tasks here is to assess whether these plans are based on sound projections or merely reflect wishful thinking.

Moroccan Contexts: Historical, Cultural, and Institutional

During the 1970s and 1980s, Moroccan films appeared only rarely in the theaters, and Moroccan audiences had little opportunity to develop a taste for them. In the early 1990s, two films had remarkable success at the box office: Abdelkader Lagtaa's *A Love Affair in Casablanca* (*Hobb fi Dar al-Beida/Un amour à Casablanca*, 1992) and Muhammad Abderrahman Tazi's domestic comedy *Looking for My Wife's Husband* (*Bahthan 'an zawj imra'ati /A la recherche du mari de ma femme*, 1993), which was seen by approximately one million spectators, remaining to this day the most successful Moroccan film ever. Both films began what was termed the "reconciliation" between Moroccan cinema and its national audience.[2]

Moroccan film production attained unprecedented levels in the new century, averaging about eight features a year (Armes 2008) and sometimes exceeding ten. Many did very well at the box office: two Moroccan films were among the top three in box office and receipts in 2007 and in 2008. Their average attendance was several times higher than those of films from the main importing countries, the United States and India, and was rivaled only by Egyptian films. While Moroccan films made up only around 5 per cent of those shown, they garnered approximately 16 per cent of audience and of box-office revenue.[3]

Numerous film festivals are held throughout the country. The National Film Festival, first established in 1982 as an itinerant festival and held irregularly, became an annual festival in 2007, with a permanent home in Tangiers. With each festival showing all or almost all national films produced in the intervening period, it leads to wide discussion in the press, on radio and television, in everyday conversation, and lately on the Internet. Besides the National Film Festival, some fifty film festivals are held each year, among the most important and longest-standing being the Festival of African Films (Khouribga) and Mediterranean Cinema (Tetouan).

But two disturbing trends blight this picture: a rapid fall in the number of theaters and in overall cinema attendance. In the early 1980s, Morocco's 251 theaters were attended by 45 million spectators—the highest totals ever reached—but CCM figures for 2007 showed only 80 theaters with 103 screens in operation and attendance below 2.5 million. Attendance rebounded somewhat in 2008, reaching almost 3 million, but by mid-2009 the number of theaters had fallen to 50, with 74 screens.

The main state financial support for film production comes via the Aid Fund, administered by the CCM. The amounts awarded have been increasing, reaching 60 million dirhams in 2008, approximately three times the amount awarded at the turn of the century.[4] Significant financial support for Moroccan films also comes from the two Moroccan television channels: 2M has produced an average of almost twenty telefilms per year since 2000 and often provides support for feature films; and in 2006 the state media company, which includes the television channel TVM, agreed to co-produce or pre-buy twenty movies, fifteen telefilms, four series, and twelve documentaries a year. Morocco's major filmmakers have been involved, enabling them to survive financially although they cannot count on making more than one feature film every few years.

After decades during which many lamented the lack of training institutions for film specialties, 2007 saw the birth of the School of Visual Arts, École supérieure des arts visuels, in Marrakesh, which enrolled 31 students in fall 2007, and a second school, in Ouarzazate, which welcomed some 120 trainees (Wilson-Goldie 2007). In addition, a series of collaborative seminars, workshops, and conferences was set up in conjunction with the European Union under its EuroMed program and with the Tribeca Film Festival.

Piracy is a serious problem: pirated videotapes and DVDs of Moroccan and major international films are openly on sale; with DVDs priced between five and ten dirhams and cinema tickets often costing thirty-five dirhams, consumers rarely resist the lure of pirated films. No clear remedies are in sight, despite official campaigns to stem piracy.[5] In 2007, pirated goods were estimated at 70 percent of the Moroccan market for video, audio, and software disks. Moroccan artists often complain that they do not receive royalties due, that even the state organs—television channels, radio stations, theaters, and so on—do not compensate them properly.

Digitalization makes piracy a simple affair, but it also aids Moroccan filmmakers in speeding up and reducing the cost of shooting and post-production. Some established directors adopted digital shooting and editing early; among them are Nabil Ayouch, Abdelkader Lagtaa, and Muhammad Abderrahman

Tazi, who all did this for films released in 2003. The trend in this direction is clear. Digital projection in the theaters would eliminate the significant costs of transforming digital into 35 mm, but equipping a theater for full digital projection is an expensive matter, and there has been little movement in this direction.

Moroccan filmmakers have benefited from the overall expansion in freedom of expression over the past decade. The Supervisory Film Commission (Commission de contrôle des films cinématographiques), charged with overseeing and enforcing permissible expression, is composed of one representative each from the CCM, the Ministry of Culture, the Ministry of Communication, distributors, and theater owners. Imposed infrequently on Moroccan films, although with greater frequency on foreign films, censorship remains a threat and self-censorship a widespread phenomenon, with creative artists knowing not to cross the "red lines" by challenging the monarchy, religion, or the nation's territorial integrity.[6]

Signs of Creative Vitality: Filmmakers, Genres, Themes

With healthy audience response to many Moroccan films, much of the credit must go to the filmmakers and their films. In at least three respects—the composition of the filmmaking cohort, the range of genres employed, and the variety and relevance of themes treated—the film sector displays remarkable creative vitality.

A significant number of the first and second generations of filmmakers—roughly, those born in the 1930s through the 1950s—whose work provides a canon for further creative inspiration, have established a considerable *œuvre*; Hakim Noury, Mustapha Derkaoui, and Nabyl Lahlou each has directed about ten films, and Farida Benlyazid, Jilali Ferhati, Abdelkader Lagtaa, and Muhammad Abderrahman Tazi have at least five each to their credit.

Since the late 1990s, young Moroccan filmmakers have been replenishing the ranks: twenty filmmakers produced first features between 2001 and 2005 (Zyad 2007, citing Mohamed Bakrim), and among the twenty-five feature films at the 2007 National Film Festival, eight were first features. Many of these first features have been received very positively, including those directed by Nabil Ayouch (born 1969), Hakim Belabbes (1961), Faouzi Bensaidi (1967), Ismail Ferroukhi (1962), Yasmine Kassari (1968), Noureddine Lekhmari (1964), Leila Marrakchi (1975), and Narjess Nejjar (1971).

More women directors are emerging. The first film made by a Moroccan woman director was Farida Bourquia's *Embers* (*al-Jamr/La braise*, 1984), followed soon thereafter by Farida Benlyazid's *A Door to the Sky* (*Bab al-sama' maftuh/Une porte ouverte sur le ciel*, 1988). These two were the only women filmmakers until almost the turn of the century, and Bourquia had to wait more than twenty years for her second feature to appear. In 1998 Fatima Jebli Ouezzani became the first woman to win the Best Film award at Morocco's National Film Festival with *In My Father's House* (*Dans la maison de mon père*, 1998). Thereafter films directed by women began to appear in greater numbers, including three more by Benlyazid as well as first features by Imane Mesbahi, Narjess Nejjar, Yasmine Kassari, Leila Marrakchi, and Zakia Tahiri. Kassari's *The Sleeping Child* (*al-Raqid/L'enfant endormi*, 2004) won the Best Film award at the 2005 National Film Festival; Marrakchi's *Marock* (2005) and Tahiri's *Number One* (2008) were box-office successes.

New trends in genres include a growing number of comedies. Despite its great success, *Looking for My Wife's Husband* remained one of Morocco's rare comedies until the turn of the century, when two films by Hakim Noury signaled a surge.[7] Also successful and high-grossing were Said Naciri's *Crooks* (*al-Bandiya/Les bandits*, 2004) and its 2006 sequel. More recently, Tahiri's *Number One* pleased audiences with its light-hearted story of a man who treats his wife and all the women working for him very badly but who, after being bewitched and undergoing other humorous plot twists, turns into something of a "feminist" himself. While these relatively recent films were commercially oriented, Daoud Oulad-Syad's *Waiting for Pasolini* (*Fi intizar Pasolini/En attendant Pasolini*, 2007) and Nabil Lahlou's *Tabite or Not Tabite* (2005) were comedies in a *cinéma d'auteur* style. Other genres of growing recent importance include documentaries,[8] documentary-style fiction films, short films, and Amazigh films.[9]

Since the late 1990s new themes have appeared, and some older ones have been reemphasized or treated in new ways. Among the new themes are those that treat the country's difficult past, with several films focusing on *les années de plomb*, "the Years of Lead"—a term used to characterize the heavy repression during King Hassan II's rule.[10] A number deal with the evils of colonialism. A film that treats both is Noureddine Lekhmari's *The Gaze* (*Le regard/Al-nadhara*, 2004), in which a French soldier-photographer who had taken photos of French ill treatment of Moroccans during the colonial period returns to Morocco; there he finds an Amazigh man whom he thought dead, now mute as a consequence of ill treatment during *les années de plomb*.

Another contentious aspect of Moroccan history is the period in the early 1960s of large-scale emigration of Moroccan Jews, treated in two films released in 2007. Hassan Benjelloun's fiction film in documentary style, *Where Are You Going Moshe? (Fayn mashi ya Moshé/Où vas-tu Moshé?)* suggests that this emigration led to loss of diversity and personal liberty in Morocco while in effect assisting Israel. Muhammad Ismail's *Goodbye Mothers (Wadaan ummahaat/Adieu mères)* follows the destiny of two families, one Muslim, one Jewish, and has as a subtheme an impossible love affair between a Muslim and a Jew. Moroccan authorities selected this film as the country's submission for the Academy Awards.

Another new theme appearing on the screen in recent years might be called "meta-filmic"—films presenting various aspects of filmmaking and/or studded with film references. Among the former are Daoud Oulad-Syad's *Waiting for Pasolini*, which deals with the impact on a Moroccan village of foreign productions, and Nabil Lahlou's *Tabite or Not Tabite*, in which a film script is written based on a recent scandal. An example of the latter is Faouzi Bensaidi's *WWW—What a Wonderful World* (2006), which nods in its title sequence to the James Bond corpus and then to Almódovar, Jarmusch, Murnau, Tati, Fellini, Arthur Penn, and Orson Welles, as Olivier Barlet notes (2006c), and to Hitchcock and Brian de Palma, as the filmmaker points out (in Barlet 2006b).

The diversity of Moroccan society—a theme related to that of memory in that both challenge a view of Moroccan history and society as relatively homogeneous and unified—figured importantly in other ways. Ethnic diversity looms large in Farida Benlyazid's *The Wretched Life of Juanita Narboni (Juanita de Tanger/La vida perra de Juanita Narboni,* 2005), in which a lonely woman, daughter of an English father from Gibraltar and an Andalusian mother, recounts her life-story, mirroring the history of Tangiers. *Moroccan Symphony (al-Simfoniyya al-maghribiyya/La symphonie marocaine,* Kamal Kamal, 2006) addresses class and social diversity; Benlyazid's *Casa Nayda* and Ahmed Boulane's *The Satanic Angels (Malaikat al-shaytan/Les anges de Satan,* 2007) foreground diversity in musical tastes and lifestyles; and Marrakchi's *Marock* deals with religious diversity as well as with the complexities of youth culture.

The role of Amazigh culture and languages in Moroccan national life reflects another aspect of diversity. With the creation of the Institut royal pour la culture amazighe (IRCAM) in 2001, an important step was taken in giving official recognition to Amazigh culture. According to an agreement between IRCAM and the Ministry of Communication in 2006, each of the two state channels was committed to producing twelve Amazigh-language telefilms or theatrical plays a year, but this commitment has not yet been fulfilled. In May 2009 an official announcement indicated that by the end of the year, an Amazigh-language channel would begin broadcasting fifty hours a week, with two-thirds of its emissions to be in Amazigh languages. One vibrant area in Amazigh cultural production is straight-to-video/DVD, with one production company alone, C Brothers, turning out some ten a year and producing the first Amazigh-language animation film, *Aladdin*, in 2006. Amazigh feature films, while increasing in number, still constitute a minority genre; among the most notable are two 2007 films, Hassan Rhanja's *Argana* and Yassine Fennane's *Skeleton* (*al-Haykal al-adhami/La squelette*), a comedy portraying a noble matriarch's struggle to beat back the efforts of a corrupt local official to seize her land; it won top prize at the Amazigh Film Festival in Sétif, Algeria. Starting in 2006, some training of Amazigh-language screenwriters was being carried out by IRCAM in conjunction with the CCM.[11]

One thematic staple relates to emigration. Issues raised in recent films include the dilemmas facing emigrants returning to Morocco and a new subtheme of relations between Moroccans—or sometimes Arabs from other countries—and people from the United States. Perhaps related to this and/or to the reach of U.S. popular culture is the recent glut of English-language titles, such as *Real Premonition* (Ahmed Ziad, 2007), *Moroccan Dream* (Jamal Belmejdoub, 2007), *WWW—What a Wonderful World*, and *Wake-Up Morocco!* (Narjess Nejjar, 2006). Nabil Ayouch's *Whatever Lola Wants* (2007) deserves special mention not only for its budget exceeding that of any previous Moroccan film (it was financed primarily by the French company Pathé) and for having led all films at the Moroccan box office in 2008 but also for reversing somewhat the usual migration story in its focus on an American woman who falls in love with an Egyptian in New York and then follows him back to Cairo, where she tries to make a place for herself as a dancer.[12]

Another long-running theme in Moroccan films relates to the situation of women. Two recent innovative films are Latif Lahlou's *Samira's Gardens* (*Samira fi al-dayaa/Les jardins de Samira*, 2007), in which a young wife's sexual desires, thwarted by her elderly husband's impotence, lead her into an affair with her husband's son by a previous wife; and Aziz Salmy's controversial *Veiled Loves* (*Hijab al-hob/Amours voilées*, 2008), recounting the story of Batoul, an unmarried woman doctor in her late twenties, an observant Muslim, and her passion for an attractive ladies' man. Made pregnant by him, Batoul ends the film deciding to have the baby and marry her pious cousin, with her lover walking away without a hint of ambivalence. Salmy's film, which did well at the box office, was harshly criticized by some members of an Islamist political party for sullying the image of pious women. Many of the films having the situation of women as a theme, and in particular *Veiled Loves* and Tahiri's *Number One*, should be seen in the context of discussions over the Mudawwana, the new personal status code adopted in 2004 that greatly improved women's legal rights.

Standing somewhat on its own in terms of genre and theme is Noureddine Lekhmari's energetic, dark film *Casanegra* (2008), which follows the violent lives of two Casablanca youths as they try, through petty crime and other schemes, to reach their goals—for one finding a way to emigrate, for the other meeting a well-off woman to usher him among Casablanca's privileged. With scenes involving "alcohol, drugs, homosexuality, prostitution, battered women, street children, masturbation" (Beaugé 2009), a sound track reflecting the latest musical tastes of the country's urban youth, dialogue as raw as any yet heard in a Moroccan film, and a camera and editing style involving rapid shifts of perspective, mostly nighttime lighting, and narrative discontinuities, the film attracted much attention internationally, won several festival prizes, and topped all films at the Moroccan box office during the first trimester of 2009.[13]

The International Profile of Moroccan Cinema

In recent years Morocco has worked to promote its cinema internationally. While very few Moroccan films have gained commercial screenings abroad, many have appeared and won prizes in international festivals. Morocco's success in international festivals was first noticed at Cannes in 2003 when two of its feature films were presented outside the main competition—marking the first time in more than thirty years that the country's films were selected for the world's most prestigious film festival—and Bensaidi's *A Thousand Months* won the prize for Best First Feature in the section *Un certain regard*. Since then many Moroccan films have won prizes: according to the CCM, Moroccan films garnered twenty-nine international awards in 2005, thirteen in 2006, thirteen in 2007, and nineteen in 2008.[14]

Morocco has a long history of providing locations for foreign productions, among them films by Orson Welles, Alfred Hitchcock, David Lean, John Huston, and, more recently, Martin Scorsese, Ridley Scott, and Oliver Stone. While Morocco has benefited from Western filmmakers' desire for Middle Eastern locations, it is facing increasing competition from other countries, such as Jordan and the Gulf Emirates of Dubai and Abu Dhabi. Yet the first half of 2008 was an extremely successful period for Morocco's foreign productions, with a record 845 million dirhams invested, some 50 percent more than in all of 2007 and almost double the amount for all of 2006.[15]

On the regional level, Maghreb Cinemas was formed in 2005, joining many Moroccan filmmakers with their Algerian and Tunisian colleagues, with the aim of promoting Maghreb cinemas and strengthening relations with the European Community. This went together with the establishment of an annual festival of Maghreb films to be held in Oujda, but only one session, in 2005, appears to have been held as of this writing. Morocco participates actively in the EuroMed Cinemas program, which supports cross-border distribution of Mediterranean and European films in member countries. Morocco is engaging in a systematic effort to join with other countries of the South in co-productions. In 2006 it co-produced and/or post-produced two films from Tunisia, two from Senegal, and one each from Chad and Burkina Faso. This collaboration continues.

Perhaps the most striking symbol of efforts to enhance Morocco's international film profile was the establishment in 2001 of the annual Marrakesh International Film Festival. Attracting global celebrities, Morocco has gained greater visibility in the international film world, projected its attraction as a location for foreign films, and, with the festival often offering a panorama of Moroccan films, succeeded in publicizing its national cinema. One sign of the growing recognition of Morocco's contribution to world cinema is the choice of Ahmed Maanouni's classic *Trances* (*al-Hal/Transes*, 1981) to be among the first films fully restored by the World Cinema Foundation, founded by Martin Scorsese at Cannes in 2007 and dedicated to the preservation of films from around the world.[16]

Responding to the Challenge: Sound Projections or Wishful Thinking?

The world media landscape is dominated by large-scale producers based in a few metropolitan centers, with creators in smaller countries struggling against great odds to reach their own publics and against even greater odds to reach international audiences. In this very difficult context, what are the prospects for a small national cinema like Morocco's to persevere and grow locally while also progressing internationally?[17]

In 2006 the CCM commissioned a "diagnostic and strategic study for the development of the film sector in Morocco" that took up this challenge and proposed significant expansion over the next ten years: annual production would increase from eight feature films to forty; state financing would double; incentives would promote theater construction and renovation, with a target of some 250 theaters; support would be provided for distributing and screening

Moroccan films; and educational programs would develop the public's taste for films. To promote the internationalization of Moroccan cinema, the number of Moroccan films shown on foreign screens would grow, and foreign productions would double—some thirty feature films, twelve television films, and fifty advertising spots would be shot annually, creating eight thousand new jobs and contributing 180 million euros a year to the Moroccan economy. The plan was adopted as national strategy in 2007.[18]

There already has been significant progress in several areas, with substantial increases in the amounts awarded by the Aid Fund for film production and records set in attracting foreign productions. Cinema is more available to the national public through a program of film caravans—in the first ten months of 2008, these provided some two hundred days of projections in remote areas.[19] And Morocco has raised its profile at foreign film festivals.

However, the situation as regards distribution and exhibition remains dire. The effort to open new cinemas and to rehabilitate old ones has not yet borne fruit. An encouraging, if modest, development lies in the birth in 2007 of Save Morocco's Cinemas (Sauvons les cinémas au Maroc), bringing together Moroccan film professionals and cinephiles to draw attention to the problem and to propose remedies.[20]

Whether the sanguine approach formulated in the diagnostic study will achieve the desired results depends not only on the continuing dynamism of Morocco's creative forces and a relatively flexible if not actually welcoming international context but also, in large part, on the political will of those in power to promote Moroccan cinema. Notwithstanding the significant steps that have already been taken in these directions, the Moroccan authorities, film professionals, and the small army of cinephiles face a daunting task.

Where does this leave the Moroccan filmmaker on his or her odyssey? We might recall that Odysseus, like Moroccan filmmakers, had modest beginnings coupled with large ambitions. Although poor in his early days, Odysseus rose to become one of Helen of Troy's suitors and, when rejected, rose again to marry Penelope, daughter of the king of Sparta. Odysseus and Moroccan filmmakers are also similar in being persistent, dedicated, and sharp-witted. How else could he and they have endured extended and perilous voyages and finally succeeded in assuming an eminent place at home?

But here Homer's *Odyssey* ends, and we can only speculate about what happens afterward. Some stories have Odysseus leaving Ithaca, marrying again, and finding new audiences away from home. Others have him leading a full life and dying only of old age, as prophesied by the seer Tiresias. Still others see him unintentionally slain by Telegonus, his own son by the magician goddess Circe. Stretching the allegory somewhat playfully, although the matter is serious, we might imagine Telegonus, infused with his mother's magic, "reproducing" Odysseus much as a pirated copy mirrors its master and thus, perversely and unwittingly, killing him.

Which of these scripts Moroccan filmmakers will bring to the screen and whether that screen will be a public or private one are impossible to know at this stage. And there are, of course, other scripts yet to be written. But for now we see these filmmakers no longer satisfied with life at home—they have spent so much time in so many places that the word "home" has lost its parochial meaning and become very difficult to distinguish from "abroad." It is perhaps in this sense, too, that we should think of Moroccan cinema as becoming an integral part of world cinema.

NOTES

1. For the comparison with Odysseus see Dwyer 2002a, 358–359; on Moroccan cinema's international outlook see Dwyer 2004a, 341–342.
2. The main English-language references for Moroccan cinema include my own works (Dwyer 2002a,b; 2004a,b; 2007), those of Armes (2005, 2006, 2008, forthcoming), and the recent book by Carter (2009). See also some contributions in Dönmez-Colin 2007. For a fuller bibliography see Dwyer 2004a.
3. These figures come from CCM tables. See, for example, http://www.ccm.ma/inter/phactualite/nation20071.pdf and http://www.ccm.ma/inter/phactualite/boxoffice20071.pdf, both accessed July 12, 2008, and http://www.ccm.ma/inter/phactualite/national2008.pdf, accessed July 17, 2009.
4. In late 2008 one U.S. dollar equaled about 8.6 Moroccan dirhams; by mid-2009 it was worth roughly 8 dirhams.
5. The BBC reported that up to October 2006 "the authorities carried out 17 raids in Casablanca, Fez, Marrakesh and Meknès, seizing more than 1.5 million illegal CDs and DVDs," but it also reported that "many more are being sold at stalls and souks across the country" (Hamilton 2006).
6. In one notable recent case—in which none of the lines was crossed—Nabil Ayouch's *One Minute Less of Sun* (*Une minute de soleil en moins*, 2003) was ruled unsuitable for screening unless several sexual scenes were shortened or cut. The filmmaker refused, and as of this writing, the film has not yet been allowed in the theaters.
7. For a comprehensive exploration of M. A. Tazi's films and career in the context of the history of Moroccan cinema see Dwyer 2004a; for a discussion of the comedic

nature of Tazi's film and the first of Noury's pair, *She Has Diabetes and Hypertension but Refuses to Die* (*Fiha al-melh wa al-sukkar wa ma bghatsh tmout*/*Elle est diabétique, hypertendue, mais elle refuse de crêver*, 2000), see Dwyer 2004b.
8. Documentaries are excluded from Aid Fund support and are often financed in part by TV channels, including sometimes al-Jazeera. For a discussion of the Aid Fund's shunning of documentaries see Quilty 2009.
9. The term "Amazigh" has replaced "Berber" in Morocco.
10. Olivier Barlet (2006a) distinguishes between films that attempt to reconstruct the period and those that show the effects on the present. In the first group he puts *Jail Girl* (*Jawhara*, Saad Chraibi, 2003) and *The Dark Room* (*Derb Moulay al-Shareef*/ *La chambre noire*, Hassan Benjelloun, 2004); in the second, *A Thousand Months* (*Alf shahr*/*Mille mois*, Faouzi Bensaidi, 2003), *Face to Face* (*Face à face*, Abdelkader Lagtaa, 2003), *Mona Saber* (Abdelhai Laraki, 2001), and *Memory in Detention* (*Dhakira muʿtaqala* /*Mémoire en détention*, Jilali Ferhati, 2004). Leila Kilani's documentary *Our Forbidden Places* (*Amakinuna al-mamnooa*/*Nos lieux interdits*, 2008) focuses on the Instance d'equité et reconciliation that was set up in 2004 under King Mohamad VI to shed some light on the repression during the rule of his father, King Hassan II.
11. For an early discussion of Amazigh videos and a partial list see Carter 1999 (569–581, 709); on *Aladdin* see Hopewell 2006. For an optimistic assessment of the current situation of Amazigh filmmaking see Idtnaine 2008.
12. Ayouch also plays a major role in Moroccan cinema as a producer. His production company, Ali n' Productions, joined with the National Radio and Television Company (Société national de radio diffusion et de télévision) to form The Film Industry—Made in Morocco, which announced in 2007 that it planned to produce thirty feature films over a two-year period.
13. First-trimester 2009 attendance figures were the latest available from the CCM at the time of writing.
14. See http://www.ccm.ma/inter/phactualite/filmprime05-06.pdf, http://www.ccm.ma/inter/phactualite/films2007.pdf, and http://www.ccm.ma/inter/phactualite/filmsprimes2008.pdf. According to the CCM site, the lists for 2006, 2007, and 2008 are not exhaustive.
15. These figures are reported by the CCM, at http://www.ccm.ma/inter/news.asp?code=486.
16. Maanouni remains active; his *Burned Hearts* (*al-Quloob al-muhtariqa*/*Coeurs brulés*, 2007) won top prize at Morocco's National Film Festival, Tangiers.
17. For more detailed discussion of the global context and international initiatives to adopt and implement a Convention on the Protection and Promotion of Diversity of Cultural Expressions see Dwyer 2007.
18. The study was carried out by the international firm Valyans Consulting and is available at the CCM's website, http://www.ccm.ma/inter/news.asp?code=320.

19. See http://www.ccm.ma/inter/news.asp?code=528.
20. See its website at http://www.savecinemasinmarocco.com [sic].

REFERENCES

Armes, Roy. 2005. *Postcolonial Images: Studies in North African Film*. Bloomington: Indiana University Press.

———. 2006. *African Filmmaking: North and South of the Sahara*. Edinburgh: Edinburgh University Press; Bloomington: Indiana University Press.

———. 2008. *Dictionary of African Filmmakers*. Bloomington: Indiana University Press.

———. Forthcoming. "The Filmmaker and the State in the Maghreb." In *African Cinemas: A Continental Approach*, ed. Josef Gugler.

Barlet, Olivier. 2006a. "*Memory in Detention* by Jillali Ferhati." *Africultures*. http://www.africultures.com/php/index.php?nav=article&no=7084.

———. 2006b. "'Pourquoi un Marocain ne pourrait-il pas faire du polar?' entretien d'Olivier Barlet avec Faouzi Bensaïdi à propos de *WWW—What a Wonderful World*." *Africultures*. http://www.africultures.com/index.asp?menu=affiche_article&no=4599.

———. 2006c. "*WWW—What a Wonderful World* de Faouzi Bensaïdi. *Africultures*. http://www.africultures.com/index.asp?menu=affiche_article&no=4602.

Beaugé, Florence. 2009. "'Casanegra,' film-vérité sur Casablanca, dévoile la face sombre du Maroc." *Le Monde*, January 28. http://abonnes.lemonde.fr/afrique/article/2009/01/27/casanegra-film-verite-sur-casablanca-devoile-la-face-sombre-du-maroc_1147066_3212.html.

Carter, Sandra Gayle. 1999. "Moroccan Cinema: What Moroccan Cinema?" Ph.D. diss., University of Texas at Austin.

———. 2009. *What Moroccan Cinema? A Historical and Critical Study, 1956–2006*. Lanham, MD: Lexington Books.

Dönmez-Colin, Gönül, ed. 2007. *The Cinema of North Africa and the Middle East*. London: Wallflower Press.

Dwyer, Kevin. 2002a. "Moroccan Film-Making: A Long Voyage through the Straits of Paradox." In *Everyday Life in the Muslim Middle East*, ed. Donna Lee Bowen and E. A. Early, 349–359. Bloomington: Indiana University Press.

———. 2002b. "'Hidden, Unsaid, Taboo' in Moroccan Cinema: Abdelkader Lagtaa's Challenge to Authority." *Framework* 43 (2): 117–133.

———. 2004a. *Beyond Casablanca: M. A. Tazi and the Adventure of Moroccan Filmmaking*. Bloomington: Indiana University Press.

———. 2004b. "Un pays, une décennie, deux comédies." In *Cinémas du Maghreb*, ed. Michel Serceau, Paris: Corlet/Télérama; *CinémAction* 111:86–91.

———. 2007. "Moroccan Cinema and the Promotion of Culture." *Journal of North African Studies* 12 (3): 277–286. Reprinted in Andrea Khalil (ed.), *North African Cinema in a Global Context: Through the Lens of Diaspora*, London: Routledge, 2008, 1–10.

Hamilton, Richard. 2006. "Piracy Harming Moroccan Artists." *BBC News*, October 1. http://news.bbc.co.uk/go/pr/fr/-/2/hi/africa/6040072.stm (accessed October 12, 2006).

Hopewell, John. 2006. "Abdeni Attached to Berber Puppet Movie 'Aladdin' to Be Produced by Morocco's Chkiri Brothers." *Variety*, December 6.

Idtnaine, Omar. 2008. "Le cinéma amazigh au Maroc: Eléments d'une naissance artistique." *Africultures*, October 20. http://www.africultures.com/index.asp?menu=affiche_article&no=8117.

Quilty, Jim. 2009. "Funding and Regulating a Country's Representation." *Daily Star* (Lebanon), January 9. http://www.dailystar.com.lb/article.asp?edition_id=1&categ_id=4&article_id=98876.

Wilson-Goldie, Kaelen 2007. "Training Morocco's Next Generation of Filmmakers." *Daily Star* (Lebanon), December 15. http://www.dailystar.com.lb/article.asp?edition_id=10&categ_id=4&article_id=87488.

Zyad, Nouri. 2007. "La réglementation du secteur cinématographique s'impose à Ouarzazate." *Libération* (Morocco), April 17.

*Ali Zaoua, Prince of the Streets**
The Harsh Life of Street Children and the Poetics of Childhood

JOSEF GUGLER

Ali Zaoua, Prince of the Streets, set in Casablanca, is the story of four boys who have broken away from a gang of street children that is ruled by an abusive older boy, Dib. During a confrontation with the gang, Ali is killed by a stone. His three friends decide to bury him "like a prince."[1]

Nabil Ayouch presents fine psychological portrayals of his child protagonists, even if they appear rather naïve at times. Working with street children, he succeeded in eliciting performances to match their realities in spite of the formidable difficulties he encountered.[2] All the while he avoided miserabilism. Ayouch depicts the harshness and precariousness of these children's lives, if in an understated way; he shows how these children find companionship with each other, troubled though it is; and his film transcends the reality of street life with a poetics of childhood. The poetics is conveyed in delightful animation sequences that enhance the excellent wide-screen production. Ayouch created a beautiful film that emotionally engages viewers and elicits their sympathy for the condition of street children, all the while eschewing social critique.

Ali Zaoua was a big success in Morocco. Selling close to 500,000 tickets, it eclipsed all previous Moroccan productions except for a few comedies. Quite likely it was the most successful film from anywhere in the Maghreb. Internationally it has been the most successful Moroccan film ever (Dwyer 2005), garnering forty-four prizes at international festivals, according to Ali n' Productions, among them the Stallion of Yennenga, the top prize at FESPACO, the premier festival of African film.[3] In the United States the film found distribution as a selection of the Film Movement.[4]

---

* *Ali Zaoua, Prince of the Streets/ Ali Zawa/ Ali Zaoua, prince de la rue*. 2000. Film directed by Nabil Ayouch; written by Nathalie Saugeon and Nabil Ayouch. Produced by Playtime (France), TF1 International (France), Ali n' Productions (Morocco), Alexis Films (Belgium), Ace Editing (Belgium). Distributed in the United States by Arab Film Distribution and Film Movement. 99 minutes.

Design by Uli Gleis

Nabil Ayouch with, from left, Hicham Moussoune, Mustapha Hansali, and Mouniïm Kbab. Frame from "Making of" on the French DVD of *Ali Zaoua*

The Portrayal of Street Life

In *Ali Zaoua*, the boys steal, prostitute themselves, sniff glue, and have murderous fights with each other; they get raped by other boys; they are chased by the police. The children use a language of the streets that is considered rather vulgar, and many Moroccans were shocked by it; the English and French subtitles fail to do it justice (Barlet 2003). Nevertheless, the reality presented in *Ali Zaoua* is rather gentle when compared to the grim representations of street children in classics like Mexico's *Los olvidados* (Luis Buñuel, 1950), Brazil's *Pixote* (Hector Babenco, 1981) and *City of God* (*Cidade de Deus*, Fernando Meirelles and Katia Lund, 2002), and India's *Salaam Bombay!* (Mira Nair, 1988). If Ali gets killed, such was not the intent of the boy throwing a stone at him. To some extent this contrast may reflect differences between these settings. The armed youth gangs of Brazil presumably are not found in Morocco, nor have Moroccan police been reported to systematically kill street children. Still, when Saugeon, who had worked on the screenplay in France, came to Morocco for the first time, she was shocked to discover that the conditions of street children were harsher and more violent than their script allowed (2001b). At that point Ayouch told her that they were not doing a documentary, that there are things that cannot be put into a fiction film.

Ali Zaoua is moving, touching, indeed enchanting. The children find companionship with each other. Kwita's encounter with a puppy may be taken as emblematic of the relations among the boys. Like the boys who fight and seek companionship, so Kwita repeatedly throws the puppy down a stairway, but the puppy keeps coming back and eventually settles around Kwita's neck. Ayouch's street children escape their harsh reality into a dreamworld. He has argued that the poetics in the film is part of street life:[5]

> The street holds a strong attraction; it has also a form of poetry and of a nearly tragical-lyric dreamworld that is difficult to imagine if one is not there, if one does not live there. Their life is made of deliriums, of phantasms coming from nowhere. They take off from anything; they have that poetry in themselves which is very strong and constitutes a pillar of their existence and helps them manage.[6] (In Barlet 2003)

Ayouch's Ali has created a veritable dreamworld of journeying on a boat, taking a girl aboard, and reaching the Island of the Two Suns. His friends get drawn into that dreamworld as well. The children, used to sniffing glue and escaping their reality, now see images on billboards and graffiti transform and become part of Ali's story. His magnificent mural painting of that island, which eventually becomes animated, and the animated designs of the boys' daydreams, the handiwork of Sylvie Leonard, are delightful.[7]

The Avoidance of Social Critique

Ali Zaoua is a new departure for Moroccan film and indeed Arab film, in focusing on street children, in conveying a good deal about their condition, in going so far as to allude to them prostituting themselves and being raped by other children. But if Ayouch brings attention to a social problem, he stays clear of social critique.[8]

In this film's telling, poverty is not at issue. We see the children on an old quay, at an abandoned factory site, on a vacant lot, but only once can we catch a brief glimpse of shanties. Beyond the street children we do not encounter poverty. The prostitution of Ali's mother is quite removed from the more sordid varieties of the sex trade. She picks up her clients at a nightclub and takes them to her apartment. She appears to enjoy a modest level of comfort. Poverty did not drive Ali into the streets. *Ali Zaoua* starts out with a television reporter

The Island of the Two Suns

interviewing Ali. He tells of his mother preparing to sell his eyes. Ali is street-smart and knows how to impress. The interviewer is taken in, and so are viewers until they learn the real reason Ali left home and come to know his caring mother. He ran away from home because he could not endure children taunting his mother about her occupation.

The film does not tell how any of the other children came to live in the streets. We do not hear of poverty, and neither is there mention of family conflicts; at most there may be a hint: as little Boubker keeps talking about his caring uncle, we hear his friends' dismissive rejoinders, see his scarred face, and begin to wonder whether mistreatment brought him to join the street children. The concluding song, "Come my dear son / Come under my wings," tells of parents ready to welcome them to homes with "green gardens, embedded with flowers and roses"—as if it were a perfectly simple choice to make, and a most attractive one at that.[9]

The vulnerability of children is central to the condition of street children, but violence in *Ali Zaoua* remains limited and originates within their own ranks. There is not a single instance of either public authorities or individual adults victimizing these children. Indeed, a couple of adults sympathetic to the children are shown helping them escape their condition. Most people literally overlook the street children. Kwita repeatedly seeks to approach a high school student, but she virtually ignores him—they live in separate worlds. When street children do manage to connect with others, they are put down. Ali's mother berates Omar and his friends for their personal hygiene and for sniffing glue. The three friends follow Muslim injunction in washing Ali's body and wanting to bury him the very next day, but when Kwita meets an age mate at the cemetery, he is told that he and his friends are not pure because of their lack of religious practice and that Ali cannot be buried at the cemetery because of his impurity—which, it seems, could be overcome if they had the money to pay for the burial. The children are ignored or put down, but we witness no repression. The three friends perceive their neighbor as the witch Aicha with the feet of a camel of the popular imagination, and she complains to the police about the racket they make in the middle of the night. The police officers, however, never catch up with the children, and we do not learn what treatment they might mete out.

All the people who come into contact with the children are kind. The two principal adult protagonists care a great deal about the children. Ali's mother cares for her own child and eventually takes Omar into her home. The fisherman Hamid was going to hire Ali as his assistant, keeps looking for him when he disappears, gives him the decent burial his friends cannot manage, and in the end takes on Kwita. The meeting between Kwita and the boy at the cemetery ends on a conciliatory, inclusive note when the boy, as an afterthought, makes a final comment about Kwita's dead friend: "You find him up there praying with the angels." And while the high school student never talks to Kwita, her face and demeanor suggest a kind person, and she gives him a little smile at their last encounter.

Ali Zaoua puts the blame for the condition of the street children squarely on the gang leader, Dib,[10] and on the children themselves: on those who tease Ali about his mother's profession; on Ali, who lets himself be shamed into running away from home and confronting Dib's entire gang to defend her honor; on a gang member who fells Ali with a stone; on children who turn violent, most dramatically when Omar sets out to cut Kwita's throat. In this story it remains for children to take the initiative to escape their condition: Ali was committed to becoming a sailor and persuaded, we infer, Hamid to take him on as an assistant; Omar seeks out Ali's mother.

The overall thrust of *Ali Zaoua* is clear. The life of street children in Casablanca is hard and precarious. No adults are to blame. No social policy or lack thereof comes into play. The blame rests on children running wild and an abusive gang leader. *Ali Zaoua* has viewers conclude that the reason Ali became a street child is trivial and that the only harm the street children experience is brought on by other children when it is not self-inflicted. Rather than address the causes of children coming to live in the streets and their condition, the film asks for sympathy and education. The film offers individual solutions to the social problem as Ali's mother comes to accept Omar and Hamid takes Kwita under his wings.

Censorship, Funding, and Audiences

Self-censorship may go a long way toward explaining why Ayouch toned down the reality of the life of street children and avoided social critique. *Ali Zaoua* was shot about the time Hassan II died, bringing to a close a long period of fierce repression of all opposition that has come to be referred to as the Years of Lead.[11] Apart from the threat of outright censorship, we may surmise that the French television networks that invested in the film and the Moroccan, French, Belgian, and European agencies that contributed to the financing would have balked at supporting a shocking film like *Pixote* or *City of God*.[12] Finally, by avoiding any suggestion of adult responsibilities, *Ali Zaoua* could reach a large Moroccan public that felt itself "neither denigrated nor disfigured, but on the contrary loved and understood," as Brahimi put it (2009, 44).

While the violence of the streets remains limited in *Ali Zaoua*, the film is notably venturesome in other respects. Not only is a prostitute a principal protagonist, but Ali's mother is portrayed in favorable terms. As for her trade, she comments on children taunting her and Ali: "I could have answered them. What could I tell them? Why their fathers come to me? You can't tell children that." She is shown having sex with a client, a sequence on which, as Ayouch wryly remarks, "a lot of ink was spilt in Morocco" (2001).[13] Showing Omar frontally in the nude was also problematic. Ayouch touches on other sensitive topics as well—Boubker being raped by Dib, references to Kwita and other boys having been gang-raped by other boys, Kwita prostituting himself—but he does it in a manner sufficiently subtle that they are unlikely to be picked up by young audiences. The success of the film demonstrates that Ayouch made savvy choices.

Ali Zaoua was seen by close to a half-million people in Morocco. If it affected the attitudes of some, if it moved them to act differently, it will have served a good purpose. Ayouch, for one, has stated (in Barlet 2003) that public attitudes toward street children changed a good deal since the film played in Morocco:

> Putting forward all the sentiments we share with them, universal sentiments, love, joy, fraternity, humor. Somehow making them more human in the eyes of people, and that is what happened when the film was released in Morocco. Many people were taken aback: "We did not know that." Inevitably, they now look at these children differently. There has been a debate, a polemic ensued that demonstrated that the film was the beginning of a new consciousness.

NOTES

This is an abridged and revised version of Josef Gugler, 2007, "Ali Zaoua: The Harsh Life of Street Children and the Poetics of Childhood," *Journal of North African Studies* 12 (3): 369–379. Reprinted in Andrea Khalil (ed.), *North African Cinema in a Global Context: Through the Lens of Diaspora* (London: Routledge, 2008), 93–103. By permission of Taylor and Francis.

1. The German poster, reproduced here, shows the four friends—Omar, Boubker, Ali, and Kwita—against the Casablanca shoreline.
2. Ayouch spent two years becoming familiar with street children and recruiting his actors among them. Boubker was played by Hicham Moussoune, who went on to a television series and a major role in Ayouch's next film, *A Minute of Sun Less* (*Une minute de soleil en moins*, 2003). Most of the children, however, went back to the streets after the film was shot, according to Ayouch, despite efforts to get each of them into school, training, or a job (Lormans 2001). On the recruitment of the child actors, their backgrounds, the love story on the set that brought the shooting to a halt, and the difficulties Ayouch encountered working with street children see Gugler 2007.
3. The chairman of the jury, the distinguished Tunisian director and critic Ferid Boughedir, praised *Ali Zaoua* for the powerful emotion it evoked, the excellence in the direction of the cast, and the sensitive description of the cruel existence of abandoned children in Africa (Quist-Arcton 2001).
4. The DVD distributed in the United States does not include the important supplementary materials provided on the French DVD: a running commentary on the film by Nabil Ayouch, a "Making of" by Ayouch and the actor Said Taghmaoui, a presentation of the characters by co-writer Nathalie Saugeon, and comments on the production by the producer Jean Cottin and Saugeon. The French DVD also offers English subtitles: they are more satisfactory and, in white, less jarring than the yellow subtitles on the U.S. DVD. The French DVD includes Ayouch's first short, *Les pierres bleues du désert* (The Blue Stones of the Desert, 1993).
5. Shafik characterizes *Ali Zaoua* as "a far more imaginative and not at all melodramatic Moroccan version of *Salaam Bombay*" (2007, 222). Carter calls the film "touching in its humane treatment of the problems of street kids" (2009, 270–272). Serceau (2004) relates the film to Italian neorealism but concludes that a perhaps excessive act of faith takes the place of the neorealist observation. Khayati (2005) takes a critical view of what he characterizes as "Disneyfication." Armes (2005, 175–176) relates the dream sequences to Luis Buñuel's *Los olvidados*.
6. Translations from the French are mine.
7. Nathalie Saugeon, who co-authored the script with Nabil Ayouch, wrote a novella, *Ali Zaoua, prince de la rue* (2001a), for young teens. The novella forgoes illustration,

but Saugeon succeeded, even without the poetics of images, in movingly conveying how the children's imaginations transcend their harsh reality.
8. Ayouch's successful first feature, *Mektoub* (1997), also focuses on an aspect of Moroccan society not readily acknowledged—the immunity that comes with power. Based on a political-financial scandal that shocked the country, the thriller was a huge success.
9. The maudlin lyrics of the song are not translated into either French or English on the French DVD.
10. For a closer look at the character of Dib see Gugler 2007, 375–376.
11. For a possible interpretation of *Ali Zaoua* as an allegory of the rule of Hassan II see Gugler 2007, 376.
12. Commenting on new developments in Moroccan cinema in the 1990s, Ayouch has observed: "When UGC [a French production company] or TF1 or Canal Plus [French television networks] agree to co-produce a film on the basis of the proposed screenplay, the screenplay is certainly not accepted as is, because those who invest in the film subsequently demand modifications and that also requires a great deal of work" (in Samie 2001).
13. Ali's mother was played by Amal Ayouch, a cousin of the director, because it would have been very difficult for other Moroccan actresses to appear as a prostitute, let alone simulate sex with a client (Ayouch 2001, Saugeon 2001c).

REFERENCES

Armes, Roy. 2005. *Postcolonial Images: Studies in North African Film*. Bloomington: Indiana University Press.

Ayouch, Nabil. 2001. "Film commenté," on French DVD of *Ali Zaoua*.

Barlet, Olivier. 2003. "Entretien avec Nabil Ayouch à propos de *Ali Zaoua*." http://www.africultures.com/php/index.php?nav=article&no=2897.

Brahimi, Denise. 2009. *50 ans de cinéma Maghrébin*. Paris: Minerve.

Carter, Sandra Gayle. 2009. *What Moroccan Cinema? A Historical and Critical Study, 1956–2006*. Lanham, MD: Lexington Books.

Dwyer, Kevin. 2005. Personal communication to the author.

Gugler, Josef. 2007. "*Ali Zaoua*: The Harsh Life of Street Children and the Poetics of Childhood." *Journal of North African Studies* 12 (3): 369–379.

Khayati, Abdellatif. 2005. "Picturing the Homeless in Casablanca." *Moving Worlds* 5 (1): 21–32.

Lormans, Erwin. 2001. "Nabil Ayouch." *Film + video en televisie* 510:20–21.

Quist-Arcton, Ofeibea. 2001. "Africa: Coveted Fespaco Prize Goes to Moroccan Director." http://allafrica.com/stories/200103040001.html.

Samie, Amale. 2001. "Le cinéma marocain s'émancipe." *Maroc hebdo international* 459 (April): 6–12. http://www.maroc-hebdo.press.ma/MHinternet/Archives_459/html_459/cinema.html.
Saugeon, Nathalie. 2001a. *Ali Zaoua, prince de la rue*. Toulouse: Editions Milan.
———. 2001b. "L'aventure du tournage vue par," on French DVD of *Ali Zaoua*.
———. 2001c. "Personnages," on French DVD of *Ali Zaoua*.
Serceau, Michel. 2004. "*Ali Zaoua*: Un anti-*Sciuscià*?" *CinémAction* 111:92–95.
Shafik, Viola. 2007. *Arab Cinema: History and Cultural Identity*. Revised edition. Cairo: American University in Cairo Press.

CONTRIBUTORS

WALTER ARMBRUST is the Albert Hourani Fellow of Modern Middle East Studies at St. Antony's College and a lecturer at the University of Oxford in the Faculty of Oriental Studies. He is the author of *Mass Culture and Modernism in Egypt* (Cambridge University Press, 1996) and editor of *Mass Mediations: New Approaches to Popular Culture in the Middle East and Beyond* (University of California Press, 2000). His research focuses on mass media and popular culture in Egypt.

ROY ARMES is Professor Emeritus of Film at Middlesex University. He has published widely on world cinema for the past forty years. His most recent books are *Postcolonial Images: Studies in North African Film* (2005), *African Filmmaking: North and South of the Sahara* (2006), and *Dictionary of African Filmmakers* (2008), all published by Indiana University Press. His current project, *Arab Filmmakers of the Middle East: A Dictionary* (2010), also for Indiana, is his twentieth book.

FAKHREDDIN AZIMI is Professor of History at the University of Connecticut. He is the author of four books, the most recent of which is *The Quest for Democracy in Iran: A Century of Struggle against Authoritarian Rule* (Cambridge: Harvard University Press, 2008). In addition to many articles and book chapters in English, he has written widely in Persian, has regularly visited and conducted research in Iran, and has maintained an active presence in Iranian intellectual and scholarly circles.

OLIVIER BARLET is the author of *Les cinémas d'Afrique noire: Le regard en question/African Cinemas, Decolonizing the Gaze* and directs the *Images plurielles* collection on cinema at L'Harmattan. He is a member of the Syndicat français de la critique de cinéma and the African Federation of Film Critics, a delegate for Africa at the Cannes Festival Critics Week, and a film critic for *Africultures*, *Afriscope*, and other journals. Chief Editor of *Africultures* from 1997 to 2004, he is today in charge of the journal's Internet development.

DENISE BRAHIMI taught modern and comparative literature in the Maghreb—she lived ten years in Algeria after 1962—and in France (University Paris VII). Her first publications were devoted to European travelers in the Maghreb and the Middle East in the eighteenth and nineteenth centuries. She is the author of *Taos Amrouche romancière* (J. Losfeld, 1995), *La peinture au féminin, Berthe Morisot et Marie Cassatt* (J. P. Rocher, 2000), and *50 ans de cinéma maghrébin* (Minerve, 2009).

RINI COBBEY chairs the Communication Arts Department at Gordon College, where she teaches Media Studies. She has written on religion in mainstream film as well as celebrity studies. Her current research looks at the interplay of aesthetics and politics in Middle Eastern and Indian film.

KEVIN DWYER is the author of *Moroccan Dialogues: Anthropology in Question* (1982, published in Arabic in Morocco in 2008), *Arab Voices: The Human Rights Debate in the Middle East* (1991), and *Beyond Casablanca: M. A. Tazi and the Adventure of Moroccan Filmmaking* (2004). He has been Professor of Anthropology at the American University in Cairo and a Fellow at the Woodrow Wilson International Center for Scholars.

ERIC EGAN is the author of *The Films of Makhmalbaf: Cinema, Politics, and Culture in Iran* (Mage, 2005). He has written extensively on Iranian cinema as well as on Third Cinema, Egyptian cinema, Pakistani cinema, and early silent cinema. He teaches film at University College Dublin, Ireland.

NURITH GERTZ is Professor of Cinema and Literature, Department of Language Literature and Art, at the Open University, and Head of Theoretical Studies, Department of Cinema and Television, Tel Aviv University. She is the author of *Myths in Israeli Culture* (Vallentine Mitchell, 2000) and of several books published in Hebrew. The English version of her *Landscape in Mist: Space and Memory in Palestinian Cinema*, co-authored with George Khleifi, was published by Edinburgh University Press and Indiana University Press.

EDWARD GIBEAU received his bachelor of arts degree in Southwest Asian Studies at the University of Connecticut, where he continues his studies as a graduate student in the Department of Anthropology, pursuing a master of arts program in Evolution, Culture, and Cognition.

CONTRIBUTORS

JOSEF GUGLER is Professor Emeritus of Sociology at the University of Connecticut, where he has continued to teach on the cinemas of the Middle East and Africa. A late convert to film studies, he is the author of *African Film: Re-Imagining a Continent* (James Currey, Indiana University Press, and David Philip, 2003). At this time he is preparing an edited volume, *African Cinemas: A Continental Approach*. He served as member of the jury for fiction films at PanAfrica International, Montreal, in 2010.

GAL HERMONI teaches courses in film theory in the Department of Film and Television at Tel Aviv University and at Sapir academic college. His research interests include film theory, critical theory, cultural studies, and popular music.

KIM JENSEN's novel, *The Woman I Left Behind*, was published in 2006 by Curbstone Press, and her poetry collection, *Bread Alone*, was published in 2009 by Syracuse University Press. In 2001 Jensen won the Raymond Carver Fiction Prize, and her writings have appeared in *Liberation Literature, Poetic Voices without Borders 2; Come Together: Imagine Peace, Ezra Journal of Translation; Left Curve; al-Jadid; Boston Book Review;* and *al-Ahram Weekly*. She is Associate Professor of English at the Community College of Baltimore County.

LINA KHATIB is a Program Manager and Research Scholar at the Freeman Spogli Institute for International Studies at Stanford University. Her research interests include the relationship between media and politics in Middle East. She is the author of *Filming the Modern Middle East: Politics in the Cinemas of Hollywood and the Arab World* (I. B. Tauris, 2006) and *Lebanese Cinema: Imagining the Civil War and Beyond* (I. B. Tauris, 2008) and a founding co-editor of the *Middle East Journal of Culture and Communication*.

GEORGE KHLEIFI, director and script writer of documentaries including *The Stone Throwers, Shorook,* and *You, Me, Jerusalem,* assisted his brother Michel Khleifi in producing and directing *Fertile Memory, Wedding in Galilee, Canticle of the Stone,* and *Tale of the Three Jewels*. He is the line producer of *Shara'a Simsim,* the Palestinian version of *Sesame Street*. He wrote and directed the series *The House of Abu Yousef* and the Palestinian soap opera *Matabb*. George Khleifi led the training of Palestinian crews for television and cinema from 1992 until 2007.

FLORENCE MARTIN, Professor of French and Francophone Studies at Goucher College, is Associate Editor for *Studies in French Cinema*. Her most recent scholarship focuses on Tunisian cinema and filmmakers Raja Amari, Moufida Tlatli, and Nadia El Fani. She is the co-author of an introduction to French and Francophone cinema, *A vous de voir!* (Editions Casteilla, 2010). Her book on Maghrebi women filmmakers is forthcoming with Indiana University Press.

YAEL MUNK is Senior Lecturer in Film and Culture at the Open University, Israel. She was program director at the Jerusalem Cinematheque, then at the Tel Aviv Cinematheques, from 1987 to 1994 and the artistic consultant of the Israeli Documentary Filmmakers Forum from 2000 to 2003. She has published articles on various issues in Israeli cinema in Hebrew, English, and French. Her book, *Exiled in Their Borders: Israeli Cinema between Two Intifadah*, will be published in Hebrew by Open University Press

JUDD NE'EMAN is Professor Emeritus of Cinema Studies and Filmmaking at Tel Aviv University and has been a Visiting Professor at the Tisch School of the Arts, New York University. He has published on Israeli cinema and on cinema and war. A laureate of the Israel Prize for cinema, his feature films and documentaries have been shown at festivals and on television. *The Dress* (1970), *Paratroopers* (1977), *Streets of Yesterday* (1989), *Nuzhat al-Fuad* (2007), and *Zitra* (2008) are some of the films he has directed.

LISA WEDEEN is Professor of Political Science at the University of Chicago. She is the author of *Ambiguities of Domination: Politics, Rhetoric, and Symbols in Contemporary Syria* (University of Chicago Press, 1999) and *Peripheral Visions: Publics, Power, and Performance in Yemen* (University of Chicago Press, 2008).

NADIA YAQUB is Associate Professor of Arabic language and culture at the University of North Carolina, Chapel Hill. She is the author of *Pens, Swords, and the Springs of Art: the Oral Poetry Dueling of Palestinians in the Galilee* (Brill, 2006) and of numerous articles on Arab and Palestinian literature and film.

FILM INDEX

Abi and Rabi, 39
Adventures of a Hero, The, 298
Afghan Alphabet, 95, 102n2
Ahlaam, 6, 26, 34n25
Aladdin, 331, 336n11
Alexandria . . . New York, 18, 247–248n18, 269n4
Algeria in Flames, 294
Ali in Wonderland, 297
Ali Zaoua, Prince of the Streets, 14, 19, 339–348
Almaz and Abdul al-Hamuli, 246n3
Ambassadors, The, 275
American Abracadabra, 247n18
Ania's Tea, 303
An-Naim Route, The, 196n6
Apple, The, 99
Argana, 331
Arna's Children, 195
Around the Pink House, 142
Ascent to the Abyss, 247n15
As Long as There Is Film Stock . . . , 292n11
At Five in the Afternoon, 95–96
Autopsy of a Plot, 298
Autumn–October in Algiers, 14, 23, 33n21, 301
Autumn Song, 299
Avanti Popolo, 11–12, 16, 27, 31n1, 159, 160–161, 177–186
Avoda, 155, 156
Ayrouen, 303

Bab Aziz, 280
Bab el-Oued City, 23, 270n10, 301–302, 303
Bab el Web, 303
Back Stairs, The, 247n14
Band's Visit, The, 163
Barakat!, 303
Baran, 52, 99

Bashu, the Little Stranger, 51
Bath House of Malatili, The, 247n14
Baton Rouge, 313–314n2
Battle of Algiers, The, 25–26, 28, 247n9, 319
Baya's Mountain, 302
Beaufort, 163, 184
Bedwin Hacker, 8, 13, 19–20, 22, 279, 284–293
Behind the Sun, 242, 247n15
Beirut, the Encounter, 135, 136, 141, 142
Beirut Phantoms, 142
Belt of Fire, The, 141, 142
Ben Boulaid, 303
Beyond the Walls, 161
Bezness, 280
Bicycle Thieves, 15, 100–102
Big Man, Small Love. See Hejar
Birds of Darkness, 242
Birth of a Nation, The, 8
Bitter Day, Sweet Day, 247n17
Blackboards, 30
Black Market, 249n25
Blacksmith's Son, The, 249n25
Blue Stones of the Desert, The, 346n4
Bookshop, The, 279
Bosta, 136, 141, 142, 143
Breakdown, 300
Bride of the Nile, 268, 270n9
Buddha Collapsed out of Shame, 95
Bullet Is Still in My Pocket, The, 232
Burned Hearts, 336n16
Bus Driver, The, 233

Canterbury Tales, The, 319
Canticle of the Stone, 188, 196n6
Captain Khorshid, 51
Caramel, 144
Casa Nayda, 330

Casanegra, 332
Chaos, 12–13, 250n34
Charcoal Burner, The, 297
Chatter on the Nile, 247n12
Cheb, 313–314n2
Children of Lenin, The, 292n13
Children of Silence, 247n15
Children of the Wind, 300
Choice, The, 27, 34n28
Chronicle of a Disappearance, 28, 34n29, 194, 196n10
Chronicle of the Years of Embers, 7, 25, 296, 304n2
Chronicles of the Coming Year, 108–110
Cinecittà, 281
Citadel, The, 300
Citizen, Detective, Thief, 241–242
City, The, 248n20
City of God, 341
Civilized, The. See Civilized People, A
Civilized People, A, 136, 137–138, 140, 141, 142, 143, 144
Clay Dolls, 280
Closed Doors, 19, 24, 242, 250n33, 258, 261–270
Cow, The, 46–7
Crazy Years of the Twist, The, 13–14, 300
Crooks, 329
Cry of Men, The, 300
Cry of Stone, 299
Cup Final, 162
Curfew, 17, 193, 202
Cut, 196n10
Cyclist, The, 75

Dark Room, The, 336n10
Dawn, The, 274
Dawn of Islam, The, 248n23, 249n27
Dawn of the Damned, 294
Day after Day, 167
Day I Became a Woman, The, 103n3
Days of Glory, 7, 14, 20, 306–14
Death of a Princess, 269n3
December, 296
Defiance, 196–7n11
Delbaran, 99

Denial, The, 297
Desert Ark, The, 300, 304n7
Destiny, 18, 19, 24, 241, 252–60, 261, 268, 269n4
Devarim, 167
Dinanir, 248n23
Disco, Disco, 249n29
Divine Intervention, 28, 191, 194, 196n8
Djomeh, 52, 57, 99
Dol, 30
Door to the Sky, A, 329
Dove's Lost Necklace, The, 280
Down with Colonialism, 246n3
Dreams of the City, 111n3
Dress, The, 158
Dupes, The, 18, 27, 113–124
Dust of Life, 313–314n2

Eden, 167
11'9"01. See September 11
Embassy Is in the Building, The, 235
Embers, 328
Emigrant, The, 19, 241, 253, 256
Empire of Dreams, 299
Essaïda, 280
Esther, 167
Every Bastard Is a King, 157
Excuse Us, We're Being Humiliated, 248n22
Explosion, The, 136, 137
Extras, The, 9, 16, 108, 125–133, 153n5

Face to Face, 336n10
Faith, 248–249n23
Falafel, 134, 144
Fatma, 280
Fatma 75, 275–276
Fear, 247n14
Fellow Traveler, 161
Female Devil, The, 301
Fertile Memory, 16–17, 188, 196n6
Fictitious Marriage, 161–2
Fifth Reaction, The, 55
Fifty-Fifty My Love, 292n12
File in Vice, A, 233, 249
Filming in Algiers, 33n21
First Step, 297
Fishermen, The, 297

For a Moment, Freedom, 33n13
Forbidden Love, 299
Ford Transit, 196n7
Forgiveness, 163, 164, 164n4
Forgotten Hillside, The, 302
Forgotten Ones, The, 341, 346n5
For Pleasure, 292n9
Free Zone, 167
Friends or Business, 235
From Hollywood to Tamanrasset, 300

Gabbeh, 75
Gates of Steel, 299
Gate of Sun, The, 26, 34n27
Gaze, The, 329
Girl from Carthage, The, 273
Girl in the Sneakers, The, 55
God Is with Us, 229
Golden Horseshoes, The, 13, 277, 278
Goodbye Mothers, 330
Good Families, The, 297
Grass, 39
Great Beans of China, 248n20
Greetings, Didou, 298
Guilty, The, 247n15
Gulf War . . . What Next?, The, 280

Haifa, 193
Haji Agha, Cinema Actor, 39
Haji Washington, 55
Halfaouine, 281
Half Moon, 30
Hamam in Amsterdam, 248n20
Hamlet of Women, 20, 23, 31n1, 303, 315–324
Hamsin, 159
Harvests of Steel, 299
Hassan Terro, 296
Hejar, 34n30
Hello America, 248n18
Hello America, Africano, 248n20
Hemlock, 55
He Walked in the Fields, 157
Hey, Children, 301
Hidden Half, The, 11, 55, 63–73
Hide and Seek, 158
Himo King of Jerusalem, 161

Hirbet Hizeh, 158, 160
Honor of the Tribe, The, 301
Houria, 299
House Built on Water, A, 57
House Is Black, The, 54
Hunt Feast, The, 132

I Am Not with Them, 24, 244–245
I Exist, 299
I Love Cinema, 250n32
I'm Taraneh, 15, 55, 56
Independence, 194
Inheritance, The, 297
Inland, 303
In My Father's House, 329
Innocent, The, 233, 242
In Our House There Is a Man, 241, 246n3
Inspector General, The, 246n4
Inspector Tahar's Holiday, 298
In the Battlefields, 134, 136, 140, 141, 142
In the Ninth Month, 194, 196n10
In the Shadows of the City, 13, 16, 134, 135, 136, 138, 139, 142, 146–153
Introduction to the End of an Argument, 196n8
Invasion, 196n9
Iran: A Cinematographic Revolution, 3, 10, 77
Iran Is My Land, 57
I Want a Solution, 229

Jail Girl, 336n10
Jamila, the Algerian, 23, 34n24, 247n9
Jasmine, 196n10
Jenin, Jenin, 191
Journey to the Sun, 29–30
Joy of Madness, 95

Kadosh, 167
Kandahar, 95–96
Karnak Café, The, 242, 247n15
Kedma, 11, 16, 26, 163, 166–176
Kilometre Zero, 30
Kippur, 167, 184
Kite, The, 142, 143

Lady, The, 55
La Zerda, 298

Laila's Birthday, 17, 195
Land of Dreams, 247n18
Land of Honey and Incense, 139–140, 143–144
Land of Peace, 230
Lashin, 248n23
Last Image, The, 296
Late Summer Blues, 161
Lebanon, 184
Lebanon in Spite of Everything, 138, 141
Leila and the Others, 298
Lemon Tree, 164
Leopard, The, 16, 18, 131
Letter from a Time of Exile, 142
Life According to Agfa, 186
Light at the End of the Tunnel, The, 189–90
Lights, 299
Little Senegal, 312, 313–314n2
Little Wars, 138, 139–140, 141
Lion of the Desert, 6, 25
Lizard, The, 55–56
Lonely Tune of Tehran, 60n19
Long Days, 18
Long Night, The, 10
Looking for My Wife's Husband, 326, 329
Look-Out, 162–163
Lor Girl, The, 39–40
Lotus Flower, 301
Love Affair in Casablanca, A, 326
Love Before Bread Sometimes, 240
Love on the Pyramids Plateau, 232

Mafia, 248n20
Magician, The, 196n10
Making Of, 280
Maloul Celebrates Its Destruction, 196n6
Man of Ashes, 13, 277
Man Who Watched Windows, The, 298–299
Ma'raka, 142
Marathon Tam, 301
Marco Polo, the Missing Chapter, 185
Marjan, 54
Marock, 329, 330
Marooned in Iraq, 30, 57
Marriage of the Blessed, 10, 15, 51, 74–83
Martyrs, 136
Mascarades, 303
May Lady, The, 54, 89–90, 91

Maxx, 55
Mektoub, 347n8
Memory in Detention, 336n10
Men Under the Sun, 123n2
Mercedes, 249n29
Message, The, 6, 22
Milky Way, The, 194, 196n10
Minute of Sun Less, A, 335n6, 346n2
Misri Efendi, al-, 249n25
Mohamed Chouikh, a Filmmaker Who Resists, 324n1
Mohammed, Messenger of God. See The Message
Moment of Innocence, A, 33n17, 55, 75
Mona Saber, 336n10
Monsieur Fabre's Mill, 14, 297
Moonlighting, 301
Morituri, 300
Moroccan Dream, 331
Moroccan Symphony, 330
Moussa's Wedding, 300
Mongols, The, 45
Mummy, The, 118
Mustafa Kamil, 246n3
My Private Map, 193
My Sister My Friend, 303
Myth, 196n11

Nahla, 298
Nargess, 54
Nasser 56, 246n7
Nazareth 2000, 196n7
Near the Poplar Tree, 297
Neighbor, The, 303
Neon Children, The, 300
Never Too Late to Unite!, 292n12
Night, The, 111n3, 111–112n7
Night Bagdad Fell, The, 248n22
Night of Fate, The, 248–9n23
Night of the Baby Doll, 248n22
Nights of the Jackal, 111n3
Noa Is 17, 161
Nobody Knows about Persian Cats, 60n19
Nomads, The, 297
Noua, 297
Nouba of the Women of Mount Chenoua, The, 298, 304n3
Number One, 329, 332

Omar Gatlato, 13, 298, 302, 303, 304n4
Once upon a Time, 33n21, 302
Once upon a Time, Beirut, 143
Once upon a Time Cinema, 75
Once We Were Dreamers, 159–60, 161
One Laugh Too Many, 279
One Minute Less of Sun. See Minute of Sun Less, A
On Whom Do We Open Fire?, 247n15
Open Door, The, 229
Opium and the Stick, 296
Osama, 23, 102n2
Other, The, 241
Other Half of the Sky, The, 280
Other Side of the Mirror, The, 303
Other World, The, 23, 303
Our Forbidden Places, 336n10
Our Times, 92n5
Outside Life, 139–140, 143–144
Outside the Law, 20

Paradise Now, 18, 28, 194–195, 218–227
Paratroopers, 158
Pardon Me, Law!, 229
Paris Love Story, A, 299
Party, 57
Pasha Nightclub, The, 234
Passport, 196n10
Pay Attention to Zuzu, 239–40
Peddler, The, 75
Perfect Day, A, 134, 142
Perhaps the Sea, 313–314n2
Pixote, 341
Plunderers, The, 297
Police Station in the Street, 232
Pomegranate Siestas, 279
Port Said, 230
Prince, The, 279
Prince Ehtejab, 45
Prince Who Contemplated His Soul, The, 280
Prisoner of Abu Zabal, The, 246n7
Promenade of the Heart, 164
Protest, 47

Qaisar, 47

Rachida, 20, 23, 303
Radhia, 301
Rage and Glory, 161
Rai, 299
Rajab on a Hot Tin Roof, 247n16
Ramadan on the Volcano, 247n16, 249n29
Rana's Wedding, 18, 189, 220–4
Real Premonition, 331
Red Satin, 274, 281
Reel Bad Arabs: How Hollywood Vilifies a People, 31n2
Return My Heart, 246n3
Return of a Citizen, 247n17
Return of the Prodigal Son, 27, 34n28, 247n15
Revolution of Yemen, The, 246n8
Rome Rather Than You, 303
Roof, a Family, A, 299

Sacrificed, The, 300
Sacrifices, 9
Salaam Bombay!, 341, 346n5
Saladin, 230, 248n23
Salama, 248n23
Salt of this Sea, 195
Salut Barbès, 270n9
Samira's Gardens, 331
Sand Storm, 296
Satanic Angels, The, 330
Scabby Khlifa, 274–275
Scream of the Ants, 75
Sealed Soil, The, 54
Season of Men, 280
September 11, 18
Settlers, 155–6
Sex and Philosophy, 75
Shaban below Zero, 247n16
Shadow of the Earth, 277
Shaymaʿ, al-, 248n23, 249n27
She, the Sindibad, 190
She Has Diabetes and Hypertension but Refuses to Die, 335–336n7
Shelter, The (Lebanon), 136
Shelter, The (Palestine), 196n10
Silence, The, 15, 75
Silences of the Palace, 278–279, 281
Silent Cinema, A, 110n

Si Mohand U M'hand, 303
Simple Event, A, 45
Sixth Day, The, 256, 259n7
Siyavosh at Persepolis, 45
Skeleton, 331
Sleeping Child, The, 329
Smell of Camphor, Fragrance of Jasmine, 57
Smile of the Lamb, The, 159, 160, 162
Song on the Pass, 231, 232, 247n13
Sons and Murderers, 240
So That Algeria May Live, 297
Sparrow, The, 27, 34n28, 118, 247n15
Sparrows Don't Die in Jerusalem, 280
Stars in Broad Daylight, 9, 105–108, 111n3, 111n6
Stars of the Day. See Stars in Broad Daylight
Still Life, 45
Story of a Meeting, 300
Strangers, 164
Strangers, The, 249n27
Stray Dogs, 15, 23, 57, 94–103
Streets of Yesterday, 161
Such a Long Journey, 280
Such a Young Peace, 294
Sultan of the Medina, 278
Sun of the Hyenas, 275
Survivor, The, 300
Suspended Life, A, 134, 135, 143
Syrian Bride, The, 164

Tabite or Not Tabite, 329, 330
Take a Thousand Quid and Get Lost, 300
Tale of the Three Jewels, 17, 27–8, 188, 190, 196n6, 208–217
Taste of Cherry, The, 53
Taxi Driver, 139
Tempest of Life, The, 41
Tenants, The, 51
Ten Shorts, Ten Feature Films, 279
Tension, 196n10
Terrorism and Kabab, 249n29
Terrorist, The, 240–241, 243, 244, 249n29
They Made Me a Criminal, 248–9n23
They Were Ten, 156–7, 159, 160
Thirst, 195
Thousand Months, A, 33n16, 336n10

Three Days and a Child, 158
Tick Tack, 52
Ticket to Jerusalem, 17, 205
Time for Drunken Horses, A, 30, 57
Time Has Come, A, 136, 138, 142
Time of Love, 15
Time That Remains, The, 29, 195
Tornado, The, 134, 138–139, 141, 142
Torn Years, The, 313–314n2
Touchia, 301
Toughest People, The, 247–248n18
Trace, The, 276
Trances, 333
Tranquility in the Presence of Others, 45–46
Turtles Can Fly, 30, 57
Two-Legged Horse, 15, 102n1
Two Women, 55

Ultimate Wedding, The, 246n8
Uncovering the Hidden, 240, 249n29
Under the Bombs, 29, 138, 144
Under the Skin of the City, 21, 54, 84–93
Upper Egyptian in the American University, An, 242, 247–248n18, 248n22
Uprooted, The, 297
Ushpizin, 186

Vagabonds, 247n17
Veiled Loves, 331–332
Veiled Man, The, 143
Victory of Islam, The, 248n23
Violin, 270n9
Visa, 274, 280
Visit of Mr. President, The, 247–248n18

Waiting, 17, 27, 31n1, 123, 193, 198–207, 226
Waiting for Pasolini, 329, 330
Waiting for Salah al-Din, 192–193
Wake-Up Morocco!, 331
Waltz with Bashir, 12, 164, 184
Wanderers, The, 280
Wanderings, 301
War, Love, God & Madness, 34n25
Water, Wind, Earth, 51
Way, The, 294
We Are the Bus People, 242, 247n15, 249n29

Wedding in Galilee, 17, 188, 190, 196n6
We Shall Go onto the Mountain, 300
West Beirut, 134, 135, 136, 137, 140, 141, 144
What about Tomorrow?, 275
Whatever Lola Wants, 331
When Maryam Spoke Out, 141, 142, 144
Where Are You Going Moshe?, 330
Where Is the Friend's House?, 52
White Shadows, 301
Widad, 248n23
Wife for My Son, A, 300
Wildflowers, 247n14
Wind from the Aurès, The, 294, 319
Wind from the South, 297

Wooden Gun, 158
Wretched Life of Juanita Narboni, The, 330
WWW–What a Wonderful World, 330, 331

Yacoubian Building, The, 12, 23–24, 242–245, 250n34
Years of Torment, 25
Yol, 29
Youssef: The Legend of the Seventh Sleeper, 14, 23, 300, 304n6

Zionist Aggression, 196n2
Zohra, 273

NAME INDEX

Abassi, Hamadi, 285
ʿAbd al-Hamid. *See* Abdelhamid, Abdellatif
ʿAbd al-Khaliq, Ali, 231
ʿAbd al-Salam, Shadi, 118
Abdelhamid, Abdellatif, 106, 111n3
Abrahamian, Ervan, 80
Abu Ali, Mustafa, 196n2
Abu-Assad, Hany, 17–18, 28, 188, 189, 191, 194–195, 196n7, 218–227
Abu-Remaileh, Refqa, 34n29
Abu Seif, Salah, 18, 247n14, 248n23, 249n27
Abu Wael, Tawfiq, 191, 192, 195
Abu Warda, Yussef, 168
Adib, Adil, 248n22
Adon, Raida, 210
Afkhami, Behrooz, 55
Aggar, Salim, 33n21, 317
Ahmadinejad, Mahmoud, 11, 58, 60n19
Akkad, Moustapha, 6, 12, 25
Akrami, Jamsheed, 48
Alawiyeh, Borhan, 135, 280
Alexander, Livia, 226
Ali, Hatem, 10
Allamehzadeh, Reza, 50
Allouache, Merzak, 13, 23, 270n10, 298, 299, 301–302, 303
Almódovar, Pedro, 330
Aloni, Udi, 163, 164
Aman, Raja, 274
Amarger, Michel, 289, 291
Amari, Raja, 274, 279
Ameli, Rasoul Sadr, 55
Ameur-Zaïmèche, Rabah, 303
Amin, Muhammad, 248n22
Annabi, Amina, 292n10
Ansari, Ali, 53

Antonius, Soraya, 118
Anzour, Najdat, 25
Aractingi, Philippe, 29, 136, 138, 143
ʿArafa, Amru, 235, 248n20
ʿArafa, Saad, 240, 249n27
ʿArafa, Sharif, 242, 248n20, 249n29
Arafat, Yasser, 194
Arbid, Danielle, 134, 140, 141–142
Arcady, Alexandre, 290
Ariss, Ibrahim Al-, 138
Aristotle, 259n3
Armbrust, Walter, 5, 12, 23, 228–251, 268
Armes, Roy, 4, 7, 31n, 32n3, 32n9, 33n10, 294–305, 326, 335n2, 346n5
Arthuys, Philippe, 296
ʿAryan, Tariq al-, 234, 248n19
Asad. *See* Assad, Hafez
Assad, Hafez, 5, 105, 106, 107, 110, 131, 132, 133n5
Assaf, Leyla, 136
Assaf, Roger, 141
Assyouti, Mohamed El-, 34n27
Aswany, Alaa Al-, 242
Atatürk, Kemal, 32n4
Attia, Ahmed Baha Eddine, 280
Auer, Claudia, 11
Averroës, 24, 254, 256–257, 258, 259n3, 259n7, 260n10
Avisar, Ilan, 157
Ayouch, Amal, 347n13
Ayouch, Nabil, 14, 19, 327, 328, 331, 335n6, 336n12, 339–347
Azimi, Fakhreddin, 63–73
Azizi, Mohamed Nadir, 297
Azmi, Ahmed, 269n2
a-Zubeidi, Subhi, 189–190, 191, 193, 196n5

Babaï, Brahim, 275
Babenco, Hector, 341
Baccar, Selma, 275–276
Bachir-Chouikh, Yamina, 20, 23, 303
Badie, Mustapha, 295
Badr, Sawsan, 269n3
Badrakhan, Ahmad, 229, 246n3, 248–249n23
Badrakhan, Ali, 247n15
Badri, Ahmad al-, 24, 244–245
Baghdadi, Maroun, 138, 139–140, 143–144
Bahloul, Abdelkrim, 303
Bakhti, Benamar, 301
Bakhtin, Mikhail, 104, 183
Bakri, Muhammad, 189, 191, 210
Bakrim, Mohammed, 33n16, 328
Bancal, Damien, 291n4
Bani-Etemad, Rakhshan, 3, 15, 21, 54, 84–93
Banna, Hasan al-, 239
Bar, Sandi, 173
Barabash, Benny, 161
Barabash, Uri, 159, 161
Barak, Oren, 150, 151
Barakat, Henri, 229, 246n3, 247n16
Barlet, Olivier, 19, 33n15, 270nn8–9, 281, 291, 306–314, 315, 330, 336n10, 341, 342, 345
Barmak, Siddiq, 23, 102n2
Béar, Liza, 1
Beaugé, Florence, 332
Bedarida, Catherine, 200
Bedjaoui, Ahmed, 295
Béhi, Ridha, 275, 280
Belabbes, Hakim, 328
Belmejdoub, Jamal, 331
Beloufa, Farouk, 298
Ben Abdallah, Tarek, 290
Ben Ali, Zine El Abidine, 13, 272, 276, 286, 288, 290
Ben Brik, Taoufik, 277
Ben Halima, Hamouda, 274
Ben Mabrouk, Nejia, 276, 280
Ben Mahmoud, Mahmoud, 279
Ben M' Hidi, Larbi, 25
Ben Mokhtar, Rabie, 301
Ben Mrad, Bchira, 276
Ben-Shaul, Nitzan, 160, 162, 174n1
Benali, Abdelkader, 274

Benallal, Rachid, 301, 303
Benchiha, Larbi, 324n1
Bendeddouche, Ghaouti, 297, 299, 303
Benhadj, Mohamed Rachid, 300, 301, 302
Benjamin, Walter, 174n7
Benjelloun, Hassan, 330, 336n10
Benlyazid, Farida, 328, 329, 330
Bensaidi, Faouzi, 33n16, 328, 330, 332, 336n10
Berrah, Mouny, 295, 298
Beyer, Bero, 18, 219n, 220
Beyzai, Bahram, 37, 44, 51, 59n3, 60n12
Bhabha, Homi, K. 174n2, 209, 216n3
Bialik, Haim Nahman, 171–172
Bishara, Khayri, 232, 247nn17–18
Blancan, Bernard, 307
Bornaz, Kalthoum, 280
Bouajila, Sami, 307, 314n2
Bouamari, Mohamed, 297
Bouberras, Rabah, 301
Bouchareb, Rachid, 7, 14, 20, 306–314
Bouchemha, Rabah, 300
Boughedir, Ferid, 279, 281, 346n3
Boughermouh, Abderrahmane, 299, 302
Bouhired, Djamilah, 25
Boukai. See Bukaee, Rafi
Boulane, Ahmed, 330
Boullata, Kamal, 118
Boumediene, Houari, 295
Bourguiba, Habib, 13, 271, 272, 274, 276
Bourquia, Farida, 328, 329
Bouzid, Nouri, 13, 118, 277, 280, 281, 290
Boyarin, Daniel, 216n1
Bozarslan, Hamit, 34n31
Bradshaw, Robert, 101
Brahimi, Denise, 296, 304n5, 315–324, 345
Brandano, Nicole, 152n2
Bréhat, Jean, 308, 313–314n2
Bresheeth, Haim, 34n29, 196n1
Brooks, Xan, 197n14
Bukaee, Rafi, 11–12, 16, 27, 159, 160, 177–186
Bukai. See Bukaee, Rafi
Buñuel, Luis, 341, 346n5
Bush, George W., 23, 290
Buzaglo, Haim, 161

Calhoun, David, 95

NAME INDEX

Carter, Sandra Gayle, 335n2, 336n11, 346n5
Caruth, Cathy, 174
Cedar, Joseph, 163, 184
Chahal Sabag, Randa, 136, 140, 143, 151
Chahine, Joumane, 226n2
Chahine, Mohammad, 123n2
Chahine, Youssef, vi, 5, 6, 7, 12, 18–19, 24, 25, 27, 31, 118, 230, 241, 247n9, 247n15, 247–248n18, 248n20, 248n23, 249n30, 250n34, 252–260, 261, 267, 268, 269n4, 275
Chamkhi, Sonia, 278
Chamoun, Jean Khalil, 13, 16, 32n5, 134, 146–153
Charef, Mehdi, 303
Chaudhuri, Shohini, 100
Che Guevara, Ernesto, 68
Cherabi-Labidi, Nadia, 303
Cheriaa, Tahar, 117, 120
Cherif, Nour El, 259n5, 260n11
Chikhaoui, Tahar, 275, 276
Chikli. *See* Samama
Chirac, Jacques, 307, 308, 311
Choueiri, Christine, 151
Chouikh, Mohamed, 14, 20, 23, 300, 303, 304n5, 315–324
Chouikh, Yamina. *See* Bachir-Chouikh
Chraibi, Saad, 336n10
Chubak, Sadeq, 44
Clinton, Hillary, 23
Cobbey, Rini, 84–93
Codsi, Jean-Claude, 136, 144
cooke, miriam, 9
Cooper, Merian C., 39
Coppola, Francis Ford, 141
Cottin, Jean, 346n4
Curry, Ann, 10

Dabashi, Hamid, 34n29, 46, 54, 76, 99
Dàc, Trân, 301
Damardjji, Djafar, 297, 301
Danesh, Mehrzad, 57
Dar, Giddi, 186
Daryabegi, Ali, 41
Daradji, Mohamed Al, 6, 26, 34n25
Daw, Salim, 185, 189
Dayan, Assi, 186

Debboub, Yahia, 301
Debbouze, Jamel, 307, 308, 309, 314n2, 314n5
de Gaulle, Charles, 310
Deleuze, Gilles, 174nn4-5, 177, 181, 182
Dembrow, Michael, 269n7
De Palma, Brian, 330
Derkaoui, Mustapha, 280, 328
De Sica, Vittorio, 15, 101
Devictor, Agnès, 76
Dhouib, Moncef, 278
Dighidi, Inas al-, 229, 249n29
Dinar, Baruch, 156
Diop, Amadou, 308
Djebar, Assia, 298
Dönmez-Colin, Gönül, 32n4, 34n30, 56, 335n2
Dotan, Shimon, 159
Doueiri, Ziad, 134, 137, 140
Driguez, Michèle, 292n6
Duagoo, Mohammad-Mehdi, 52
Dupont, John, 60n12
Dwyer, Kevin, 32n8, 325–338, 339

e Ahmad, Jalal Al-, 45, 59n5
Echenberg, Myron, 314n7
Egan, Eric, 4, 11, 37–62, 74–83, 94–103
Elbendary, Amina, 34n27
Elena, Alberto, 53
Elias, Hana, 189
Ellenson, Hannah Miriam, 177
Eloui, Laila, 254, 259n5
Elsaesser, Thomas, 174

Fadil, Muhammad, 246n7
Fairouz, 152n2
Fakhry, Majid, 258
Falkat, Lilia, 290
Fani, Allia El, 291
Fani, Bechir El, 291, 292n13
Fani, Ghalia El, 291
Fani, Nadia El, 8, 13, 19–20, 22, 279, 284–293
Fani, Sofian El, 291
Fares, Tewfik, 295
Farid, Samir, 188, 213
Farmanara, Bahman, 44, 45, 57
Farrokhzad, Forugh, 44, 54

Farzanefar, Amin, 267, 268, 270n8
Fauzi, Husayn, 249n25
Fawal, Ibrahim, 34n24, 34n28, 249n30, 253
Fawzi, Usama, 250n32
Fellini, Federico, 330
Fennane, Yassine, 331
Ferdowsi, 40
Ferhati, Jilali, 328, 336n10
Ferroukhi, Ismail, 328
Fetter, Sid Ali, 299
Finn, Howard, 100
Folman, Ari, 12, 164, 184
Ford, Alexander, 155
Forutan, Mohamad Reza, 92n2
Fouladkar, Assad, 141
Francis, Yusuf, 247n14
Freud, Zigmund, 174, 187, 216n1
Friedman, Regine Mihal, 159
Frodon, Jean-Michel, 259n7
Fuad, Ahmad, 247n16

Gabous, Abdelkrim, 291
Gadant, Monique, 295
Gaddafi, Musammar al-, 6, 22, 25
Galal, Nadir, 240, 247–8n18
Ged'oun, André, 138
Georgakas, Dan, 226n2
Gertz, Nurith, 17, 34n29, 154–165, 166–176, 187–197, 201, 202, 205, 208–217
Ghafouri, Ebrahim, 33n19
Ghalem, Ali, 300
Ghanam, Oussama, 127
Ghobadi, Bahman, 30, 57, 60n19
Ghorbal, Khaled, 280
Gibeau, Edward, 146–153
Gitai, Amos, 6, 11, 16, 26, 31, 32n5, 163, 166–176, 184, 185
Gleis, Uli, 340
Gogol, Nikolai, 246n4
Golbu-Kardavani, Farideh, 63n, 65
Golshiri, Housang, 44, 45
Gordon, Joel, 231, 246n1, 246n5, 246n7, 246n10
Gören, Şerif, 29
Goudet, Stephanie, 76
Goupil, Romain, 290–291

Greenberg, Judith, 174
Grossman, David, 159
Guattari, Felix, 174n4, 177, 181, 182
Guevara. See Che Guevara, Ernesto
Gugler, Josef, 1–36, 125–133, 252–260, 261–270, 284–293, 339–348
Güney, Yilmaz, 29
Gutman, Amos, 161

Habchi, Samir, 134
Haddad, Moussa, 297, 298
Haddad, Suheil, 185
Hadjadj, Belkacem, 33n21, 302, 303
Hadji Thomas, Joana, 134
Hafez, Sabry, 34n26
Hajjar, Rafic, 136
Hakkkar, Amor, 303
Hamid, Marwan, 12, 242
Hamid, Rahul, 89, 90
Hamid, Sacid, 247–248n18, 248n20
Hamilton, Richard, 335n5
Hamza, Sonia, 291
Hansali, Mustapha, 341
Harel, Amir, 195
Hassan, Azza al-, 189–190, 196n5
Hassan II, King, 14, 329, 336n10, 345, 347n11
Hassan, Nizar, 188, 189, 194, 196–197nn9–11
Hatami, Ali, 55
Hatamikia, Ebrahim, 51
Haugbølle, Sune, 152
Haydar, Haydar, 131
Hazaz, Haim, 172
Hellal, Abderrazak, 301
Hemeida, Mahmoud, 269n4
Hemingway, Ernest, 51
Hennebelle, Guy, 115, 118, 121, 123n4, 196n1
Hermoni, Gal, 166–176
Hetata, Atef, 19, 24, 242, 258, 261–270
Hetata, Sherif, 19, 267
Hilmi, Mohamed, 301
Hilwani, Widdad, 151
Hitchcock, Alfred, 330, 332
Ho Chi Minh, 68
Hoang, Mai, 140
Hojeij, Bahij, 141
Hojeij, Wassim, 141

NAME INDEX

Homer, 325, 334
Hopewell, John, 336n11
Hussein, Saddam, 6, 18, 26, 30, 289
Huston, John, 332

Ibn Quzman, 257
Ibn Rushd. *See* Averroës
Idris, Ali, 235
Idtnaine, Omar, 336n11
Imam, 'Adil, 247n16
Imam, Hasan al-, 239–240, 249n26
İpekçi, Handan, 34n30
Ismail, Muhammad, 330
Issari, Mohammad Ali, 41, 46
Iz'har, Smilansky, 158

Jabes, Edmond, 177
Jacir, Annemarie, 195
Jadid, Salah, 105
Jalili, Abolfazl, 37, 52, 57, 99
Jam-pour, Esmat, 33n18
Jarmusch, James R., 330
Jarre, Maurice, 6
Jelejel, 275-276
Jensen, Kim, 261-270
Jhally, Sut, 31n2
Johnson, Penny, 222-223
Joreige, Khalil, 134
Jumblatt, Walid, 259n5

Kaes, Anton, 174
Kahena, Queen, 275
Kamal, Husayn, 247n12, 247n15
Kamal, Kamal, 330
Kammoun, Michel, 134
Kanafani, Ghassan, 27, 113–117, 122–123, 123n2
Karimi, Niki, 66
Kar-Wai, Wong, 307
Kassari, Yasmine, 328, 329
Kbab, Mounïm, 341
Keshales, Aharon, 174n3
Khalaf, Ghazi, 136
Khalaf, Samir, 135
Khalidi, Rashid, 216n3
Khalili, Laleh, 206n2

Khamenei, Ayatollah Ali, 60n13
Khan, Mirza Ebrahim, 38
Khan, Muhammad, 232, 247n17
Khan, Reza, 39
Khan, Shah Rukh, 132
Khatami, Mohammad, 11, 47, 53, 54, 56, 57, 58, 63, 88
Khatib, Lina, 31n2, 134–145, 150, 151, 152n1
Khayati, Abdellatif, 346n5
Khayati, Khémaïs, 115, 118, 120, 121, 123n4, 196n1
Khemir, Nacer, 280
Khleifi, George, 17, 34n29, 187–197, 202, 208–217
Khleifi, Michel, 16–17, 27–28, 188–189, 190, 191, 192, 193–194, 208–217
Khlifi, Omar, 274
Khodja, Liazid, 303
Khomeini, Ayatollah Ruhollah, 48, 50, 59n8, 67, 79
Khouri, Elias, 26
Khouri, Makram, 160, 210
Khouri, Malek, 259n1
Kiarostami, Abbas, 37, 44, 52, 53, 59n3
Kilani, Leila, 336n10
Kimerling, Baruch, 214
Kimiai, Massoud, 47
Kimiavi, Parviz, 44, 45, 57
Klemm, David E., 180–181
Kolorin, Eran, 163
Koussa, Bassam, 131, 133n6
Kramp, Fritz, 248n23
Kronop, Oscar, 199n
Ktari, Naceur, 275
Kuttab, Eileen, 222-223

Labaki, Nadine, 144
Lagtaa, Abdelkader, 326, 327, 328, 336n10
Lahiji, Shala, 54
Lahlou, Latif, 331
Lahlou, Nabyl, 328, 329, 330
Lakhdar-Hamina, Malik, 14, 33n21, 301
Lakhdar-Hamina, Mohamed, 7, 294, 296, 301, 319
Lallem, Ahmed, 295, 297
Laor, Dan, 172

Laradji, Rabah, 299
Laraki, Abdelhai, 336n10
Laskri, Amar, 295, 297, 299, 301
Leaman, Oliver, 258, 259n3
Lean, David, 332
Lebcir, Mohamed, 303
Lee, Spike, 267
Lekhmari, Noureddine, 328, 329, 332
Leonard, Sylvie, 342
Lerski, Helmar, 155
Letaïef, Ibrahim, 274, 280, 281
Linor, Irit, 195
Lledo, Jean-Pierre, 299
Loevy, Ram, 158
Lormans, Erwin, 346n2
Loshitzky, Yosefa, 154
Louhichi, Taïeb, 277
Lubin, Orly, 163
Lund, Katia, 341

Maanouni, Ahmed, 333, 336n16
Machmouchi, Majdi, 151
Maghsoudlou, Bahman, 59n7
Maherzi, Lotfi, 294
Mahfouz, Naguib, 19, 247n12, 256
Mahir Pasha, Ahmad, 241
Mahmoudi, Alireza, 55
Majidi, Majid, 52, 99
Makhmalbaf, Hana, 15, 31, 95
Makhmalbaf, Maysam, 33n19, 103n4
Makhmalbaf, Mohsen, 1, 10, 15, 22, 31, 37, 47, 51, 55, 57, 74–83, 95, 99, 102n2
Makhmalbaf, Samira, 15, 30, 31, 54, 95, 99, 102n1
Malas, Muhammad, 111n3, n7
Maleh, Nabil, 9, 16, 18, 108, 123n2, 125–133
Malih. See Maleh, Nabil
Mammeri, Mouloud, 296, 302
Mandur, Sharif, 248n22
Mansur, Caliph Al, 256, 258
Maoz, Samuel, 184
Mar'i, Hamid, 105
Marks, Laura U., 180
Marrakchi, Leila, 328, 329, 330
Marsaud, Olivia, 285
Martin, Florence, 271–283, 291n2

Marzuq, Sa'id, 229, 247nn14–15
Masharawi, Rashid, 17, 27, 123, 188, 189, 191, 193–194, 195, 196n7, 196n10, 198–207, 226
Masri, Mai, 16, 151, 153n7, 189
Massad, Joseph, 34n26, 260n9
Mazhar, Ahmad, 230
Mazif, Lotfi, 295, 297, 298, 299
Mazra'eh, Hamid, 73–74n2
McGill, Hannah, 95
McLarney, Ellen, 116, 122
McNeece. See Stone McNeece, Lucy
Mdanat, Adnan, 188
Meddeb, Abdelwahab, 257, 259n8
Meddour, Azzedine, 302, 304n8
Mefti, Tayeb, 300
Mehrabi, Massoud, 44
Mehrjui, Dariush, 21, 37, 46, 51, 55, 59n3
Meirelles, Fernando, 341
Mekachera, Hamlaoui, 308
Mengouchi, Mustapha, 300
Mer, Juliano, 191, 195
Merbah, Mohamed Lamine, 297, 301
Mesbahi, Imane, 329
Meshkini, Akbar, 33n19
Meshkini, Marziyeh, 15, 31, 54, 57, 94–103
Migdal, Joel, 214
Milani, Tahmineh, 10–11, 15, 21, 54–55, 63–73
Millo, Joseph, 157
Mimouni, Rachid, 302
Mirbakhtyar, Shala, 46, 59n9
Misleh, Hanna, 189
Mizrahi, Togo, 248n23
Modelski, George, 255
Mohammad, Oussama, 9, 16, 105–108, 111n3, 111n5, 130, 131
Mohammadi, Ali, 55
Mohammed VI, King, 14, 336n10
Mohiedine, Mohsen, 256
Mohr, Jean, 192
Moknèche, Nadir, 303
Moqaddam, Saman, 55, 57
Morrison, Toni, 277
Mosaddeq, Mohammad, 41, 66–67, 68
Moshinson, Ilan, 158

NAME INDEX

Motahhari, Ayatollah, 78
Motavalli, John, 49
Mouazzen, Marwan, 123n2
Mounir, Mohamed, 259n5
Moussoune, Hicham, 341, 346n2
Mozaffar al-Din Shah, 38
Mubarak, Hosni, 232, 243
Muhammad. *See* Mohammad, Oussama
Munk, Yael, 154–165, 166–176, 177–186
Murnau, Friedrich Wilhem, 330
Mustafa, Hani, 150, 151
Mustafa, Husam al-Din, 232, 248n23
Mustafa, Niyazi, 246n7, 248n23

Nabili, Marva, 54
Naceri, Samy, 307, 314n2
Naciri, Said, 329
Naderi, Amir, 44, 51
Naficy, Hamid, 43, 49, 85, 92n6, 203, 225–226
Nahhal, Mohammad, 210, 215
Nair, Mira, 341
Najar, Najwa, 189, 196n5
Nasr, George, 135
Nasrallah, Yousry, 26, 248n20, 249n29
Nassar, Ali, 189, 191, 194, 196n10
Nasser, Gamal Abdel, 12, 27, 116, 214, 215,
    229, 230, 231, 232, 239, 246n5, 247n9,
    247n12, 247n15
Nativ, Guy, 164
Ne'eman, Judd, 158, 159, 161, 164, 177–186
Nejjar, Narjess, 328, 329, 331
Ne'meh, Hana', 211
Nesher, Avi, 161
Nesselson, Lisa, 133n3
Nikbin, Mohammad, 65, 66, 72n1
Nomani, Farhad, 78
Noury, Hakim, 328, 329, 335–336n7
Novak, Marcos, 279

Ohanian, Avanes, 39
Omid, Jamal, 58
Ouezzani, Fatima Jebli, 329
Oulad-Syad, Daoud, 329, 330
Ould Khelifa, Saïd, 301, 303

Pahlavi, Mohammad Reza Shah, 41
Pahlavi, Reza Khan, 39, 41
Panahi, Jafar, 21, 47, 57
Parsa, Vahid F., 92n6
Pasolini, Pier Paolo, 319, 329, 330
Penn, Arthur, 330
Petit, Soazig, 306
Peysson-Zeiss, 304n3
Polanski, Roman, 291
Pontecorvo, Gillo, 25–26, 247n9, 319
Popham, Peter, 25
Prince, Yves, 208
Prokhoris, Sabine, 194

Qaraman, Bushra, 210
Qasim, Abd al-Karim, 116
Quasim, Mahmud, 4, 32n2, 248–9n23
Quattan, Omar al, 188
Quilty, Jim, 147, 336n8
Quist-Arcton, Ofeibea, 346n3

Rachedi, Ahmed, 14, 294, 296, 297, 303
Radi, Muhammad, 247n15
Rafla, Hilmi, 246nn3-4
Rafsanjani, Ali Akbar Hashemi, 51, 53
Rahim, Hadj, 301
Rahnema, Ali, 78
Rahnema, Fereydoun, 45
Rakha, Youssef, 269n3
Rand, Shuli, 186
Raveh, Yair, 173
Rhanja, Hassan, 331
Riad, Mohamed Slim, 294, 297–298
Riahi, Arash, 33n13
Rida, Muhammad, 247n15
Riding, Alan, 140
Riklis, Eran, 162, 164
Riyahi, Shahla, 54
Rogoff, Irit, 209
Rosen, Miriam, 118, 142–143
Rosenstone, Robert A., 32n6
Roy, Anne, 202
Ruby, Rich, 226n2
Rugh, William, 246n5

Saab, Jocelyne, 134, 142–143
Saadawi, Nawal el-, 19, 267
Sabag. *See* Chahal Sabag, Randa
Sabcawi, Ahmad al-, 247n16
Sadat, Anwar El, 231–232, 239, 240
Sadr, Hamid Reza, 34n26, 39, 46
Saedi, Gholam Hossein, 44, 46
Safaee, Hamed, 92n6
Sagi, Eran, 174n3
Sahafbashi, Mirza Ebrahim Khan, 38
Saheb-Ettaba, Nawfel, 279
Sahraoui, Djamila, 303
Said, Edward, 192
Saiji, Nadia, 292n10
Saladin, 193, 211, 230
Salah al-Din. *See* Saladin
Salam Shehada, Abed el-, 189
Saleem, Hiner, 30
Saleh, Tawfik, 5, 18, 27, 113–124, 153n5
Salem, Lyes, 303
Saless, Sohrab Shahid, 45
Salhab, Ghassan, 144
Salih. *See* Saleh, Tawfik
Salim, ʿAli, 247n13
Salim, ʿAtif, 246n8, 247n14, 248–249n23
Salim, Hiner. *See* Saleem, Hiner
Salim, Muhammad, 246n8
Salmy, Aziz, 331
Salti, Rasha, 16, 110n, 111n6
Saltz, Barbara, 226n2
Salur, Samam, 60n19
Samama, Albert, 273
Sami, Samar, 131
Samie, Amale, 347n12
Sarhan, Shukri, 230
Sarkozy, Nicolas, 311
Saugeon, Nathalie, 339n, 341, 346n4, 346–347n7, 347n13
Sayyid, Daud ʿAbd al-, 232, 241, 247nn17–18
Schatz, Kevin, 90
Schirazi, Asghar, 51
Schoedsack, Ernest B., 39
Scorsese, Martin, 332, 333
Scott, Ridley, 332
Scott, Stephanie, 72n2

Scorcese, Martin, 139
Sepanta, Abdolhossein, 39
Serceau, Michel, 304n8, 346n5
Shafik, Viola, 5, 6, 33n20, 34n22, 34n31, 118, 188, 196n1, 228, 229, 232, 246n1, 249n28, 34n31, 291n3, 346n5
Shaheen, Jack G., 31n2
Shakespeare, William, 160, 182, 184
Shammut, Ismail, 118
Sharaf al-Din, Duriyya, 231, 247n11
Shariati, Ali, 78, 82
Sharif, Midhat al-, 247–248n18
Shauqi, Farid, 230, 246n6
Shaykh, Kamal al-, 230, 247n15
Shaymaʾ, al-, 249n27
Shohat, Ella, 11, 33n14, 155, 162, 174n1, 196n1, 214
Shor, Renen, 161
Sidami, Obeida, 146
Sid-Ammi, Louiza, 316
Sider, Yosef, 184
Sidqi, Husayn, 246n3, 248–249n23, 249n25
Sisley, Tomer, 290
Slackman, Michael, 235
Solvay, Muriel, 290
Soueid, Mohamad, 141
Spaas, Lieve, 279
Stam, Robert, 96, 183, 196n1, 214
Stone, Oliver, 132, 332
Stone McNeece, Lucy, 278
Stora, Benjamin, 295
Suleiman, Elia, 28–29, 34n29, 188, 189, 191, 194, 195, 196n8, 196n10, 280
Suner, Asuman, 32n4, 34n31

Taboulay, Camille, 304n7, 324n1
Tadmor, Erez, 164
Taghavi, Nasser, 45, 51
Taghmaoui, Said, 346n4
Tahami, Massoud, 53
Tahiri, Zakia, 329, 332
Takmil Homayoun, Nader, 3, 10, 77
Tarr, Carrie, 33n10, 304n10
Tarraf, Marwan, 141
Tati, Jacques, 330

NAME INDEX

Taylor, Richard C., 257
Tayyib, 'Atif al-, 232, 233, 240, 242, 249n29
Tazi, Muhammad Abderrahman, 326, 327–328, 335–336n7
Teguia, Tariq, 303
Tesson, Charles, 170, 173
Thackway, Melissa, 313n, 324n
Thomas, Antony, 269n3
Thomas, Kevin, 92n1
Tilmisani, Kamil al-, 249n25
Tirawai, Ghada, 196n5
Tlatli, Moufida, 278, 280, 281, 282
Tolbi, Abdelaziz, 297
Toubiana, Serge, 173
Touita, Okacha, 299–300
Truman, Harry, 287
Tukhi, Ahmad al-, 248n23
Tsaki, Brahim, 300, 303

Umm Kulthum, 248n23
Ustaoğlu, Yeşim, 29–30

Vautier, René, 294

Wahab al-Moadeb, Abed al-, 213
Wahbi, Yusuf, 249n25
Wavelet, Christophe, 194
Waxman, Daniel, 159
Wedeen, Lisa, 9, 31n, 33n11, 104–112, 130, 131, 133n5
Welles, Orson, 330, 332
Westmoreland, Mark, 150
Wettig, Hannah, 140
Willemen, Paul, 168, 169

Wilson-Goldie, Kaelen, 327
Wolman, Dan, 158
Wood, Jason, 28
Wright, Lawrence, 9, 130, 131, 132, 133n7

Yacef, Saadi, 25
Yahiaoui, Allel, 317
Yahya, Ahmad, 232
Yala, Mohamed Meziane, 299
Yaqub, Nadia, 113–124, 198–207, 218–227
Yasin, Isma'il, 230
Yektapanah, Hassan, 52, 57, 99
Yeshuron, Itzhak, 161
Youssef, Khaled, 12, 33n15, 255

Zalman, Amy, 12
Zanger, Anat, 174n6
Zayyat, Latifa, 229
Zeffirelli, Franco, 291
Zem, Roschdy, 307, 314n2
Zemmouri, Mahmoud, 13, 300, 301, 302
Ziad, Ahmed, 331
Ziad, Tawfik, 170
Zikra, Samir, 108–110, 112n10
Zinai-Koudil, Hafsa, 301
Zinet, Mohamed, 298
Zizek, Slavoj, 182
Zohar, Uri, 157, 158
Zonnour, Mehrdad, 94
Zran, Mohamed, 279, 280
Zulficar, 'Izz al-Din, 230, 246n3
Zvi-Riklis, Dina, 162
Zyad, Nouri, 328

www.ingramcontent.com/pod-product-compliance
Lightning Source LLC
Chambersburg PA
CBHW030332240426
43661CB00052B/1608